Nail Soup

By Jane Eden

Lauric Press
www.LauricPress.com

Copyright 2021
ISBN: 978-1-932113-77-8
All rights reserved

Disclaimer: Events in this book are true, and I've described them to the best of my memory as they occurred. Some liberties have been taken with timelines for the sake of drawing the "then and now" life parallels I found curious and interesting and wanted to share. Names have been changed or omitted of all except members of my most immediate family for the sake of privacy. If I said something you didn't like, then it must not have been you. If you liked it, then it was indeed you that I described. Everyone recalls events differently. If your recollection is different from mine then I invite you to write your own book.

Table of Contents

Acknowledgements..	5
Prologue..	9
Chapter 1 – What to Do About Dad...	13
Chapter 2 – Roasted Possum..	25
Chapter 3 – Frog Legs..	37
Chapter 4 – Chicken Stew..	53
Chapter 5 – Nail Soup..	71
Chapter 6 – Mountain Oysters..	85
Chapter 7 – Daddy's Veggie Patch...	103
Chapter 8 – Going Fishing..	119
Chapter 9 – Barbecue, Roasted or Fricassee................................	137
Chapter 10 – Don't Badger Me...	153
Chapter 11 – Wine and Kitty Valium..	165
Chapter 12 – Betrayal...	189
Chapter 13 – Nut Hunt..	203
Chapter 14 – Poor Man's Lobster...	217
Chapter 15 – Rattlesnake Sandwiches..	233
Chapter 16 – Squirrel, the Other White Meat..............................	251
Chapter 17 – Black Beauty...	265
Chapter 18 – Chipmunks and Peanuts..	285
Chapter 19 – We All Scream for Snow Cream............................	297
Chapter 20 – Ladies Wear Hose...	309
Chapter 21 – Sink Strainers..	317
Chapter 22 – Gopher Stew..	325
Chapter 23 – Thanksgiving Gobbler...	335
Chapter 24 – Turnip Greens and Wire Sculpture.........................	345
Chapter 25 – Fresh Roasted Corn and Plum Pits.........................	355
Chapter 26 – Diapers and Knives...	363
Chapter 27 – Amazing Grace Cookies...	375
Conclusion..	385

Acknowledgements

Hock Hochheim, marrying you is the best thing I have ever done. You are supportive, kind, respectful, and you challenge me to be a better person every single day. You are a man among men, and a man of steel. You're a wonderful, talented writer, and editor in your own right. Thank you for being a fantastic listener, loving life partner, and for leaving me room to figure out things on my own without judgment. I love you.

Sherry Laurence, you are the best daughter anyone could ever wish for. I am so proud of the person you have become, the priceless gift of two granddaughters, and all that you are and do. Thank you for your support and for never making me feel guilty when I am less than perfect.

Thank you to my sister, for being my partner caring for both our parents and for loving me. Your sound medical advice and advocacy for our parents, as well as your support and love for us all was a priceless gift. While I came in and helped as I could, you provided care for both our parents when they were critically ill as well. Often you helped search for unique medical treatments that prolonged their lives, found the best doctors, and facilities. No doubt you could write several books about your own experiences caring for elder parents and the consequences of such undertakings.

Special thanks to Leanna Ellis who provided feedback on the project during the concept in the early days of writing and encouraged me not to give up. And also, giant thanks to Dennis Scharnberg for reading the entire manuscript and making excellent suggestions and many saves. Dennis, you are the best editor I've ever know as well as a good friend.

Thank you to my many extended family members Freeda Richardson and Beverly MeHaffey who lifted me up in their thoughts and prayers, provided support via visits and emails and offered sound advice during my many adventures with Dad and Mom.

> *"Bye-o, baby bunting,*
> *Daddy's gone a-hunting,*
> *For to catch a rabbit skin,*
> *To wrap the baby bunting in."*
> – English Nursery Rhyme. Exact composer unknown.

"In his defense Jesus said to them, 'My Father is always at his work to this very day, and I too am working.'" (John 5:17)

Prologue

When I was 13 years old on the side of a steep hill near the Cumberland Valley of Tennessee, Dad took a job for our family doctor bulldozing off the hill near a lake so the doctor could build a lake house. The hill sloped so steeply that to doze down the trees Dad had to tie one end of the logging chain to the side of his dozer and the other to his heavy-duty, tandem truck at the top of the hill as a counterbalance. The weight of the truck helped keep the dozer from rolling down the hill as Dad moved side-to-side pushing down trees and scraping up the shrubs.

One day Dad invited Mom and me to see the place, and to watch him work, and afterward we planned to share a picnic lunch. As Dad worked, Mom put a tablecloth over the hood of our family car to the side of the job site, and she and I watched Dad on the dozer until lunchtime. It quickly became obvious that what Dad was doing on that steep hill was extremely dangerous.

"Louis, you're going to kill yourself one of these days," Mom said when she saw one end of the log chain hooked to the side of the dozer and the other hooked to the truck at the top of the hill.

Her words nearly came true seconds later as the dozer's weight on the truck suddenly grew too much for the counterbalance. Under the weight of the dozer, the truck tipped off the far-side wheels once, fell back, tipped again, then tottered, wobbled, and finally rolled on its side toward Dad. It made a metallic crunching sound when it hit the ground, and as it slid it sounded like the screech of a wounded elephant. Without the counterweight the dozer slid down the hill several feet. Fortunately, a tree prevented it, and Dad, from toppling into the lake. Startled crows flushed from the treetops called out the danger to their companions like when a hunter shoots a deer.

Dad watched the truck settle more firmly against the tree high above him. No doubt he wondered if the tree could hold the weight, or if it might break loose and slide down the hill. It slid a little toward him several times, before finally stopping for good.

Dad turned off his dozer and jumped down. The world had gone still except for Dad. As I watched him walk up the hill, I could hear my heart pounding and his footsteps crushing the fresh dirt with every step. Nothing else moved. He looked over the truck to assess the damage. He took off his cap and scratched his head. He whistled, squatted, looked under the truck to see if it was intact. Apparently, he determined all was well, so he unhooked the chain and calculated how to get the truck back up on its wheels again.

Having devised his plan, Dad hiked down the hill, got the dozer and crawled it back up the hill to where the truck lay on its side. He placed the blade of the dozer slightly under the bed of the truck and lifted it back onto its wheels with a bouncing crash and a cloud of dust. Dad then got the front-end loader he had nearby, and he loaded the dump truck with dirt to make it heaver. Then he went straight back to his hillside cliff-hanging act with the dozer until he was ready to eat lunch. More dirt, more weight, no more truck rollovers!

How Dad, the dozer and the truck didn't slide into the lake that day taking a good portion of the hillside with them, I still do not fully understand.

The event crystalized in my mind. I can still recall it as clearly as if it happened yesterday. I can see the startled birds and I can smell the fresh-turned earth and the crushed bushes and trees combined with the scent of smoke and diesel fuel. I can hear Dad's low whistle as he examined the truck.

The whole thing left me with a lasting impression of both how crazy, but also how brave, Dad really was. God had his hand on Dad for sure. Dad was smart in so many ways, but he also faced many personal challenges. Yet, for some reason, God really loved him. And God protected him, time, after time after time. Even more than that it was a lesson about how when life comes crashing down, the only thing left to do is get up, pick yourself up, figure it out and get back to work.

My brother, sadly, was not so lucky as Dad was that day. He barely made it to adulthood before, at the age of 24, he tragically passed from a work accident where he too was doing something really dangerous to put food on the table— and it did not work out for him. Yet he too had done many a more dangerous thing that *had* worked perfectly fine—until it didn't.

Why one man died and the other lived is not something I can explain. Part fate. Part circumstance. God decides. Those were different times. Life—was different. However, death is timeless and universal. It's terrible for those who remain. Often what remains is forever broken. Yet, somehow humanity goes on.

My brother's death changed all our lives forever. Deep down I believe Dad blamed himself, partly because of the example he set, and partly for simply not being there at the time. Maybe he felt a bit responsible because of the pressure he put on my brother to "be a man". I have no doubt Dad was often afraid …yet he courted danger daily himself. He said it was to feed, clothe and shelter us, but I suspect it was more than that. Perhaps he had his own standard of manhood set by *his* father, and by men larger than life at the time that survived WWI and then WWII. Dad was not healthy enough when he was called to service to go off to war. So maybe he felt he had to prove he was a man at home by taking extraordinary risks. Perhaps taking chances and living life on the edge made him feel more alive.

As for me, I discovered that life lessons learned under the influence of fear and adrenaline have a way of sticking with you. Adrenaline is what I felt when I saw Dad hanging from the side of a hillside; or from the edge of the roof by his fingertips, hammer in one hand, a live electric wire in the other; or when I heard a shotgun explosion under the house where Dad had gone only moments before—followed by perfect stillness. At times like that I prayed a lot. Dad was a brilliant man in a mad-scientist kind of way. He was also a world-class hoarder, hillbilly, strange food connoisseur, cranky tightwad and daredevil. He had the blood of both Daniel Boone and President Andrew Johnson running in his veins. But the common sense of both ancestors appeared to have skipped Dad at times, or did it? Somehow Dad found a way to resolve his bizarre, unique, and creative mishaps every time. Well, nearly every time.

Yes, Dad taught me a lot and spoon-fed me daily from his metaphorical recipe for life I called "Nail Soup". Real nail soup was sipped by prior generations to build blood iron levels and in essence to give them strength. Its bitter contents made a person stronger, if it didn't kill you. Sometimes people found comfort through sharing it.

Nail Soup made me stronger, more appreciative, more observant; and it made me grateful for what I had. I could not wait to move away and try to forget its evil taste. Yet, once away I could not stop thinking about those hard times, those blessed times before my brother died, when we were a unique, complex, gritty, loving, and perhaps —to the outside world— a wheels-off family. Yes, I thought I had moved away from it all, had forgotten it all, was perhaps above it all, until I found myself sucked into a court hearing and a judge appointed me conservator and caretaker for Dad in his old age and ordered me to liquidate his estate to pay for his care. Suddenly I had to sort and sell all the junk he'd collected for more than 60 years; and in the process I had to confront a lot of things about Dad and about me. Did I inherit a portion of the grit Dad had? Could I take on the hard, dangerous tasks, learn a thing or two in the process, spend some good quality time with Dad, and still live to tell about it? Between us, did we have the makings for our own healing version of NAIL SOUP?

<>

"God has decided the length of our lives. He alone knows how many months we will live, and we are not given a minute longer." (Job 14:5)

Chapter 1 – What to Do About Dad

"No, dying isn't always painful. Only sometimes." — Mom

2002

I am cleaning out the kitchen cabinets on a Friday. As I'm cleaning, I look up and for a moment I can almost see Mom standing in front of the dining room windows at my house in Texas. That, of course, is impossible. Mom has been dead more than a year now. She never even saw this house. She passed away September 9, 2001, two days before 9-11. We sold our house in Georgia the following March and moved back to Texas where our kids live so we could resume our life there. Lately, I've been catching up on a number of things I let go while Mom was sick. Last week I went to the dermatologist, and, at my insistence, he removed a tiny mole from the inside of my right leg below the knee. After he did it, I felt relieved, even though he said it was nothing. This was just one more thing to check off my list.

    I don't really think about it again until I see Mom standing there with a worried look on her face. She's there—but not. I know she's in my mind, not actually in front of the dining room window; yet I can see her so clearly. The last time I envisioned someone who was dead like that was when Mom was still alive and at her house and she fell and broke her leg just below the hip suddenly while she was walking down the hallway. I wasn't there to see it. She only told me about it later. She had beans cooking in the kitchen. Her phone was on the kitchen table, and the house nearly caught fire before she managed to drag herself to the kitchen, somehow grope the phone off the table and call 911. They sent EMTs and the fire department broke down the door to get to her just in time to prevent the beans from igniting on the stove.

    At my house at the same time, I'd just gotten out of the shower. As this was all unfolding at Mom's house, I suddenly felt strange and needed to lie down. I crawled into my bed and curled up—waiting, feeling something was wrong. My husband, Hock, came into the room and asked me what I was doing. I told him I didn't know. He asked if I planned to get up, and I told him I didn't know. He went upstairs; and as I lay there, I saw my grandmother, who was long since dead, standing in the doorway to our bedroom. I knew she was dead. She'd been dead since the 80s, and yet there she was standing in the door, her arms hanging loosely at her sides, one arthritic hand gently patting her thigh, over and over. It was a gesture I knew well. It meant *she* was worried.

    A few minutes later I got the call from my sister, that Mom had fallen, and she was on her way to the hospital following the ambulance in her own car. That was the beginning of the end for Mom.

So, what does it mean for me now, today, to see my dead Mom standing in front of my dining room window looking at me with worry and love in her eyes? I don't know, but I suspect it isn't good.

About that time my phone rings. It is the dermatologist's nurse. Her voice sounds solemn. She does not give me the results of the biopsy. Instead, she insists I come to the office and bring my husband as soon as possible saying the dermatologist needs to speak with us both. I schedule the appointment for the following Monday and hang up. When I turn to look again at Mom, I can no longer see her. I feel a fresh pang of grief and loss. I miss her.

At the dermatologist office the following Monday it is quiet when we go from waiting room to exam room. The dermatologist comes right in and sits down. "The biopsy came back, and you have melanoma. We need to do a wide excision as soon as possible."

I ask all the questions anyone who hears something like this might ask. All he tells me is that we will know more after the surgery. Then they will know how advanced the cancer is and what my prognosis will be.

Somehow, I find a general surgeon who can do the surgery the following week. Every day until the surgery I look at the butcher knife in the kitchen and consider taking the cancer out myself. I don't know a lot about melanoma, but I know it is not good. Suddenly I no longer want my leg to be attached to my body.

The next week as I wake up from anesthesia after the surgery the first thing I think about is Mom and how I don't want to worry her. Not even in the hereafter. I remember the pact we made shortly before her death.

Eventually they release me and I go home and try to pick up the threads of our life. It is difficult because the wound is large and located in the part of my leg where —when I bend it— there is significant strain on the stitching. The surgeon has taken out tissue about the size of half a soft ball. Soon the stitches fail, and the wound opens. They cannot re-close it, so it must heal from the inside out. This takes months, and every time I look at my leg I think of the prognosis. Stage II melanoma. They do tell me if it does not reoccur within five years my chances of a normal lifespan are good. And so, we begin counting the days toward the goal of five-year survival. As we count, memories about my childhood and early life and death encounters begin to flow to the surface of my brain at odd times during the days and nights when I can't sleep. And so, efforts to write an unplanned yet unavoidable memoir begin.

* * *

1968

"If your dad doesn't change the way he eats, he's going to die before he turns 45!" Mom's voice echoed off the yellow, butterfly-covered paper on the kitchen walls. She scraped the last of the table scraps from a pan into the dog bowl before plunging the pan, along with the rest of the lunch dishes, into a sink filled with hot sudsy water. As the dishes settled into the water with gentle thumps, she squeezed out a wet dishcloth and wiped down the kitchen table with vigor. Drying her hands on her apron, she turned to the refrigerator, opened it, and took out a carton of buttermilk. She poured herself a glass with her perpetually nervous hands and sat down at the table next to me. Mom and I sat, like always, at the red Formica table in our small kitchen in the house that Dad built before I was born yet never seemed to stop adding on to. Sunshine streamed in the windows; and when I looked out at the yard, I saw my Aunt Gretta's fruit-filled orchard across the road lined with rows of cherry, apple and peach trees. Purple grapes grew along the fence bordering the garden to the south, visually shielding it from the gravel road that ran on the other side. That road was named Hinkle Lane after Dad's family, and it wound alongside Aunt Gretta and Uncle Dave's farm leading down a steep hill where the sawmill used to be and then on to the farm where Dad was born about a quarter of a mile away. Aunt Gretta was Dad's half-sister 13 years older and birthed by a different mother. Her mother died young under mysterious circumstances. That is another story.

Everything looked so innocent and peaceful at that moment. I imagined myself, sitting under one of the trees in the orchard reading a book, or maybe picking the sweet, firm grapes from the vine and popping them, one by one, into my mouth as I listened to the birds sing and watched butterflies sip water from the stone watering trough under the well pump. It was a fantasy I indulged in often over meals to escape the arguing between my parents. But at age 9 I had never actually lived out my dream. Sometimes life wasn't as peaceful as it appeared on the surface. Sometimes real life got in the way of dreams.

Only yesterday, I stood at the back door and listened as my pony Black Beauty screamed horrific screams from her stall in the barn across the field behind our house. Pony death screams flowed out of the barn at regular and increasingly close intervals until the sun began to set. Sometimes when I looked that way the barn appeared to vibrate with them, so I quickly looked away. Then, suddenly, the screams stopped. Even at age 9 I knew what that meant. She had been in foal, and a few days earlier when my horse Misty kicked Beauty in the stomach causing her to die.

Dad did not call the vet before he left that morning not knowing how bad it would get. No money. No way to reach him. So, now we listened to her screams until long after sunset. If I'd only known how to do it, I would have shot her myself. But I didn't know how to shoot. I could barely lift the shotgun, let alone fire it.

Instead, I stepped up on the bottom wooden part of the screen door at the back of the house that opened out onto the back porch and swung out and back, and out, and back, and listened and watched the barn off and on until there was nothing to hear anymore. My toes stretched the screen wire out of place at the bottom ruining the door. Dad would spank me for that later. But I didn't much care.

After the pony screams stopped, I thought why couldn't I think of something to do about all of it? Something to fix Beauty, to fix it? But what could a 9-year-old girl do to fix anything in life anyway, really? Still, I felt guilty for doing nothing. I felt useless. I also felt relieved that the time to do something had passed. Either fate or God had taken the decision from my hands. And then I felt guilty about thinking that.

Why hadn't God saved my pony? I wondered. Too busy? She never hurt anybody. It looked like he would know that and would have put his hand on her and saved her all that pain! There was a lot about God I didn't understand.

"Mom, is Beauty still in the barn?" I asked her as we sat at the table now a day later.

"No, she's gone," Mom said.

"Gone where?" I asked.

"Gone." Mom did not elaborate. Her mouth formed a straight line across her face turning neither up nor down at the corners.

"Is dying always painful?" I had never known anyone to die. My mind filled with questions.

"No, dying isn't always painful," Mom said. "Only sometimes."

I guessed the pain ended as soon as you died. But what came after? That is the part I didn't know and could only guess at. I decided not to ask Mom about the pain because she was pregnant, like Beauty, and I didn't want to upset her. In Sunday school they told us God saw everything. I wondered what God made of all of us as he looked down from heaven at our little family—assuming folks in small, rural Tennessee had not entirely escaped his notice. Maybe he only had time to take care of all the soldiers fighting in Vietnam. Mom tried not to let us watch the news—but I knew about the war. I didn't know everything, but I saw enough to guess a lot.

On Sundays Dad lead the singing at church and Mom hesitantly played the piano, as if playing softly would draw less attention to any wrong note she might strike. You see, Mom wanted to be perfect. And if she slipped up, she wanted to draw as little attention as possible to her mistake. I followed her example when I could.

Every night Dad read us a Bible story and helped my brother and me to say our prayers. After devotion, he set us in a row on the edge of the bathtub and then he sat on the toilet with the lid closed and brushed his teeth and instructed us about how to brush ours. Once we were done, he patted us both on the shoulder with his big work-roughed hands, kissed our foreheads and sent us off to bed.

The barn was quiet now as I finished eating. And outside the kitchen window I could hear the mockingbird sing a happy song. A song about life bursting with joy and hope. Birds know that bad things happen and how important it is to sing—sing while you can. Sing even if you don't know why, because singing just makes you feel good.

Lunch was over. Or "Dinner" if you are from the South. The meal at the end of the day is called "Supper". Moments before Dad had stomped out the back door going back to work. He was always either coming from work or going to it. The screen door slammed behind him with a loud screech and thump. He took a thermos of coffee and a cold hot dog to eat on his way to the next job site.

Dad farmed, but it didn't pay the bills, so he built houses too. It was an honorable trade, Dad said. He reminded us from time to time that Jesus was a carpenter. Dad lectured Mom and me soundly before he left about all the things we needed to do and gave us our verbal marching orders. One list for Mom. One list for me. I needed to feed the horses, except for Beauty of course, sweep the patio, and clean up the tack room. I needed to shell corn if the sheller would work. My hands were too small to shell it by hand. That was often the job for my brother, Franky. Mom had the 20-dollar bill Dad gave her for the week's groceries tucked into the pocket of her apron. She needed to weed and water the garden, prepare dinner, and iron our clothes for Sunday services.

My parents were always busy. So was I.

In the wake of his departure the house felt larger, lighter and quiet somehow. Dad was the kind of man who commanded full attention—on a good day. On a good day, his face shone like the sun. If he was angry, we'd slink off into a private place to hide. All too often he seemed angry. When he was angry, he'd yank me right up and spank me for nearly nothing, and if I got in his way, he would accidentally step on me; so, I tried to stay out of his way. Sometimes he seemed angry at us, but Mom said he was angry at life. Mom's hands shook when she poured coffee, and I quivered like a dog at the vet when Dad got angry. But he was not always like that. Sometimes he was kind. Some nights he read to my brother and me and then helped us say our prayers. He told us God always listened and loved us. Did God hear Beauty?

The sound of Mom's stomach rumbling brought me back to the present. I saw her reach for another piece of cornbread. She picked it up and crumbled it slowly between long tapered fingers into a frosted glass of cold buttermilk. Her wedding ring glistened in the sunlight the band worn thin from 20 years of matrimony.

Once the last crumble fell into the milk with a tiny plunk, she picked up an ice-tea spoon, stirred the cornbread several times, then dipped out a spoonful and took a bite. She sighed. Chewed. She stared straight ahead out the window into Aunt Gretta's orchard. Sighed again. I saw the tension in her shoulders visibly unwind. Cornbread was Mom's comfort food.

I shivered and the motion caught Mom's eye. She looked at me intently while absently rubbing the small of her back with her fingers. She was pregnant, the baby due at any time.

I thought of Beauty, also pregnant. Now dead. And the unthinkable popped into my mind. Could Mom die having this baby? If pregnant ponies died, I suddenly realized a pregnant mom could die too.

Brushing my hair out of my eyes I wondered for a moment about the nature of life and who made the life and death decisions for the world. Suddenly I felt extra aware that I was alive and separate from my surroundings and other people. Here we were together in this room, hearts beating, breathing, thinking, sharing this meal, yet I didn't know what Mom was thinking; and she didn't know my thoughts either. We might as well be on opposite sides of the planet, I realized. As if intuiting something, she reached out her hand and pushed back my hair gently tucking it behind my ear, as if to reassure me she was, after all, right there beside me. Her fingertips felt cool. I could smell the cornbread on them. Her touch calmed my mind. Thoughts of death receded into the background, and I felt part of a family unit once more. Safe. There was safety in numbers and in belonging to a family, wasn't there? It kept a person from spinning off into the universe.

Mom's touch made me feel pretty—but the truth was, I was plain. Plain Jane. My arms were too long, feet too big. I was muscular yet skinny and tanned from long hours playing in the pastures behind our house. I didn't have the blue eyes of my namesake, Aunt Jane. Instead, my eyes were green, an expression of the Native American portion of my genes I got from Mom's side of the family. I got my muscles from horseback riding, swimming, and running away from my brother.

I was happiest when I could forget what everyone else thought about me and lose myself instead, running barefoot through the hills and tree-lined fields of our farm behind our house. Normally, there was no death there, only cows and horses, rabbits, squirrels, and bobcats to see. On our farm the trees tilted happily toward the sun as it moved across the sky, day after day. The wind tickled the lush grass in the fields and made it whoosh beneath my feet when I walked. Seasons passed one after the other in an endless cycle of sunshine, snowfall, wind and rain. We lived in God's Country, as opposed to Devil's Land, which is crouched only just down the road from our house. Dad comes from beyond Devil's Land. That's where his family farm still is. I asked Mom once why there is a sign that said Devil's Land right down from our house.

"That's an area that isn't included in any survey," Mom said with a laugh. "It doesn't really mean the devil lives there. It just means it belongs to no one. It's no man's land, really. You didn't think it belonged to the devil, did you?"

I told her I didn't; but really, I did. I'm not sure anyone should live so close to a place called Devil's Land and not give that some serious thought. Truthfully—I'd wanted to move.

But we did live there, and I was growing up as I walked the paths of our farm beneath those tall trees. And sometimes as I walked, I heard the echo of my footsteps vibrate in the deep caverns below our property. At those times I knew I was walking on hollow, not hallowed ground. Those caves beneath our farm had likely been there since time began. I had never seen them, probably never would, but I knew they were there because I could hear them. I did not know what slept in those caverns, or if whatever was there would ever harm us. Maybe the devil lived there, but I'd not yet seen him even though I looked for him underneath my bed every single night.

I ran whenever I could across those fields, I pushed myself, so I didn't have to think too much about what lived underfoot. I ran fast, so nothing could reach out and grab me and drag me under the ground.

I wondered for a moment about what Mom had said about Dad dying, but I couldn't imagine this so I shook the thought out of my head. To me, Dad was immortal.

While it seemed like I'd been thinking for hours sitting at the table, I guess it'd only been a few minutes because only half of Mom's buttermilk and cornbread mix had disappeared. I drank down the rest of my milk and asked Mom, "May I be excused?"

"Did you clean your plate?" she asked.

"Yes, Ma'am! May I have a Rice Krispie treat?"

"Yes. Put your plate in the sink, please! And go do your chores."

I pushed back my chair, got up and gathered my dishes to put them in the sink, and then I grabbed the last treat from the plate on the counter and took a giant bite. It tasted crisp, smooth and sweet.

"Thanks for lunch," I told her and turned toward the door.

"You're welcome," she said, looking at me briefly clearly taking in the state of my dirty shorts and dust smeared top, but she didn't comment on that. Instead she said, "Keep your shirt on, you're too old to be running around without a shirt! If the neighbors see you, there'll be horrified."

How did she read my mind so well? It was so hot outside it could just suck the life right out of a person. I had been known on hot days to hang my shirt on a bush and leave it while I worked or played. My chest was still as flat as a baking pan, and I saw no reason why I should wear a shirt when my brother didn't have to wear one. There was no one around for miles most of the time. But I also knew my behavior shocked Mom, and it would likely shock the neighbors too if they saw me. So, I resolved to keep my shirt on unless I was sure no one, and I mean no one, could see me. I also firmly resolved that when I grew up, I would live so far out in the country that I would be able to walk naked to the mailbox if I wanted to without horrifying anyone.

Mom reached for the *Ladies Home Journal* magazine on the counter. The page was turned down on the section titled 'Can This Marriage be Saved'? She began to read, and I headed outside.

In bed later that night I did what I always did to take my mind off things that worried me. I read a little from *Bambi*, or *Bally the Blue Whale*. I prayed until I got so tired, I didn't really worry about a devil sneaking into my room while I was brushing my teeth and hiding under the bed to wait and eat me after I fell asleep. Sometimes I thought he might come disguised as a tiger. But most of the time it was the devil, all red with horns. But I was too tired tonight to care. Instead, I sang a bit of "You Are My Sunshine" or "Jesus Loves Me" until I couldn't think of the words anymore. Then I recited, "Now I Lay Me Down to Sleep, I Pray the Lord My Soul to Keep, If I Should Die Before I Wake, I Pray the Lord My Soul to Take." And then, finally, my thoughts seemed to fall into place, and I felt okay. It was like Dad said, "God is in control." He controlled everything. He controlled whether Dad was safe. Whether the devil got me or not. Beauty was with God now, and I knew she was safe and free from pain. That thought gave me peace. God would make sure Mom delivered her baby safely. I knew that.

The next morning, I heard footsteps at my bedroom door. I opened my eyes and Aunt Gretta came into my bedroom and gently shook me the rest of the way awake. "You have a baby sister," she said softly with a smile. I looked up into her warm brown eyes; her weathered face was closely framed by curling brown hair thinly laced with gray. It was a kind face. A loving face. Her smile was warm, and she smelled, like she always did, of fresh baked bread and sunshine. Her blue, flower-printed dress was gently wrinkled around the hips and back as if she'd been wearing the same clothes she had on yesterday, and I got the impression she'd been at our house for a while.

I sat up and rubbed the bleariness from eyes. My heart beat fast. "And Mom?" I asked. My voice quivered.

"She's fine! We can go see her after you get dressed and eat breakfast!"

"And what about Dad?" I asked.

Just then Dad came to the door and leaned against the doorframe smiling that Frank Sinatra smile filled with large, even, white teeth. He crossed his tan, muscular arms over his chest. He was not wearing his worn overalls today; instead, he wore a white, freshly pressed Sunday shirt and dark dress pants. He looked handsome and confident. He looked happy.

"I'm fine too, but I nearly had to deliver your baby sister myself! There was some construction at the hospital entrance, and I missed the drive and hit a culvert. For a minute I thought your mother might have the baby in the car!" He laughed the kind of laugh that showed he was a little scared. But now everything was okay.

"Oh, Louis," Aunt Gretta sounded shocked. "I'd hate to think of you delivering a baby."

"Think I couldn't do it? Well, I could do it! I've delivered calves, and pigs and baby rabbits. I could deliver a baby!"

"Well, I'm glad you didn't have to," Aunt Gretta said, her cheeks glowing pink, and she patted her forehead with her apron.

"But everyone's okay, the baby too?" I asked again.

"Yes, they're fine," Dad said.

I lay back in bed, with a soft thump, relief flooding over me. All the worries, all the fears I had were for nothing. Mom was fine. The baby was fine. Dad was standing in the doorway smiling from ear to ear. The whole imaginary devil under the bed thing...that was just stupid, baby stuff. There was no devil here!

"I have a baby sister?" I said, in disbelief. One day there was not a sister, the next there was. Life was a miracle!

And that's how I got a sister. Just like Dad said. No matter what you worry about…that's rarely if ever what actually happens. What really happens is nearly always something you never even thought about. So, there's no point in worrying, right?

Living and dying. Do we have any control over it at all? What was God thinking when he made us all subject to both? There doesn't seem to be any rhyme or reason to it. One day your pony is dying; and then, the next thing you know, you have a brand new sister.

There was so much I don't understand about the world. When I did die and go to Heaven I had a lot of questions for God.

* * *

2002

The wound in my leg from the melanoma has finally healed, but it took a while. Hock and I are trying to put the unpleasant brush with cancer behind us. We work hard. Plan our future. Travel as often as we can when work allows. We talk of other things, carefully avoiding the big "C" word that haunts us. At nights when I can't sleep, I search the Internet for statistics on melanoma that will give me hope. I even write a woman whose melanoma had spread to her brain to ask how she's managed to survive years with it. She sends me a recipe for herb tea she swears has kept her alive. She credits that and dramatic lifestyle changes to avoid stress for her longevity. I keep the letter in my desk drawer and learn to make the tea. Hock and I make plans for work and vacations. We try to act normal. We visit our kids as often as we can.

Then one day the phone rings and I answer. "Jane, if we don't do something, Dad's going to die," my sister tells me over the phone. It's not the first time we've had such a conversation. It reminds me of the conversations with Mom so long ago. The calls from Tennessee seem to come with increasing frequency these days.

"He was fine when I visited last month." I say, standing in my kitchen. I clinch the phone tight, not wanting to go back so soon. I need to control my own stress level.

Over the years I've made the drive through Texas, Arkansas, across the Mississippi, and then finally into Tennessee more times than I can count. I've rolled down that road past flatlands, pine trees, and up and down hills lined with limestone walls in a Mustang, Toyota, Ford, Oldsmobile and Porsche. My best time to make the drive was nine hours. That was in the red 944 Porsche — of course. That was when Mom was sickest yet before I moved to Northern Georgia to be closer. The worst time took 21 hours in a blinding snowstorm.

Sometimes I've traveled with Christmas presents tucked into every corner of the trunk. Other times I've traveled light with only a weekend bag in the passenger side floor.

"What happened this time?"

And so, she launches into the story of Dad's latest misadventure. "He was working in the heat, his blood sugar got too low when he was operating the loader on a job site in town," my sister says. "When he realized it was low, he said he thought maybe he shouldn't try to climb off the loader, so instead he drove it to McDonalds to get some orange juice. As he pulled through the drive-thru he tore the canopy over the customer window right off with the top of the loader. He's in the hospital now. Mostly his pride is hurt. They just want to stabilize his blood sugar and run some tests before they send him home."

"Jane, I just can't do this by myself anymore," she continues. "I have to work. I'm getting a divorce. It's too much. I wish Franky were here," she says, wistfully. "I think he could handle Dad better than I do?"

I nod but don't say anything.

While I had moved to Georgia when Mom was sick to be closer and help take care for her, my sister did the heavy lifting on that one. And with my brother dead, now I know—it's my turn to take the lead in caring for an elder parent, regardless of how inconvenient it is.

"Can you come and keep an eye on him for a while?" she asks.

I know from the tone in her voice, she's had enough, and understandably so. The stress from caring for Mom likely contributed to the end of her marriage and took away from the time she had with her two girls who are not yet grown. No doubt she'd like a few days of not having to worry about what Dad's up to and spend some time with them.

"Of course, I'll come," I tell her, wishing—like her—that our dead brother was still alive. Dad has more respect for men than women, I thought. He'd have been way more likely to listen to Franky.

"If I leave in the morning, I'll be there late tomorrow night," I tell her.

We talk a little more about Dad and what the doctors plan to do. We run over the possibilities of what we might do if he does not get better. Few of the options seem workable. Most seem downright impossible. Dad will not easily surrender the reins of his life to others, and we are reluctant to wrestle them from his hands.

When is it appropriate to start making decisions for someone else? I wonder after I hang up. Neither of us feels equal to the task. Yet our concern that he will hurt himself or someone else grows stronger each day.

The next morning, I kiss my husband goodbye in Texas and point my car toward Tennessee once again. As I drive my mind drifts back to all the history and all the memories that come with my family home. It is a place where I galloped my horse through pastures of thick tall grass and threw myself off like cowboys did on television shows. Confident as only a child can be, I felt invincible, made of rawhide and a bit rubber, and there was nothing I could not do. There were also very few bones that I had not broken, yet I persisted in this optimism of hope and survival despite all the plaster casts I chalked up.

But I'm older now. I know from experience that life and bodies are fragile, and they can and do break. Dad's is breaking now. What on earth are we going to do about Dad? I wonder as I drive.

◇

"For as in Adam all die, so also in Christ shall all be made alive."
(1 Corinthians 15:22)

◇

Cornbread and Buttermilk
Fill chilled glass ¾ full of cold buttermilk.
Crumble freshly-made (but cold) cornbread into the milk.
Stir until cornbread is saturated with buttermilk but not soggy.
Eat with a spoon.
Enjoy.

Chapter 2 – Roasted Possum
"Is she dead? Or is she just playing possum?" — Jane

2005
Not far from my old Tennessee home now. As I drive the sun sets behind me and the sky darkens to a deep blue in front of me. The limestone hillsides of Nashville rush up to meet me in the glare of my car headlights, then flash past and fall away into the black night behind.

It is sometimes easier to let history fade into the background of your mind replaced by every-day new, life. Physical distance sometimes provides the space we need to break free of the past. At least it worked for me, for a while. If you work hard at it, you may almost entirely forget your past. But like old bones buried, the slightest thing can scratch memories to the surface. A smell, the way the sun shines on a spring day.

In my new life I feel sorry for that other younger Tennessee girl who lost her brother, her mother, and, in many ways, her entire family. Moving away to Texas really didn't change anything about my past. It only made me think I'd changed it. But, in my new life, most of the time, I no longer feel like that girl.

But as I drive back to where it all happened, I suddenly become her again.

Finally, I pull up at a hotel in my hometown. I take my things from the car and go inside, fall onto the bed in my room and close my eyes without undressing. Here I am…again…. where the earth still feels hollow under my feet.

The next morning, I drive out to the old country house where Dad lives. Dad built this house, but it is not the house I grew up in. That house is across a horseshoe-shaped subdivision that Dad developed during my childhood. The original house was the one Dad built when he was young, and he and Mom were only just married. They built the first house before they had children back in the mid-to-late 40s when their world was filled with hope and possibilities shortly after WWII ended.

The house where Dad lives now is also the house where Mom died.

While glad for a much larger, nicer, cleaner home than the first one, Mom never forgot that this home was not originally built for her. None of the nice new houses Dad built during his career as a house builder were ever built for her.

This house was built on the foundation of shattered dreams that never came true. While it is a lovely house down a winding drive nestled in the trees, there is no shelter here. The house lacks the warmth and homecoming it once had now that Mom is gone. I turn in and drive down the driveway, then stop, turn off the motor, and step out. I take the well-worn path around back to the kitchen door, tap lightly, call, "Dad", then open the door and go inside without waiting for a response.

Dad stands in the kitchen, newly home from the hospital. His arm is in a sling, but otherwise he looks pretty much like he did the last time I saw him. He is attempting to wash dishes with a long-handled sponge. He turns and smiles at me, and I say again louder, "Hello Dad!"

"Well, hello you Great Big Beautiful Doll," his nickname for Mom. "Where did you come from?"

I kiss his head and say, "I drove up yesterday. Got in last night. Late. I'm staying at a hotel in town." The kiss leaves a lipstick print, and I gently the it off before giving him a hug.

The only place for me to sleep if I spend the night here is in Mom's old room. It still has the rose-colored carpet she had the day she died. The spread is the same one she had on the bed. It has been 5 years, but I'm still not ready to sleep in her room. Honestly…I'm not sure I'll ever be ready to spend the night here again.

"Well, it's a good thing you are here," he says smiling that crooked smile of his. Dad's teeth are yellowed and cracked from 80 years of chewing. He brushes them daily with pride, the last of his peers still using his God-given original set.

The pajamas he wears were a Christmas present from my sister 10 years back, minus the white tasseled Santa hat.

"Why's that?" I ask, thinking he will mention his recent hospital stay.

He taps his hand against the red- and white-striped pajama leg and says…

"Well, Jane. It appears I've forgotten how to cook."

"What do you mean, you've forgotten how to cook?" I ask, moving the cereal boxes a comfortable distance from the hot stove.

"I put the muffins in the oven in a plastic dish, and it melted," he says. "The muffins were still good. I ate the last one this morning."

I pat his arm. "Dad, they make silicone ovenware these days that looks like plastic, but it's not. You can't put real plastic in the oven. They do look a bit alike though, so I can see why you might find it a little confusing." I smooth aside the strands of hair that he's attempted to comb over to cover his scalp.

"Well, I wanted to make you breakfast," he said.

"Dad don't cook. Let me take you out to breakfast. Okay?"

"Okay, if you'll let me ride in your fancy car," he says as he hands me my coffee. He always picks the crustiest cup. The coffee comes from his trusty little, dented aluminum percolator, despite several modern coffee makers in the kitchen. This ancient percolator has that clear, glass top that might allow an impatient witness to visually count the burst progressions and guess the thickness content of the brew. Sometimes Dad forgets to screw the glass cap on tight enough, and the cap and coffee can shoot off in the air like a wildcat oil well. This time, however, the glass top appears secure.

"Breakfast with my rich daughter, the writer. Wow!" he calls out from his bedroom while changing. He is no doubt changing into what I know will be threadbare clothes and shoes with holes in the toes and heels.

I hear drawers open but don't hear them close, and something falls over beside his bed with a muffled thump on the well-worn carpet. It sounds like a glass of water. With a firm mental-discipline I resist the inclination to rescue him and clean up the mess. Instead, I empty a nearby chair of heavy equipment and sales catalogs and magazines so I can sit down to wait.

"Rich daughter?" I'm not rich. I'm a struggling writer with a 5-year-old car. But it's all new to Dad who drives a 1972 Toyota pickup with a fish and chips box wedged under the frame of the headlight to keep the light centered. A nameless, small-town gossip wrote the local newspaper last Christmas saying all they wanted for Christmas that year was for Mr. Hinkle to buy a new truck.

I have traveled...a lot. And I've lived far from home since I first married... young. Dad lives a mile from where his mother gave birth to him in Middle Tennessee. Once I asked him to come and live with me in Texas, but he refused. He does not want to die so far from home.

Gazing around I see my blacksmith-grandfather's ancient shotgun leaned, business end up, next to Dad's desk that's squeezed into the corner of the kitchen. I know without checking—the gun is loaded. A single careless sneeze and either of us could be chatting with St. Peter before we ever swallow a bite of breakfast. I gingerly pick up the gun and shove it under some old coats thrown down on the floor behind the desk. Judging from the musky dust on the clothing, with luck, he won't find it for months, years maybe—if ever.

Dad believes in saving everything from old furniture to nails for that rainy day. When working in the garage, he carefully straightens each nail he finds one by one, with a hammer against his father's blacksmith anvil and puts them into an old Leo peppermint stick can. He uses the same bath towel and washcloth for a week to avoid unnecessary wear on his washer and dryer. He opens and shuts the refrigerator door quickly to avoid letting the cold air out. Dad lives largely in the dark only turning on lights if it's "absolutely necessary".

He comes from a long line of Depression Era folks who believed in thrift in all things and survival of the fittest. But the most significant accomplishment I attribute to Dad's survival instincts remains his uncanny ability to eat almost anything, in any state of sanitation or decay, and keep living. He modestly credits his microwave for much of this biological survival as, "Those magic waves kill all bacteria."

Still drinking the coffee, I meander around the kitchen. Junk lines the kitchen table and the counters. I know without looking, the freezer still contains the carton of butter pecan ice cream I scooped from two days before 9-11. That was the day Mom died. I can't discern a single square inch of his wooden desktop under the stacked, waist-high piles of dried orange peels and pecan shells, mixed between layers of more industrial catalogs and endless bills. I lean in and can easily determine the relative age of the fruit peels, much like an archaeologist, by looking at the date of the bills. I stare in disbelief at the date on his phone book. 1967! My thoughts shot back to the child I once was, growing up, before Mom died, before Dad had to learn to cook.

* * *

1967

"Your father likes food best if it's free," Mom once told me when I was still a child. We stood at the kitchen sink washing turnip greens a neighbor gave Dad, preparing to blanch them and scoop them into freezer bags.

At that time, the full depth of his survivalist obsession was still unknown to my Mom brother and me. Always prone to the unexpected even when I was a child, Dad often had odd thoughts or behaved in what we thought were strange ways. Of course, all this really blossomed after my brother's unexpected death. But even before that, Dad had an unusual take on life. It was true, he liked food, but he liked it better if he didn't have to pay for it. And he liked women to stay at home and not get out without their "man folk". This resulted in Mom not getting her driver's license until well after she had children. If we needed to go somewhere, Dad took us.

"A woman's place is in the home," Dad always said. "Nothing good ever came from a woman going to town by herself," he added. And he wasn't taking any chances with Mom. She was beautiful, and without trying she attracted attention of both men and women alike wherever she went. She did not welcome that attention, and I recalled many times when she would catch someone looking at her, and her cheeks would flame red, and her hands would shake. Before Mom learned to drive, Dad did most of the shopping. Once a week, I'd stand in line at the meat counter of the local grocery with Dad.

The store was so close to the railroad tracks in town that the canned goods sometimes danced along the shelves from the sheer vibration of a passing train. The engine whistle threatened to shatter the windows and made conversation impossible.

"How much is that pot roast?" Dad asked the meat clerk once the train sounds faded.

"Twenty-five cents a pound, sir."

Dad hung his head and curled his shoulders forward in defeat. He uttered a low two-tone whistle like some men used to compliment pretty girls.

"How do people afford that?" he gasped. "That must be for rich people! How much is the shoulder?" He lifted his cap and scratched the black hair on the top of his head, then proudly smoothed it back and reseated his cap with the name of his construction company printed across the bright yellow fabric.

The clerk looked at Dad's hair and work-roughened hands. "Well, it is a day old, maybe I could mark it down to 20 cents a pound, just for you?"

Dad groaned. "That must be for your million-dollar clients. What do you have for the likes of poor folks like us?"

He motioned at me and, unable to help myself, I hung my head down too, so my blonde hair fell over my face. I sucked in my stomach until my pants dropped down below my belly button, and I tried to look pathetic and hungry like the children I saw on the cover of *National Geographic*. I coughed a little thinking it rounded out the effect nicely and didn't take much effort since I had an allergy to wood burning fireplaces anyway.

There I stood, a pathetic sight and, often, the clerk would put a red sale sticker on the chuck roast, and Dad would walk out with a satisfied smile on his face. The great hunter had bagged another catch. The clerk had no way of knowing that, yes, we might drive an old car with springs poking through the seats and holes in the floor, and Dad might wear old clothes, but we also had the only swimming pool in town. A nine-foot deep, Cinderella Pool, special, all the way from Chicago, complete with vinyl sides and white coping around the perimeter.

There was even a fiberglass diving board. But Dad hadn't gotten around to installing that yet. My brother had temporarily solved this problem by rolling up a huge tree stump to the edge of the pool for us to dive off and into the cool, deep water on a summer day. It didn't bounce us up and down, but it gave us some extra height. Elly May Clampett would have been proud of this "cement pond" diving board.

In the 60s, Dad had established himself as a fine homebuilder. Sometimes he took my brother and me to the job site to work for 10 whopping cents an hour. While other girls in my class tried out for cheerleading or gymnastics, I worked for Dad. I'd run twine between stakes he set to mark what would eventually be the perimeter of a new house. I'd firm up the stakes, pounding them into the ground with the flat end of my favorite little red-handled ax. (The axe was a special present from Dad, as he felt all little girls need axes.) With my own axe, he'd have me chop down small bushes, and then I'd pick up rocks and stack them while he whistled, "You are My Sunshine" to me and point where I should hammer in the next stake.

One Saturday mornings I would put on frayed denim shorts and a tee-shirt and ride along with Dad to the job site in his lowboy hauling the loader, a beautiful, little, yellow John Deere 450 loader with…as in…well…a big shovel on the front, if you are new to the heavy equipment world. While other girls lay in their beds late on Saturday reading *Teen Magazine* mooning over their favorite records and movie stars, I recited names of trucks and heavy equipment in my head as I bumped along the highway riding beside Dad in his truck before sun-up.

"This new loader may be small, but it's highly man-eu-ver-able," Dad said as we rumbled along. He knew big words but didn't graduate from high school. However, he came close; lacking only a few months. He dropped out in 1938 to help on the farm when his dad caught a bad case of the flu. No farm? No food.

Before that he'd been a straight A student. He liked using the big words, as he said, "with four or more syllables." A large vocabulary, he felt, improved his ability to sell houses and garnered the respect of rich engineers who worked at the air force base near our town. People who could help him "make it." People who were "big shots." They were "some-body." Dad wanted to be a big shot, some-body too, some-day. Dad was also a wizard at math and at diagrams so building came easy for him. And he also had a gift for persuasive writing proved by the fact that Mother married him based largely on years of correspondence between them.

    I nodded and gazed with longing out the window at the passing greenery. Each time he hauled me and my little red axe out for a trip, I wondered if he'd make me work until noon or until past dark. You never knew for sure with Dad. The rumbling noise of our arrival that day at the job made the earth shake and the trees quiver and startled all the birds, causing them to fly away in one giant whooshing of wings. Dad shut the truck engine down when we arrived and we both got out of the truck. He studied the site for a moment. The silence reigned briefly until Dad started up the loader and began uprooting trees! He piled them in one corner of the lot to clear a driveway for the house he planned to build. I watched from the sidelines in fascination prepared to do anything he asked.

    He pressed down on one tree with the bucket of the loader. I saw a mother with her children clinging for dear life to her back, run out of the brush nearby. Nothing escaped Dad's notice on his turf, especially a potential "free" meal. He spotted her at once. And the possum chase was on.

    Dad ignored the trees and gunned the loader engine. Black smoke boiled out the overhead exhaust pipe. Under my feet, I could feel the ground pitch and rumble. Quickly, he backed away from the tree, expertly maneuvering the loader as if on an obstacle course. With incredible race car driving skill, he started to chase down the possum. Could a loader outrace a possum? These are questions country folk need answers to. Giving the engine another blast, Dad gripped the ever-present toothpick tighter between his teeth, cocked it skyward like a dueling sword and set out to corner the possum with the loader. I ran alongside the predator and the prey. I had to scurry aside to get out of his way at times. He nearly ran over me more than once as I dodged and leaped to escape.

    The possum kicked into high gear, waddling rapidly toward the woods, a blur of dirty white fur and spinning gray legs. Her bare, pink tail flowed out behind her like a flag at half-mast. Dad intercepted by running the loader between her and the woods. She paused in confusion as only a possum can, and then struck out in an entirely new direction. Dad backed up and set out to cut her off again. This happened half a dozen times in scant minutes as he advanced and retreated on the loader like it was one of Patton's tanks. Through a clear patch in the dust, I watched the possum, her mouth slightly open, panting. Her little button eyes bulged. She seemed puzzled, and unsure what to do next.

    Halfway on yet another misguided attempt to reach the woods, possum children lost their grip one after the other and fell from their mother's back like tiny sailors abandoning ship. One dropped and rolled in the grass to scurry under a bush. Another fell off backward and rolled into a small ditch. A third catapulted into a wild azalea; a fourth rolled into a tangle of uprooted honeysuckle vine as its mother raced to escape the fast-advancing metal menace.

Finally, unable to get between her and the woods with the loader again, Dad threw the machine into park and bailed out chasing the possum down on foot. His heavy work boots hurled thick clods of dirt into the air behind him with every step. As he ran, he picked up a softball-size rock with the clean sweeping hand of a professional third baseman retrieving a grounder. With the sweep and the rock up, he aimed, wound up and let it fly. I heard a sickening thud, and the possum pitched over into the dirt, its skull crushed.

"Is she dead? Or is she playing possum?" I asked Dad once I made it over to where he stood.

"She died before she hit dirt," he replied using his tongue to pass the toothpick from one side to the other of his mouth. He pulled out his pocketknife, rolled her over and neatly slit her throat. Blood trickled into the dirt.

"Your Mom sure is going to be surprised when I bring this home for dinner."

Dinner? Behind us I heard possum children scurrying to hide deeper in the undergrowth. Briefly, I considered joining them. My eyes remained on the dead mother possum, my heart felt like a lump of coal in my chest. It was the first time I'd seen anything dead up close.

"What will happen to her babies?" I asked Dad, but what I really wanted to know was: did he really intend to feed us a possum momma for dinner?

"Don't worry about them. They're big enough to take care of themselves." He walked to the truck and pulled out a machete he kept under the seat to cut weeds. With one swift hack against a nearby stone, he severed the possum's head from its body and tossed the head into the bushes. Then, with his pocketknife, he slit it down the middle and down each leg before pulling the white fur off in one long, stretchy piece that resembled a baby's coveralls. In only a few minutes, he'd dressed the possum and placed her on ice in the Coleman cooler we'd brought for drinks. The meat looked clean and pink. Dad wiped off the machete with a paper towel from a roll he kept behind the seat, then placed it back in its sheath. He rolled up the pelt and stuck it in beside the machete. Later he'd nail it to the back wall of our garage with the various rabbit and raccoon skins he'd already collected. He secured the lid on the cooler and set it in the back of the truck.

Dinner? Possum? Never! No one I knew ate possum. What's Mom going to do? I wondered as I went back to work picking up rocks and sticks.

Later Mom stared into the ice chest sitting on the kitchen counter. "A possum, Louis? You've got to be kidding me. I have a roast thawing in the refrigera-

Page 31

tor. I'm not cooking that filthy possum in my oven. I just cleaned it!"

She placed her fist on her hip and stared meaningfully at Dad for a moment as if to size up his determination. Something in her assessment gave her encouragement and she continued, "You know, my father told me the best way to eat a possum was to throw it out the window and eat only the potatoes cooked with it."

"Why did he say that?" I asked.

My older brother Franky, home from his day with Scouts where he'd been working to earn his survivalist training badge, walked up behind me, looked over my shoulder at the possum and said, "Mmmm…" He rubbed his stomach. "Looks good to me! When do we eat?"

"What a fake!" I punched backward into his stomach with my elbow. "Seeing a dead bird makes you puke!"

"Does not!" he punched back catching me in the side.

"Does too!"

"I killed it. I brought it home, and you'll cook it." Dad glared at Mom. "We can't waste food!"

Mom sighed. "I'll cook it. But I'm not eatin' it."

While Dad and Franky went to wash up, Mom turned the oven on with a flip of her wrist, pulled the broiler out of a cabinet and slung it on the counter with a metallic thump. She picked up the possum from the ice chest with pinky fingers extended and washed it under a steady stream of cold water from the sink faucet. Then she salted, peppered, and placed it in a baking dish. With expert hands, she created a foil tent—open at both ends for viewing—then placed it over the dish and slid it all into the oven to cook at 375 degrees.

During the afternoon, I peeked through the oven window more than once. Will that possum look like a chicken? What will it taste like? Are we really going to eat it? Dad worked at his desk behind folding doors in a corner of the den that adjoined the kitchen. The possum bubbled away. Its shoulders turned a lovely brown and shrank to less than half their original size. I gathered from the shrinkage that possum had more than average quantities of fat and moisture. If I hadn't known better, I could have mistaken it for a very long, small chicken. What meat remained seemed hardly sufficient to feed one person, let alone a family. Finally, I settled down in my bedroom, just across a large foyer from the kitchen, piled up with pillows on the bed to read. I heard Mom check the progress of the possum in the oven once or twice. It smelled…unusual. It gave off a bit of an oily, wild, fetid mushroom-ish smell.

Eventually, I heard Mom open the oven door for the last time and remove the casserole dish setting it down with a thump on a trivet on the kitchen table.

Moments later Dad called, "Jane, what would you like? A set of ribs? A shoulder?" There was a lilt to his voice that I deeply disliked. It happened when he felt particularly satisfied and happy with himself about something he'd done that he knew really bothered the rest of us. It seemed to say, 'See-there, now that I've forced you to see things my way, now you will recognize that I am right after all.'

"How about you, Franky?" he asked, with the same tone.

Franky didn't answer from his room next to mine. Had he fallen asleep? I wondered.

"I'm really not hungry," I called back.

"Come on! Try it!" Dad suggested. "Possum's just like catfish or shrimp—they're scavengers, but there's nothing wrong with the meat. It's good eatin'." He tried to tempt me by mentioning my two favorite dishes. I shuddered. There was no way I could eat the oily, crusty meat, after seeing the furry little thing all wild-eyed and fearful right before he slit its throat. In the kitchen, I heard Dad taking a plate from the cabinet preparing to eat his prize. Several minutes later Mom peeked into my bedroom and motioned me to put shoes on and come with her. She also signaled my brother from his room, then gathered her keys and purse from atop the sewing machine table in the foyer. When Dad turned his back in our direction, we snuck out of the house, closing the screen door slowly so it wouldn't slam. Dad had recently begun to lose his hearing, so we managed this easier than you might imagine. Carefully, we opened the car doors and got in real quiet so as not to tip him off we were leaving. Thank goodness Mom had recently learned to drive—! Though she did drive super-slow and tended to "hug the ditch" at times, it gave us much more freedom; and we were glad for that freedom now.

Mom started the car and turned to us. "Want to go to Dairy Queen and get a hamburger?"

"Yeah!" A hamburger sounded better than possum.

When we came home that night, Dad had washed all the dishes before retiring. On the table sat a plate piled high with dry, naked bones, the entire skeleton of the possum reconstructed on the plate. To me, his work appeared worthy of a museum exhibit.

Staring at them I asked Mom, "Why did Dad spend so much time and energy chasing down that possum?"

Mom folded her arms around my brother and me and hugged us close. "Your father remembers a time when people had to kill if they wanted to eat. When his father brought his mother home as a young bride, he killed a dozen pigs and left her to butcher them and render the lard while he took a team of horses and went to Indiana to buy a new wagon."

"Wow," I said, thinking this was not my idea of the perfect honeymoon!

"Doesn't sound like much fun, does it?" Mom asked.

"Not much." It was hard for me to imagine the life she described.

Looking at the pile of bones on the plate, I realized, if I'd wanted to, I could take Dad's reconstruction of the entire possum to school and teach a science class about possum anatomy with it. I could have—but I wouldn't. The sight of that skeleton made me feel proud and embarrassed all at once. Thinking about my friends, I realized not one of them could relate to my life with Dad.

In Sunday school sometimes, the teacher told us stories and then helped us see the lesson in the story. I looked at the bones and tried to see the lesson in the day's events but couldn't find one.

Mom patted my head. Then she lifted the plate of bones and tipped them into the trash can with a thump before placing the plate in the sink.

"Time for bed," she announced and flicked off the kitchen light.

In my bed, eyes spread wide in the blackness, I pictured the scared baby possums still out there somewhere huddled motherless under the bushes. They too must be staring into the blackness, wondering what happened to their mom. I wondered if they'd found their mother's head yet. Would they cuddle up to it, or would they eat it? I wondered. They were, after all, scavengers.

* * *

2007

"I'm ready to go." Dad's words from the bedroom startle me back into the present. When he comes into the kitchen, I see he's changed into a worn light-blue shirt and navy pants with a paperclip replacing the zipper pull. He keeps his pencil and pen in his front shirt pocket by securing the opening with red yarn tied to the buttonhole and wrapped several times around the button. The excess yarn hangs limply down his shirtfront like a medal. His pants hang on an old leather belt on which he's used an ice pick to make new holes so he can pull the belt tighter. Like that old possum in the oven way back when, he too is shrinking. He wears a soft slipper on his bad foot and a dress shoe on the good one. He picks up his straw hat and Mom's old cane, the one with a brass duck head for a handle. Together we head for the car; his large, calloused arthritic hand rests in the crook of my arm.

"I want waffles," he tells me as I close the door behind us.

"Not possum?" I ask.

"Possum! Why would I want possum?"

And then I realize—all those things I can't stop thinking about? He's completely forgotten them.

◇

"And to every beast of the earth and to every bird of the heavens and to everything that creeps on the earth, everything that has the breath of life, I have given every green plant for food." (Genesis 1:30)

◇

Roasted Possum

Take one fresh possum.
Cut the head and tail off and discard.
Gut.
Skin.
Wash thoroughly in cold water.
Soak for 2 hours in brine of 2 tablespoons salt and ¼ cup apple cider vinegar and sufficient water to cover possum.
Rinse.
Place in baking dish with 1-inch water in the bottom.
Salt and pepper to taste.
Add pearl onions and potatoes to water once it reaches 120-degree internal temperature.

Cook at 350 degrees until internal temperature reaches 180.
Suggested side dishes turnip greens and steamed carrots sprinkled with fresh dill and butter.

Chapter 3 – Frog Legs
"I could have been someone," Dad says again, and on more than one occasion. I want to say, "You are someone now! You are my Dad!" — Jane

2006
"This may be the last time I'm here when you visit," Dad tells me over the phone during my next trip to Tennessee.

I am here yet again trying to sort out what's best for Dad.

"When do you plan to come out to the house?" His voice sounds matter of fact, as if he's announced he plans to change coffee brands or car tires, not about changing from a house to assisted living. But I understand what he is really doing. He's flirting with this new reality, feeling the words on his lips, bringing them into the conversation as bait to see if I'll bite. If I do, he will yank the words back and argue that he's just fine, that he doesn't need to move into assisted living and that he doesn't need help. In short, he wants to pick a fight with me. So, I say nothing.

"I could have been someone," he says out of the blue.

I want to say, *You are someone now! You are my Dad!* But I can't seem to choke out the words. We both know that he's not the father I wanted, and I'm not the daughter he ordered. The love that connects us is as thin and taunt as a spider web. It feels like a single puff of wind could break our connection, and not just the phone connection.

I am across town staying at my sister's apartment this time, sitting on her balcony, watching the sun come up over the trees, drinking coffee.

When I'm in town and can't afford a hotel, I stay here. She rented the apartment when she left her husband as a temporary move until the property settlement is arranged. I still can't bring myself to spend the night at Dad's house. I remember my nieces, my sister, and me circled around Mom's bed as she took her last breath. It is not something I talk about with Dad, but I think he knows why I don't stay.

The apartment is quite different from the little house my sister and her husband built and own nestled deep in the woods close to where Dad lives. She lived there for more than 20 years. That was the house where she yearned for children and finally had them. It was the house where her marriage frayed away at the seams due, in part, to the heavy burden of helping out aging and sick parents. That was the house where she grieved Mom's death and tried to build a life for herself again.

She's moved out of the house and into an apartment thinking a fresh start in new surroundings would help. But pain is not something you can move away from. It follows you like a shadow sometimes. Her ex-husband lives at her little house alone now, for the time being, as they negotiate the divorce. It is my hope she will get her house back someday. With all its imperfections, it is part of her heritage a lot of which was actually good. Maybe if she can only find a way to recall those good moments again, everything will work out.

We both carry wounds, inside and out mental and physical. Recently I've had surgery on my thumb to correct damage caused by osteoarthritis. During the recovery I learned to write with my opposite hand. The surgery forced me to slow down and think about what I wanted to say before I wrote it. Taking time to compose your thoughts can be a very good thing.

My husband and I took a much-needed vacation to Cabo two weeks ago to celebrate the success of my reconstructed thumb. There we held hands as we walked along sandy beaches and ate and drank more than was wise. No worries could find us there as we stepped leisurely through crystal clear waves and watched the fish curiously inspecting our toes. There, only happy thoughts lingered in my head, thoughts of all the possibilities ahead of us in life. Perhaps I would attend law school or write a book. My husband and I rode horses at sunset side-by-side and raced across the beach laughing, sand flying out behind the hooves of our mounts.

How quickly all that has become a distant memory. It feels like someone else's life, certainly not the life of this girl who sits on a balcony in Tennessee staring at coffee she can't swallow wondering how to keep her Dad from accidentally killing himself or someone else. Tennessee is filled with complications. My nieces are growing rapidly. I still have no idea what to do about Dad.

This time I came to visit because a neighbor called the police claiming she met Dad driving on the wrong side of the road carrying the dozer on his tractor-trailer truck. She reported he nearly forced her off the road. No one was hurt. Dad denied it happened. But my sister and I both know—it's just a matter of time before he injures or kills himself or someone else.

The discussion of an assisted living facility creeps into nearly every conversation. Dad has finally agreed to visit a few places just to look. And that is my mission today.

Dad is not an easy guy to deal with. He has his rules, and they apply to everything in his world. The rules are, "touch nothing, move nothing, take nothing. And leave him alone." There is hell to pay for anyone who breaks the rules. Hell can take many forms – from verbal assault to suddenly finding yourself facing the business end of a shotgun.

Mom had a knack for knowing what Dad would tolerate and what would send him into orbit. It is the kind of knowledge that comes from living with someone for more than half a century.

But she is gone now. And my sister has found herself, more than once, on the wrong end of Dad's shotgun AFTER she cleaned the house, or "helped" him with something, uninvited.

When I was a kid Dad padlocked the door to his office in our house after Mom cleaned it one day. After that, no one entered the room or dusted it for more than 20 years. Dad's rules have a long history that likely date back to his childhood. Mom told us the doctor delivered him with forceps and that the pressure crushed part of his brain. Whether this is true or not, it's clear that the only way to get along with Dad is to let him have his way whenever possible.

Often, I marvel at how patient Dad is with non-family members and how impatient he is with the rest of us. It is one of many quirky contradictions. Since Mom's death he's hired a succession of misfits, malcontents, and a few gold-digging women with questionable reputations to "clean" his house under his unique directives. Sometimes they "kept books" for him. For a few months he even hired a parolee to run errands. Dad believes everyone deserves a second chance. The parolee stole one of his cars and took it to Florida. Dad said she must have needed it, and he thought she would bring it back–eventually. So far, she has not.

However, the "DON'T MOVE ANYTHING" rule applies to help as well as family. Most of the time, the "help" stays only long enough to exploit him in some way or ask for their pay in advance and then move on. One backed his car up to Dad's garage and took a good portion of his tools. Another ex-con stole a roll of copper wire that would barely squeeze into the back of his car. Copper brings a high price at the recycle center in town.

One sweet, young thing, with only a few missing teeth, rubbed his bald head and asked him to marry her. She then stole his wallet and bought all the cases of cigarettes and beer at the local convenience store she could before tossing his wallet into the garbage can on her way out the door. The one that worries him the most is the one that took his phone and made international phone calls running up his cell bill several thousand dollars. That one, for some reason, bothers Dad more than all the others combined. He has a long list of the dates and calls he's made to the cell phone company trying to get the charges removed from his bill. I'm not sure how this will settle out, but I think if diabetes doesn't kill him his blood pressure during these calls will most likely do the trick. All this and we, his family, can't dust off his windowsill or put away his oatmeal box without him yelling.

Long-lost relatives and children of dead friends with hard luck stories parade through his life with uncanny regularity. They all have one thing in common. They all need money. Only last year Dad arrived at his shop to find one of our relatives loading Craftsman tools into his trunk along with several practically new skill saws. Dad gave him the tools and took him to lunch. He gave him 20 dollars from his wallet when they parted, along with a hug, big-handed pat on the back and the cautionary shake of his finger while saying, "Don't do it again, or I may have to shoot you."

It is clear Dad needs help. Despite doctor's advice he continues on much as he has always done. He worries friends and terrifies neighbors. They will call me and my sister regularly to keep us informed about what our crazy Dad is doing this time. They relate all his near misses if we aren't there in person to witness them first-hand. One week he's up on the roof in the rain adjusting the TV antenna. The next he's working outside in 90-degree weather with a cutting-torch cutting up steel to haul for salvage. He writes angry letters to the neighbors and to us and overall seems angry at life. Yes he prays daily, attends church regularly and loves his God. These are two very difficult behaviors to reconcile.

I've tried to talk to Dad about his driving and his other bizarre habits more than once. But he won't listen. "It's time for you to stop working," I tell him. I explain how if he sells off his assets, he could have enough money to support himself, go fishing for the rest of his life and leave a good-sized nest egg to all his children and grandchildren. But he refuses to sell and refuses to stop working.

"Work is the only thing I have left," he replies. "I hate to give it up."

And I must admit, the thought of finding things to entertain Dad other than work is intimidating. His blood sugar soars and plummets like a kite and this is a big part of his problem. Sometimes he finds it hard to think and focus. He slurs his words. However, he still somehow manages to drive…and to work. Once home, he collapses. Sometimes he skips supper and bath. Once in a while I'll ask him if he's bathed and he responds, "Why? Do I smell?"

The truth is—sometimes he does. It seems he is afraid he'll fall in the tub and no one will find him until it's too late. Yet off he goes to work every day with absolutely no fear that I can discern. At home again, sometimes he gets up in the night and can't find his way back to bed. He hired a handyman to carpet over the linoleum in the kitchen so when he gets lost, he can lie down comfortably wherever he is until he can make his way back to his bedroom.

Yet he lingers on like a relic inhabiting his old life the best he can. He is like an actor, reluctant to leave a familiar stage after years of holding his audience captive. It is a stage where various dramas that attract highly emotional and controversial reviews have unfolded. Most of the dramas require regular participation from us—his often unwillingness and ever so shocked audience-family. It is difficult for him to face the last curtain call for his lifelong performance or for him to move to a smaller stage, one where there are other actors playing similar roles in their own family dramas. Our home, once the scene of conflict, anger, joy and tears, sits all too silent among the oak trees skirted with junk, broken-down cars, trucks, cast-off equipment of every kind, relics of a life that is fading away. Somehow all this junk makes Dad feel safe. The why of this entirely escapes me.

Though he still works, on some days Dad stays a little longer at home in the mornings. He spends more time stretched out in his recliner watching the birds and squirrels through the sliding glass door in the den, or feeding his blue beta fish, Gus, too much. Sometimes he invites in the cat Tom for breakfast and then together they plan what he will plant in the garden next spring when he feels better.

I can tell we are approaching a point of no return. Some sort of alternative living arrangements needs to be made—and soon. But he is far from the typical "rest home" candidate. Dad is still incredibly physically fit despite a host of ailments that should indicate otherwise. His brain does sometime check out on his body. But often he continues on much like the energizer bunny and doesn't miss it all that much. My sister and I want him to be part of the decision-making process while he is still able. Yet, he remains undecided. If he does not make the decision soon, we will be forced, for the sake of his safety and everyone else's, to make the assisted-living decision for him. But when is the appropriate time to take such a step? Once taken, you cannot take it back. How will we know if what we are doing is right for him…and for us?

Eventually, I stir from my place on the balcony at my sister's apartment where I've sat alone since she left for work. I toss my cold, ignored coffee down the kitchen sink, and put on some clothes. I drive through at a fast-food restaurant and purchase breakfast. Thirty minutes later I arrive at Dad's door holding a bag containing biscuits filled with eggs and bacon in one hand, my car keys in the other.

Before knocking and entering, I stand on the patio to let the dew dry on my feet and appreciate the sun's warmth on my face. Across the yard I see Mom's old plant stands, piled in a heap. On the ground nearby lay discarded flowers that have taken root and bloomed in thin, unfriendly soil under the oaks. There are abandoned truck doors leaning up against several decomposing tree stumps.

Almost every square inch of the yard is covered in jumbled array of discarded items of every description that only a man who owned a construction company could find and hoard. And yet there is a kind of beauty about it all despite the disarray. His house sits in a subdivision of very fine houses that he built in his youth. All are well-kept and well-manicured except for his. A jungle of green vines and trees grow up around his collection, raccoons have moved into a downed tree trunk, birds' nest here and there, deer frolic around twisted metal, broken doors and railroad iron. I marvel at the forgiveness of nature, which can make even the most horrid object beautiful if you give it enough time.

Next to Mom's cracked and tipped over flowerpots, I spot the discarded ladder from our old swimming pool from the 60s. It was the pool Dad built in my childhood at our old home half a mile away before he started his collecting. The pool has long since been filled in, an insurance risk. Dad rents the house to a young girl named Doris. She is a renter in a long line of renters who mean well, but just won't or can't pay. The ladder's an odd relic from a previous life, a tiny corner of it shimmers in the early morning sunlight casting a prism of light upon a sea of discarded and useless objects imprisoned in spider webs that shine like diamonds at that moment.

The reason Dad chose that particular item to move from his old house to his new one escapes me. Maybe a dream of another pool…someday? A moment of recaptured youth when the kids were still home and his future yet to be made? And yet there it is, bent and rust-encrusted, waiting for him to think of some use for it, just like everything else he's saved—enough to fill several houses, warehouses and tumble-down garages and acres and acres of land he owns. Indeed, he's filled more than 25 acres with things he plans to use—someday, maybe, when he retires.

I peeked through the glass of the back door before opening it to go inside. The door is, of course, unlocked. Dad never remembers to lock it before bed. That was Mom's job.

"Hey, Dad!"

"Jane? When did you get here?" He raised his arms despite arthritic shoulders to collect a hug. Once he had to bend down to hug me and then would lift me to ride on those shoulders, now I must bend at the knees for him to reach round my neck. He smells a bit like aftershave, and the ever-present scent of diesel fuel. He holds a whittled-down, very short toothpick precariously between his clinched teeth so as not to stab me.

"Do you still want to visit Valley View?" I ask.

Valley View is an assisted living home Dad says he wants to go to when he can "no longer care for himself." He's asked me to take him for "a look," wanting to know what I think.

"Today's as good a day as any." He eyes the fast-food bag and licks his dry, cracked lips. "What ya got there?"

In the kitchen I clear a 6-inch space on the table for him to eat among all the pill bottles, pamphlets, and countless items he insists he must have at his fingertips. On the table for years is the small toy, an orange wind-up kangaroo, that does somersaults. He also has a wind-up ladybug that runs across the table when he, like Moses parting the Red Sea, clears a path of rubble for a good run. He always has a floating lantern flashlight on the kitchen table as well, in case of emergencies.

"How do you undo a lake?" he asks as we eat. He tells me about a former employee of his. The man lived on a houseboat moored in a man-made lake Dad constructed years ago. The man never paid Dad for constructing the lake. Dad is unsure how you "undo" a lake for someone who didn't pay for it. I murmur and nod without a clue of how to handle such a scenario either. As I chew the egg sandwich and listen, I look out the window at the pool ladder. I recall the pool. Children laughing, diving off an upended stump into sparkling water. I think of Mom sitting with her shorts rolled up getting sun on her pretty, shapely legs and sipping fresh-made ice tea from a tall, frosted glass. I think of myself playing with my Barbie dolls in the sandbox next to the pool. I think of birds singing a tune and Dad in his bathing suit swimming from one side of the pool to the other and then back again with swift, sure, muscular strokes. I think about the picture I have of my Mom age 44 rocking a bikini quite well. I wonder if I would look as good.

Beyond the pool, beyond the wooden property fence I picture the fields I rode my horses in. Or the road I traveled coming back from a swim in the lake in the evening. The horse hurries home because she knows there's grain and a roll in the fresh green grass of the pasture waiting. I think about spring, and it all seems like only yesterday. Where did those happy days go? And how exactly did the grief we all feel now overwhelm those the good, wonderful, yes sometimes scary and dark but often happy times of youth?

My mind wanders to all the frogs that inhabited the green water of the pool in the winter where that same pool ladder hung. There were hundreds of frogs once at the old house in that pool...

* * *

1964

My love for frogs started when Mrs. Brasier, my third-grade teacher, accepted frog eggs from one of my classmates. She put them into an aquarium in our second grade, room for the class to observe. Every day before school I pressed my nose to the cool side of the,glass aquarium setting on the window ledge over the radiator. I could see the eggs swelling, literally vibrating with life. Soon a tiny tail appeared. Then odd legs popped out and dangled along behind as the tadpoles explored their tiny glass enclosure. Eventually, I saw shiny black frogs the size of my pinky nail setting on the plastic lily pads in the aquarium looking back with wide, downturned-mouth expressions. To me, it looked like a better trick than any Houdini ever performed. Escaping into life!

At home our new swimming pool became a massive haven for frogs during the winter months when the weather got cold and Dad shut down the filter. With the filtration off, the crystal-clear, blue water where we swam all summer quickly turned brackish and filled with algae. Frogs from nearby fields and ditches invaded. As winter turned to spring, happy frogs croaked loud recommendations to their friends, and the frog population in our pool exploded. I lay awake at night listening to their throaty calls and thinking how God had a sense of humor to make such funny looking creatures, that made such strange sounds.

One spring evening, as I studied spelling in my room at home, the screen door on the back porch opened with a reek and Dad, in his usual way, stomped into the house wearing his heavy work boots. Bam! The door slamming behind him always made me jump a bit.

"Your father's home!" Mom announced from the kitchen where she spent most of her day planning, cooking, serving or cleaning up after meals.

"Kids, let's go frog gigging," Dad called from the den after putting his rusty, lunch pail and beaten notebook on the kitchen counter. "Get your boots on! We'll round up some frogs and clean out the swimming pool—tonight! We could be swimming by tomorrow! Jane, you ready to catch some frogs?"

"Yeah! Sounds great!" I couldn't wait to swim in the pool.

Somewhere in the back of my mind, I knew Dad hunted frogs in the spring; and frog legs sometimes appeared on our dinner table. But my child's brain had not yet made the connection between dinner and the miracle of frog birth I had witnessed at school.

Before we built the pool, Dad and my brother Franky sometimes gathered gigs —long poles with tiny, barbed forks on the end—pails and flashlights, picked up our aluminum rowboat by the ends and headed to the far corner of the pond out of view of the house. There, in some mysterious way I neither knew about nor cared to know, they collected frogs, killed and cleaned them. The rest of the year, the gigs lay in evil repose on the back porch with their tips accumulating rust like small satanic pitchforks. I knew they looked scary and dangerous, but I didn't really understand what they were for.

It all might have remained a mystery to me had the pasture fence not collapsed. When that happened, we could no longer keep our Shetland pony, Bupp, at home. He kept wandering off until Dad got the bright idea of tying him to the aluminum rowboat with a long lead.

"He might wander a bit, but he won't get far tied to a boat," Dad said satisfied he could out-think the pony any day of the week—and twice on Sunday. I wondered why he didn't just fix the fence, but this simple idea apparently did not occur to Dad.

For a full year Bupp dragged the boat around the yard. It was not good for the boat; however, it had given Bupp an impressive set of neck and shoulder muscles. To graze he dragged it up and down the edge of the dirt road beside our house, the ditch between the house and the road and around our overgrown garden. Graze, graze, heave, drag. Graze, graze, heave, drag. The sound of him cropping grass in this manner often lulled me to sleep on summer nights when Mom had the windows flung open to capture the fresh night breezes. I grew accustomed to the boat drag sounds.

After a year of heaving a boat around dry land in pursuit of edible grass, Bupp had no trouble pulling the pony cart. Unfortunately, the boat was no longer good for frog gigging. Somehow this fact seemed to take Dad by surprise when he and my brother set it in the nearby pond to provide their perch from which to gig frogs, and it immediately sank into the thick swampy habitat. Bupp, now psychologically attached to the boat, followed them over to the pond watching his constant companion, the boat, sink with no small degree of pony surprise. He lowered his nose sniffing the bubbles as they popped up to the top of the water, then tossed his head and snorted several times in sadness and fear.

"Go on!" Dad shouted at the pony and kicked the last part of the boat that remained above water until it sank too. Then he swung again at the pony. Bupp shied away and rolled his eyes before walking on a few steps and dropping his head to crop grass, no doubt feeling much lighter yet lonelier. The relief was short lived, however, and he soon found himself tethered to a tractor tire instead of the worn-out boat that remained at the bottom of the pond from then on. The sound at night was different with the tire, but the results for Bupp were much the same. And so, time passed, we all grew older, Bupp got stronger, his hooves grew out to further hinder his escape, and now Dad had a new idea about how to hunt frogs. Without the boat Dad realized frog hunting might work better, say, in the backyard pool!

Outside once more he summoned us again with a throaty bellow "kids", and soon we stood, outfitted in old clothes and Wellington boots, ready for action. I collected brooms, shovels and buckets per Dad's instructions. Franky, Dad and I trudged to the side of the pool in the twilight, buckles on our unfastened boots rattling, a rag tag bunch. The frogs were customarily silent, as if sensing the pending slaughter with all froggy eyes cast warily upon us.

The white vinyl edge of the pool encircled what had, over the winter, become a virtual frog metropolis. We flicked on the outside floodlights in the fading evening light, and hundreds of fat green bodies sling-shotted themselves under water leaving multiple concentric ripples in their wake. Overhead, bats darted, eating moths and other insects attracted to the light. Their wing beats sounded like random laundry flapping in the wind, making me want to hunker close to the ground because, frankly, they creeped me out. For once I felt glad Franky towered over me by at least a foot. They would most likely claw and bite into his hair and eat him first.

Unsure what Dad had planned, my brother and I looked expectantly at the pool water, which had evaporated to less than half its normal depth, then back at Dad in unison, waiting. Seeming to enjoy our attention, he thoughtfully bent and rolled the legs of his blue overalls above his boots. In a few movements Dad started the pump designed to suck the rest of the water out of the pool. He threw the sucking pipe into the deep end and then turned back to us. Over the loud noise the pump made he cried, "Well, don't just stand there, let's catch some frogs!" He flashed a big film-star smile and then picked up the skimmer net and started skimming with gusto. Franky handed me a gig, then moved out to carefully select his prey, his instinctive stalking movements equal to any of our Creek Indian ancestors from Mom's side of the family.

For the next hour, our pool and backyard turned into a scene straight out of the "Twilight Zone" as Dad and Franky dismantled the utopia that was once Frog World while I mostly watched cowering next to the pool fence in horror, slimy pool water running down my skinny legs, glad I was young enough Dad didn't expect much of me. They skimmed out frogs, bopped them on the head with a hammer and lined the limp bodies up along the low roof of the pump house to await either the frying pan, or the freezer bag. The ones that struggled the most usually got the frying pan. The pump did its work quickly and soon all that remained at the bottom of the pool was a thick sludge and a large population of frantic frogs. When the pump started sucking air, Dad shut it off and returned to catching frogs.

"Bruised frogs don't keep well in the freezer," Dad commented on one catch.

I laid down my gig and pressed myself into a dark shadowy corner next to the fence and watched in stricken fascination as they speedily collected an amazing number of frogs—to me it looked like hundreds, but in hindsight I'd guess they collected 50 or so large enough to eat. Giant frogs, almost as big as small chickens, sprang high in desperate attempts to jump out of the pool. By this time the water level had dropped so low it became virtually impossible even for the strongest frog to escape over the high pool walls. Their metropolis had become their prison.

Things went as smoothly as a frog hunt could for a while, but then, as the night wore on, fatigue set in and little things started to go wrong. Franky stabbed at a frog with his gig and missed, sinking it into the side of the pool, puncturing the vinyl liner. This propelled the frog onto the patio near the edge of the yard with an unappetizing splat.

"He's getting away!" Dad yelled. Franky climbed out of the shallow end of the pool in one fluid motion, sank to all fours and grabbed the frog, bonked him headfirst on the patio to stun him, then threw him in a bucket. Still in the pool, Dad made a grab for another high jumper. When he missed, he took off his hat and tossed it over the frog instead, easily scooped him up and tossed him into the bucket as well. However, in the process he lost his balance, and the hand skimmer went flying backward. Completely out of control, Dad fell into the remaining brackish water with a huge splash sending frogs, and thick, smelly water flying in all directions. The slimy mess flowed over his head and, for a moment, I thought that might be the end of the frog hunt—or Dad! Then Dad reappeared in a spray of mist and spew. He wiped his eyes with a sodden hanky, struggled to his feet and climbed out of the pool with a whish and trickle using the shiny pool ladder. It was a scene fit for any Grimm's Fairy Tale. Dad scraped the ick off his arms and legs and picked up the skimmer, his jaw set.

At some point I realized there wasn't much I could do to change the fate of the larger frogs, but I might save a few little ones. Hoping the shocking events would end soon, I rose from the corner where I'd hidden. While Dad and Franky focused on cutting up the frogs and skinning them, I worked capturing the more youthful, walking, crawling teen frogs along the perimeter of the battlefront.

Every chance I got, I tossed the small healthy ones out into the dark yard beyond the pool of light coming from the floodlights. In hushed tones, I pleaded with them to hop in the opposite direction quickly before Dad saw them and put them back into the bucket.

I collected the ones that escaped the bucket or those thrown my direction whenever I could if they seemed healthy enough to survive. Each cold, plump body wriggled in my hands and then dropped like old, lime Jell-O onto the ground. Slanted eyes looked up at me surprised, worldly, yet somehow resigned. I guess frogs know their place in life. If a fox, cat or hawk didn't get them, then a lawnmower probably would. Such is the fate of frogs everywhere. Often after a soulful look, as if to say thank you, they frantically hopped off into the darkness presumably to croak another day. For those that remained, my mind latched onto the comforting thought that Dad's hammer bonking their heads was more humane than many alternative fates. Say a car on hot asphalt, or a bush hog or rotting away in some huge snake belly somewhere.

My activities went unnoticed as Dad continued working at the cleaning station between the pool and patio. He cut off legs with expert care to save every scrap of edible meat. Some frogs only faked death until the leg cutting began. Then they woke up with frantic struggles and croaks, legs kicking as they tried to escape. Dad quickly foiled their attempts to live by slamming the frog's head against the corner of the well house wall. "Smack!" That generally put an end to all frog plans.

As he worked, Dad told us a story, to take his mind off the work.

"When I was a little boy, my Uncle Leslie kept a pet frog, named Herman. After dinner each night, while Mom cleared the dishes, Uncle Leslie would set this frog on the table. Under the candlelight it didn't take long for the frog to start catching moths, or candle flies. In his pocket, Leslie carried a tobacco pouch of buckshot, the beads that you put into shotgun shells when you make them yourself. He'd roll a piece of buckshot across the table, and the frog would swallow it. We'd laugh, and he'd take another piece out and roll it across the table again. That frog's tongue rolled out and grabbed the next piece of buckshot, just like a fly.

"Leslie kept going until the frog completely filled up on buckshot and couldn't hop. Then he'd pick up the frog and shake him by his hind legs until all the buckshot fell out. He'd put the shot back in his bag, pick up the frog, put it in his shirt pocket and then we'd go to bed. Leslie would sleep with that frog on his pillow every night."

"Didn't the frog get sick?" I asked.

"Not that I know of. In fact, the frog seemed to enjoy the process, like he knew he was putting on a show for us."

"What happened to the frog?" Franky asked.

"I don't know. But Leslie had that frog for a long time. He said it ate the flies and mosquitoes that buzzed around him at night while sitting on his pillow. And when it went to sleep it would rest its chin on his ear. He said it snored ever so slightly. So, I guess it worked out pretty well for both of them. That frog made Leslie really popular at school."

Eventually Dad finished butchering the frogs. All the walking wounded were accounted for, and I headed for the house for a much-anticipated bath. Later, I found Mom in the kitchen preparing frog legs for the freezer and frying others to golden tenderness in her stainless-steel pan.

"You've got to cut the leg tendon—like this," she demonstrated to me, "so they don't jerk hard enough to splash grease on you, after you put them into the pan." A frog's version of postmortem revenge, I thought, keeping my distance from the sizzling, randomly twitching legs. Mom cast another collection of battered, trim ankles and muscular calves into the hot grease where they splashed down and immediately began to sizzle. The smell of cooking frog legs filled the kitchen and made my mouth water despite myself.

"Dinner will be ready in a minute," she added.

The okra and cooked carrots steamed in bowls already on the table. A tiny grease explosion sent a frog leg shooting out of the pan, narrowly missing my head before it skittered across the floor. Somehow a barn cat had snuck into the house, and when she saw the leg she grabbed it. She raced toward the door with her unexpected delicacy pausing along the way to drop the hot meal and pat it with her foot until it cooled enough to carry outside.

"See, I told you they'd jump out! I guess I didn't cut the tendon on that one enough." Mom smiled, her knowledge gained from experience.

Then back outside I watched Dad and Franky collect the awful remaining body parts and haul them down behind the barn in a wheelbarrow where they would leave them to rot on the manure pile. Then they filled buckets with hot soapy water and scrubbed the well house roof, pool and patio clean. Dad rinsed everything with a hose. Before the evening was over, all sign of Frog World was obliterated, and Dad had crystal-clear water running into the pool with the hose.

Later that night, I stared at my plate. I could tell Mom knew how I felt. The legs smelled delicious, but the battle scene, still fresh in my mind, prevented me from enjoying the meal. I silently cursed my carnivorous nature. I longed to be Catholic so I could give up eating frogs for Lent. But we were Church of God members. Women had to wear dresses; we couldn't wear makeup or take the Lord's name in vain. We couldn't dance, but we could eat all the meat we wanted on any day of the week! Darn! All the work had made me hungry and I reached for a trim frog leg closed my eyes, thought about swimming, and took a bite. Delicious.

* * *

2007

After Dad finishes eating his ham and biscuit, I help him bathe and dress. We do this in Mom's bathroom because Dad's bathroom is no longer suitable for bathing. His tub is filled with tools where he's working on some project there that I can't quite make out. It takes the rest of our morning to get Dad ready.

Looking at him after his shower, I notice his head still looks dirty. So, I rewash and rinse it with medicated shampoo and a clean cloth. I cut his toenails, which have grown long and ragged. I clean the dead skin from underneath his toes. It had been so long since he bathed that it looks like he has a second row of toes sprouting underneath his real ones. That's something I did not know could even happen, and yet it has. I ask him about his toes, and he shrugs and tells me he can no longer reach his feet. As I clean them, they remind me of the feet the tadpoles sprouted long ago in the aquarium in my classroom. I clean his fingernails and rub lotion into the rough folds of his hands.

Cleaned, bathed and dressed, we depart for the retirement home. As we proceed in the car down the road he motions and says, "There is where I went to elementary school." He points at a building not far off. I know this, but I pull in the drive anyway because it is the same building where I attended elementary school and saw tadpoles and frogs for the first time. We make a slow circle of the building in my car. Dad seems lost in thought, likely seeing everything as it once was rather than as it is now.

Eventually, we drive on. It's a road Dad and I have both traveled riding our horses as children. Trees still line the curves, and we spot Hereford cattle in the roadside pastures. Once in a while we see horses too. Horses, cows and a few goats dot the various pastures. Why not sheep? I wonder. But there have never really been sheep in our area. Lots of pigs…but no sheep. In one field an old Jersey cow drops an early calf just as we pass.

"What a lovely place to begin life," I say to Dad. He looks out the window and doesn't say anything. I'm not sure he hears me, so deep is he in thought. The fields are filled with spring wildflowers that cover the ground like purple carpet.

"That's the field where I used a bulldozer for the first time," he comments a moment later. Through the years, he's owned a dozen dozers, loaders and trucks in various stages of working order. Some lay scattered and abandoned around his property like arthritic, iron dinosaurs even today. Dad tends to keep his equipment. He keeps everything long after it is no longer useful.

A little later, we wander into the assisted living facility lobby where a group of male residents gather and are deep in conversation. The sight seems to appeal to Dad.

"They look like they're friends," he says as we search for the administrator. We find her and sit for a while in her office discussing what Dad wants in the way of a new home.

He shifts a little self-conscious, in a wheelchair she offered for the tour.

"I'm just a dumb old country boy, so you'll have to talk slow."

She looks at him, raises an eyebrow, and then looks at me, questioning.

I smile my encouragement.

"Mr. Hinkle, do you have a Will?" she asks.

"Well, no, I'm working on a Trust—but it's not finished yet."

The Trust he's working on he started before I left for college, and he's never completed it. I have never seen it, and I've come to think it's merely in his head with nothing put on paper yet. I suspect he has a deep fear that his death will follow quickly on the heels of any organized plan he makes, so he keeps putting it off.

He drops his hat on the floor. I pick it up, and he takes it.

"Mr. Hinkle, do you have Advanced Directives?"

"What's that?"

He drops his hat again. I pick it up and hand it to him.

"That's what you sign when we admit you, so your family know what your wishes are. Have you discussed your wishes with them?" She looks at me.

I shake my head side-to-side.

"Mr. Hinkle, how do you intend to pay for your care?"

He drops his hat again. Again, I move to pick it up. He looks at me and growls loud enough I'm sure the men at the other end of the hall hear him,

"Leave it!" It is the sound of Papa Bear growling at his cub.

The growl sends a chill through me even as an adult. It makes the administrator jump. I do not pick up the hat again.

He turns to the administrator and says, "I want to see if Medicare will pay for it."

Dad's property alone is worth hundreds of thousands of dollars. But growing up in the Depression instilled in him a lifelong commitment to scrimping, and penny wise, pound-foolish kind of saving. In his garage are the Styrofoam box for every hamburger he's ever eaten and many that he has not. In an era when roads, easements and large houses have sprung up on most all the neighboring farms, he still owns half the prize bottomland his father left him. The other half that his brother inherited was eventually sold to developers.

Dad rents the part that remains that he has not cluttered up to a large farming corporation, and they alternately sow it down each year with wheat, soybeans and corn depending on crop predictions.

I've tried over the years to explain to Dad how Medicare works. I've also tried to explain a spend-down policy, which basically means you must spend what you have before Medicare will pay. He has not yet acknowledged this fact and does not do it now. The administrator suggests we speak to a financial advisor who offices down the hallway. However, today she is unexpectedly out of the office. So instead, she takes us on a tour of the facility.

I am pleased to see the people who live there are clean. The air smells fresh, and there are many amenities I think Dad will appreciate like a big screen television in the reception room and a lovely walking path with gardens. I wonder as we walk if my standards of "clean and fresh" are set too low, but I've also seen what facilities are available to Dad, and the reality is that most of them are not a place you want your parents to be. Most are not places YOU would want to be. This is a sad commentary on the world in which we live and what we value. I have yet to reconcile myself to this fact. We complete the tour. Dad does not necessarily seem shocked or unhappy. However, when the administrator presses him about when he will join them, he declines to set a date.

Back in the car I ask, "Is this what you want to do?"

"I guess—someday! But not today." He looks across the field at the wildflowers.

"Would you like to eat supper out?" I ask him, starting the engine.

"Let's go to Mrs. Catfish's. I'll buy."

Thirty minutes later we arrive at the restaurant. I help Dad out of the car. He holds my elbow with one hand and his cane with the other. While the nursing home insisted on a wheelchair for his tour, he really does not need one. Their insistence was based on insurance requirements. For his current situation, the cane serves him well. In this slow fashion we make our way to the door. An elderly man opens it for us.

"Hope you left some fish for us," Dad jokes. The man nods and smiles as we pass.

Inside as we wait for the hostess to seat us, I notice a blackboard on an easel with today's special scrolled in pink chalk, "Frog Legs, $5.99 a dozen."

The elderly waitress with silver-threaded hair twisted up into a giant bun on the top of her head picks up menus and ushers us toward a table. Even though her face is wrinkled like a fan with age, she quickly outdistances us.

Dad makes it halfway across the restaurant and declares, "I've got to sit now, or I'm going to fall down."

We take the booth closest, and I motion to the waitress that we will sit here. She nods and waves to indicate it's okay. We settle in.

Of all the things wrong with Dad, prostate cancer, arthritis, diabetes and a host of weird and strange psychological issues, I never anticipated his legs would be the first thing to go.

We study our menus.

"Dad, they have frog legs. Would you like some?"

"Frog legs? Never had 'um. But I hear they're good," he says reading his menu through the bifocals of his glasses.

This is when I realized that everything that haunts me, he's totally forgotten.

◇

"Do not cast me off in the time of old age; forsake me not when my strength is spent." (Psalm 71:9)

◇

Fried Frog Legs
Cut frog legs off at hip joint.
Skin legs.
Remove feet and discard.
Discard rest of frog.
Cut tendon behind knee and again at back of ankle ¾ of the way through.

Wash legs in cold water.
Soak legs in saltwater brine for 30 minutes with 2 tablespoons of salt per 2 cups water.
Rinse and dry legs.
Batter with egg, plain flour, and cornmeal mixed.
(Dip in egg and shake up in plastic bag containing flour and cornmeal.)
In a stainless-steel skillet, place one cup of corn oil and bring to temperature that makes oil swirl in pan but not smoke.
Drop legs into pan.
Cook on medium heat until done.
Drain on paper towels.
Suggested side dishes are green onions, collard greens, sliced tomatoes.

Chapter 4 – Chicken Stew

"Mom would rush out to the garden with a pair of kitchen shears, and she'd grab those chickens up. She'd take a whack out of their tail feathers and a whack out of one wing, then she'd heave them over the fence back into the chicken yard. They couldn't fly anymore because she'd whacked them, so they'd fall with a great big thump on the other side of the fence." — Louis

2007
"Do you want one egg or two?" my sister asks from the kitchen of her apartment where she is preparing breakfast. It is the morning of her first divorce hearing; and while I am here in Tennessee, I plan to testify on her behalf. Outside the screen door I see a green and ruby-throated hummingbird hovering around a red artificial geranium in a pot she uses as her ashtray on the deck. The bird inspects the flower, then looks right at me as if in disappointment at the ashes, and then it flies on.

"One," I call back across the living room. I stop to check my email on my laptop. My nieces crunch away on dry cereal while watching cartoons on television. Their fine childish hair falls in silky abandon around slender shoulders. We are all still wearing our pajamas. I check my email, then carry my empty coffee cup into the kitchen for another splash of coffee. I lean against the smooth white counter to watch her cook.

"How did your visit to the assisted living home go?" she asks swirling yellow clouds of egg around in the skillet with a fork, fluffing them the way Mom did.

"Okay. It looks clean, and the patients seem comfortable. Better than most."

For 11 years my sister, a nurse, was the primary caregiver for Mom. She lived close by making this possible. Then, two years before Mom passed, I quit my high-paying sales job and partnered with my husband in his business. It was a decision we made together so I could help my sister and spend more time with Mom.

Going into business with my husband allowed me to control my schedule. We moved closer to Mom and Dad, so my sister and I could work in tandem to take care of Mom as she fought her battle with bone cancer. During this time, my husband and I decided to launch a magazine for our self-defense company because it was something I could do while sitting by Mom's bed at her house—or at the hospital, depending on how she was. In the final stages at home, while she slept and I spelled my sister, I sat at an old wrap-around high school desk, solicited articles from writers all over the world by phone and email and then edited and laid out a magazine and sent it off to print. In less than a year our magazine was in major bookstores and sold by subscription in 26 countries.

That magazine allowed me to be there for Mom. On good days we watched "Golden Girls" on TV and ate butter pecan ice cream or Goo-Goo bars. On bad days she didn't always recognize me. Instead, she referred to me as "that woman" who sat beside her. She slept a lot while I worked. Sometimes, when she felt like it, Mom and I would talk.

One morning after I came in from a run, I sat beside her on her bed. She looked out the window and said, "Let's go for a walk." Mom had not walked in a long time.

I looked at her and said, "Let's go after you've have your breakfast."

She nodded with a wistful smile on her face. We both knew that walk would never happen, but we both remembered other walks, not that long ago, and I longed to have those moments back. There are a finite number of talks…a finite number of walks for all of us. But no one knows how many and no one counts them as they are happening. It's only afterward that you realize this. The thought squeezed my heart deep inside my chest as I realized I could still recall precisely when the last walk was and how fast that time past.

My first walk with Mom happened when I was maybe six. Mom called it a penny walk. We left the house in the cool afternoon, walked to the end of the driveway, and flipped a penny to decide which way to go. We did this for an hour, just flipping the penny at each crossroad, and eventually it led us home again as if by magic. I loved the random element of those walks.

Looking back, I wonder if Mom somehow controlled that penny or if it really was magic. I can't ask her now, so I guess I'll never know for certain. Later in life, after I left home, when I visited her, we'd take walks through Tim's Ford State Park a few miles away. On these walks we looked for Suzie the deer. She and Mom were long-time friends. Mom walked with her friends often in that park when I was away, and early on Suzie began to join them. Sometimes we would take Suzie apples. Sometimes, if we were particularly quiet, we could catch a glimpse of her latest fawn. Sometimes there were twin fawns. Those were the days when I felt I could just keep going home forever and could take a walk with Mom whenever I wanted! I took it for granted that she'd always be there because that was the way it had always been. I thought everything would stay the same. But life is constantly changing. We just don't always notice.

With my sister and I in the kitchen, I wonder, has it already been four years since we brought Mom home from the hospital to die at home? You know it is time for someone to die when you become more afraid of what will happen to them if they live, than if they don't. Eventually we reached that point with Mom. It was time for her to go, and we wanted her to die with us in a familiar place – not in some cold, sterile, unfamiliar hospital far from home.

I held her hand as she took her last breath in her own room. As she slipped away my sister recited the 23rd Psalm. I swear I could hear Mom's heart beating. And then I heard it…stop. I do not understand how, but that is how it happened. After she stopped breathing, I began to count. Somewhere I read that you could live for 3 or 4 minutes without your heart beating? As I counted the bed began to vibrate. I do not know what caused the vibration. It was as if some high-powered mixer was churning away under the covers. At the foot of the bed Dad stood with his arms around the shoulders of my young nieces. One was biting her fingernails; the other chewed on the neck of her shirt. Both stood big-eyed and silent.

Recently, I asked them what they saw in that moment? They said they saw fairies wearing green and blue dresses fly in the window and they saw them take Mom away. I did not see fairies. I felt, for a moment, that Mom's loving spirit entered my body through my chest and settled somewhere near my heart. And even as I felt her alive inside me and I wanted her not to die, I also felt fear from this experience. Silently I thought, *Oh no. I love you, but you can't stay. Two spirits in one body cannot be.* I think she rested there for a moment, and we held each other's hearts close. And then…she was gone.

As she departed her physical body exhaled deeply and then lay still. In place of her spirit, I was left with the strongest sense of love and peace I have ever known. The closest I can describe it is the feeling I got the first time the nurse lay my baby daughter, Sherry, in my arms. I am not a fan of organized religion. For some I believe it is a comfort, but not for me. But I do believe in a higher power, and I felt it working in my life every day. And in that moment of Mom's departure, without any explanation or definition, I knew without a doubt that we are much more than our bodies.

We are infinite beings living temporarily inside clay jars. But we are NOT the jar. For what purpose we are here I do not know, but I felt a sense of celebration that Mom had slipped outside her jar and moved on—I cannot fully explain it. It defies language. Yet I know that now she is one with the mystery and the infinite world we cannot see but instinctively know for certain is there.

I was so happy for her, but oh so sad for the rest of us. How do you say goodbye to the one who gave you life and always loved you unconditionally? The truth is you can't.

Now there are no more walks with Mom except in my memory. There is only now. It seems I've spent my life always returning from—somewhere—always busy with–something–that took me far from home and Mom. Each walk was as precious as a jewel–I know that now. How few walks. How few precious jewels.

Now when I take a walk with my daughter (which is often—but not as often as I would like), and even my granddaughters (who I cherish beyond words but who have their own lives)—so many, many years later, I think of walks with Mom. Unique. Finite. I appreciate each one as if it is the final one because you never know when God will take you home.

For months when Mom was trying to crack out of her clay pot and fly into the next world, my sister and I took turns sleeping on lounge cushions thrown down on Mom's rose-colored carpet next to her bed in her bedroom. We took turns dozing, and pushing the morphine pump button as often as the timer would allow to ease her pain when she could not push the button herself. We cleaned every inch of her, fed her, dressed her, fixed her hair and painted her nails. We kept her like a porcelain doll, pretty, clean, dressed, waiting…

On the outside she looked normal, beautiful, but on the inside her bones were fragile as glass and literally dissolving as the disease ate her away from the inside out. Taking care of her was like taking care of a precious figure knowing the slightest bump, the slightest movement, might break her. And, once broken, horrible, unending pain would consume her.

Sometimes she would feel restless from the medication, so I gave her washcloths to fold to keep her hands busy. She would fold an entire basket full, then look at me and say, "Now don't mess them up again!" And we'd laugh. When she got tired of folding wash clothes, I'd give her an extension cord to coil. Anything to keep her hands busy.

My sister's voice pulls me back to the present and renews mindfulness of our current challenge – Dad – and what to do about him. We don't have the luxury of keeping Dad at home like we did Mom. My sister is working long hours, and I am recovering from hand surgery and live far away. I have a bulging disc in my back from lifting Mom far too many times during her illness. The doctor tells me it's dangerous now for me to lift almost anything. And Dad is not Mom. Dad is combative, argumentative and sometimes dangerous.

"Assisted living and nursing homes are all the same," my sister says. She pulls a plate out of the cabinet and heaps it full of scrambled eggs. "All different shades of bad."

"Surely not all of them?"

She nods her head. "Pretty much. They are all simply different versions of bad and worse."

She thrusts slices of whole wheat bread into the toaster and pushes the lever down.

"Do you think Dad's going to go to an assisted living place if we can find one, he likes?" she asks.

"I don't know." I load my fork and take a bite of egg. "I'm afraid if he doesn't, we'll find him dead on the kitchen floor, or he'll kill someone while driving."

She joins me at the table with her plate. "That or he'll have a stroke while on the dozer and level half a dozen houses in the neighborhood."

"He's still driving the dozer?"

She nods between bites. Chews thoughtfully. "He was on a ladder in the garage taping up a naked wire with duct tape only last week!"

"Jesu--!"

"Juice?" she said, raising the pitcher. She cocks one dark eyebrow, a life-long habit that punctuates her sentences from time to time. My brother did this too. I wonder if it's genetic. For the life of me, I cannot do it. Expressive eyebrow trait must come with the Native American gene. I do not have eyebrows that can articulate thoughts with a fine arch like a billboard.

There is much I still don't know about my family history. As children we don't think to ask the questions often until it is too late and all the people with the answers are long gone. There are many questions I wish I'd asked Mom. They are questions pushed so far back in the recesses of my mind that even I didn't remember them except at odd moments. Big questions, Dark questions.

"I'm going out to see him this afternoon to take a prescription he needs," I say. "Guess we'll talk about the assisted living facility again then, now that he's had time to sleep on the idea."

"What are we going to do if he doesn't go? I don't have time to take care of him like I'd like, and he really won't let me anymore," she says. "With the divorce, the girls, work—there aren't enough hours in the day." She looks out the sliding glass door at the trees behind her apartment.

Outside that hummingbird lingers around the fake flowers again not wanting to give up. He tries unsuccessfully again and again to insert his thin tongue into the flower with no success. Rays of sunlight form a star burst pattern across the carpet of my sister's living room. In a few minutes we will head off to her divorce hearing. I to testify on her behalf, she to find a path to a new life that I hope will result in her getting her house back.

"It's going to be okay," she says. She puts her plate in the sink and looks in the refrigerator again.

"What do you want for dinner?" she asks. "How about this evening I pick up some chicken from the Colonel?"

I pause mid-bite and look at her for a moment, as my mind flies back over the years thinking about chicken.

* * *

1964

"My Mom says I shouldn't play with you!" my friend Jean snarled at me. Friday afternoon after school. We were standing with the other girls from my 2nd grade class waiting for our bus to pull up and take us home! Often, we passed the time playing hide and seek in the trees near the parking lot.

"Why?" I asked.

"Your grandfather was a murderer, that's why!"

Jean whispered something to a circle of three other girls, usually my friends, but now they pulled closer to each other physically excluding me from the group. When I tried to stick my head in, they drew their heads closer still, crowding me further away.

When I persisted Jean stepped on my foot.

"Ouch!" I yanked it back. "What gives?"

"We don't want you as our friend anymore. That's what!" she said.

"Why not? I didn't even know my grandfather! He died before I was born!"

"Cause, we don't!" Jean glared. Her blonde hair seemed to curl even tighter as she spoke the words. Her blue eyes sparkled, and she drew her red lips into a little circle puffing her cheeks out as she shouldered me away.

"You know!" She tauted.

"What are you talking about?"

"Your grandpa was a murderer, that's what. Everyone knows he killed your grandma," Katie said, tossing her blond curls.

"Wha–?"

Jean turned her back on me before I could get the words out and said to the others, "There's the bus, let's sit together and not let her sit with us."

"I'll sit with you if I want," I said, shouldering my own way past several of the other girls and onto the bus.

"No, you won't. All murderers are chickens, anyway" Jean said. "You won't dare try to sit with us."

"But I didn't kill anybody?" I said.

"Doesn't matter. You're related to a murder, and that makes you as good as one yourself," she said. She turned her back blocking that seat, and I found myself forced to find another seat alone at the back of the bus. The ride home seemed to take an exceptionally long time.

I lived three houses down from the school. Unfortunately, the bus always picked me up first in the morning and dropped me off last in the evening and took more than an hour to pick up and drop off all the other kids. The rejection felt like chilly fingers running up my spine as I stepped off the bus an hour later onto the gravel road that ran beside my house. The sun hung low over the horizon, peeking at me from behind our barn as I trudged up the hill. My shadow stretched out long behind me making me feel like someone from another world was following me. The back of my neck prickled.

"Who knows what evil...the Shadow knows" came to mind. Well now, did he really? Why me? I wondered? What did my shadow know about me? All while I knew nothing. And I was afraid to ask anyone because I was afraid that I wouldn't like the answer. Murder!

The trees had already dropped most of their leaves and they rustled behind me as I walked up the drive to the house as the spooky wind whispered unintelligibly in the shadows. Leaves swirled around my feet as I walked, and I could not help but think about how Halloween was fast approaching. Halloween always made me think of the headless horseman of Sleepy Hollow. I hurried on to the house drawing my coat closer around me as I walked, my heart pounding. Who's a chicken? You're a chicken. Once inside, I threw my books on the foot of my bed relieved to be home.

"Did you have a nice day?" Mom asked when I reached the foyer, which also served as the sewing room for our house. I hurried past it and into the kitchen knowing I'd have the safe and warm feeling that I always did when I was with Mom. I also hoped being with her would make Jean's voice stop echoing in my head. Murder she said. My grandfather was a murderer. Not Mom's dad. He was virtually a saint. But Dad's dad? I knew nearly nothing about him. Was it possible?

"Not really" I replied to Mom's question as I slid into a chair near her. This was not my usual response, so Mom stopped what she was working on and looked closely at me from over the top of her reading glasses.

"What happened?"

"The girls won't play with me. We were playing hide and seek, and they just left me hiding behind a bush, and then they wouldn't let me sit with them on the bus on the way home!"

"Why would they do that?" she asked.

"I don't know." Somehow, I couldn't quite tell her what Jean said about me being the granddaughter of a murderer.

"Don't worry," Mom said. She drew me into her arms and patted and rubbed my back in a comforting rhythm. I lay my head on her shoulder, enjoying the soothing feel of her touch. Tears welled up, and I brushed them away with the back of my hand so she couldn't see because I did not want to worry her.

"They'll get over it, and you'll all be friends by Monday. Want some chocolate milk and cookies?"

I nodded.

Saturday, I woke groggily and stumbled into the kitchen where Mom polished the counter tops with a clean, damp cloth then turned to scrub the pots soaking in the sink from the night before.

"Would you like some breakfast?" she asked.

"Yes." I sat in the dining room chair with one foot crossed under my hip, the way I always liked to sit on one foot.

"Feet on the floor," Mom said. She had her back turned to me. How did she know? I wondered adjusting my position to place both feet on the floor.

"Oatmeal?"

I nodded again. I sat up straighter.

"Where's everyone?" I asked, unsure why Mom let me sleep late.

"Your brother's going to work with your dad. They're in the backyard getting ready to go."

I had only taken a sip of my juice when a disturbance in the backyard erupted.

First the ruckus of what sounded like a dozen pairs of flapping chicken wings, accompanied by chicken squawks as if a dog had attacked the hen house.

Mom and I rushed out of the house to the backyard.

Before my amazed eyes, I saw Dad, taking swift steps around the yard. He grabbed first one hysterical, fluffy-white chicken by the neck, and then another. Each time, he'd wind the chicken round three times holding it by only the neck, then, like a whip, he'd crack the chicken, and the headless body would go flying across the yard. Dad laid the head down on a tree stump by the firewood pile, the surprised golden eyes of the now body-less chicken head still open, still blinking, its little beak making surprised, lung-less cries. Without noticing, he moved on to the next chicken. The discarded chicken body that belonged to the head now sprawled on the grass jerking, wings outstretched as if in flight. Some of the already headless chickens would get up and run for amazing distances before flopping down again. In less than 5 minutes Dad had killed 20 chickens or more, and my brother rowed the bleeding, headless bodies up along the edge of the patio under a shade tree. The yard, now adrift in white chicken feathers and blood, seemed to echo with the cries of the now-dead chickens.

"Louis, what are you doing?" Mom screamed! "I don't have time to clean all these chickens! We can't possibly eat them all!"

I sat down in a yard chair on the patio and buried my face in Mom's castoff apron and tried to block out the sight of all the dead chickens. The smell of fresh blood welled up in my nostril making me feel sick.

Dad didn't answer. Instead, he let the last body drop from his big, blood-spattered hands, and then walked over to the well house. Turning on the faucet, he hosed off his hands and washed them with a bar of dried-out Lava soap we kept sitting by the tap in a chipped porcelain bowl.

"Well, my Great, Big, Beautiful Doll," he said to her. "You said you didn't have time to feed them. I don't either, so we might as well put them in the freezer and forget about raising chickens."

"Well, you didn't have to kill them all at once! You could have done it over several days–maybe even weeks. Now I won't get anything done today but cut up and freeze chickens. And there's so many, I'm not sure if I can do them all before they ruin."

Ignoring her protest, he said, "Well, we're off to work!"

It was not uncommon for Dad to work on Saturday and take my brother and sometimes me with him. Now, he seemed satisfied that his part of chicken preparation was done. He walked to Mom and brushed a kiss across her cheek. She turned her head to avoid his lips and the kiss landed near her temple. He smiled a tight smile and walked to the edge of the patio to a red-plaid thermos bottle he'd left on the morning grass earlier. He picked it up along with his lunch box and a rolled-up Sunday-school book and tucked the items under his arm. He'd study and underline passages in that book while he ate his lunch learning how to be a better man. I wondered if directions about not overworking your wife might be in the Bible. I also wondered if there weren't a more humane way to kill chickens. But now was not the time to ask.

My brother didn't comment, but his face looked chalky. He hated the sight of blood. A nosebleed made him pale and sometimes he threw up after. Probably he'd throw up the first chance he got when Dad wasn't looking. But, for now, they both climbed into the truck. Dad started the engine, shoved it into gear and backed out of the driveway. The truck rattled off with them both inside. The last thing I saw as they turned the corner was my brother, his face looking pinched, with a hand held over his mouth like he was trying not to vomit. I knew him and thought likely this was a battle he wouldn't win.

"Jane, help me get them inside in the cool," Mom sighed. Even though it was fall, the day promised to be unseasonably warm. She walked over, picked up the first chicken, created a basket out of her apron she'd tied back on, and lay the chicken gently inside. Then she picked up the next one, and then the next. I didn't have an apron, so I picked up the first chicken I came to by its feet in one hand and another one in the other hand and followed her inside, blood dripping down in thin trickles leaving a tiny, dotted trail behind me. We lined them up on clean newspaper Mom spread out in the large foyer. And Mom started preparing to de-feather and gut the chickens. The hall soon filled with the smell of bloody chicken feathers still wet with dew. I could feel the warmth of sunshine clinging to them as I lay them out in neat rows. I saw henhouse dust floating in the air as sunlight streamed through the open back door. Grief filled my heart as I realized they would never live again. I wondered, as I looked at them, where their tiny spirits went? Would we see them again on the other side?

Occasionally one of the little chests shuddered as the last bit of oxygen escaped from lifeless lungs through their headless necks. I sat down on the floor, put my arms around my ankles, rested my chin on my knees and gazed at the dead chickens. I had no idea where to start. The room smelled like a combination of chickens, sunshine, grass, grain and other mysterious outdoor scents.

"What do we do now?" I asked.

"The clock's ticking. The day's warming up. We've need to scald, pluck, clean and wash them and put them in the freezer in the next few hours. Why don't we both pluck until we have a few done, then I'll clean and bag while you pluck."

Mom picked up a chicken and handed it to me.

I accepted the limp body gingerly. Holding onto the chicken with one hand, I tried pulling feathers out with the other. I was surprised at how firmly they were attached. Only a few came out each time. I kept trying and thinking the job would probably take me forever.

"This is impossible!" I threw the chicken down. "We'll never get them all done!"

"'By the mile, life's a trial, by the inch, it's a cinch.' We'll get as many done as we can," Mom answered. "Here, let me have that one. We'll try scalding it under the bathtub faucet. That should make it easier to pull the feathers out. Make sure and pull off all the little pinfeathers, too. We don't want them in the soup."

She smiled encouragement.

"What do I do with the feathers?" I asked.

"I'll get some flour sacks. You can stuff them in those. We'll dispose of them later."

For hours, Mom and I worked feverishly plucking, cleaning and cutting up chicken. Occasionally we'd looked at each other, at the feathers in our hair and on our clothes, and Mom would make a face. She looked so funny and red-faced from her efforts I had to laugh. Sometimes she'd blow her hair upward to shake a feather out of the front. And we'd keep plucking. As we worked, we talked to take our mind off what we were doing. Sometimes we'd sing songs. My favorite was, "She'll Be Coming Round the Mountain." We sang that several times. Then we sang "My Bonnie Lies Over the Ocean". We started substituting six white chickens for six white horses in "Coming Round the Mountain" and this really made us laugh. Then we started singing "My Chicken Lies Over the Ocean" and making up additional lyrics and soon we both collapsed into laughter on the floor laughing until we sobbed.

"Why did Dad kill all the chickens?" I asked as I plucked methodically once the laughter had spent itself. Pulling feathers out of a chicken felt something like pulling the stick off the last bit of Sugar Baby caramel sucker. They stuck for a while, but if you pulled hard and firm, they would turn lose and come off eventually. Then they stuck to my fingers instead, and I'd sling my hands trying to get them off. I plucked several hands full, then shoved the feathers into the sack before scraping the wet feathers off my hands with the edge of it.

"He killed the chickens because I don't have time to take care of them, and he doesn't want to buy feed for them anymore!" Mom said. "He thinks with all the trouble, it's cheaper to buy them at the grocery store."

"But they were my pets, my friends even," I told her. I thought of all the mornings I'd gone out under protest to feed them and felt really guilty about that now. They would rush over, and I'd throw them cracked corn and chicken feed. With little golden eyes they would glance around and scratch greedily with long talons in the grass looking for nuggets of corn and barley in the mix. It made me realize how dependent they were on me, and I had not given it a thought until now. I owed them more. I should have provided for them better and without complaint. If I had, maybe they would still be alive. The thought hurt my heart.

"We live on a farm, you know; it's not good to make friends out of the farm animals," Mom said.

"I know, but I just hate to see them killed. That's all."

"I don't like it either," Mom said. "I grew up in town and we always bought our chicken at the store. We couldn't afford chicken most of the time. Instead, we ate biscuits and vegetables – when we could get them. Your grandmother and your grandfather knew just about every edible plant there was, and they often fed us by foraging. The War, you know. Your grandfather ran a vegetable market from a corner basement in Fayetteville for a while when he could get vegetables to sell. Did you know that? He kept a milk cow in the country, and every day he'd walk three miles to the edge of town. Milk the cow. Then he'd walk three miles back so we could have fresh milk and butter. The cow gave a lot of milk, and he would sell what we didn't need. There were people that didn't even have that! With milk you can make cottage cheese, butter, buttermilk, and you can cook a lot of things. Without it, not much is good."

I thought about this. Walking three miles for a gallon of milk seemed drastic. I couldn't imagine living that far from a field. I remembered the conversation with Jean…and murder…and the "other" grandfather.

"For a while your grandfather, my father, served as sheriff of the town we lived in," Mom continued. "He broke up a ring of chicken thieves by following a trail of white feathers to the thief's back door."

I considered this for a moment. How the dead chickens left a trail of feathers like Hansel left a trail of bread crumbs in the fairy tale, and the trail of feathers lead my grandfather to the home of the chicken thieves. I thought about how smart that was, to follow the feather trail.

"What about Dad's family?" I asked.

"Your Dad's family was…different," Mom said. "They were big farmers and owned hundreds of acres of fertile valley land, hundreds of cattle and pigs. They did things in bulk. When your dad's father married your Dad's mother, she was his second wife. His first wife died. He was kind of a rugged, pioneer-type man. He expected his woman to work the fields alongside him and still keep up with the house and children."

I shook my head. It didn't sound like much fun to me. "Why did Dad's mom marry him?"

"She was nearly 40, past her prime, some would say. Never a beauty, really. Most considered her an old maid. She was a serviceable woman, not really the type of woman a man dreams about marrying. Mr. Hinkle used to call her a good "help-mate." I don't think your grandfather cared much about her looks at that point. Everyone said he loved his first wife best, and there was no love left after she died. She was the one love of his life. When he married the woman, who became your father's mother, I think he only wanted someone to cook and help him on the farm. It was a marriage of convenience. Not all that uncommon back then."

"What do you mean by convenience?" I asked.

"He needed someone to look after his daughter by his first marriage and help on the farm. Maybe give him sons to help him when he got old. I don't really think he loved her. He was a handsome, tall widower. A descendant of Daniel Boone and President Andrew Johnson. One of his relatives was mayor of Columbus, Ohio. His family back home was well-to-do. I think they made their fortune by building a soap factory. Your grandfather could have had anyone. I'm not sure why he picked her except maybe because he knew he'd never have to worry about her leaving him for someone younger and more attractive. His first wife, the one he brought with him from Indiana to Tennessee, was very pretty. He was lucky to get her, some said. But she died. And after she died, he never talked about her again."

"What happened to her?" I asked, thinking back to Jean's tauts.

Mom stopped plucking. She looked out at the back yard through the open door. For a few moments her thoughts seemed far away, then she startled a bit and seemed to realize where she was again. I could hear the clock ticking loudly in the kitchen. She pressed her lips together with tense firmness and started slowly plucking again. Her hands shook a little as she plucked.

"Did she get a disease?" I prodded.

Mom sighed. "I'm really not sure what happened," she squinted as if trying harder to focus on removing the pinfeathers from the nearly-bare breast of her chicken. "It all happened years before our family moved here. Your grandfather said she went out to check on the chickens in the henhouse and something scared her. They say he found her dead on the floor in the henhouse."

"Dead from what?"

"I don't know," Mom said. "A heart attack maybe? Now, let's go put these under the faucet and wash them really well."

"But she wasn't old enough to have a heart attack, was she?" I asked.

Mom suddenly got terribly busy and no longer seemed to hear me. Instead, she washed the chickens while I thought about what I could recall Dad telling me about his parents.

I thought back to my rare visits to Dad's hometown. His dad, my grandfather…the so-called murderer…died before I was born. But my uncle still lived on Dad's family farm with his wife and kids. I recalled the dark, wood paneling inside that house. The mahogany floors were always layered in thick dust and grime. I remembered the giant pantry right off the kitchen how it was lined with rows and rows of dusty jars filled with fruit, vegetables and soup stock. The house always smelled of farm dirt, rancid bacon and an indefinable smell of sweaty people and burning coal. I already knew Mom's opinion regarding my paternal grandmother's cleaning habits. Mom said she never ate at Dad's house when they dated. His Mom never mopped a floor, ever, as far as she knew. That they lived "Colonial-style" during the week by spreading newspaper on the table on Monday and, instead of washing the table, they just tore off sheets of newspaper each day all week until Sunday when they took the rest of the paper off, scraped the table and applied fresh paper for the coming week. This was directly the opposite of Mom's mother's house where a guest once commented that he'd feel comfortable eating off her floors because she kept them so clean.

I'd also seen Dad's family tree, all written down with tiny notations tracking our ancestors back to 1544 in Southern Germany. According to that tree, we really were related to Daniel Boone and President Andrew Johnson. Johnson was not the most-famous president. Some said he was deathly boring. He only became president by default after Lincoln was shot. Not everyone was happy about the compromises he made to bring peace to the South after the war. But later he did negotiate the deal for the U.S. to purchase Alaska! I also thought about the relative that became the mayor of Columbus, Ohio. These were strong men. They were good men, as far as I knew. I found it hard to believe one of their descendants could have murdered his wife.

Mom and I plucked feathers in silence as I waited for more details. I thought about Jean's accusations again. Finally, I collected my courage and asked, "Was my grandfather a murderer?"

"Heavens no!" Mom said. "My father was a sheriff for a while, but he never killed anyone, let alone murder. He didn't even carry a gun! He didn't need one! Most of the people in town respected him so much all he had to do was talk to them—look at them even to make them behave—he had a very distinct gaze—those ice blue eyes could cut right through you. Even the criminals were a little afraid of him, and they respected him. All my father had to do was look at me in a certain way, and it made me shiver. He never had to spank any of his children. That look was enough to make any of us stop what we were doing immediately."

"Not your father — Dad's father! Jean told me he was a m-u-r-d-e-r-e-r." Mom stopped plucking and looked at me with cool blue eyes the color of a spring sky after a rain. Her face shone red from work and heat. Her arms were covered in chicken feathers up to her elbows, and some of them floated down into her light brown hair. "Your Dad's father?"

I nodded. "What happened to his first wiffffe?"

Mom waited another long moment before she answered. She looked down at the chicken in her grasp. "There were rumors…" she said softly.

"What do you mean, rumors?"

"We heard rumors, but I have no idea if they are true." She took the chicken to the kitchen, and I followed. She made a fuss over washing and gutting the chicken and patting it dry with a cup-towel much like she'd dry a baby after its bath. Then she laid it in a white enamel washtub with two others she'd already washed. Soon she'd cut them up and put them in freezer bags, and we'd stack them in the freezer.

"The rumor was that your grandfather went on a trip to Indiana to buy mules and left his first wife at home. When he got back, a neighbor saw him in town and told him he'd seen Mrs. Hinkle across the valley with a single, neighbor man. That they'd seen her go there several times. Well, rumor had it, Mr. Hinkle got very jealous. He confronted her. She denied it. But that didn't satisfy him. He stewed on it for a while. The next thing you know, she turned up dead. Some say he mistook her for a chicken thief and shot her as she came out of the chicken house. Some said he knew the sheriff and paid him to keep quiet about it. But most people don't believe that. A neighbor told me once that he shot her because he was jealous. But another one said he was inside late one night and heard something chasing the chickens, that he went out to see what it was and shot a round into the air to frighten what he thought was a fox. That the gunshot scared Mrs. Hinkle and she had a heart attack in the chicken house and died as a result."

"How old was she?" I asked.

"I don't know. Maybe in her 30s?" Mom answered. "She was a bit overweight and had a heart condition. It was one of the reasons they sold their farm in Indiana and moved here," she added.

"Isn't that kind of young to have a heart attack?"

Mom didn't answer.

"Do you think he shot her on purpose?" I asked. The Bible verse about the sins of the fathers being vested upon the children until several generations came to mind. The thought made me shiver.

"I don't know," Mom said.

"Do you think Dad knows?"

"I don't think so. And don't you ask him!"

"Where is she buried?" I asked.

"In Indiana with her family," Mom answered.

That gave me food for thought. "Sounds like my grandfather stayed mad at my grandmother even after she died. Otherwise, seems like he would have buried her in the small cemetery next to the house, wouldn't he?"

Mom had cut up a wash pan full of chickens while we were talking, and I'd been putting them into the freezer bags. Now we squeezed all the air out of each bag and tied them up with yellow, paper-covered twist wires. She didn't respond to my question, just looked thoughtful.

"So, it could be true. My grandfather might have been a murderer."

She bent down and put her arms around me. Despite all the sweat and hard work and knee-deep in chicken guts, Mom always smelled like fresh baked bread to me. I inhaled her warm scent and relaxed into her hug wrapping my arms around her.

"Darling, what I do know is, you can't believe rumors. He was never charged. All this happened long before your father was even born. Your grandfather and your Dad's mother sat on the front pew of the Methodist Church every Sunday for 30 years, after they married. Your grandfather was a church deacon! People respected him. He and your grandmother ran a successful farm. Could he have done all that and been a murderer? I don't think so. I don't think you have anything to be ashamed of, and I want you to tell Jean that the next time you see her. You hold your head up! You stand up to her! Now let's get the rest of these birds into the freezer, and then you and I can clean up this place and take a bath!"

* * *

2007

The court hearing that morning goes well and my sister regains custody of the house. And her divorce is granted. That afternoon, when I round the corner and pull up into Dad's driveway, I see Dad standing on the patio, encircled by Mom's old walker, throwing something out into the overgrown garden. Beside me I have the prescription I picked up in town.

As I watch, he hurls a missile of some sort into the thick undergrowth behind the house. Despite his age, I am amazed at how far he can throw something that looks heavy.

I roll down the window and ask, "What are you doing?"

"The freezer in the garage came unplugged again! Did you unplug it?"

"Me?"

"Yes, you!"

"No! I didn't even know you had a freezer in the garage."

He looks at me, doubtful. "Been off for days. Everything in it is rotten. I'm throwing the chickens out for the neighbor's dogs to eat."

As I watch, Dad flings another rotten chicken into the undergrowth where it lands with a thud.

"I brought your prescription." I hold up the bag so he can see it.

He pulls his hanky out of his back pocket and wipes his hands. "Come on inside. I was just about to make a sandwich and pop some popcorn for a snack." He walks back into the kitchen pushing Mom's old walker ahead of him. On the front of the walker, he's duct-taped what appears to be a wire, freezer basket from our old freezer to the front handles. He's mounted it much like the wire basket I had on the front of my bicycle when I was a kid. This one contains used hankies, a dried-up orange, Afrin nasal spray and an earmarked and underlined Sunday school devotional, as well as a handful of used insulin needles and several hearing aid batteries in a jar lid. It also contains a spiral notebook that I know records the logged details of all his insulin readings written in red pen, every day for what may go back years.

It appears he's used the walker for a while inside the house, but this is the first time I've seen him take it outside. Usually, he uses his cane.

I don't want one of his sandwich concoctions or popcorn, especially after he's been handling rotten chickens, but I park the car and follow him inside anyway.

He washes his hands, fills a brown bag with kernels and puts it into the microwave. Then he pulls out packaged meat and bread and begins to make a sandwich. As we listen to the kernels exploding, he leans against the counter to catch his breath and tells me, "My Mom raised Dominique Red chickens, and Rhode Island Reds, you know. Did I ever tell you that?"

"No." Immediately my mind zips back to one of the many questions held deep inside my brain for more than 30 years. What was the real story about my grandfather? The grandfather I'd always thought of as a successful farmer, deacon of the church, father, husband — and more. So, I might ask, "Dad, did Grandpa kill his first wife?" But I don't have the courage to ask him, even though I knew I'm running out of time.

"She raised some of the biggest, prettiest chickens you ever saw. But she hated when they got in her garden and ate her tomatoes." My father's shoulders begin to shake with suppressed laughter as he recalls some distant summer day where the chickens dared fly over the fence and eat his mother's tomatoes. The sound he utterers in mirth are difficult to distinguish from cries of pain these days. Only his lips turn slightly up at the corners indicating he is indeed laughing.

"She'd rush out to the garden with a pair of kitchen shears, and she'd grab those chickens up. She'd take a whack out of their tail feathers and a whack out of one wing, then she'd heave them over the fence back into the chicken yard. They couldn't fly anymore because she'd whacked them, so they'd fall with a great big thump on the other side of the fence."

The timer chimes on the microwave; the popcorn is done. Dad opens the door, takes out the bag, opens it and puts half in a bowl for himself, half for me. We sit at that cluttered kitchen table. He splits his sandwich into two parts and gives me half, and together we munch the tough popcorn and sandwiches in silence for a bit.

The question burns inside my head. The age-old question. It rises to my lips, but I push it down with each kernel of popcorn. It rises again and again. I insert another piece and push it down again. The moment is here. The time to ask is now. If not now, when? Time is running out. But the question remains sealed in my chest like a body in a crypt.

Instead, an endless round of logic circles in my head. If he knew, he wouldn't tell me the truth, and by asking the question, I'll shatter the rare and comfortable silence between us. Such a question might irreparably damage the hard-earned peace we are enjoying at this moment together. And if I'm related to a murderer, do I really want to know? Do I really even need to know?

Isn't it enough to be saddled with the fact that I'm a descendent of one of the most boorish, unpopular presidents in the history of our country? Do I really need to know if there's also a murderer in the family? Maybe it's better not to know. Maybe there's another way to find out.

I decide to check the old issues of the town newspaper, first chance I get. For a moment I consider finding my grandfather's first wife's grave, digging her up to see if there's buckshot, or a bullet rolling around in the casket. But I know that I won't. Can't! And so, we finish off the popcorn and the sandwich in companionable silence, and I resolve that God will just have to sort out what happened to my first grandmother. There are some things you just can't know.

As I pull out of the driveway later, I realize I've completely forgotten to ask him about the assisted living home. Has he made up his mind yet? I guess that answer too will just have to wait.

◇

"Fathers shall not be put to death because of their children, nor shall children be put to death because of their fathers. Each one shall be put to death for his own sin." (Deuteronomy 24:16)

◇

Fried Chicken

Take one whole chicken.
Wash thoroughly and dry.
Cut off legs, thighs, cut breast in half and cut back in half. Retain liver.
Retain neck and use to season rice (then discard neck after cooking).
Beat up whole eggs sufficient to dip chicken, add ¼ cup buttermilk to egg mixture.
Dip chicken parts (including liver) in egg, then roll in half-half mixture of self-rising flour and cornmeal.
Add cup of corn oil to cast-iron or stainless-steel copper-bottomed skillet.
When oil is swirling but not smoking, add battered chicken pieces.
Brown quickly on each side, then reduce heat and cover.
Cook on low heat until done.
Salt and pepper to taste while cooking.
Drain on paper towels.
Possible side dishes are
rice cooked with chicken neck (discard neck).
Green beans.
New red potatoes cooked in skins (cut eyes out before boiling).

Chapter 5 – Nail Soup

"I made a boo-boo yesterday. That's all. The kids helped me fix it last night." — Louis

2007
The next morning I arrive at Dad's house to take him to the grocery store so we can replace the food items he lost when the freezer got unplugged. I arrive just in time to see him striding across the patio toward his battered, tan, 1965 Dodge van. The walker is nowhere in sight. No cane. Through the back window of the van, I can see acetylene tanks he uses for welding stored behind the back seat in an upright position. They look like small robots with green caps peering out through vertical eyes from behind the dirty, back window of the van. There are enough tanks in the back to have him chatting with St. Peter by lunchtime should someone rear-end the van on his way to town.

Dad has on his work clothes and an oil-stained, canary-yellow hat with his business logo embroidered across the front. "Dozer Work, Fill Dirt–We Aim to Please" the hat reads. He wears a work boot on one foot and a house shoe on the other to spare his foot still sore from recent ankle surgery. His cheeks look flushed to me as he climbs into his van and slams the door shut with a clank and a rattle of several, old, shattered window glass fragments trapped inside the door panel.

"Where are you going?" I ask, getting out of my car.

"Doris, the renter called this morning. The bathtub won't drain. I think the previous renter stuffed something down the drains before she left—one last shot at me for evicting her is my guess."

He is talking about our original house, the one I grew up in, which is now being rented.

"Want me to call a plumber?"

"You can't get anyone to come the same day. It will be several days before anyone good will come out. Those sorry, low-down, scoundrels. All they do is take your money and tear up more than they fix. There was a guy I used once; he was fair, not sure where I put his number. He's only slightly less worthless than the rest..." He pats his shirt pocket, the one tied with red yarn twisted round the button, as if hoping he'll find the number there. He leans out the open van window and studies his back tire. "Do you think that tire looks low?"

"Maybe. Think you picked up a nail?"

"Could be." He shrugs. "Go inside, look on the desk in the kitchen. See if you can find a phone number for the plumber. I'll go see what I can do about the drain." He starts the van and backs down the driveway as I watch, my heart in my throat, hoping he won't hit my car and blast it, himself and the van clean to heaven. It amazes me that only yesterday he needed a walker, today he feels fine to drive.

Inside the house a moment later, I hurriedly shuffle through piles of discolored and moldy paper on his desk looking for a plumber's number he thought he remembered but does not know from when. The minutes tick by. I've promised to meet old school classmates for a late lunch after I take Dad to the grocery store—friends I haven't seen in years. I don't have their numbers with me to call or reschedule. I scheduled it all through email. I need to return home to Texas soon and resume my normal life, catch up on my writing, handle a mountain of business duties, try to make up for lost time with my daughter and granddaughters. I feel torn apart between my life in Tennessee and my life in Texas. No matter where I am, I feel I should be somewhere else.

We still haven't found an assisted living facility Dad likes. Despite my time in Tennessee, we appear no closer to deciding than when I arrived. Dad avoids the topic, and this morning he looks normal and capable, so I wonder, are we rushing things? Maybe he is still fine on his own after all. Dad has never been "normal" in the traditional sense of the word. He has good days. Won't we know when it's time? Won't God tap us on the shoulder and say "now"? The truth is… I really don't have a clue what I'm doing.

I shuffle frantically through the pile of numbers. There are hundreds maybe millions of phone numbers on the backs of torn envelopes, catalogs, phone books, pink artificial sweetener packets, torn slips of yellowed paper, old photographs, but none say "plumber." I'm not even sure if I find the right name that I will recognize it.

My head aches from the fast search made without bifocals. I go to the bathroom to hunt for Tylenol. I open the medicine cabinet and, no surprise, find it still contains all of Mom's old prescriptions, her nail polish, and colognes. The colognes are named things like Happy. Longing. Obsession. I open each and sniff, then close my eyes and remember better days. The nail polish we used on her nails the day before she died still sits in the cabinet. I pull it out and absently slip it into my coat pocket. Somehow, I find comfort in its weight there, like a tiny piece of her is still with me.

Knowing I can't afford the time, but nonetheless compelled, I find myself drawn down the hallway to her room. I open the door Dad keeps tightly shut. I have not seen her room since a few days after her funeral. I find storage boxes stacked to the ceiling. Sun streams in at the window bleaching the rose-colored carpet a lighter shade of mauve. The peach and mauve Ralph Lauren comforter and drapes look yellow from years of sunlight streaming in through the curtains. Dust cakes the furniture. Yet the scent of Mom somehow still lingers in this room. The sickly-sweet scent of death persists too. I look up and notice that a dark circle stains the ceiling where the roof has leaked. Dad had the outside roof repaired last year but has not fixed and painted the ceiling in Mom's room. I can see where the nail heads have rusted leaving faint prints like upside-down squirrel footprints.

I find the sight of the disrepair unbearable and go to the utility room searching the shelves feeling I must do something to restore order in Mom's room—right then. After a moment I find what I'm looking for, the spray-on white ceiling primer. I used it once when Mom was still alive to fix the ceiling in the guest room. I slept there during the last months of Mom's life when I wasn't sleeping on the floor next to her bed.

Despite the time constraints, I pick up the can and grab a small tub of wall repair filler as well. I must fix it—now. I locate a hammer, stand on the bed, and pound the nail heads back into the sheetrock, then I cover them with the filler. Then I spray. I cannot believe my luck. A perfect storm for my effort. The stain disappears almost like magic. I feel relief having restored at least some order to what feels like a world crumbling apart around me.

I put the can, hammer and filler away, then—back to the desk to find the plumber's number.

As I sort, I find one of Dad's lab reports. "Hem-o-chrom-a-to-sis," I read the diagnosis. I Google it on my phone. "A metabolic disorder involving the deposition of iron-containing pigments in the tissues characterized by bronzing of the skin, diabetes, and weakness," according to Webster. I glance down to the treatment portion of the medical report, which recommends Dad have his blood drawn once a month to rid him of the extra iron. They recommend his blood either be thrown away or donated. If left untreated, iron builds up within the tissue and may prove fatal. I don't have to ask him; I knew he's not following the treatment.

So, now I know Dad's not a man of steel—instead, he's a man of iron. Truly. For years I suspected as much. Now, I hold the proof in my hands. It is not the first time I've considered the reason for Dad's hard resiliency, nor the first time I've had rusty nails teach me something and at the same time alter the course of my day.

* * *

1968

"Jane, get up! Get dressed! There's something I need you to do."

"What? I'm sleeping!" I said. I jerked my shoulder trying to pull away from his big, calloused fingers that were now pulling my toes. I looked at the clock and it said 2:00 a.m.

He tugged at my shoulder again. "Get up. I need you and your brother to help me. Put some clothes and shoes on, and then meet me in the driveway."

As I fumbled for my clothes, moonlight streamed in my window. And I heard him wake my brother in his room down the hall from mine in a similar fashion. I could not find a shirt, so I pulled a sweater on over my pajama top. I stumbled around for my tennis shoes, but couldn't find them, so I went into the hallway barefoot.

"Does Mom know?" I asked.

"Ssshhh," he answered.

We quietly left the house and went out to the driveway. Dad did not notice my feet were bare in the darkness.

"Jump in the truck," Dad said, his voice tense. He placed some buckets, cardboard boxes and empty nail crates in the back of the flat-bed truck and covered them with a tarp, tying it down so it wouldn't blow off and would keep the contents in the truck. This was the truck he used to carry sheetrock and supplies back and forth to the houses he was building. In the last three years Dad had developed quite a name for himself building houses.

"I'm sleepy!" I whined, yawning. The inky darkness of the night felt thick with humidity and blanketed us in a vast blackness as only country nights in Tennessee can do.

"Where are we going?" my brother mumbled.

"Hush up. You'll see," Dad said and started the truck.

"Did you tell Mom we were leaving?" I asked. I could see by the dashboard lights, Dad's face looked glossy with sweat, his hair tousled and greasy, and his jaw tense. Sweat stained his shirt down the front and under the arms, and he smelled of dirt and grease.

"You're Mom's asleep. She's tired. I didn't want to wake her. We'll be back before she wakes up."

He turned the key and the truck engine purred to life, and he quietly backed it out of the driveway. Dad pulled the stick into forward, accelerated and turned the truck onto the highway where he gave the engine a burst of gas and, when the RPM wound out, he changed gears. The truck was new—to us—but typical of Dad he did not buy it on the car lot. He bought it from a salvage yard in wrecked condition because the previous owner drove it off a cliff and likely died as a result. For a long time, it sat in front of his shop on blocks, and my brother and I played in it. Like TV detectives, we determined the former owner died quickly based on the pieces of dried, torn skin, scalp, and other organic matter we scraped out of the dash with our fingers and the blade of a penknife to examine more closely. We pretended we were Dick Tracy and his sidekick. Eventually, Dad reconstructed the truck with parts he bought from another wrecked truck of the same model.

Now we flew down the highway Dad at the wheel, one arm hanging out the window in the breeze, and the powerful engine purring. The wind poured in the windows blasting our faces with cool night air. I shivered in my pajama top and thin sweater, and my teeth chattered. As we drove, I wondered if my brother and

I had found all the scalp pieces from the former truck owner, or if there were more still lying dried, fuzzy, and leathery under the seat.

I thought about life and death and if that man whose scalp we found suffered much before he died. I wondered if he knew he was going to die, and if it hurt a lot to have your entire scalp ripped from your head when you bounced into the windshield and then back out again, or if the first blow rendered you unconscious. As we rode my hand searched for seat belts, but I found none despite the recent model of the truck. Eventually, I found the frayed ends where, apparently, Dad had cut the seatbelts off. He always said they bothered him, or they got in his way. So instead of belting myself in I clung to my brother's arm for stability and security.

We headed out the Shelbyville Highway, a drive I'd only taken a few times in my life but one that I recognized even in darkness. Long straight stretches, then steep, winding curves and hollows that made Dad shift gears a lot. I sat in the middle of the wide truck seat, so when Dad shifted, I had to move my legs over close to my brother's to make room.

Light from the truck headlights skimmed along thick woods and fields, sending deer bounding and rabbits hopping and then wriggling under woodland shrubs in search of cover. Fast cars with their lights on bright nearly blinded us sometimes as we drove, then whooshed by going fast in the opposite direction. The drive took a while. I was just beginning to feel sleepy nestled against my brother's arm, when Dad slowed the truck.

Soon he turned onto a dirt road and slowed even more until the truck was virtually at a crawl. This narrow dirt road ran parallel to the highway, but sometimes I could still see the main road through the bushes that separated the two. Every now and then Dad stopped the truck, turned out the lights and looked out across the narrow field at the main road. He listened.

After a few minutes, he said, "Okay. It's clear."

He turned on the truck lights, and we pulled back onto the highway once more and headed back in the direction we'd come before turning off. He crept along in the truck until he found a wide driveway with a gate that led to a field. The driveway was almost hidden by large cedar trees. Dad pulled into an opening I couldn't see completely, but he clearly knew well. He followed the drive deep enough so no one could see the truck from the highway. It looked like the entrance to someone's hay field. I did not see a house beyond. He turned off the headlights and killed the engine.

"Okay, boys and girls, I have a job for you."

We got out of the truck and handed each of us a cardboard box from under the tarp.

"What are we doing here? It's the middle of the night. I'm cold!" I shivered more with nervousness than with actual chill.

"Let's go home. Can't this wait till tomorrow? I think it's about to rain," my brother said.

"No! We must do it now. We do it now, or your dear ol' Dad might just be in jail tomorrow."

"JAIL!" His voice sent shivers down my spine. Was he kidding?

Dad picked up several crates and buckets. He handed us each a bucket. "Listen to me and listen good! Follow me and watch for cars. If you see or hear a car, jump in the ditch, lay flat and put your hands over your head. And close your eyes!"

Goose bumps spread along my arms as I followed, my bare feet making pattering sounds as we walked down the warm asphalt on the highway. A painful little knot pressed against my heart. He didn't have to tell us—we knew what we were about to do was very dangerous and the TV detective in me knew it was jailhouse trouble.

We walked a way down the highway. Steep hills fell away from the road into a valley on one side and the road was divided from the field by a deep ditch. On the other side a sharp hill rose. We kept walking until we reached a wide curve.

In the moonlight I could see mounds in the road. As we walked closer, I saw the mounds were really busted nail crates. There must have been a dozen crates and millions of nails scattered all over the highway and along the gravel edge. Looking behind us I could tell that fast-approaching cars would not see the nails until they were right upon them because of the hill and turn—a terrible accident waiting to happen. Exploding tires! Out of control cars and trucks! I thought only a miracle had kept someone from hitting the nails, busting the tires out and causing the vehicle to crash.

"Work as fast as you can. Pick up all the nails and put them in the buckets. Bring them to me, and I'll put them in the crates and nail the tops back on. I'll be filling the crates here on the side of the road. I can't afford to lose all these nails."

The night took on a surreal quality as my brother and I walked out into the middle of the highway in the dark of night in our bare feet wearing pajamas and began to pick up handfuls of nails to put in our buckets. As soon as we filled our buckets, we took them to the side of the road and dumped them in the crates Dad brought. As each crate filled, Dad nailed the tops back on and carried them back to the truck, loading them into the back under the tarp.

Between trips to load crates Dad grabbed a push broom he'd brought along and began to sweep the nails up into neat piles at the side of the road yet still on the blacktop. This made the process of collecting them go much faster. Soon my fingers felt scraped and raw, and I wished for gloves, but I kept working as fast as I could. As we worked a soft drizzle of rain started falling. But we continued working. Nerves made me break out in a sweat despite the cool rain and caused me to shiver until my teeth chattered even more. I listened for the distant whine of a car engine. I fumbled to pick up as many nails as I could in each hand. All the while listening. The sound of an oncoming car came far too soon.

"Car coming!" My brother yelled almost as soon as I heard the sound myself. We all ran and jumped in the deep ditch on the far side of the road. As Dad ordered, I lay flat and ducked my head under my hands, curled my legs to my chest in a fetal position and closed my eyes. Seconds later, I heard the car tires squeal as the driver saw the nails at the last minute. For a second, I thought he might lose control and crash into the ditch where we lay and crush us all. I heard nails ping like sharp bullets flying out in all directions under the force of the tires sliding across them. The car skidded and stopped a few yards down the highway. The driver rolled down his window. He was so close I could smell the smoke from his Camel cigarette.

"Son of a gun," the driver yelled, and pounded the steering wheel.

I held my breath. He's going to get out of the car and kill my Dad. He's going to kill us all, I thought. We've probably punctured all his tires. We're lucky he didn't crash into the ditch and kill himself *and* us. A scream rose in my throat. I pulled the neck of my pajama top up to chew on it to keep from screaming. It was all I could do not to yell at the top of my lungs. Moments passed. I held my breath until I could feel my face turn red and the sky started spinning overhead in a kaleidoscope of diamond stars and blackness.

After a few moments, the man decided his tires could get him home. He tossed his cigarette out the window and spun off in a spray of gravel and nails back onto the highway and quickly disappeared over the next hill. I gasped to fill my lungs with fresh air and stumbled to my feet.

After the light from the red taillights faded, we ran back out onto the highway and picked up more nails again like mad. Soon my hands and feet were covered with asphalt grime, and bleeding from the sharp nails, but I kept working. I longed again for a pair of gloves and wondered if Dad might have a pair in the truck, but I didn't ask. The process repeated itself over and over in similar ways with other cars until I lost track of the number of time cars screeched, we jumped into the ditch, the cars halted and the drivers yelled. Every few minutes I wiped my bleeding hands on the back of my pajamas.

Eventually Dad inspected the road, and said, "That's enough kids. Let's go." I nodded, too tired to speak, and we stumbled back to the truck in silence. The sun peeked over the treetops as he started the engine and backed out onto the highway, headed for home.

"What happened?" my brother asked when we were halfway there.

"Smoky Bear," that's what happened, Dad said.

"A bear?" I asked.

"No, stupid, the cops!" My brother said, nudged me in the ribs like I didn't know anything.

"What about a cop?" The word felt foreign on my lips. I'd never heard the police referred to as "Smokey Bears" or "cops" and the words made me suddenly feel like I was somehow part of an "in crowd," one of the "cool and dangerous people."

Dad was silent for a while as if weighing whether to let us in on his secret. Finally, he said, "I was coming home late last night from Builder's Supply in Shelbyville with cases of nails on the back of the truck. The police had a roadblock set up. I didn't see them until I topped the hill. I hadn't gotten around to changing the license tags on the truck, and I guess too…I was going faster than I thought."

He referred to his habit of buying one set of license plates and changing them to the truck he was driving to avoid having to buy tags for all his trucks.

"So, I threw my brakes on thinking I'd turn around and go the back road. But when I braked, the truck swerved, and all the nail cases spilled out onto the highway. I got away, but I had to come back. I couldn't lose all these nails. And, too, maybe, somebody was bound to get a blowout or worse maybe get themselves killed from nails in the road."

I tried to picture all these events.

"You kids did a good job tonight." He patted me on the head and squeezed my brother's shoulder. Then he withdrew his hand, placed it on the steering wheel again and stared out through the windshield.

I stared at the smooth, black gearshift knob with the white diagram that showed Reverse (R), 1st, 2nd and 3rd gears and wondered when Dad would teach me to drive. I wondered if I even wanted to learn. It seemed the world of adult driving could be filled with unexpected pitfalls. And Smokey Bears! I wasn't sure I was ready for that world yet.

The house was quiet when we pulled into the driveway. After the engine stopped, and before I followed my brother out of the truck, to satisfy my curiosity, I reached my hand deep under the seat where I'd been sitting, searching with both excitement and dread…for a bit of hair and skin that might remain there. Perhaps a little something we'd overlooked. My hand only encountered an old grease rag and an empty thermos of Dad's. No scalp or other organic human matter remained. I let out a sigh of both relief and disappointment.

By some miracle, Mom appeared to have slept through the entire night oblivious to our adventures. I pulled off my bloodstained pajamas, pulled on fresh ones, washed my cut-up hands and feet in the bathroom then fell into bed exhausted.

When I slid into my place at the breakfast table an hour or so later, Mom looked up from her coffee and asked, "What happened to your hands?" I looked down. My swollen hands were covered with rust stains and scratches. I looked at Dad.

"Hold out your hands," Mom instructed me. Then she turned to my brother. "Let me see your hands too."

He dutifully held his out as well. I saw they looked even worse than mine. Mom looked at Dad.

He took a bite of his toast, chewed. He looked up. Mom was still staring with a questioning look of disbelief on her face.

"I made a boo-boo yesterday. That's all. The kids helped me fix it last night."

Mom sat holding the coffee pot as if frozen in mid-air. "A boo-boo? You made a boo-boo?"

Mom carefully set down the coffee pot and laid the red checked potholder beside it.

"Louis, I need to see you in the bedroom, please?" She took off her apron, folded it twice and placed it across the back of her chair then headed for the bedroom her back straight, chest thrust out, nose high. She did not look back to see if he was following. Dad took his napkin out of his shirt neck, threw it down in a wad on the table and scooted his chair back, rose and followed her into the bedroom with slow and heavy footsteps. The door slapped shut. My brother and I looked at each other, then down at our food.

"How long do you think they'll be?" I asked.

"A long time," he said with a crooked smile.

"Think we should go ahead and eat without saying the blessing?"

My brother bowed his head and said quickly, "Good food, good meat, good God, let's eat! Dig in," he said looking at me with a smile.

We ate. Muffled voices grew louder until it became obvious a heated argument was underway in the bedroom, first Mom, then Dad, then Mom again yelling quietly. Drawers slammed, something fell on the floor, books toppled from shelves and hit the floor with explosions as loud as gunshots. I heard Mom crying. I heard loud nose-blowing (Mom) followed by more crying. More murmured voices (Dad). Then more loud nose blowing (Mom).

Then I heard Dad praying out loud, "Lord move upon the scene! Please see what I must deal with, Lord. Help her understand!"

Franky and I chewed our food while we looked out the kitchen window at the squirrels playing in the trees across the road in our aunt's yard. The voices rose and fell punctuated by loud shushing noises from Mom and pleading from Dad. After a while they seemed to recede into the background as I grew more interested in watching what the squirrels were doing.

We ate everything on our plates, and then my brother ate what was on Dad's plate.

"No sense letting good food go to waste," he mumbled, his mouth full in a gruff higher-voiced impression of Dad. He washed it all down with a large glass of orange juice and smacked his lips. "Ah!" he rolled his eyes, which made me laugh as was the intent.

A few months later I walked over to Dad's shop behind our house to call him to dinner. Walking down the path I noticed a nail crate sitting alongside the old, converted school bus Dad used to carry his tools from one construction site

Chapter 6 – Mountain Oysters

"No sir, I came into this world a bull, and I'm not going out a heifer!" — Louis

2007

"I ain't taking any more of those pills! Nor shots either," Dad yells. "Those shots give a fella breasts." He shakes a worn-out nylon-bristled broom at me that he's been using to sweep dirt off tomatoes he's gathered from the garden. The red orbs Mom called love apples are rowed up along the edge of the patio, gleaming with water droplets in the morning sunshine. Despite his difficulty walking again this morning, Dad hobbles through the overgrown garden to collect any volunteer vegetables that might have ripened from last year's planting, along with the tomatoes he planted this year.

"Dad, you have prostate cancer! You've got to get treatment or it's going to kill you!" I follow him in my light-colored sandals, unsuitable for gardening, or chasing gardeners, trying to walk down the barely discernable rows, trying to ignore weeds brushing my thighs. The moist dirt clings to the bottom of my shoes making them uncharacteristically heavy. I back away just in time to avoid the worn-out bristles waving uncomfortably close to my white linen shirt. He is wearing his house shoes and thin, brown, work pants torn around the back pockets until I can see his equally thin white underwear underneath barely concealing the pale pink of his backside. His pants hang on his hips like an old shirt on a coat hanger. He is so very thin now. I have bought him clothes and bought him clothes, and he will not wear them. This is his outfit of choice. I do not understand why.

His broom bristles barely miss the end of my nose. This morning I've postponed yet again my return trip to Texas and made my apologies to my husband, again. Hock is doing my job and his too for our business now as I try to persuade Dad to see reason and get the medical help he needs. He has not yet selected an assisted living facility, and I am exhausted from exploring all the possibilities both in person and online. For the millionth time I wonder if I need to just leave him alone; but the responsible side of me says that won't end well. So, I persist.

"These doctors don't know what they're talking about! All they want is your money. They'll do anything to get it! Now, I've been reading *Bottom Line!* There's a man who knows a thing or two! The man who wrote that says doctors want to keep information from you, not help you. They've had a cure for cancer for years, but they aren't telling anybody. How would they make any money if they told us? That quack doctor would do well to read *Bottom Line*." He shakes the ragged broom at me again for emphasis.

"All that training and I bet he doesn't know half of what Mr. Bottom Line knows. He needs to forget all that junk he learned in medical school; I tell you. Now this fellow who wrote *Bottom Line*—"

"Dad, I know you don't believe you have cancer, but you do. Several doctors have confirmed it. Not all doctors are evil. Now, if you like, I can take you for your treatments, or someone else can. I don't care who or how, but you have to go!"

"I'm not going! That last shot cost 16 hundred dollars! That's right, 16 and four zeros! That's nuts, and I'm not going to pay it I tell you!"

"But Medicare will pay for it!"

"Medicare! Me-eye. What insurance! I can't even figure out how to fill out the forms!"

On this point we totally agree. I've wrestled with my own insurance issues over the years, and mountains of insurance claims when Mom was sick. Even at my age, I find the struggle to file claims for myself almost a full-time job—and I'm relatively healthy! These days insurance companies seem more intent on wearing people out filing claims, so they die rather than helping people get better.

Dad goes back to scrubbing the tomatoes with amazingly gentle strokes cradling them in darkly arthritic, hands. He lets a tiny trickle of water from the hose run over them to wash away the loose black soil. When I consider his tender cleaning of these tomatoes in the chaos of dirt and wreckage of broken parts and salvaged oddities and absolute garbage surrounding us in his yard and garden, the irony of it causes me to sigh and wonder for the millionth time—what really makes Dad tick? Why this? Why now? Why MEEEE!

"They want to cut off my balls—ya know. They say that'll cure it and there'd be no need for more shots! They're crazy, I tell you! Maybe, I'm not sexually active NOW—but that doesn't mean I won't be again–SOMETIME! And I don't want to have to wear a brassiere when I do it! I've had balls all my life—I'm kinda attached to them, ya know!"

I take a deep breath, unsure what to say and not comfortable with the visuals this conversation causes to spring to mind. My last conversation with Dad about the facts of life took place when I was about 13 years old. All he said then was that if I gave a fellow his way, he would lose all respect for me. Somehow, I wasn't sure how to spin that knowledge back into this situation in any form that would help me make my point, so I chew the corner of my lip instead and say nothing.

When I look up, I see robins in a mating dance. I watch the delicate air ballet, and I am filled with wonder at the certain indicator of spring. Heady with love, they intertwine in the air. Briefly they catapult over and over. Between rapid sessions, they take a break and hungrily skitter along the ground on toothpick legs, fanning their wings to fool worms into surfacing. When one pops up, the robin pulls it from the ground like a red rubber band. With a backward fling, the worm is gobbled down, and the robin exhibits the same quick relish my granddaughter does when she devours gummy bears.

"Isn't that just a sight?" Dad says. At first, I think he's talking about the pile of junk that begins at the edge of the patio and extends as far as I can see through the overgrown garden and woods beyond. But he's not.

"Having sexual intercourse in front of both of us. Birds have no shame—a lot like some women I know." Dad smiles, a yellow, crumbled smile. I sense he is talking about me. I'm married to my third husband, and Dad never lets me forget it. It doesn't matter to him that both prior husbands broke their marriage vows with me first, or that I've been happily married for many years to my current husband—happily, and faithfully. Dad has never asked, and I don't enlighten him. And so, we have it, all women are harlots to him—all except Mom.

"Why do you hate women so much?" I ask him.

"Did you bring me breakfast?" he asks, ignoring the question. I am unsure if he is acknowledging what I've asked, or ignoring it. Likely I will never know. I hand him a crumpled fast-food bag. We go inside and for the next 20 minutes we sit with a cleared six-inch strip of kitchen table between us. It might as well be a football field.

He says, "When I was recovering from foot surgery the attendants at the hospital slept with the patients, even my roommate. I know because I heard bed springs squeaking all night in the bed next to me. All they think about is sex. All everyone thinks about is sex. I'm not sexually active anymore—you know," he says again. He pauses, as if to let this surprise sink in.

"My renters are moving out. Getting a divorce. The new one is named Delilah; she's named after the woman in the Bible that tempts Sampson. I bet she's never even read the Bible to know who she's named after. She's living with another woman's husband, you know that?"

"If you don't like her, why are you renting to her?"

"I have to rent it to someone. Everyone lives like that. I'm going to tell her it's wrong. But she won't listen. A Delilah never listens. No one listens to an old man."

"Maybe she will help you clean your house," I say hopefully. Dad cannot keep a housekeeper; his most recent one weighed more than 300 pounds and was unable to do the work because of her size. She stayed less than a month.

"She's too busy supporting another woman's husband to clean my house," he grumbles.

"What happened to your other housekeeper?"

"She left because she saw all that trash literature you get in the mail laying on my desk—all that stuff about sexual aids." He flushes. "I meant to throw it out, but I guess she saw it in the trash. Must have thought I was that kind of guy."

"What kind of guy?"

"One of those guys that thinks about sex all the time. Anyway, she just disappeared, stopped answering my calls, no notice, no nothing."

He gets up and walks back outside with me following him closely behind. He picks up the tomatoes he washed earlier which are now dry from the sun. His chin juts out in the way it always does when he doesn't intend to budge.

"I am not going to let anyone cut my balls off!"

"Well, I guess I don't blame you. And I'm sorry for asking about the housekeeper. That's more information than I ever wanted to know about you."

I'd had no idea that castration was one possible treatment for prostate cancer. Maybe if I were in his shoes, I'd feel the same way. But then again, I've already had a hysterectomy and—in the end—it didn't slow me down all that much…so who knows? Are balls necessary for orgasm? At the time my gynecologist patted my hand and reassured me ovaries and a uterus were not necessary for orgasm. But he is a man. I am not. How could he know? Who do you ask about such things? What does a doctor really know about any of it anyway? Now I sound like Dad!

In my case I took my own poll among friends to see if they were truly orgasmic post hysterectomy—just to see. The shocking surprise was that most women over 40 I talked to hate sex with their husbands anyway…ovaries, uterus, or not. So, it was extremely hard to find an authentic poll from which to make my decision. In the end the decision process was taken entirely out of my hands. My uterus finally ruptured due to endometriosis and started bleeding into my abdomen making the surgery totally necessary, in fact…an emergency. Thankfully, everything that mattered to me worked afterward, but in the end, I will never know if I would have had the courage to have it all out or not if the decision hadn't been made for me. What did I know about male orgasm anyway other than the obvious? How could I possibly make this decision for Dad? It was difficult enough listening to him. It was impossible for me to open my mouth and talk about it.

"I don't know," I mumbled.

"Well, if you don't know and don't *want* to know my business—then stay out of it!" Dad raises his voice in a way that makes me jump like a 7-year-old, and he glares unblinking at me for a moment over the top of his glasses. Then he leans down checks that the outdoor faucet is truly off, then hobbles back toward the house with his tomatoes. There is a coltish stiffness to his walk that softens my heart toward him. I recall the fluid confidence of his stride and his well-muscled form from back when he was in his prime. And here we are now. A little time can change things so much, it's difficult to wrap my mind around it all. His chest and arms are still muscular from endless years of work, but his legs and buttocks are so thin, it hurts me to watch him.

Mom once told me about a friend whose husband had prostate cancer that went undiagnosed until it was too late.

"It was a terrible death, Jane. At the end, he lay writhing in pain, screaming until people down the street could hear him. Not an end I'd wish on my worst enemy, even if he did cheat on his wife—and heeEEE DIDdddd," she'd told me with a shudder and an arched eyebrow that spoke volumes. That arched brow just like that of my brother and sister seemed to have an opinion of its own. In this case it seemed to indicate what words could not, that God has his own way of dealing with cheaters. I wonder anew at what all she knew. Briefly my mind flickers over the male cheaters in my own past, and wonder if what Mom loved and believed in was holding a special consequence in store for them as well. I shuddered to think of it. I prefer to believe in the all-knowing, all-loving, all-forgiving God. I was happy now and bore my previous two husbands no malice. We are all works in progress. But occasionally I do see the benefit of there possibly being the other kind of God who hands out rough justice as he sees it. While I don't wish death on anyone...I might...like my grandmother...wish all cheaters, both male and female, a nice home without air conditioning in Texas during summertime. Or better still, a good case of diarrhea while stuck in traffic in their favorite, very-expensive car would do nicely too. It all makes me grateful that husband number three is a keeper; and so far, God has not found cause to separate him from his private parts.

My gaze drifts off across the yard as I search for something to shake dark thoughts of cheating, castration, and cancer. What was once a glen where I used to ride my horse as a girl is now covered over in broken salvaged concrete from building demolition Dad's hauled home for "fill". Behind the garage are broken storm doors and coils of discarded fencing, car batteries and wire are scattered everywhere. Underneath the weeds lay piles of discarded soda bottles, oil cans that I can't see, but know they are there, along with worn out cars and dozer parts.

Someday someone will need to clean this up. Mother always said it. I know it. I sigh. It won't happen while Dad has any say in the matter. For some reason I cannot fathom, he likes it the way it is. He saves everything as if he's on a desert island and thinks a Styrofoam hamburger container from Burger King or some other disposable object may rescue him from an untimely death? But anyone who looks at his place would think he was bent on self-destruction instead.

I know Dad doesn't have much money in the bank, but his land and houses and shops are worth a lot if he just wouldn't pile so much of it sky-high with torn down buildings, old equipment, cars and more...for years. He hoards cash too, putting it inside peppermint candy tins. Once when Mom was sick, my sister confiscated a pile of money he had hidden in a folder in a file cabinet. We used it to help pay for Mom's medicine for years right up to her death.

If Dad gets any sicker, we'll have to sell something quick to pay his medical bills. But he'll never let us sell anything if he has any say in it. And if not for his own care, what is he saving for? Unless he dies in his sleep, or kills himself driving his truck or bulldozer, we'll need funds to take care of him, someday. And that "someday" is breathing down our necks right now. And, when that happens, someone is going to have to clean all this up so it's fit to sell. A sense of dread fills me.

"Your lip's bleedin'," Dad says calling to me from the door with his little recycled, metal basket of fresh scrubbed tomatoes strapped to the walker. I pull a Kleenex from my pocket and dab my lip where I've chewed right through the skin.

* * *

1970

"The bull's out again," Mom told Dad one morning, her voice raised just high enough to make sure he heard.

The steady audible sound of Dad crunching his crisp, breakfast bacon stopped mid-chew. He dropped the bacon on his plate and cupped his hand to his ear. "You said the bull's out? Where? When?"

Too many years of sinus infections and long hours using floor sanders and other loud power tools and heavy equipment had left Dad nearly deaf. I suspected he'd been reading lips for a while. Sometimes he misunderstood Mom, or me; others he couldn't hear at all. He often complained that Mom mumbled, so she tried to speak louder than normal and spoke slow. Now that she had his attention, she raised her voice and drew out the words, "Mrs. Brasier called. Said that bull bellowed all night. Your BULL kept her, and her husband awake. And when she went out this morning, her garden was trampled to the ground."

Mrs. Brasier lived to the south of our farm. To the north lay a horseshoe-shaped subdivision that Dad developed over several years on property that once belonged to Mom's family. When my grandfather died, they split the farm between my mother and her sisters. The sister's sold their portions, but Dad eventually bought that part back and developed it. Gradually, Dad cut a horse-shoe shaped road and started building houses and selling them. The development consisted of about 12 lots with well-manicured lawns, and fine houses framed with large oak shade trees. The houses were owned by schoolteachers, doctors, and even a retired military colonel. While no one liked having escaped cattle running across their property, most of the time it was an idyllic place to live. Still…when the cows got out, no one liked us very much.

"Oh boy," Dad said. "I guess he got himself a girlfriend."

"That, or he wants to fight another bull," Mom said. "That bull is a testosterone driven maniac! If he isn't off fighting other bulls, he's worrying the bushes down to the ground around here with those big horns of his! Louis, he's a menace! What if he were to catch one of the children out in the field! That's the third time he's escaped this month!"

Mom was right. I missed our old bull. Dad could sit on that bull when he lay in the shade chewing his cud. Sometimes Dad even let me ride him when he was leading him to the barn. But the year before Dad felt he was getting too old and had sold him and bought a new bull. The new bull had been a headache ever since we got him.

Mom picked up her coffee cup, little finger delicately extended outward, and sipped it with full, pursed lips. I watched as her lips made a perfect red lipstick print on the rim of the cup. Can there be anything more feminine than that? I wondered. Well maybe silk stockings, but they were totally out of the question for me, for now. Mom said I was too young for such things. I looked down at the wispy blond hairs sticking up like soft fur on my unshaven legs. I really didn't have much hair anyway. The Native American in me, I guess. We were hairless body-wise. But still I was horrified at what I had and wanted to shave it all off immediately. I looked at her again and watched her lips move as she talked. I wanted to wear lipstick someday. The week before she'd let me drink coffee, so long as I mixed it half-and-half with milk. I liked it with three teaspoons of sugar.

"What's tes-tis-to-rone?" I asked Mom.

"You…never mind what it is! Eat your breakfast!" she snapped.

Her tone and the look in her piercing blue eyes hurt my feelings. I knew I was being too sensitive, but I couldn't seem to help it. Mom said it was because "puberty" was knocking on my door. I wasn't sure what puberty was or what door it was knocking on. Likely, I wouldn't recognize it if I saw it at the door, but I already knew I didn't like it if it was going to make me cry all the time.

"I suppose the fence is down again, I better check. I just have not had time to maintain the fences like I should since I started building houses; and the cattle sure can spot a weak piece of fencing. Once they start getting out, they keep getting out; and I declare, I just can't keep up with them." Dad shook his head, then tossed the last bite of bacon into his mouth and washed it down with a large gulp of coffee before he lowered the cup to the saucer again with a clatter.

"Louis don't swallow things whole. You'll get choked and maybe even ruin your digestion!"

"Who's got time for digestion?" Dad retorted. He slid his chair back from the table with a screech and sprang to his feet. He grabbed a toothpick from the small ceramic decanter on the table shaped like a milk can.

Mom said with a sigh, "Last week the cows got out and trampled Mr. Murry's yard. He nearly cried right in front of me when the kids and I went down to herd them home. With all this rain they left huge holes in his beautifully manicured grass. Before they got there, it looked like a golf course. Now it's pitted and ugly. We'll be lucky if he doesn't sue us!"

"Cry, you say. What a baby! A grown man crying over some grass! I thought he was an ex-marine! Must a been wrong about that. Guess he's some sort of sissy boy!" Dad grinned. "Marine, me eye! Boo hoo!" he jeered and mocked rubbing his eye with his fist.

I remembered the last time the cows got into Mr. Murry's yard. I went down and tried to drive them home. Scoop, our dog, somehow rose to the occasion and behaved like cow dogs I saw on television. Without him, we would never have gotten the cows organized enough to herd them back to our property.

Poor Mr. Murry. I recalled how he looked white-faced and tight-lipped standing behind the white, wrought-iron gate on his back patio as the cows, their tails looped over their backs with excitement, crisscrossed his lawn, sinking nearly up to their knees at every step into the soft soil of his perfectly manicured yard. Personally, I loved to wade around ankle deep in fresh mud after a clean rain, but I could tell Mr. Murry didn't think much of it when our cows were doing it. I'd seen pictures in magazines of women who went to spas and paid good money for someone to smear mud all over them. We had lots of mud, and I could smear it on my hands, feet, even my face almost any time I wanted, a real beauty treatment—for free! I guess cows feel the same.

"Sissy or not, he could sue us. You need to take care of the fences—today!" Mother declared.

Dad bellowed, "You don't have to remind me! Tell me, when do I have the time?"

"Well, if you don't have time to take care of the fences and the cows, you need to sell them!"

"Then, what will we eat, my Great, Big, Beautiful Doll? We've already killed all the chickens."

"I don't know, but if he sues you, what will we eat then?"

Dad didn't answer. He just chewed his toothpick, apparently considering his options.

Franky and I watched the encounter from our customary places at the table. We knew enough not to say anything. I could tell there was a very real difference between the humor I found in the situation and the reality of what might happen if neighbors really did sue. I didn't know much about lawsuits, but I knew enough to know they were bad.

Cow problems had come up more and more often at breakfast since Dad purchased the new Hereford bull, Gus. Dad bought Gus at an auction. He paid a lot of money for him, and he was a beauty. He had a long Hereford pedigree, red with white face, his coat rippled along his back in rich, shiny, auburn waves. Gus came complete with a large brass ring in his nose. Dad said that ring was there so he could hook a chain in it and move him from field to field without him wanting to "argue" about it.

Compared to the new bull, the rest of our cattle looked scraggly. They came from the herd Dad's father left him when he died. Dad had kept them on our place for years, mostly old culls and the like, but good enough to provide us with a few calves for the freezer. We had a couple of Jersey mix cows for milking, and the rest Dad raised so we'd have meat in the freezer—good enough to keep us in milk and meat, but they wouldn't bring much at market. In all about 50 head of cattle. However, Dad hoped to improve the bloodline by adding Gus to the mix.

Before Gus came, our cows stayed in their fields. Even though the fence wire hanging on cedar posts sagged heavily and looked old and worn in places, they seemed to remember the fences as solid and didn't test them. Gus, on the other hand, came from out of town. He did not know our ways of respecting threadbare, tumbledown imaginary fencing. He knew weak fences when he saw them. And ours were weak. With no hesitation and scarcely any trouble, he pushed the rotted cedar posts right over and stepped over the rusty, barbed wire to escape at every opportunity.

With his first assault on the fencing the veil of imagined imprisonment seemed to fall from all cow eyes, and they happily followed him out as if he were the leader of a happy prison break. Once they realized they could get out, there was no stopping them. It was, essentially, a bovine party every time they left the farm. Like a group of teenage girlish pranksters following their James Dean, they ran away every chance they got. Their tails flowed out behind them like thin, fluffy flags flying. With every step they emitted loud, intermittent gaseous explosions of delight that only seemed to fuel their speed and lift their mood even more.

Usually, they headed for Mr. Murry's place because he had the softest, greenest yard in the neighborhood. It must look like heaven to a cow. A virtual paradise for lovesick heifers would immediately want to go there where they could wallow with glee and frolic. The scene would have inspired a Renaissance painter to grab his easel and paints and begin a great work of art! They ate and fornicated with Gus all they liked, leaving cloven hoof prints everywhere in the soft turf. Through the windows Mr. and Mrs. Murry gazed upon the spectacle with downturned mouths before tugging the curtains tightly together so their young children couldn't watch.

The bull however was not satisfied with only making Mr. Murry's yard home for his new harem. Once he served the local, available cow population in his neighborhood, he quickly left the Murry yard and high-tailed it over the countryside bellowing challenges to any local bulls within earshot professing his sex appeal to everyone within hearing and challenging all comers. If he received any audible response from the others of his kind and gender, he considered them fightin' words, and out he'd go to demonstrate his dominance. If he found another bull, he'd quickly wrestle him to the ground and pound away until the other bull knew who was boss and bowed out of the fight.

By the time Dad got back from fixing the fence, Mom had confirmed by phone that Gus was still hanging around Mrs. Brasier's house some miles away. Since their last talk, the bull had trampled through her flowerbeds and worried one of her rose bushes down to sticks to demonstrate his strength to the young impressionable bullocks on their lot who likely already regretted audibly replying to his challenge.

Mom drove Dad over so he could walk the bull home, and we rode along in the back seat of the old, but still good, maroon Ford Galaxy 500. When we got there, Dad hooked the lead rope he brought to the bull's nose ring easily. The night's adventures had drained most of Gus' vim and vigor and, for the moment, he appeared quote docile. However, a bull doesn't lead like a horse. All the fields the bull trampled at a gallop the night before he now covered at a much slower pace on the way home.

Looking back over his shoulder every chance he got he continued to bellow slobbery challenges, something to the effect of, "I may be leaving now—but just you wait—I'll be back; and then you'll be sorry!" Every few steps he grabbed a mouthful of grass clearly needing to fortify his energy. He bellowed anew between bites, off and on. Dad said, it looked like the sleepless nights of cow chasing and tough talk had really taken a toll on Gus. He looked tired; but he still talked a good talk.

Mom and I left Dad to walk the bull home alone and we drove back to the house where, from inside in the air conditioning, I watched out the window for Dad to come up the drive leading Gus. By the time I saw them rounding the corner down the road, the sun had reached high noon. Time for lunch. I ran out of the house to greet Dad and pat the bull who seemed somehow resigned at this point to field confinement. Once Dad led him into the pasture and released the rope from the ring in his nose, the bull dropped his head and started grazing intent on replacing the pounds he'd no doubt run off during his adventures.

"Hey, Dad. Hot, ain't it!" I said, trying to make conversation.

"Yes, and I had a million things to do today," Dad answered. "Don't need to be chasing a bull all over the countryside."

I could tell he was furious and exhausted.

"Did he give you any trouble?"

"Nope. Too tired. Walked right along. He seemed ready enough to come home. Probably ran off a hundred pounds of hamburger on his little adventure. That's a hundred pounds we could be eating!"

"You wouldn't butcher him, would you?"

"One more trip like this, and I sure will. He's going to cost us more in damages than he's worth if this keeps up!"

"What are we gonna do?"

"Well, I fixed the fence the best I could. We'll just have to wait and see if he decides this is home and stays put or decides to break out again. I'm giving him one more chance."

His tone made me shiver.

For a couple of weeks, Gus seemed to have decided to "stay put". Occasionally, I'd catch sight of him following the cows we owned around the place. Now they looked like one big happy family. Life settled back into rural bliss, in a manner of speaking. Dad's chest swelled with pride when he talked about his new bull. Over dinner he'd count to us how many fine calves he'd have to sell at market over the next few years.

    The 4th of July rolled around. The day dawned bright and cloudless. Mom had agreed to let me host a slumber party in a huge tent we pitched in the nearest field behind our house. We closed the gate to that field to keep the cows out, and my brother helped me raise and stake out the large, green Army surplus tent. My girlfriends started to arrive in the late afternoon.

    The day before Mom had bought charcoal, marshmallows and graham crackers for smores, and hot dogs with all the fixings. She'd gotten chips and even Cokes—a huge treat for us. My friend Jennifer and I swept the grass and dirt out of the tent after we got everything all set up. We tightened the tent stakes where the ropes had gone lax in the heat and decided it might even stay up overnight. We laid out the makings for a campfire and put the lighter fluid close-by to help us light it when it got dark. All the while we worked, we talked about boys. I didn't have any boyfriends.

    Both Mom and Dad said I was too young to date. But Jennifer was older and had started double dating that summer. Now she pressed her white shorts and ruffled blouses carefully with a hot iron before she walked the quarter of a mile down the road to my house so we could go for a "walk", just in case she met "one of the guys". She also carried a pink rat-tail hairbrush with her everywhere she went and frequently teased her hair just a bit on top to give it some "lift". Every night she slept in brush rollers and wore a hair net so her hair would be curled and bouncy during the day. She also applied Vaseline to her lips to make them look shiny and kissable like the girls in fashion magazines that lay scattered all over her room. And she shaved her legs and rubbed them with baby oil, so they always looked sleek, trim, and moist.

    Having Jennifer camp out with the rest of us added a few novel twists to our overall camping experience. For one, most of my friends wore old, frayed shorts and tee shirts to sleep in like we did when we were younger. Bras were optional because essentially there was little for them to hold up at this stage. However, tonight we ALL planned to wear baby doll pajamas, and sit around the fire in thatched lounge chairs in case some of the neighborhood boys might happen to drive by and see us *from a distance*. How we knew that they knew we were camping at my house, I'm not sure. But we knew.

    And that's exactly what we did. After all the girlfriends arrived and settled in, darkness fell, and we lit up the campfire. Then we sat with toes curled toward its warmth and teased each other and told stories about escaped, insane prisoners-of-war ripping the doors off cars of unsuspecting teens parked in the woods where they went to neck. I didn't know what necking was, but it sounded exciting. Mom said teenagers who necked were sex maniacs. When she said things like that, I nodded seriously like I knew what she meant, and I never wanted to be a sex maniac, ever; but I really had no clue what she was talking about. It was like all the times on television when actors were having entire conversations that I didn't understand, and I never really got the point. Mom never had an answer about those either when I asked her. She always just said, "You'll see!" But I never did see. Or I hadn't seen yet—anyway. Now my brother, on the other hand, seemed to get everything and said he did see, and the point was to do what you loved until you only needed glasses. Do what? I asked. He laughed. And I gave up ever understanding at that point.

  We cooked our hotdogs and smores, we talked about boys we liked who lived in the neighborhood. Word had it these same boys along with my brother had suddenly decided to camp out at the lake about two miles from our house! I thought my brother was a real pain in the neck, but Jennifer and some of the other girls liked him and thought he was "gorgeous". It had occurred to me more than once that maybe they were friends with me so they could see Franky occasionally. Jennifer said she wondered if they'd sneak up to visit us that night. I told her I didn't think so. The thought made my stomach tighten in little strangling, frightened circles shutting off my airway. What if they did? An entire abyss of things I felt instinctively yet didn't know about opened up in front of me and made me hope the boys would stay away.

  Suddenly, grass snakes and barn rats didn't frighten me so much. Boys sneaking into our camp did. And the fear that Dad might catch them, scared me to death! Honestly, I thought, he'd likely beat us all if that ever happened! But I didn't want to throw cold water on Jennifer's hopes, so I kept silent when I went up to the house to get more chips and just kept saying in a kind of prayer, "Oh, God, Oh God, Please, no!"

  When I returned, Jennifer threw another log on the campfire and wadded up more paper to feed it. She held her cigarette lighter to the paper and a blaze flared. She stuffed the paper under the log with slim fingers, and it soon caught. She didn't smoke, but she camped out at the lake often with her family, so her dad let her keep the lighter. She made it look chic to light paper with the silver lighter. The sound of it clicking shut sounded magical. Oh…the magic of fire. We settled in and Jennifer naturally steered the conversation toward the extensive time and process to maintain hair, makeup, and nails. Then of course there was the white, Mach I, Ford Mustang her dad planned to buy her in a few months for her 16th birthday. None of this was native terrain to me. I felt thrilled for her to have a new car, and happy that now I'd have a friend who had a car; but I knew next to nothing about this particular car, only that it was beautiful. And I knew almost nothing about makeup either. I didn't wear makeup, and I wore mostly tee shirts and cutoff jeans and had absolutely no hope of owning my own car—ever. So, it was a bit like listening to a fairytale.

  I was growing up and trying my hardest to be cool and learn about this other life, and as much as possible be like everyone else my age. Someone pulled out a *Seventeen Magazine*, and we used Wendy's flashlight to go through the pictures and see what clothes we could dream about buying and wearing for fall.

Gradually the chips and Cokes disappeared, and talk fell to whispers. Jennifer held court as she described her previous weekend with her boyfriend, who played in a rock band in town. She told us how he kissed her for the first time. She rolled her eyes, and someone let out a moan and fell backward onto their sleeping bag when she finished her story.

"Let's tell another ghost story," Valerie said suddenly. Leave it to Valerie, I thought. She had two more years of braces and no hope of a boy's kiss until they came off. We'd all heard the stories of how braces could cut a boy's lip wide open, and he'd never kiss you again. And heaven forbid if your boyfriend had braces too—you might get locked together during the kiss and must be separated by pliers in the hospital emergency room! It was a fate too embarrassing to contemplate. I was grateful that all my teeth had come in straight, and I would never need braces. We would never have been able to afford them anyway.

"I've got a good one," Tess said.

Countless stories later, the tension around the fire grew to fever pitch. It was my turn to tell a ghost story, and I started to tell them about the one-armed convict who lived out near the lake close to the military base, and how he cooked and ate unfortunate lovers he caught kissing in their car. I hoped this might steer the conversation back to the topic of kissing because I didn't know a lot about it and wanted to make sure I knew enough so that when the time came, I wouldn't embarrass myself. I was just getting to the good part, when a huge bellowing roar echoed across the field. We all jumped. Several of the girls screamed. Tess jumped up, took a few steps, and peered out into the darkness. And Karen, who was short, jumped right into Tess's arms.

"Get down!" Tess yelled. She dropped Karen to the ground with a thud.

"What was that?" Wendy wailed.

My own heart pounded. "I'm not sure."

"Think it's one of the guys sneaking up on us to scare us?" Valerie asked.

"It didn't sound human," Tess murmured.

"Think it's that one-armed man?"

"Ahhhh....!" We all screamed, spontaneously.

"M-roar!" The sound came again....but this time we could sense movement out in the darkness. The rest of us stood in unison and strained our eyes looking into the dark beyond our campfire to see what it was.

Suddenly, there were multiple grunts and bellows, and thumps and the sounds of huge bodies impacting one another.

"Oh my gosh! Gus is out again," I said.

"Gus? Who is Gus?" several of the girls said in unison.

"Our bull, Gus. He keeps getting out and fighting other bulls and running around the neighborhood destroying yards."

"Are you sure?"

"I don't know what else it could be."

We all listened intently. Soon my ears tuned in on the location, and I could see huge shadowy bodies moving and writhing in the field next to ours. There was no moon, and the only light came from the campfire and the light streaming from the windows of our house behind us. The noise and motion came from the far side of the field across the road from where we were camped. We listened for several minutes.

"Are you sure it's not the boys?" Jennifer asked with a Mona Lisa smile. She tucked her wispy bangs back under one of her brush hair rollers and ran her tongue over her lower lip to moisten it.

"I'm sure!"

"Are you positive?" she smiled.

"Positive!"

The fight in the next field intensified. Suddenly there was a cracking sound. I realized they were tumbling against the fence that separated them from the very field we were in. They were rolling over the tall stalks of corn in their path as they fought! In a few seconds they rolled into the fence line in our very field again, and I heard the cedar post crack, the wire fencing fell to the ground.

"Run!" I said, "They're breaking through the fence into this field!"

"Run where?" Wendy cried. She made running in place motions with her legs, unsure which direction to head. "Run for the house…or.. no, run to the barn, it's closer!"

I ran for the barn. So did Jennifer. The others ran for the house. Jennifer and I sprinted for all we were worth, floral printed baby doll pajamas pressed to our chests the backs fluttering out behind us in the wind as we ran. I glanced over my shoulder once and saw the other girls running full tilt toward the house, which was farther away—but they were making good time. Even though Jennifer had long legs I was more muscular and soon I out distanced her on my way to the barn.

We had sprinted about 50 yards, when something tripped me, and I fell in a somersault over the electric fence stretched across the empty space where we sometimes kept a wooden gate to the field. Jennifer stopped just in time to avoid somersaulting over the fence and me. Fortunately, Mom had turned the fence off in preparation for our camp out. I sat in the soft grass for only a moment—stunned. Then, behind us the bulls bellowed and fought and pawed their way in our direction. We could hear them breathing heavily as they tumbled into the field we'd just left, crunching and rolling over the fence posts in their quarrel.

"Jane, get up! Run!" Jennifer cried.

I jumped to my feet. She stepped over the fence, and we both ran to the barn, pulled opened the door and climbed up into the loft where we looked out the opening down to the field we'd just vacated now between us and the house.

"I think I lost one of my hair rollers back there in the field, Jennifer moaned, breathlessly. They're new and they all match. My favorite shade of blue! Should I go back and get it?"

"Are you kidding me? No!"

Jennifer didn't say anything; she just began immediately to re-subdivide and rewind her hair on her remaining rollers with trembling fingers, so rearranging her hair once more into an even procession of rows.

The bulls fought for several more minutes until both appeared exhausted, and eventually they meandered out of our field and across the road where they settled to cropping grass side-by-side as if they'd reached some sort of truce.

"Are you girls alright?" Mom called from the house after the noise of the fighting had stopped.

"We're fine!" I called back.

"You better come to the house."

"Okay. We're coming!"

"Quick! Better run before they get started up again!"

She didn't have to tell us twice.

That was the end of the camp out. Mom collected blankets and sleeping bags, and we all slept on the living room floor the rest of the night.

The next morning, the girls took turns calling their mothers to come and pick them up. Jennifer walked home saying she'd return later for her things, that she simply had to have a long soak in the tub first.

The chairs around the tent lay scattered and smashed. The radio was destroyed. During their fight, the bulls had tumbled into the tent, collapsing it down over most of our clothes and other possessions. The outside was muddy with large hoof prints, but inside the clothes were mostly clean, though a bit wrinkled and squashed smelling of damp tent and grass.

"Guess I better go look for the bull," Dad said as we stood outside surveying the fallen tent and scattered camping supplies.

"No need, Mr. Murry called," Mom said. "He saw him standing in his back yard under his pear tree eating the pears this morning when he went out to collect his newspaper. Louis!"

"I know!"

About 2 p.m. I heard a rifle shot but didn't think much about it. People hunted squirrel in the woods at the back of our place all the time. I went back to hose the mud off the tent like Dad told me. After I finished, I took a bath. That evening I walked out onto the back porch to let my hair dry in the sun before supper. On the shelf on the back porch sat a small white enamel bowl. Inside the bowl were what looked like two perfectly symmetrical lobes of pink meat. What type of meat I wasn't quite sure? I had even less idea where it came from.

"Mom?" I called. "What's this sitting on the back porch?" I asked.

"Mountain oysters," Mom called back.

"What are mountain oysters?"

"Beef testicles."

My mouth was just forming the "What..." word when she interrupted. "Now, don't ask me anything else. Come set the table for supper."

As I set the table, Mom cut up the delicate pink orbs and mixed them up in the skillet with scrambled eggs she had cooking. She folded in some fresh spinach to wilt at the last minute and added salt and pepper.

"Louis, time to eat," she called out the back door toward the barn.

When I looked out, I saw the local meat packer wagon backed up behind the barn, the back door opened wide. They had skinned, gutted, and quartered that bull and were hauling the carcass into the refrigerated wagon. No one had to tell me, I just knew they planned to take Gus back to the shop and cut and grind the meat into portions they could package for our freezer. Gus the bull became Gus the lunch and supper.

The next time I was in Dad's office I saw Gus' nose ring resting on his desk serving as a paperweight.

* * *

2007

At the doctor's office I sit in the chair, and Dad sits on the exam table where the nurse has helped him settle in.

The doctor comes in and, after a few pleasantries, asks, "How's your flow, Mr. Hinkle?"

"I urinate like a racehorse," Dad tells him. "How about you? How's your flow!"

The doctor's cheeks turn slightly pink, and he ignores the question and continues with his examination. "Are you getting your blood drawn every month like we talked about for the hemochromatosis?" he asks.

"I don't have hemochromatosis," Dad tells him. "That lab made a mistake."

"Well, let's go ahead with the Lupron shot for your prostate cancer then."

"I don't have prostate cancer," Dad laughs, his shoulders go up and down with each spasm, but no sound comes out. "You boys just like to take my money. That's all. I'm perfectly healthy, see!" he makes a muscle. For his age, even I'm impressed. I've seen 25-year-olds with smaller biceps. Despite his age...Dad looks a bit like a mini-Atlas from the waist up.

"I've heard you can do radiation implants to kill the prostate cancer. Is that an option for him?" I ask the doctor.

"It's one way to treat it."

"Is there anything else we can do?"

"Well, there is one other option," the doctor pauses for a second, then continues, "You see, the cancer is sensitive to testosterone. That's what makes it grow. The shots cancel out the testosterone."

"Ain't going to take no more shots," Dad rants.

"Well, then the other choice would be to remove what's producing the testosterone," the doctor says. Folding his arms across his chest, he leans back against the patient room sink.

"You're taking about castrating me!" Dad says.

"Well, yes…"

"I knew it! Well, I'm not doing it! No sir-ree! I've castrated roosters and made them hens, I've castrated bulls – but ain't nobody going to do that to me! It's criminal to even suggest it – that's what it is! You guys are knife-happy! That's what you are! Quick to make a buck at some other fella's expense! No sir, I came into this world a bull, and I'm not going out a heifer!"

The doctor raises an eyebrow as he turns to wash his hands in the sink.

"You boys just need to read *Bottom Line*," Dad continues in a more even tone. "I'll even give you a subscription if you want."

"Well, Mr. Hinkle, I can see you have us all figured out. Why don't you go ahead and get dressed?" The doctor dries his hands and then pats Dad's shoulder.

"Jane, haven't seen you in a while, why don't you come out here and catch me up on what you've been doing while your Dad's getting dressed."

In the hallway outside the exam room, I ask, "How's he doing, really? Is the prostate cancer getting worse?"

"Well, really it's not that much worse. His PSA is only slightly higher than it was last year when he was here."

"What about his iron level?"

"That's serious, he really needs to donate blood periodically to reduce the extra iron build-up. If he doesn't, he's going to start having organ failure."

"Like his kidneys?"

"That, or his heart. Honestly, with his high blood pressure, a heart attack or stroke's likely to kill him long before the cancer ever does. Still, it would be better if he'd at least take the shots."

"I'll talk to him."

The doctor, who has known Dad and his ways for years, and understands him as well as anyone, nods. Smiles. Pats me on the back.

Once back home Dad stops and gazes down at the remaining tomatoes, he's left to ripen on the patio table. He places some of the best ones in the plastic basket fastened to the handles of his walker and starts toward the house. "I can go all night and not get up except maybe once to go to the bathroom. There's nothing wrong with my plumbing. I bet you can't go all night."

"No, Dad, I can't. I have to get up at least twice, every night."

"Want a tomato sandwich?"

"Yeah, Dad. A tomato sandwich sounds good."

"They've got lycopene," Dad says. "Sounds a little like Lupron, maybe it's almost the same. Good for your prostate, though. I read it in *Bottom Line*."

◇

"For a man ought not to cover his head, since he is the image and glory of God, but woman is the glory of man." (1 Corinthians 11:7)

◇

Mountain Oysters

Take fresh, skinned bull testicles and place in brine of salty water mixed with 2 tablespoons of vinegar.
Marinate for 3 hours in the refrigerator.
(Some like to marinate in beer. Brand does not matter.)
Remove from refrigerator, rinse, slice ¼ inch thick crosswise rather than lengthwise of the testicle.
Dip in freshly beaten egg, batter in a mixture of cornmeal and plain white flour, salt, and pepper to taste and fry in corn oil until done.
If calf testicles (smaller) you can fry whole.
Serve with hot sauce to taste.
Side dishes include cold slaw or potato salad, black-eyed peas (for lunch) or may be served with eggs and toast for breakfast.

Chapter 7 – Daddy's Veggie Patch

"Is Dad rigging up his own Jacuzzi in the bathtub using a cattle trough warmer?" — Jane

2006
Dad seems better for a while and again picks up the threads of his life. He goes back to work as best he can; and for a while, things seem quiet. I drive back to Texas, but in the back of my mind I know our situation is temporary. Dad is fragile and his ability to take care of himself limited. He isn't mentally or physically able to care for himself the way I'd liked to see him cared for. And I knew he won't let me do it for him. Increasingly, he lives an isolated and precarious existence. And truthfully, I have enough on my plate trying to keep my own business going, building my writing career, attempting to spend time with our kids and grandkids and keeping myself and my husband healthy. It's a full life even without dealing with Dad's challenges.

For several months we go on like this until finally I get the dreaded phone call from my sister.

"Jane, Dad's had a mini-stroke and is in the hospital. They say he's going to be okay, but I'm really scared. He's not right. He's not able to take care of himself, and really hasn't been able to for a while now. He's combative and won't even talk about getting someone to help him at home now or about finding a place to live where he can get the support he needs. He's refusing to speak to me and hasn't let me in the house for a while now!

"After he went to the hospital, Jane, I went to the house to pick up some clothes for him. Oh! It's terrible. I can't even describe it; the place is so bad. I could hardly walk through it for all the trash. It smells. I can't believe he's been living like this. There's garbage everywhere. Rotten food. Flies. Maggots. I don't think he's taking his medicine right. It looks like he's slept on the same sheets ever since you made his bed the last time you were here. For weeks now his blood sugar has been rising and falling; he calls and tells me about it. But he won't let me check it for him. I'm not really even sure he knows where he is half the time. It doesn't look like he's bathing, and I'm not sure what he's eating. Jane, I don't think Dad can go home even if he does get better."

I listen as she tells me everything, my heart feeling heavy in my chest. I look out the window at the beautiful green grass, the small, yellow butterflies on the white Morning Glory vine outside my kitchen window. The trees around our Texas house are slowly bending under a soft breeze. All around me I can feel the cycle of life humming. But inside I feel my own life screeching to a halt. Finally, I say, "It does sound terrible. What do you think we should do?"

"Home probably is not a safe option for him anymore. I think it's time for us to apply for Conservatorship and find an assisted living facility for him. I've got a lead on a place in a town nearby called Autumn Manor. It's close to where I work. I can check on him regularly there, and he'd get the care he needs. They will monitor his blood sugar, make sure he eats, and keep him clean. Jane, there are people there he knows. People he went to church with. We can't let him drive anymore. He's going to kill someone if he keeps driving. I know the administrator who runs the place. She's an old friend of mine from the home health care days. She's very good. Very caring."

The realization that many people Dad's familiar with are at this location is very encouraging. Dad has been active in the church community since his youth. He and Mom met when my grandmother invited him to attend church with them. My parents worked hard to organize church groups, and Dad contributed his time, skill, and materials to build several churches even cutting trees from family land and sawing the boards and smoothing them into usable timbers for walls, roof, and floors in one church. Dad led the singing in several of the churches over the years, and Mom played the piano, and they both led youth group activities. So, to reunite him with old friends from these wonderful days would be an incredibly positive thing.

"Okay," I said. "Let's apply for Conservatorship. Do you know a good attorney?"

"Yes, I think I do. He's a friend of someone I know."

"Can you give him a call?"

"I'll call him tomorrow. We need to move fast, while Dad's still in the hospital. He really can't go home."

"Okay," I say again. "Do what you feel is best. I'm heading your way tomorrow to help."

The next morning, I reluctantly pack my car, yet again, and make the 15-hour trip to Tennessee my heart filled with sadness and dread. Again, I drive through the piney woods of East Texas, through the flat fields of Arkansas, over the Mississippi River to the land of my birth. Then I spiral down the twisting winding roads cut through limestone cliffs in Nashville, and finally home. Alice, down the rabbit hole—again.

I arrive in my hometown with no answers; I drop my things at a hotel, then head to the hospital and find Dad in his room. He is staring out the window wearing a hospital gown and a deep frown. All things considered; he looks good. The stroke was a minor one leaving only the slightest drooping on one side of his face, but there's a disorientated look to him I don't like. I talk to the doctor, and he confirms what my sister has told me. Clearly, she's right. He can't go home.

"Dad, how you are feeling?" I ask brushing his cheek with a kiss and taking his hand in mine. He allows me to hold it briefly before tugging it away.

"Well, I'm doing pretty well, how about yourself?" He turns toward me and smiles a little, the smile twists a bit as he attempts to avoid the metaphorical elephant in the middle of the room.

"Did you have a nice drive up?" he asks.

"Yes, rather good. Some construction around Memphis."

He shakes his head in sympathy.

We visit for a while about his medical details. Finally, I broach the subject we are both dreading, "Dad, we are concerned about you going home by yourself. Do you have someone that can stay with you?"

"You girls worry too much! I'm fine by myself. I came into this world alone, and I can sure go out of it alone! No one gets to do it for you."

"I know Dad, but you know, you might not have to go out of the world so soon if you'd let us hire you some help. We'd like to keep you around as long as we can, you know!" I smile encouragement. We've tried hiring attendants to stay with him but no one trustworthy has lasted more than a few days. So, this is a thin attempt on my part to find a workable, less dramatic solution.

"You girls can't be spending money on help for me. I'm just fine. If I need any help…I'll hire them myself."

"Dad, we are just afraid that if you are at home alone and your blood sugar gets too low you might pass out. Or if it gets too high you might have another stroke like this one…or worse. You could fall and hit your head on the coffee table or something and might not wake up again."

"I'm old. What difference does it make if I go out hitting my head on the table or in a car accident? When it's my time, it's my time; and the Good Lord's just going to take me. I'd rather die alone on the floor in my own house or in a car accident than in one of those blasted homes."

"Well, Dad, that's another thing. I'm worried about you driving. You nearly ran one of the neighbors off the road a while back when you were driving on the wrong side of the road and…."

"That lying, conniving woman…I never even came close to being on the other side of the road. She's just out to get me, that's all there is to that. She's hasn't liked me since I delivered that load of dirt to her that happened to have a snake in it. Wasn't my fault it had a little green snake in it. A snake is one of God's creatures too, you know. But she didn't quite see it that …."

"Well…that's kind of beside the point…the fact remains I'm not sure you need to still be driving. She's not the only one complaining about it. And another neighbor saw you on the roof the other day. Dad…really…the roof? What were you thinking?"

"Well, I needed to check to see if the roofers fixed the leak. You can't trust what they say…." he trailed off.

I continued more firmly, "The doctor told us it's not a good idea anymore for you to live by yourself, Dad. Your blood sugar got so low that you've already driven the loader through a fast-food restaurant and tore the canopy off with the top of it a while back. Dad, even you must admit, that was a little crazy!"

"I am not crazy! You'd like to prove that I'm crazy, but I'm not. I'm completely sane."

"You're right. You aren't crazy. But you've got to admit, it was not a wise decision to drive the loader through the drive thru!"

"No, but what choice..."

"Dad, you weren't thinking straight. You can't think straight when your blood sugar is too low or too high."

"Well, maybe not all that straight...but straight enough! Nothing terrible has happened yet. I'll do better."

"Well...even if you think that wasn't terrible enough. Do you really want to wait until something terrible happens? We aren't just talking about you dying anymore. What if you run over a neighbor, or even worse, a neighbor's child? What if you fall asleep with the stove on and burn down your house and all the houses in the subdivision besides?" I ask him.

Dad's face seems set in stone. His brown eyes turn even darker. He mumbles, "Well, I don't really like most of those people in the subdivision anyway... they never even have the time of day for me. All they do is complain about Mr. Hinkle, the noise, the mess...the..." he trails off into silence and looks out the window.

I'm shocked and I sense he's shocked himself a bit.

A smile touches his lips a little and we both chuckle in a dark way, and then the smile fades. Really, we both know it's nothing to joke about. I can tell the conversation is upsetting him, so I change the subject and we talk of more pleasant things. When he gets better, we agree to go to a local park and feed the rainbow trout, a favorite pastime that we've not done in a while. Before I leave, I kiss his cheek and he puts his work-roughed hands on my shoulders to give me a few pats. The pats are meant to be gentle but the size of his hand and the way they are delivered feel more like a bear cuffing me. Somehow, I enjoy it anyway.

"I love you Dad." I grab onto his hand again and squeeze it, and he squeezes back a little.

"I know you do." He looks off to the side.

"I'll see you tomorrow."

"Bring me some clothes. I'm breaking out of this place tomorrow."

"Not tomorrow the doctor has to release you before you can leave, but soon, okay!"

"Tomorrow," he shouts as I'm going down the hall. "No one will give a fella any pants in this place! I'm a good mind to just walk out with my back side shining to the world in one of these worthless, backless gowns.... why they want to put a grown man in something like this I have no idea. Of all the fool things..." his voice fades out a little more with every step as I leave the hospital and walk out into the sunshine. Outside everything looks normal. Just a beautiful day for the rest of the world, but not normal for us. I'm not sure anything will ever be normal again.

As I walk back to my car, I wonder how long we can keep him in the hospital and how long it takes to get Conservatorship.

It would be one thing if he was the kind of elder gentleman who could be content to sit at home and have a family member drive him to and from the store. Maybe do a little gardening, maybe a little woodwork. But that isn't Dad. Dad's accustomed to power, to driving tandem trucks and dozers and huge dump trucks. Dad has loaders and dozers and every imaginable power tool. His tools are big, his projects are big, and increasingly he is less and less capable of handling any of them.

More than once Dad's mentioned that his own father died after building 12 gates in one day. It is a man's death, one that I believe Dad wants to replicate in his own way. A death that's honorable. Working right up until the day you die. I know he doesn't want to die a slow lingering death in a nursing home. Who does? Part of me wants so much to grant him this wish. But the fact is, it's too risky. The man is clearly engaged in some sort of strange suicidal spiral. My sister is right. Conservatorship seems to provide the only answer. My sister is local. She is a nurse. It makes sense for her to become his Conservator. I will help with finances and business organization and whatever needs to be done from Texas and come back as often as necessary to see about him. Maybe once we've got everything in place, Dad may even like it. He may make friends and decide he really wants to live a few more years and have people around him. This thought cheers me considerably.

Where he will go after he leaves the hospital we don't yet know, but Autumn Manor sounds like a good place to start. We can try it, and if he doesn't like it, we'll think of something else.

Much as I don't like our situation, I resolve that it truly is time to contact an attorney and apply for Conservatorship with my sister as Conservator. It is not something I want to do, but it is something that must be done.

The next day I drive out to Dad's place with my sister, and we go inside. It is as she said, only worse, far worse than my last visit. There are maggots in the half-eaten cans of sardines on the kitchen table. Everything in the refrigerator is spoiled. There are waste cans filled with used insulin syringes overflowing under the kitchen table and cotton balls covered in blood on the table next to where he's been eating. A coat hangs from the back of a chair in front of a space heater where it could ignite. The heater is plugged in using two bare wires, the plug having been cut off entirely, for some mysterious reason, something he's always been prone to do.

In the bedroom dirty clothes cover the floor. Dust and paper cups and newspapers are scattered everywhere. The bed is filthy and in the bathroom the bathtub does not look like it's been used in months. Standing next to each other my sister and I try to make sense of the bathroom. The toilet in his bath next to his bedroom doesn't work, and there's an electrical device next to the bathtub that takes us a bit to recognize as a cattle trough warmer. In the bathtub Dad has built a rough wooden seat to sit on.

"Is Dad rigging up his own Jacuzzi in the bathtub using a cattle trough warmer?" I ask looking at all the wires splayed out by the tub.

"I guess!" she answers.

"He's going to electrocute himself, isn't he?"

"Most likely!" She raised one dark eyebrow.

We spent the next 30 minutes taking pictures of the house to support our case in court. Once that is done, she says, "Jane, I'll meet you back at the apartment. I need to pick the girls up. Let's talk about what we can do this evening to persuade the judge to allow us to place Dad in our care so we can make things a little better for him. This just won't do anymore."

After she leaves, I see Tom, Dad's yellow-striped tabby cat. He is thin and uncared for much like Dad. He sits on a dirty piece of plywood laid out over two sawhorses in the sunshine behind the house cleaning his fur, trying to remove the burs from his coat.

I remember another time, another visit, when Dad was standing next to me looking out this same window. That time too Tom was stretching across the same plywood atop the same sawhorses cleaning himself. Tom was in better condition then. So was Dad.

Many years earlier Dad threw the sawhorses together to serve as legs for a worktable in the garage behind his house. They provide a large work surface for almost any project. There is always something that requires space to repair. The garage is filled to the brim with all kinds of lumber, cans, used insulation and scrap metal and tools. Massive coils of copper wire hang from the rafters like splayed out intestines emerging from inside some discarded, scrap metal robot body, all salvaged from various jobs he's taken over the years.

***

2001

It was morning and I was home for a visit with Dad. Mom had just passed away. I was helping Dad wash the dishes. Dad has two garages at the new house, a two-car attached garage and another two car detached garage out back visible from the kitchen windows. The outdoor garage facing the rear of the house had no doors, so I could see the yellow cat through the kitchen window as I helped Dad organize and put things away. The cat appeared young and sinewy, without a spare ounce of fat on his frame beneath thick, matted, yellow fur. From the way he licked and chewed it was clear he'd been through the thickets behind Dad's house and accumulated a bumper crop of cockleburs in his fur. He seemed at home on his perch, as if bathing and sunning in this place was part of his normal routine, which puzzled me because, as far as I knew, until now, Dad had never really liked or owned a cat.

"Dad, why don't you like cats?"

"I never said I didn't like cats," he said looking up from the heavy equipment sales catalog he studied while leaning full back in his dusty, blue recliner. "I just think they need to work for a living, like Louis Hinkle. Kill a few mice, maybe a rabbit or two, a chipmunk—then they have earned the right to lay around the rest of the day and sleep in the sun. There's nothing worse than something or somebody sitting around doing nothing but swatting at flies and eating up my groceries all day. Cats, like men, should work."

"Is he yours?" I pointed out the window at the cat now repeatedly trying to spit out the bur he'd dislodged from his fur. After several tries, he scraped the burr off his tongue with his paw, then shook his paw to dislodge it from between the pads. It dropped to the surface of the makeshift sun porch, and the cat sniffed it like it might explode back into his coat. Satisfied it wasn't going anywhere, he started on another knotted mound on his back.

Dad put the catalog down, sat up and reached for a huge pair of pliers he kept in a white, plastic, 5-gallon bucket half full of pecans next to his chair. He used the pliers to crack a pecan. The pliers had the longest handles I've ever seen—18 inches at least. And they were blackened with age. When the shell splintered, he picked up a 14-inch fileting knife and carefully separated the nut from the shell before popping the delicate kernel into his mouth. While chewing, he selected another nut and cracked it in the same fashion.

In the silverware drawer in the kitchen, I knew there were nutcrackers and picks specially designed for safely removing nuts from shells. They were proud purchases made by Mom. Dad preferred to use his own selection of tools for this task, like he did on most jobs. This predilection was one of the strongest traits that differentiated him from the average man.

Dad blew on a new, choice kernel to remove the dust, then popped it in his mouth with relish. He chewed audibly with his mouth slightly open. Looking out the French doors beside his chair in the direction I pointed, he spotted the cat.

"That's Tom. Haven't you met Tom?" he smiled, chewed, swallowed.

"Don't think so."

And so, Dad introduced me to Tom. I liked Tom very much. He came to me during subsequent visits and wound his tail around my legs whenever he could, and we became friends. Sometimes Dad would feed a bit of cereal to Tom under the table. I guess Tom caught enough rats to earn his cereal.

* * *

1968

When I was a kid, despite what he said in later years, Dad often seemed to absolutely hate all cats, and our cats especially. I knew this because he'd told me he didn't have any use for them countless times. The list of reasons he hated cats included the fact that they carry rabies. One fertile female cat could seriously overpopulate one small farm in only a couple of years. And they were always underfoot and could cause a person to trip and be killed. More than anything I think he hated them because they sensed the anger in him and were afraid of him. Often if he tried to pick one up and pet it, the cat would scratch him which made him even angrier.

As a young girl, each time I asked Dad for a cat, he gave me his list of reasons why we should not have one and told me "The subject was closed."

To get my "cat fix"—as my brother called it—I went across the street to my aunt's barn and played with her cats and kittens in the hayloft. There I could hunt for newborn kittens among the stacked hay bales, then gather them all up and cuddle them in my lap to my heart's content. I carefully looked at each new one to see how close it was to opening its eyes. Sometimes my aunt would give me a bowl of milk, and I'd spend hours teaching a kitten to drink. When they got older, I'd slide them down the gently sloped grain shoot from the loft one at a time, then go and pick them up from the grain bin below, take them back up in the loft and let them slide back down again. The cats seemed to enjoy this process as much as I did. There were times when they got older, we all slid down the shoot together. However, I didn't dare take any of my little friends home.

That is, I didn't until Tigger. Tigger was special. He looked at me from his intelligent little gray eyes framed by gray bands that striped his face. I looked at him and felt true love blossom in my heart. He followed me everywhere, and one day I just had to pick him up, put him in my sweater pocket and take him home. I made the decision because eventually I knew if I left him at the barn he'd come to a bad end. All the kittens did. If an owl didn't get them, a fox would, or a cow would step on them, or the dog would eat them. Barn cats seldom lived to a ripe, old age.

"Don't let your father catch you with that cat," Mom said when Tigger poked his head out of my pocket. "He'll tie him in a sack and throw him in the pond."

"But, why?" I asked. What's he got against cats, anyway?"

She offered all the reasons; and I heard them all again, but I refused to believe Dad wouldn't change his mind once he met Tigger. Tigger...was special.

"He thinks they carry rabies," Mom said. I could tell Tigger's charm worked on her though because she stopped kneading bread, wiped her hands on her apron and reached out to tickle Tigger behind one of his gray ears.

"I had a cat once," she mused. "A white one." Her eyes took on a wistful slant as she turned to wash her hands before going back to kneading the bread dough. "He used to come and sit with me on the back porch in the evenings. I'd feed him leftover cornbread and buttermilk."

"Tigger doesn't have rabies," I said, clutching the cat to my chest. "Maybe

Dad will let me keep him?"

"I doubt it, but you can ask," Mom said. "He'll need vaccinating. And he must stay outside. Remember, Dr. White said no cats in the house. You're allergic. And don't touch your face after you handle him; and wash your hands!"

"Okay, okay!" I agreed. "I love you, love you, love you!" I said to Mom for opening the door a crack so I could own a cat. It wasn't as if I didn't hear the part about Tigger being an outside cat, I just thought if I wanted something bad enough, I could make it happen. Already I had plans about how I'd win the battle with Dad over cat ownership, and Tigger would become an indoor cat. And I figured, until that time, what my parents didn't know about Tigger and me wouldn't hurt them—or me.

Vaccinations! I looked at Tigger. He looked healthy enough. But then Old Yeller looked healthy to his master too, in the movie, for a while—and what a train wreck that turned out to be! At my age, I had only the vaguest notion of what rabies was. Once, while at city hall with Mom to get car tags, I saw a video in the lobby that showed a raccoon foaming at the mouth. Not pretty. And I happened to know a distant friend of ours had to have shots in her belly button after a stray dog bit her and then ran off. Having shots in your belly sounded like a horrible experience. I looked at Tigger but could not detect a speck of foam anywhere. I scratched his head and a deep rumbling erupted from somewhere inside his chest. At that moment I resolved to make sure Tigger got all his shots so neither of us would ever have to worry about getting rabies.

I'd heard Dad talking about a vaccination clinic scheduled at the school right down the street from our house coming up in two weeks. For 5 dollars they vaccinated both cats and dogs. Five dollars seemed like a lot of money when the going rate for washing dishes at our house and sweeping the patio or polishing shoes only earned me 10 cents. To have the money in time, I'd need to do a lot of work. I resolved to expand my services to include toilet cleaning and weeding the flower beds. The image of Dad tying the knot in the gunny sack with Tigger inside kept me motivated. Surely, once Tigger had his shots Dad wouldn't mind if I kept him. However, the lack of shots wasn't the only issue—and I knew it.

I loved cats, but I really was allergic to them. Tigger felt so cuddly, and I could tell he loved me, and I so wanted an indoor pet. Dad had given me a calf the year before, but it wasn't the same as having a cat. We of course had once had our pony Beauty, but she was dead now, and Bupp her full-grown up foal, had to stay out in the field in winter and was too dirty to cuddle. Cute calves grew up to be cows that could care less who owned them. And you couldn't snuggle with a cow or pet it for long before it ambled off and started cropping grass. And eventually they all ended up hamburger anyway. No, it was best not to get too close to your pet cow.

Tigger wasn't just another pretty face either. He quickly made himself useful in a way Mom really appreciated. When she had a mouse in the cupboard, she'd call me. I'd find Tigger and turn him lose in the cabinet and close the door.

A few minutes later Tigger would utter a muffled meow. I'd open the door, and he'd walk out with a mouse in his mouth. He always took his mice outside to kill and eat them. No mess. No bother. Tigger became quite an exterminator.

Vaccination day came, I pulled the money from my shoe box, wrapped Tigger in a towel with only his head sticking out so he couldn't scratch me, and Mom drove me down to the school where they vaccinated him. He didn't like it much, but it was over quick, and he rode back home wrapped in the towel again as if he knew somehow, he'd now become a permanent member of our family. I taped his vaccination certificate into my scrapbook, and that night I sat on Dad's lap after dinner and said, "Dad, I found a cat; can I keep it?"

Dad had just eaten a piece of Mom's pecan pie, and when I rubbed my hand across his balding head, he almost purred himself.

"Where did this cat come from?" he asked.

"From Aunt Gretta's," I answered.

"Is it a well-behaved cat, and will he stay out from underfoot?" he asked.

"Yes." I said. I pulled a comb from my pocket and began to comb Dad's hair on the sides of his head.

"Is it a he or a she?" he asked.

"I'm pretty sure it's a he," I answered, knowing this was a critical factor in our arrangement.

Dad's eyes slid closed, I finished combing his hair and then got lotion from Mom's dresser and began to massage his calloused hands.

"Well, I guess you can keep it, but he has to stay outside most of the time; and if he gets underfoot, he will have to go," Dad said.

"Thank you, Dad," I picked up his other hand and rubbed lotion into it all the way up to his elbows. Then I hugged his neck, and he patted my shoulder and smiled.

Spring nights got cold. A long narrow screened-in back porch stretched across the back of our house. The porch held a giant chest freezer and provided a place to stack firewood in the dry in wintertime. Tigger chose the space behind the freezer next to the motor to warm himself on cool nights. As soon as we went to bed at night, Tigger would cry at my bedroom window. I'd raise the screen and let him in as soon as I thought my parents were asleep. He purred and kneaded my pillow with barely concealed claws. Eventually, he'd curl up like he belonged there and fall asleep. I went to sleep with a smile on my face my hand resting on the cat's back, feeling him purring under my fingertips. The next morning I'd wake early and let the cat out before Mom came to wake me for breakfast. Then I'd carefully brush all the cat fur off my pillow, all the time rubbing my red, swollen, itchy eyes and sneezing. While this was not exactly sticking to my agreement with Dad, I justified it in my own mind that Tigger might catch cold if I left him out all night or a fox might kill him. So the risk and slight overstep of our agreement seemed worth the consequences.

I thought I'd get used to the cat, but I didn't. As a result, Mom started taking me to the doctor's office for shots and pills for what she thought was bronchitis.

"Mrs. Hinkle, you're sure you don't have an indoor cat?" the doctor asked, staring over the top of his black bifocals at my runny, red nose, my swollen eyes and listening to my croupy cough. He furrowed his brows and twisted his mouth sideways considering me thoughtfully. I looked away at the wall hangings of Jack and Jill running down the hill with the bucket about to capsize and tried not to think about whether silence was really a lie of omission. *Could I go to hell for this?* I wondered.

"I'm sure." Mom smoothed a lock of my hair back behind my ear the way she always did when she felt concerned about me. "Jane has a cat but she keeps it mostly outside and she washes her hands after handling it. Occasionally we bring him in to catch a mouse, but then she takes him right back outside."

He looked at me, in a way that made guilt chew at my insides like a rabid animal. My stomach felt queasy. I kept hoping I'd build up a tolerance to the cat. I'd heard some people did. But meanwhile, I kept imagining the doctor's floor opening and flames of hell lapping at my feet, threatening to make short work of my dishonest soul. I had not exactly lied about the cat—neither of them had asked me directly if I had slept with the cat; and who was I to stop them from believing what they wanted. But I had not volunteered the information either. My intentions were deceitful, and I knew it.

God knew it too and would soon make short work of me if I didn't confess. But that would likely mean the end of my friendship with Tigger, and I just couldn't see how throwing a little cat into the pond in a sack with rocks or letting a fox kill him could be right either. So, I held my tongue. The gnawing feeling in the pit of my stomach continued after we left the doctor's office. On the way home we stopped by Dairy Queen and Mom bought me a chocolate milkshake.

"How do you feel?"

"Okay." I sucked hard on my straw and immediately felt the pain in my head that my brother called brain freeze. We rode home in relative silence after. It was cool and moisture began to build up on the windows inside the car probably due to my nervous cold sweating. I carefully drew a portrait of Bugs Bunny in the moisture and tried not to think about hell. For the entire drive I kept thinking about my sins and my heart felt heavy. What to do. Stay silent, keep Tigger, and lose my soul, or confess, save my soul, but condemn my cat to a watery grave. It was a big decision. How long would God allow me to sneak my cat into the house at night and lie by omission to Mom before he cast my soul into the depths of hell for good? The thought, plus the ice cream, made my teeth chatter, and my head hurt, and I shook like I had a hard chill. When we got home, Mom put me to bed and gave me hot chocolate which only made me feel even worse.

The next night after dinner, Dad hauled us out to the garden. He pulled the '59 Olds up casting light from the headlights over the garden so we could see to hoe the new potatoes, radishes and onion sets. The earth felt cold and lumpy under my bare feet. With a hoe taller than me, I dug a little hole and put an onion set in the ground. Once I had inserted the plant, I covered the roots by shoving earth over it with my bare foot. Then I'd step down on loose dirt to pack it firmly enough to make sure the onion was well seated. Then I planted the lettuce seed carefully sowing it into the soil at regular intervals. Red worms and night crawlers sometimes popped up between my ticklish toes. I'd put a ladle of water from a bucket onto each planted onion. Then I'd do the same with the next onion.

I planted three rows of onions halfway across the garden by the headlights. When I was finished, I had blisters on most of my fingers and thumbs from digging with the hoe. I thrust them down into the water in the bucket to cool them off. Meanwhile, Mom and my brother planted radish seed and potato sets, working much faster than me. While we worked, Tigger caught moths in front of the headlights, stretching up tall to knock them out of the air. One quick swat and he'd throw them to the ground, pounce and eat them with relish.

Dad didn't do a lot of planting. He mostly ran back and forth preparing to plant and getting tools to plant. I liked planting and even weeding and hoeing. I just didn't like doing it in the middle of the night. Sometimes neighbors drove by in their new cars. They'd slow down and look at us all out there planting barefoot in the dirt at night by the car headlights. I wondered what they thought. We were the only family I knew that did its gardening late at night.

A fatalistic attitude hung over our family during planting season. We all knew, as soon as the weather got hot, the sun would burn the garden up, and we'd end up buying our vegetables to freeze from the grocery store or from one of the neighbors like always.

Every year, Mom would save her grocery money and buy a new garden hose. She'd use it for a while and hide it in the hall closet when she wasn't using it, but eventually she was bound to forget and leave it out where Dad would find it. And every year, Dad cut the end off every hose so we couldn't hook them together so they would reach the garden to water it. He said with the end on the hose it wouldn't fit into the truck radiator to fill it—so he cut the end off every time. Good for watering the radiator. However, when he did this, it put an end to watering the garden with the hose and put us back where we had to carry water for a quarter acre garden in cans. Eventually, exhaustion inevitably won out over water carrying. If it rained enough, we had a garden, if it didn't the garden burned up.

However, each year we planted a garden just the same. You might say hope grew perennially in the hearts of each of my parents even though they seemed to be somewhat star-crossed when it came to cooperating with one another. Every year, each one prayed the other would change. And each year the good Lord disappointed them both. But they never gave up. Neither of them ever looked to themselves to consider if they should be the change they wanted to see.

A few days later I lay sprawled across the bed in my room reading a Trixie Belden book when Dad yelled, "Velma!" Calling Mom. Usually it was "Dear" or sometimes "My Great Big Beautiful Doll." When he called Mom by her name, it was never a good sign.

"Yes Louis?" Mom went to the back door and looked out on the porch.

"The freezer's unplugged," he snarled. "All the food's ruined!"

In my bedroom I put the book down on the bed and swallowed hard. *Oh no,* I thought. This would be the third year in a row the freezer had come unplugged during the summer. We never could figure out how it happened. Personally, I thought Dad unplugged it himself to plug in some other electrical appliance—a light or a saw, maybe the vacuum—and forgot to plug the freezer back in once he finished. I had mentioned my theory to Mom, and she agreed. But neither of us felt brave enough to bring it up with Dad.

"It's that damn cat," Dad said. "I caught him sleeping behind the freezer the other night."

The fan from the freezer motor did generate some heat and this did attract Tigger like a magnet on cool nights. Sometimes he did curl up and sleep in the space on the floor behind the freezer right next to the grill on the back where the motor vented. But I knew where my cat had been the last few nights—and it wasn't behind the freezer. It was in bed with me. But I didn't dare tell my parents that.

"See here. The plug's loose. The cat knocked it out of the socket, I'm sure of it."

I rushed to the back door. "I'm sure Tigger didn't do it," I said, leaning out the door behind Mom. I avoided mentioning that I knew where the cat slept.

"He's almost never out here," I added, twisting a lock of my hair between my fingers, and stroking my lips with it.

"I better not see that cat around the back porch anymore," Dad said. "If I do, I'll kill it, do you hear me?" He shot a dark look my way, eyes sparking in anger, then slammed the freezer shut so hard it made Mom and I both jump. Over Dad's shoulder I could see Tigger dart behind Dad's truck, then peek around a tire to watch as if sensing he was in trouble. I prayed Dad wouldn't see him. Dad stomped off into the house, and Mom got some plastic trash bags and started emptying the spoiled food out of the freezer. I vowed to do everything I could to keep Tigger out of Dad's way until he cooled off.

Several weeks passed. We undertook several more night plantings in the garden, this time setting out corn and peppers. Normally, Tigger worked alongside me. When I pulled weeds, he pulled weeds using his teeth. I'd dig a hole to plant. He'd help me push the dirt back into the hole. Somehow, he just knew what I needed. He was that kind of cat. This night felt cooler than most. I hadn't seen Tigger for a while. Eventually, we had all the plants set out, and Dad called it a night. Tired, we carried our tools to the garage and put them away, then headed to the house.

As soon as we stepped onto the back porch, we saw something shoot off the freezer and behind a box on the back porch in the darkness.

"That blasted cat," Dad yelled. "Just as I suspected, sleeping behind the freezer."

He made a swift move, reached behind the freezer, and unceremoniously dragged Tigger out hissing and yowling.

"See here!" Dad fished behind the freezer and brought up the disconnected cord.

"He's the one that's unplugging the freezer."

"But, Dad, weren't you using the saw out here this afternoon to saw new rails for the fence?" I asked. "Couldn't you have left the freezer unplugged?"

"Go inside," Dad yelled, holding Tigger by the scruff of his neck so hard that he pulled his eyes back making him look like an Oriental cat. "I'll not have such disrespect. Get in the house!"

"Jane, come inside," Mom urged.

I stood frozen, watching Dad.

"What are you going to do with Tigger?" I asked.

"Jane!" she insisted.

I couldn't move.

She went in and shut the door behind her, leaving Dad and me on the porch. Tigger squirmed and fought in eerie silence, trying with futility to get a hind claw into Dad's wrist to leverage his escape.

"Maybe it was me. Maybe I used the vacuum on the car and just forgot to plug it back in. I'm sorry. I won't do it again. I promise!" I begged, tears sliding down my cheeks.

"It's this cat! Cats are always a problem!" Dad pitched Tigger as far as he could out into the darkness. My last view of him was his body somersaulting through the black night air.

Tigger didn't scratch on my screen that night asking to be let in. I spent a sleepless night wondering if he was alright and if he'd come back the next morning. Dad grabbing him so hard must have really frightened him.

The next morning as soon as it was light, I crept to the back door and looked out. I saw our dog tossing something that looked like a black rag into the air. She caught it, shook it and then tossed it up again. When she dropped it, I saw the black limp rag was really Tigger's lifeless body.

* * *

2006

As I look out at Tom, I remember Tigger and marvel that in Dad's later years, his best friend is a large, skinny yellow cat. And I wonder if he will ever blame Tom for unplugging his freezer.

I hunt through the cabinets until I find some cornflakes and some canned milk. I mix them up in a bowl and take them out to feed Tom. I call the neighbor on my cell phone and asked her if she'll feed the cat for a while. "Dad's in the hospital." I tell her, and "I'm not sure when he'll be coming home." She agrees, and I feel better about the cat at least.

I call my sister next and ask if she managed to reach the attorney.

"Yes, and he was so nice. We have a court date for next week. I talked to Dad's doctor, and he says he will keep Dad there…they need to run some more tests and get his blood sugar regulated better anyway. So hopefully we can get this all set up, take it before a judge and get the Conservatorship awarded next week."

"Are we doing the right thing?" I ask her, really though I'm asking myself too, and truthfully? I am asking God!

"Jane, we have to do it. He's going to die if we don't."

"Maybe he has the right to die the way he wants. Doesn't he?"

"Jane, what kind of people would we be if we let him die from food poisoning or low or high blood sugar. We wouldn't let a dog die like that, why should we let Dad die like that?"

"He's going to hate us forever!" I persist.

"Well, he already hates me!" she says. "But it's not about whether he loves or hates us. He's our dad. We must do this. It's the right thing to do. I've seen it before, Jane where families have just left old people to fend for themselves. It's terrible."

"I know. But taking your Dad to court. Taking his rights away. It's just really terrible!"

"Some things in life are just terrible. Sometimes there are no good choices," she says. "You make the best choices you have based on the options available."

"Dad's not left us much choice, has he?"

"No, he hasn't."

"Okay, let's get the court date set and go look at Autumn Manor…and get his place cleaned up. You are right. It's horrible."

We hang up and I go back inside. It smells so bad I must hold my breath. I grab up the worst offensive items and put them in a trash bag to take to the community dumpsters down the road. My sister and I plan to come back tomorrow and try to take care of some of the rest.

As I pack up the bag, I look at Dad's overflowing desk and notice the pile of unpaid bills. The electric bill has not been paid for months. Nor has the water bill. No insurance on the house or the cars. Phone bill is overdue. I sigh. As I go through it all in my mind's eye, I can see Dad, sitting at this very desk laughing and talking about Tom and his fleas.

"Hang around a while Jane, and I'll give you a demonstration of a flea circus. Have you ever seen a flea circus?"

"No, Dad, I've never seen a flea circus."

"Here watch," Dad says, and he blows on Tom's fur and a flea pops off and lands on the desk. Dad pulls his toothpick out of his mouth and then inches his finger toward the flea.

The flea jumps over the toothpick, lands, hops a time or two more. Dad laughs. "Did you see me make him jump? Here, I'll do it again."

"No Dad, you don't have to do it again, I get the point."

"No, watch, I can do it again." He inches his finger toward the flea. This time Tom the cat is watching too, his ears perked up, his head drops down to get a closer look as he sits on Dad's desk and studies the flea. I can't help myself; I watch too. The flea jumps again.

"See that, Jane. We are all just fleas in the circus of life together. A little bit of prodding from behind and we'll all jump. The question is…where will the flea land?"

I'm wondering what part I'm playing in the current flea circus of life, as I turn off the kitchen lights, as if I'm turning off the lights on a show ring, and walk out the back door as if I'm exiting a stage. Just another jumping flea on the stage of life.

◇

"For God is not a God of confusion but of peace…" (1 Corinthians 14:33)

◇

Wilted Country Salad
Fry several strips of bacon until crisp.
Set aside bacon (pat with a paper towel to make sure it's dry).
Drain grease from skillet into a small bowl to use later.
Prepare loose-leaf lettuce torn into chunks.
Slice radishes.
Slice green and red peppers.
Dice green onions.
Chop tomatoes.
Salt and pepper to taste.
Just before eating, crumble bacon over the salad.
Heat bacon grease and drizzle over the salad.
Eat promptly.

Chapter 8 – Going Fishing

"Even St. Peter would shoot someone if they started trying to throw him out of his house. It's justified homicide, I tell you! I really don't think God would blame me, AT ALL!" — Louis

2006

The next day my sister and I check out the Autumn Manor assisted living more closely and together. It's a lovely place, new with private rooms and attached bathes. The furnishings are homey and inviting. The smell of fresh-baked cookies wafts through the lobby. The windows in each room look out into deep woods, and there's a common room for eating, a music room for entertaining and for family gatherings. There is also a well-equipped exercise room and an assisted exercise therapy room with a full-time exercise therapist. It is a place so nice I think I would like to live there myself!

Also, since it is in a town near where Dad lives, there are many residents already living there that he knows. Many are from his church. After our visit, I feel much better. However, the price for living there is enough to take my breath away. Dad will never agree to pay it. However, less expensive places are not suitable for him, in my opinion. Many don't smell good, the curators have shifty eyes and the patients look unhappy. They aren't ranked well on government websites either. Few places are. At Autumn Manor the people living there look clean and content. They gather in the common areas to work puzzles, visit with family and play games. They exercise in the exercise room, and I see people coming and going constantly and sharing meals with family members. It is a happy place.

After the visit, my sister and I reconnect again at her apartment on the balcony. We sip from large glasses of wine as we talk.

"So, what did you think of the place after seeing it?" she asks me.

"I thought it was really nice," I answer, before taking a sip of my wine.

"As options go, I think it's a good place," she says. "And you know as well as I do, Dad's a loose cannon. He can't keep getting behind the wheel of a truck or driving a dozer or loader. He's going to hurt someone or himself for sure."

"I know. The state of his house alone is enough to convince me."

"It's really is terrible, isn't it? I haven't been able to get into the house and clean it for months. I'm concerned he's not paying his bills either," she says.

"No, he's not. I saw a pile of unpaid bills on his desk when I was there. Have you tried hiring someone to come in and help him? And does he qualify for home health care?"

"He won't let me hire anyone. He's hired several himself and none of them have worked out. And, as long as he's driving, he doesn't qualify for home health care. All the people he hires are shady characters—at best. Some of them I'm actually afraid of. He should be afraid of them too; but, unfortunately, he's not. You know how he is. He likes to 'help' people he thinks are down on their luck. Jane, many of them are really dangerous. He carries wads of money around with him, and he waves it every time he pays for something. One of these days someone's going to knock him in the head and take away that wad of money and maybe kill him in the process.

"Many of these people are known drug addicts," she continues. "One was a parolee who served time for assault and battery. They steal from him constantly. One backed up in his yard not long ago and took all the batteries out of all the trucks. Jane, they are going to steal him blind, and one may kill him. So, it's not just about his health. His judgment is impaired. At his age he's an easy target for criminals and swindlers."

"So, what do we do? How do we get custody of a parent?"

"The attorney says we just go to court and present our case. We have to have Dad served with the legal paperwork and allow him to get an attorney. If he doesn't know one, they will appoint someone," my sister tells me.

"Well, if we go to court, we are going to have to prove he's incompetent, and I'm not really sure what that means."

"I think he is. He can't manage his affairs. He has poor health and poor judgment and he's not able to take care of his own basic needs," she says.

"Yeah, but how do we prove that to a judge? We know he's dangerous, that he's making poor decisions. We see it all the time. But how do you provide examples?"

"I believe the unpaid bills, a doctor's testimony as to his mental capacity, and the state of his health, combined with our testimony will likely be enough," she says. "We have the pictures of the inside of the house too. I think the trough warmer in the bathroom pretty much sums it up. That scares the life out of me. No one should live like he's living. If that doesn't sway a judge to give us custody, I just don't know what else we can do. I guess the best we can say is that we tried. If they say no, we'll just have to wait until he nearly dies or he kills someone else. Not very pleasant options."

"He is NOT going to like this," she says.

"'Not like' is an understatement," I say. "He's going to be furious." Just thinking about Dad's reaction makes me shudder.

I have to get back to Texas to handle some business there that I can't put off. Then, in less than a week, I drive back to Tennessee the day before the court date. I immediately go to the hospital to see Dad who has had another mini-stroke, further delaying his release.

"Hi, Dad!" I say when I walk into his room at the hospital. He is sitting on the edge of the bed in pajama bottoms that I brought him during my last trip, only last week. His pajama shirt is beside him on the bed. A nurse listens intently to his heart with a stethoscope, and he is wearing a blood pressure cuff around his arm.

"Hi, Jane!" He motions me toward him with a work-roughened, arthritic hand. He fumes a little and makes a futile shrug with his shoulders. "Did you drive in all the way from Texas?"

"Yes. Had to make a quick trip there and back. I got here late last night. I'm staying in town," I say wondering why he doesn't remember that I was just here to see him only a week before. His mouth still looks droopy on one side from the stroke, but he is sitting up and seems to be pretty okay at the moment.

"Well, you didn't need to do that! Your dear old Dad just felt a little bad for a while, that's all," he smiles. "And now I feel better; but they won't let me out of here."

"Dad, we need to talk."

"Haven't you listened to my heart enough?" he yells crankily at the nurse and swats her hand away? "If it takes you this long to figure out if my heart's beating, I might as well be dead!" He yanks the stethoscope off the nurse's neck and hands it to her.

The nurse jumps back and looks shocked for a moment. Then she collects herself and she gestures offering to help him put his pajama top back on, but he motions her away impatiently. She slings her stethoscope back around her neck again and casts me a sympathetic yet a frightened and relieved look before she walks out of the room.

I know how she feels as I watch her go. I take Dad's hand in mine and turn to him, "Dad, you can't go on like this," I say. "*We* can't go on like this."

"Yea, I know what you want to talk about," he said, "but I don't want to talk about it! I am NOT leaving my home!" He yanks his hand away from mine abruptly.

"Dad, you can't stay at that house by yourself anymore. Your blood sugar is very unpredictable. And you can't keep driving. It's too dangerous. You need to retire! Think about it, if you sell the equipment, put the money in the bank you'll have enough to live off of for the rest of your life. You could go fishing whenever you felt like it. You could maybe take a trip to the Holy Land with a group of your friends. Why, you could do anything you wanted!"

"Well, I wouldn't mind taking a trip to the Holy Land, but I think I'm too old for that. I might get over there and not be able to get home. And I don't want to go fishing! I want to work until I can't work anymore! I've lived on my own most of my life. I've taken care of myself. I've taken care of you! I've never needed anyone to take care of me in all that time. I don't need anyone to take care of me now!

"I'd rather die right on the floor of my own house by myself than in some nursing home. My two beautiful daughters, me eye, you're both mean as snakes, if you ask me. You're trying to put me away, that's what you're trying to do."

I pick up a pair of house shoes from the floor and put them under the side of his bed where he can slip his feet into them if he needs them. I pick up a pair of hospital socks and offer to put them on his feet. He allows me to perform this small service.

"Dad, we aren't trying to put you away, and it's not a nursing home," I say as I slid the socks up. "It's an assisted living facility, one of the best in the state. I checked the ranking online, and it's a good one. We know people there. We know the administrator. Medicare approves of it. We just don't want you to die alone at the house in a horrible mess."

"Assisted living isn't so bad," I continue. "There will be people there to talk to. There will be someone to help you take a bath and change your sheets. It's kind of like living at Holiday Inn Express! Dad has not slept in a hotel in more than 40 years. I consider telling him about Autumn Manor specifically but think better of it. One thing at a time.

I untangle his blanket and then try to fluff his pillow, but he grabs the pillow out of my hands, "Leave that alone! Leave me alone; and leave my things where I left them! If you keep moving everything around, I won't be able to find any of it!" He looks at the ceiling and prays aloud as he usually does, "Lord, move upon the scene."

When Dad does this, I'm never sure exactly what he wants the Lord to do. Strike me dead? Or *literally* remove me from the scene? Either way, I consider the outcomes less than desirable.

"If you try to take me out of my house, I'll take that shotgun and shoot anyone who tries to come through the door," Dad says loud and firm. His chin creases in the center as he presses his lips together in a fine line, the look he gets when he doesn't want to talk about something anymore.

"Dad, you've lived this long without shooting anyone, do you really want to shoot someone right before you stand before St. Peter and have to explain yourself?"

"Even St. Peter would shoot someone if they started trying to throw him out of his house. It's justified homicide, I tell you! I really don't think God would blame me, AT ALL," Dad says, glaring at me.

"Are you willing to bet your eternal life on it?" I ask him.

He says nothing. Instead, he picks up a chewed toothpick from the nightstand and inserts it into his mouth. He clenches his teeth around it and then turns to gaze out the window.

I change the subject to something more pleasant and stay for a while longer. We visit about safer things as he lies in the hospital bed refusing to look at me. I consider telling him that we have applied for legal Conservatorship, but the words get stuck in my throat; and I just can't bring myself to utter them. I think I'll have time to discuss it with him before he's served; so for now, I let the subject of assisted living drop. I guess, deep down I want things to stay the way they are for as long as possible. Once he's been served, I know…everything will change.

He tells me about the job he was working on right before the stroke. He is worried about losing the job now and asks if I'll get in touch with my soon-to-be-ex-brother-in-law and ask him if he can finish it so Dad will get paid. We talk about things he will need from home. His socks. His Bible. More toothpicks. The doctors want him to stay for a few more days so they can run more tests. Dad apologizes again for making me make the long drive from Texas to Tennessee and back. He asks where my husband is, what country is he teaching in at present? And I tell him a little about our life in Texas and about his relatives there.

"I'm fine Jane. I didn't really need you to come. Your sister can handle things here," he says.

I don't tell him that my sister is exhausted. She has her own challenges with work, divorce in progress, and two girls. I don't mention that she called asking for help.

After a few hours they bring his supper. I kiss his forehead and leave to go back to my hotel. I unlock the hotel door and throw my keys on the desk. I lie back on the hotel bed, fully clothed, and look up at the light on the ceiling. I don't know what Dad dreads more, losing control, or losing his home. I have traveled to Germany, Spain, New Zealand, Sweden, and many other countries and have made my home in half a dozen states in my lifetime. Home to me always means people, not places. But my way of life is foreign to Dad. With few exceptions, he's spent most of his days within a 10-mile range of where he was born. Clearly his world differs from mine in ways I cannot fully comprehend.

I lie there thinking about the meaning of home, about change, about how beautiful, yet rotten, life can be. How fortunate we are in many respects, yet how horrible our circumstances have become too. I think about choices and making decisions and the price of not making them in a timely way. I think about my husband my daughters and wonder what I'll be like when I'm Dad's age. Will our children be faced with making similar decisions for me when my time comes? We are head-strong people, and that's a fact. I doubt I'll be any easier to deal with than Dad. However, I won't be a world-class hoarder, and I won't be running around using heavy equipment and running people off the road in giant trucks, will I? I also don't think the neighbors will call to tell anyone I'm up on the roof again…but then who knows, anything can happen.

As I think this, I say a silent premature apology to my children for what I will probably eventually do to worry them; and I hope I can manage to age gracefully and die conveniently and inexpensively for everyone's sake. I recall a conversation I had with Mom shortly before her death when we were discussing funeral expenses and she told me to just throw her in a ditch somewhere that she wouldn't smell when her time came. We laughed about it at the time. And when the time came...of course...we did no such thing. She had a proper funeral even though she died 2 days after 9-11 and most of her family and friends could not attend the funeral. All the flights were grounded. But I did recall the conversation and did see her point...that she really did not want to be any trouble to the people she loved. Our sweet Mom. How I miss her.

I lie there and think on all these things until I can't think anymore. Somewhere in the back of my mind I know the sun is setting, the room grows dark around me, and I stare at the light in the ceiling until it almost feels like it's drilling a hole into my brain. I've heard that light stimulates Vitamin D in the brain and wards off depression. Perhaps that's why I can't stop staring at it? Some people cry, I stare at lights. I've always done this even as a child. Mom used to say, "Stop staring at that light, you'll put your eyes out." But I stare at it anyway. And with that thought and the image of my sweet smiling Mom fixed in the back of my mind, I finally close my eyes and drift off to sleep.

* * *

1967

In the summer of '67, when I was 10, Dad stopped building houses for a while and packed his bags and carpentry tools into a rusty white Chevy pickup with a large camper on the back. He also packed cooking utensils including his favorite pressure cooker and well-sharpened Old Hickory knives. He added eggs, a side of sugar-cured ham and some white, sweet onions to his cargo. Then he threw in a 25 lb. sack of potatoes with a large thump and a bit of a hand dusting afterward. Then he turned, kissed Mom goodbye on the cheek, got into his truck and headed to Pennsylvania where he planned to take a job as a construction foreman for a building being built near a community of Quakers. These actions spearheaded his fifth career change since my parent's marriage.

When Dad married Mom, he earned his living farming and he sold vacuum cleaners on the side to make extra money. He was an excellent Electrolux salesman and used to tell us how he got the sales. He would smile that big flashing smile filled with white, even teeth and persuade the housewives to let him in their homes. Then he'd go straight to the bedroom, throw back the covers and vacuum their mattress. Then he'd dump what came out of the mattress onto the bed in a pile and just look at the wife. He didn't need to say anything more. They were always horrified with the dirt on their bed and bought the vacuum, usually through payments over time. Dad won several awards for his vacuum cleaner selling skills and won a watch for my mother that she still wore long after he quit. However, sales took him away from home and away from the farm. Farming was what he really wanted to do; and as soon as he had enough money, he quit selling vacuum cleaners and went back to farming full-time.

Then came several years of drought when the sun burned the corn stalks brown and they shriveled up before they were full grown. After the crops died,

Dad raised pigs. But soon all the pigs died of a mysterious illness, so he turned to Hereford cattle. Unfortunately, the cattle seemed to find every single hole in his fencing and escaped at every opportunity and he ultimately sold them to the local meat market.

After that, Dad started building Jim Walter Homes. That's how we learned Dad simply found it impossible to say no to a pretty woman, but not in the usual way. All the pretty wives of the men he built houses for wanted the best dishwashers and garbage disposals and the fanciest, wrought iron trim around the front of the house entrance. But none of them wanted to pay for it.

Dad built beautiful houses, but he lost money on every single house. When Dad's homebuilding debt reached $24,000, more than the average family made in four years, he mortgaged the house we lived in to secure the debt, and Mom stopped sleeping at night. I always thought the raccoon circles under Mom's eyes, at least in part, influenced Dad to start a heavy-equipment business.

So, he sold part of his inheritance from his father, approximately 75 acres of thickly wooded land down the road from where we lived, and bought…a bulldozer. While he always managed to feed himself and us, Mom took the fact that he mortgaged the house really hard. After that she refused to allow him to mortgage any more of the property. None of his professions, including equipment operator, proved particularly profitable, but Dad remained optimistic. At 42, he believed he still had time to make his fortune.

In the winter of '66, the economy slowed. Jobs grew scarce. After talking it over with Mom, they both agreed the following spring he should try his luck working for someone else.

"Let them pay my insurance for a while and pay the repairs on all the equipment. I'll just collect my paycheck and say, 'Thank you God.'"

And so, that morning Mom waved him down the driveway with a white checked dishcloth in her hand, calling after him, "Please be careful, Louis, and don't forget to write!"

And off he went to Pennsylvania.

After his truck was out of sight, she returned to the kitchen and began work again on a meat loaf to put in the freezer, adding crackers and eggs to make it go further.

My brother and I stood at the end of the gravel driveway feeling a bit orphaned, unable to imagine the house without Dad's loud voice and heavy footsteps in it. But most of all, we almost immediately felt the quiet descend around us much like the quiet after a tornado has passed. Even before his truck sputtered around the curve of the highway and the sound drifted away beyond the rolling hills, we began to wonder what we would do to entertain ourselves in his absence. A sense of change flowed into our lives in the wake of his departure. I half consciously wondered how life would unfold without a daily dose of Daddy-crisis to spur us on.

Each week Dad wrote letters home telling us how he had eaten a time or two at a restaurant down the road from his job. They served up dinner for the crew in the dining room of a lovely old Victorian home that he admired. Some of the men working on the same job were rooming there. But Dad preferred his camper. He paid an Amish family to park his camper on their land not far from where he was working. He always slept there and most of the time he prepared his own meals either in the camper, if the weather was bad, or over an open fire if it was good. He told us he liked camping out. He liked his privacy. But I suspect he camped so he could send more of his income home to us.

Dad told us Quakers drove everybody crazy, poking along the narrow Pennsylvania roads in black, horse-drawn buggies, all dressed in black themselves. They slowed traffic for miles as they plodded along with their bay horses pulling the ancient, creaky buggies. He said he had no idea how most people in cars avoided hitting and killing them in a fit of road rage. But somehow primitive life and modernity managed to coexist in this place, for the most part, alongside one another. Each side grumbled but forgave the other's perceived ignorance.

Dad told us in letters about the thin Quaker men at the post office wearing black suits tall hats and how their whiskers grew down past the length of their shirtfronts. The women went around town dressed in their long black and gray dresses and white bonnets tied firmly under their chins. They always kept their hair covered. They never talked to strangers, nor did they even meet another person's gaze. They shepherded their children around like domestic chickens, as if wolves lurked around every corner ready to snatch them away.

Mom read Dad's letters to my brother and me as we sat at the table wearing our cutoff jean shorts and tee shirts while we ate egg, sweet pickle, mayonnaise and tuna sandwiches. We couldn't imagine a world where little children had to wear long pants, skirts and hats and couldn't talk to any other kids that didn't belong to their "community". Suddenly we saw our lives as free and easy. We could wander where we wanted over the land Dad owned and even far beyond. We could say and do what we wanted as long as we didn't resort to bad language in front of Mom. Sure, we couldn't say, "darn" or "damn" or even "drat it" within earshot of our parents, but other than that, life was easy going on our farm. We both had a lot of freedom.

Mom finished reading the letter, and Franky swallowed the last bite of his tuna sandwich. "I'm going fishing, want to come?" He looked at me sideways and downed the last of his milk before wiping his mouth on his sleeve.

"Use your napkin, please." Mom folded the letter up carefully and put it in her apron pocket. She picked up Franky's plate and set it in the sink. She brushed crumbs to the edge of the table and dusted them off into her hand before she tossed them into the trash.

Franky picked up the napkin and polished his mouth with it to placate her.

"Maybe we can catch dinner? You coming?" he asked again.

With Dad gone, my brother had begun to think of himself as head of the house. Soon he started telling me to eat my vegetables and to water the garden for him. He walked taller, furrowed his brows more frequently, and seemed to always be watching me. His behavior really creeped me out. I didn't like that he felt entitled to lord it over me just because he was older. But asking me to go fishing WITH him seemed to be a bit of a departure from his normal nature, so I immediately accepted. I was eager to become his equal, and I was pretty sure I could catch a fish before he did. Dad had been coaching me privately about fishing and the special ways I could bait a hook for some time now.

Sometime back I'd gone fishing with Dad and he'd said, "You see Jane, all a fish knows about is his own little pond. It's his home and he doesn't know anything different. A fish has to eat, and he's always looking for something good. What he likes best is a healthy worm that's just unfortunate enough to fall into the water. So, think like a fish when you bait your hook. What would a fresh happy, yet surprised, slightly desperate worm look like? Then coil the worm up on the hook and make him look like that. All very natural. Not ridged or straight or suffering looking worms. Coil him around just like he happened to fall in by accident and he's wiggling trying to get out of the water. That will make the worm enticing to the fish, and the fish will try to eat him. Then you get to eat the fish."

"What happens if another fish eats that fish," I asked him?

"Then we get both the fish!" Dad told me with a laugh. "You see, Jane, no matter what pond you are in there are always going to be bigger fish than you; and while you may be looking for something smaller to eat, there's always something bigger looking to eat you. So, you have to be a crafty fish to live in a pond with the other fish and survive."

"I would just jump out of the pond and go to another pond where I was the biggest fish if I were a small fish," I told Dad.

"Well, fish can't do that, Jane. They have to find a way to live in the pond in which they were born. So, they have to be crafty or something will come along and eat them. If you are an old fish or a careless fish, there's always a smarter, quicker, bigger fish waiting to eat you? That's the way life is. Also, it's better to be in the pond you know than in the pond you don't know."

"Why is that?" I asked.

"Life teaches you over time who you can trust and who you can't," Dad told me as he baited my hook and I watched.

"If you live in the pond for a long time and manage to avoid getting eaten, do you someday get to be the big fish?" I asked him.

"If you are wise and if you are lucky, someday you may get to be the big fish," Dad said. "But you can never relax, even if you are the big fish. There's always something or someone waiting to take you down. Sometimes it's something tiny, like an amoeba, a bacteria or fungus that will kill the big fish. Sometimes it's an eagle or a hawk, and you don't even see it coming!"

"What's an amoeba?" I asked.

"They will teach you about amoeba in school, Jane. But it really just means that you never get so big that something can't take you out. And age takes us all out eventually."

"Dad, that's a sad story, now I'm not sure I want to fish," I told him. "Well, that's the big story of life, but today is only one day in a long line of days, and today we won't think about the big story anymore. Today we'll just think about what this fish out there wants for breakfast and try to make it for him. Okay?" Dad said.

"Okay," I smiled. "I like the idea of making breakfast for a fish."

Yes, Dad had been schooling me. Franky might be bigger than me and even older than me, but I was pretty sure a fish wouldn't know the difference and that I could bait a hook better than Franky. Finally, something I could do as well as he could.

"Sure, you really want to go?"

"You bet. Get your pole, and I'll meet you behind the chicken house in 5 minutes to dig worms."

Ugh! Worm digging. Not my favorite activity. But I liked to fish, so I changed into my old, dirty, outdoor shorts and folded the holey part of my socks under my toes before thrusting them into old tennis shoes.

I found Franky digging a hole in the ground with the jagged-cut top of an old coffee can. He already had a pile of black, loamy dirt at his side and a handful of worms in an old lima bean can set beside the hole.

The sun slanted from the west casting shadows over the warm dirt behind the hen house where we crouched. Recently Dad had purchased some new chickens for us. This time a specific breed. The Rhode Island Red chickens had settled down under the bushes nearby nestling with ruffled feathers for a lazy afternoon nap. Dust from their scratching floated in the afternoon air around us like a golden haze. It smelled like a combination of grass, cattle and the dusty wet smell of the chickens themselves. We heard them mutter to each other as we started to sort through our newly excavated dirt. Chicken dreams, probably of grasshoppers and beetle bugs, I thought.

I looked closely into the brown dirt. When I worked this way, I liked to pretend I was an Indian. My Mom said real Indians squatted to do all their work. They could squat for hours without getting tired. They even squatted to have babies! It was part of Indian "genetics," she said, that, and being lactose intolerant. I knew my great-great-grandmother had been a Creek Indian, during the time of the evacuation from Alabama to Oklahoma. The Trail of Tears Mom called it. Only my great-great-grandmother didn't go. Instead, as a young girl, she hid out in the mountains and foothills of Georgia and Alabama, living on berries, rabbits, and fish. She probably dug for worms to hang from the end of her cane pole to entice fish to bite her hook—just like we were doing now. Only we were doing it for fun. She did it to survive.

I imagined she must have fished the creeks and rivers regularly for her supper. Maybe she wondered what happened to her Mom who disappeared after taking her to visit some white settler friends. Maybe she thought about her father, who—unable to escape Andrew Jackson's army—was rounded up by soldiers who marched him to Oklahoma. Gone, like Dad was gone to Pennsylvania now. Maybe she missed him. And maybe she cried a little, but I bet she also caught fish for dinner. I believed my ancestors somehow learned to make wherever they were their home and to survive and even thrive. My mind hummed with a renewed sense of responsibility at how the cycle of life continued on through the generations in much the same fashion even if your parents were gone. Survival was in my blood, I decided. I imagined my eyes becoming sharp as eagle eyes. I looked harder for worms and found several. Evening approached. We needed to get cracking if we wanted to catch dinner.

Several red tails wriggled in my hand, and carefully I traced them to the worm heads. I dropped the healthy-looking earthworms into the old bean can alongside the ones Franky collected, and then added a little dirt so they wouldn't feel too vulnerable until time to put them on the hook and make them fish bait. Dad said a little dirt kept them "fresh".

"You ready?" Franky asked, standing up.

"Yep."

"Then, let's go!"

To enter the pasture from our backyard, we opened a white-picket gate that Dad made before we were born and closed it behind us with a click of the latch. Then we followed a dirt path made by the animals as they lined up to go to the pond in the evenings to drink water. It led us west from the house past the abandoned pig shed to the barn lot. From there we crawled through a slotted gate and entered the pond field, several fields over from the house. We carried long, tan cane poles slung over our backs, the line wrapped around them and red and white bobbers attached near the end. Franky carried a rusty, green fishing tackle box, and I carried the can of worms, careful not to drop it.

You couldn't see the pond until you were right up on it. A stranger walking in the field in the dark might take a nasty fall down the hill that would end abruptly in a splash in the pond during a moonless night if he happened to be walking too fast. The sides were extremely steep and the water level fully 10 feet below pasture level with the pond likely still another 8 feet deep in the middle. Around the edges it was belly high on the cows.

Several years before I was born a road crew had come through needing fill dirt to level out the roadbed. They'd dug the pond for Dad for free. The sides were craggy with sharp clay rocks jutting out in places, but smooth dirt in others. Over the years, Dad had caught fish in other ponds and lakes, and released them into our pond until it was well stocked with bream, catfish, and a few small-mouth bass. In order for the cattle to drink, from the side of the field from which we approached, Dad had shoveled out a walkway down to the pond that was steeply sided, but functional for his purpose. Over time the animal hoofs had rounded it out so now it felt as if we were descending a steep flight of stairs with a rail of earth on one side. On the far side of the pond, the hill naturally fell away so the approach from that side was much gentler and there were trees alongside the pond that made a place for the cattle to linger in the evening and chew their cud. Mosquitoes and other night creatures would hover over the pond, and quite often we would see bats there feeding on the insects.

With constant use, the animals had eventually worn a narrow path around the pond at the edge of the water. It was on this path, 10 feet below pasture level that we sat down our fishing supplies and cleared a place on the bank from stones so we could sit. By moving some of the sharper rocks, we could sit on the path and lean back against the side of the bank. From this, more or less, relaxing position, we could plop our fishing lines into the water and rest while we fished. If we picked the west side of the pond, the bank would shade us and a portion of the pond this time of day. The fish would be cooling in the shade, and that's where we wanted to drop our hooks. We settled in and baited our hooks with worms from the can. I was careful to thread the worm lengthwise like my father had taught me to make them look tasty to the fish. We always left a little tail hanging off the end, wiggling, but not too much or the fish would bite off the tail and leave the hook. Then we cast our lines into the water and sat down to wait, watching the red and white bobbers.

Franky's bobber sank almost immediately with a little plop, and his line pulled. "You've got one!" I cried, excited.

"Yeah!" he said and began winding his line around the pole in his primitive imitation of a reel. When the fish splashed into sight, we could tell by the way it parted the water that it was a mud catfish. You could see the unmistakable long fins that looked like whiskers and telltale wide mouth. The fish was about 10 inches long. It fought hard when Franky tried to grab it, digging one of the fins sharply into his hand. He grabbed it around the gills and extracted the hook with quick fingers while I watched closely. Then he slid the stringer line into its gill and out its mouth.

"Where are you going to hang the stringer?" I asked.

"Not where we are fishing, it'll scare the other fish," he said. Carefully he wound his way along the footpath next to the pond until he reached the other side. Several times he slipped, and I thought he might fall into the clear blue water of the pond, but each time he righted himself and only sent a few pebbles rumbling into the water instead. Selecting a rock about a foot in diameter that jutted out, he fastened the stringer to the narrow base of the rock and tossed the fish into the water to keep it fresh. The fish quickly dove out of site, but we could tell it was still attached by the way the stringer went taut.

We fished for most of the afternoon. One after another, Franky strung up the fish on the stringer until we had eight nice fish for dinner, of which I caught six. We were feeling pretty content with ourselves as we sat there waiting for the next fish to bite. Every now and then a gentle breeze would stir the branches of the oak and poplar trees around us freshening the air and reminding us that evening was coming. I imagined how surprised and pleased Mom would be when she saw that string of fish. I could smell them cooking in the pan, battered in cornmeal. My stomach growled letting me know several hours had passed since lunch.

The last hour the fish stopped biting, and Franky and I lay back against the clay bank and dozed a little. Once in a while a horsefly would get curious and buzz around us a bit, then move on to tastier victims in the field next to us. Dragonflies landed here and there on the water to rest before taking off again. Sometimes a small-mouth bass would jump up and gulp down a dragonfly in a single bite.

"Did you see that?" Franky would ask. "He was huge." He'd hold out his hands in estimated fish lengths. "I'm going to catch that one."

"No, you aren't. He just ate!"

A cool breeze more energetic than normal stirred up dirt devils and roused us enough to realize darkness was falling. It would soon be time for dinner.

"Guess it's time to go home," Franky said. "Get the poles, and I'll get the fish."

I wound the line around the cane poles and tucked the bobbers underneath so we wouldn't lose them.

"What the, hey?" Franky called from the far bank. "These fish weigh a ton."

I looked over at him and it seemed he was having more difficulty than usual pulling the stringer in. He pulled and tugged, and a wide ripple trailed toward him out of the water where the stringer disappeared. He tugged hand over hand several times and on the last tug, out came the end of the stringer with a huge mud turtle attached—and only a couple of fish remained.

"Heck," Franky said. "The turtle ate all our fish!" I dropped the pole and ran around the edge of the pond where he stood holding the turtle dangling from the end of the stringer. He was huge, at least 20 pounds with ancient leathery skin and lichen covered shell. He was as large as Mom's round Thanksgiving platter, and so ugly it made me shiver. He reminded me of a dinosaur. Hanging onto the stringer, his neck stretched out a full foot from his shell. Franky could barely hold him up, and the turtle refused to let go of the fish on the stringer.

"Shucks," I said, staring at the turtle. Tears welled up in my eyes. All our hard work had come to nothing. So much for Indian maiden ingenuity. The turtle had eatin' everything!

"What are we going to do?" I asked. "He ate our dinner!"

It was a disaster. Now we had nothing to show Mom. What kind of Indian girl was I if I couldn't keep a turtle from eating my dinner?

Franky thought hard. "We're going to take *him* home for dinner."

"We can't eat a turtle!" I looked at the hard shell on the mud turtle lying on the cow path next to the pond. He was struggling to crawl back into the water, the stringer still hanging from his mouth, but Franky had his foot set squarely on the turtle's back, so he was mostly just stirring up the dirt under Franky's feet and not going anywhere.

"Sure, we can. Dad told me turtles are good eaten. There are eight different types of meat in a turtle. They have meat that tastes like beef, chicken, and a lot of other things. You can make soup out of them, I heard. I'm taking him home."

"Well, I don't know. I don't think Mom knows how to cook turtles." I looked at the turtle doubtfully. I didn't see a thing appetizing about it. Mostly I just wanted it to go back where it came from.

"We're taking him home, and that's final."

"But why?"

"Because I'm the boss, that's why! Now get your stuff."

I gathered up our things, and together we hiked back to the house. From the back of the house, we could see Mom in the garden, collecting radishes and onions for salad for our dinner.

We took the turtle to the kitchen.

"What are we going to do with it?" I asked Franky. There didn't seem to be any place we could put the turtle that he couldn't crawl off.

"Let's put him in the sink. He needs a bath anyway." Franky crinkled his nose at the smell of pond scum and mud clinging to the turtle. "He sure does smell bad. I think a bath is just what he needs."

We ran water in the sink, and Franky added a little soap so it would foam up. Then he lifted and strained to get the turtle over the edge of the sink so he could drop it in the water. We both looked down into the deep sink to see what the turtle was doing. At first, he drew mostly back into his shell, but eventually he ran out of air, and peeked the tip of his nostrils just enough out of the water so he could breathe. He seemed comfortable enough there in his soapy bath. It almost looked like he was relaxing a bit in the warm water.

"Guess we better get cleaned up before Mom comes in," Franky said. "I'll go first." He headed to the bathroom to shower. I headed to my room to pick out some fresh clothes for dinner and to wait until he finished since we only had one bathroom. Going through some things, I got distracted and lost track of time. I could hear the water in the bathroom running and my brother whistling in the shower, doing his best to imitate Dad's loud clear whistle. As he showered, he whistled and sang snatches of "I've Been Working on the Railroad".

I heard the screen door slam but thought nothing of it as I put a record on my record player. The sound of "Build Me Up—Buttercup" drifted through the afternoon breeze in my room and I stacked up my clean clothes and found a towel in the linen closet. Instinct told me Franky was almost finished showering and it would soon be my turn.

"Aaaaaahhhhhh……!!!!"

The sound of Mom's scream followed closely by a crash made the hairs on the back of my neck stand up.

I dropped my clothes and ran to the kitchen sure she'd dropped a butcher knife on her foot. Franky tore out of the bathroom, sopping wet, tucking a white bath towel around his waist, following close behind me.

"What's the matter?" he asked.

Mom stood in the center of the kitchen a broken dish at her feet, pointing at the kitchen sink. The turtle, with its neck extended to its full one-foot length, stared back from its bubble bath in the sink, its mouth wide open and as surprised as Mom. If turtles could scream, it would have screamed with and at her too! With such a long neck, it looked more like a snake than a turtle.

Mom screamed. "What is that?"

"It's just a little ol' turtle," Franky said. He tucked the towel more securely around his waist, tiptoed through the broken dish and went to pick up the turtle. However, the turtle had had enough of all of us for one day. He snapped at Franky, narrowly missing his hand. Franky sprang back.

"What's a turtle doing in my sink?" Mom's screamed with only slightly less force than before.

"The turtle ate nearly all the fish on my stringer, so we brought him home for dinner instead," I said, rushing to get the words out before Mom screamed again. The sound had completely unnerved me, and now my knees were shaking.

"Get it out! Get it out!" Mom's face turned red as she pointed to the door.

"Out! Out! Out!"

More afraid of Mom than the turtle, Franky snatched it out of the water. The turtle drew its head back in and slammed its shell shut as much as possible, and Franky headed toward the door with it, his white towel flipping back and forth and nearly falling off in his haste.

Mom didn't punish us that evening, but we could tell by the look on her face, we'd made a serious error in judgment bringing the turtle into the house and putting it in her sink. She scrubbed and bleached the sink and rinsed it in steaming water until moisture clouds swirled around the ceiling of the kitchen and made her hair damp and curly. She didn't say a word the whole time, but probably she was thinking single motherhood didn't much agree with her.

Franky and I slunk off to our respective duties quietly, not talking.

That night we had radishes, lettuce, green beans, and Mrs. Paul's fish sticks for dinner. The fish sticks were burned, but we ate them anyway too afraid to complain. Mom went to lie down without even doing the dishes after dinner. She said she had a headache.

As we sat in front of the TV watching "The Flintstones," I whispered to Franky, "What did you do with the turtle?"

"I took it back to the pond."

"Sure, would have liked to see what turtle soup tasted like," Franky said wistfully. Fish sticks were not my favorite either. I had to bathe them in ketchup to make them go down even when they weren't burnt.

"Maybe Dad will catch it again and cook it when he comes home."

"Maybe."

"It's the cycle of life," I guess.

"What's the cycle of life?" Franky asked.

"The turtle is. Dad says it's the cycle of life. No matter what pond you're in there's always something waiting to eat you and often it's something bigger than you."

"That's a pretty harsh," Franky said.

"But I'm right, aren't I? The fish eats the worm, the turtle eats the fish, and we eat the turtle."

"Yes, that pretty much sums it up," Franky said, smacking his lips.

"Should we write and ask him?" I asked. Franky being the boss had its drawbacks, I decided, one of them being an upset Mom if you did the wrong thing.

"Nah. Let's just forget about it," he said.

"Okay by me." I shrugged, glad I wasn't the boss of anything.

*　*　*

2007

My cell phone rings and wakes me. I am still in the same position on the bed I went to sleep in. My feet, still in my shoes, are hanging off the side of the bed resting lightly on the floor. My arms are outstretched to my sides as if I am hanging on a cross. I lift one very stiff arm, reach for my phone in my purse beside me marveling that there's still a charge.

I push the button. "Hello?"

"Jane, it's me," my sister says. "They served Dad this morning."

"So quickly?" I gasp. "I thought I had time to tell him."

"The attorney said they had to do it quick to get it heard next week, so they went ahead and served him."

My stomach clenches. "When is the court date?"

"Next Wednesday. They will keep him in the hospital until then."

"Did Dad say who he would have represent him? Or has he even had time to think about it?"

"He said he knew someone he could use. He didn't mention a name."

"Well...I guess the cat's out of the bag."

"I guess it is."

"No turning back now."

"Nope. No turning back. Are you okay?"

I look around the room and consider the fact I'm sleeping in my clothes and say, "Sure. I'm okay."

"It feels like the end of everything doesn't it," she says.

"Yes...and the beginning of a whole new something," I say.

"For better or worse, I guess we are in this together. We did a good job with Mom, didn't we?" she says.

"Yes, we did. We were a good team."

"We'll do the same with Dad."

"Yes, the same."

"Jane, I'm tired."

"I know you are. But I'm here. I'll help. We'll get you set as Conservator, but I'll be here all the time, anytime you need me."

"Jane, I'm not sure they'll give me Conservatorship. I'm still in a legal battle to get custody of my kids in the divorce. I'm working a lot of hours. I'm not sure they'll grant it to me."

"Well, let's just see what happens. Maybe we can get Co-conservatorship and that will take some of the pressure off you. I will be here as much as you need me," I tell her. Inside, I am cringing because my home is 750 miles away, but I will do what it takes. I'm grateful that my daughter is grown and what needs to be done to take care of Dad at this time in his life is possible.

"I know you will," she says. But I can hear the strain in her voice. The guilt, the regret. We both had it. Our lives are changing. Inside I'm thinking: *Here we go again, I really need to step up and accept more responsibility this time around.*

"Let's just see how it goes, okay?"

"Okay."

"Love you."

"Love you too."

As I hang up, I think about the circle of life. Dad took care of us as we were growing up.

Whether or not we can pull it off and take care of him in return—remains to be seen. And all the while, he's going to act like that mud turtle and try to take our fingers off if we get too close.

The battle to save him is on!

◇

"Therefore, we are always confident and know that as long as we are at home in the body we are away from the Lord." (2 Corinthians 5:10)

◇

Fried Catfish

Catch the catfish using a cane pole with red and white bobber.
Keep the fish on a stringer submerged in water until you are ready to clean them.
(Clean sooner rather than later—watch for turtles that will eat your fish.)
Cut off fish head and tail.
Gut fish.
Throw away head, tail and guts.
Wash fish.
Fillet or cook whole any fish that are 7 inches or shorter.
Longer fish should be cut into 6–7 inch lengths.
Note: Our fish were usually 7 inches without their head and tail.
Mix, milk, egg and self-rising cornmeal until it's thick enough to stick to the fish, but not runny.
Wash the fillets. Pat dry with paper towel.
Add corn oil to large deep skillet.
Oil should be hot enough for specks of cornmeal to sizzle as soon as they hit the oil.
Roll fillets in batter until it adheres to the fish.
Fry fish in cast iron or stainless skillet without lid in 1 cup of corn oil on medium heat turning once until golden brown.
Replenish oil as needed. You can also use a deep fat fryer.
Keep cooked fish in oven on a foil-lined baking sheet at 250 degrees to retain warmth after frying until all are cooked.
Side dishes are fried green tomatoes or slaw, or sliced fresh red tomatoes from the garden and green onions.

(Note: There are catfish batter products. These are fine, but may contain MSG which is a no-no. Also, if you catch more fish than you can cook, place in plastic freezer bags, fill the bag with enough fresh water so the fish are submerged, and freeze. They will keep up to a year this way.)

Chapter 9 – Barbecue, Roasted or Fricassee
"I thought I'd cut the electricity off, but apparently I didn't!" — Louis

2006
At the hospital, just as I am arriving, I find a man I knew from high school is leaving Dad's room. "Paul? How are you doing?" I ask him in the hallway. A few months back, Paul had called me while I was in town and asked me to lunch. I went because I hadn't seen him in years and wanted to catch up; and it was good to see him. But to see him twice in such a short period of time after decades not hearing from him sets off an alarm in my mind. He has someone with him, someone I don't know who looks like an attorney.

"Fine, Jane," Paul says. He gives me a big hug and holds it a bit too long.

"So, what are you doing here? Someone you know in the hospital?"

"We came to see your Dad, Jane. Heard he was under the weather," Paul says. Recently, I've heard Paul has been buying up property around town from the older folks. He buys it cheap, improves it and then sells it for a great profit. Something about the way he does not meet my gaze worries me.

I liked Paul in high school, in fact Mom and I used to see him walking to school and we would offer him a ride sometimes. At one time I wanted him to ask me out; but, though we were friends, he never did. It appeared his taste ran in a different direction than tall blonde girls. We visit for a moment in the hallway, but I can tell he and his friend want to leave, so we say goodbye, and I walk into Dad's room.

"Hi, Dad! How are you feeling?" I ask, and I try to brush his cheek with a kiss, but he quickly turns to avoid me. Clearly, he's not happy to see me.

"Not great," he responds. "Your attorney served me with papers! The papers say you and your sister are in cahoots trying to have me declared crazy and that you plan to take everything I have away from me."

Hoping to hold off the argument, I ask, "Did Paul come and see you?"

"Yes, he did! Wanted to buy the property in town that I own," Dad blusters. His face is a bit red, and I wonder about his blood pressure.

"Really," I say. We call the property he's referring to the G Street property.

Dad's had it for years. He never developed it because at the time this might have impacted a small fish called the snail darter. Another person might have been able to work with the city council to get the property rezoned, but Dad has never managed to do this. Other, better-connected people would have likely been able to get permission to develop the property; but as it was, no one really wanted Dad to be the one. So, it has sat for more than 20 years and only serves as a place for Dad to store equipment closer to town.

"So, how much did he offer you?" I ask.

Dad names a figure, proud of himself for the offer.

"You didn't sign anything did you?" I ask, horrified at the offer. The property is likely worth many times that amount.

"No, I told him I wanted to think about it," Dad says.

Inwardly, I let out a sigh of relief. This is just the type of exploitation we are worried about. If I didn't know before, I certainly know now that my sister and I are doing the right thing. Every type of lowlife is likely to come creeping out of the woodwork wanting to make a deal with Dad. A sad testament to some of the people in town, I think. Dad has worked hard all his life. To be swindled in the end would be incredibly unfair.

"Well, you did the right thing by telling him you needed time to think about it, Dad," I tell him. "Let's check around and see what the actual going price is now for property like that before you cut a deal, okay?"

He nods, but I can tell he feels stung by our efforts to try to help him.

I reach out to hold his hand and this time he lets me, grudgingly.

"Dad, we aren't trying to have you declared crazy. You just aren't making very good decisions for yourself right now. We want to help you make better decisions. We want to make sure you are taking care of yourself and get the help you need. You aren't managing your money very well. You aren't paying your bills. If your house burned down right now it's not insured. And your health is rocky too. You aren't really getting the medical care you need. Things like that."

"I don't need your help!" Dad yells at me. "I can take care of myself."

"My house is fine. I'm fine! I need daughters that mind their own business, that's what kind of daughters I need!"

"Well maybe so, but I'm hoping someday you'll be grateful that I didn't mind my own business. Dad, what is that thing you have in the bathroom at the house? It looks like a trough warmer like the kind they use in cattle troughs."

He blushes. And I can tell I have him.

He stutters a bit, then says, "That fancy Jacuzzi thing you sent me that blows bubbles in the tub? That was no good! I thought I'd make my own Jacuzzi with the cattle trough warmer. It's much sturdier, and I think it would work well and last longer."

"Dad, you could electrocute yourself using something like that in a way it's not intended to be used." I notice his white hair is sticking up in the back from pressing on his pillow, so I smooth it down with my fingertips.

He shrugs, "What's wrong with a Jacuzzi I make? I know a thing or two about electricity. That would not have killed me. I can tell you that."

"Dad, this is just the kind of thing that's worrying us half to death. You do know a thing or two about electricity, but you are also forgetting things as well. Electricity is very unforgiving. We can't have you doing things that might get you killed."

"So did you get rid of it?"

"Not yet, but we will."

"I could make it work, and it would be safe enough you could put a baby in the tub with it," he says. The misguided sense of confidence in his voice makes the fine hair stand up on my arms and my skin prickle. I've seen some shocking examples of Dad's work with electricity over the years even when he was operating with what some would call "a full deck". Pictures of naked 220 heater wires plugged into sockets in our living room shoot through my brain, or house wall switches attached to table saws with wires splayed out like smashed spider legs. Sparks flying. I always check the light switches in Dad's house even today to make certain they have switch plates before I reach to turn them on. A few shocking childhood experiences instilled lifelong caution in me when I'm around him and he's playing with electricity.

* * *

1968

Pop, Zzzzzp, Crackle. Smoke poured out of the fuse box in the corner kitchen cabinet, and our house plunged into semi-darkness leaving us with only the evening twilight for illumination. My brother and I watched in surprise as the picture on the television shrank into a little pin-like dot in the center and then disappeared entirely.

"Louis!" Mom cried from the kitchen. She shook the electric hand mixer she'd just plugged in, as if by shaking it she could extract enough remaining electricity to mash the rest of the steaming potatoes in her mixing bowl. Of course, this didn't work. Disappointed, she laid the mixer on the kitchen counter and sighed.

"Daddy!" My brother and I sang out in a chorus from the den where we sprawled on the floor to watch television. Our heads rested on Mom's fluffy, blue-ruffled, gingham pillows as we lay watching Fred and Barney search for Bam Bam on "The Flintstones".

"Did something happen?" Dad shouted. His voice echoed from the bathroom where earlier I heard him splashing in the bathtub like a giant fish.

"What is it?" he called again as if this was the first time, not the hundredth, our family had unexpectedly found ourselves plunged into darkness.

Mom raised her gaze to stare questioningly at the kitchen light fixture as if consulting God for a solution to what had become an increasingly annoying problem. Power outage due to blown fuse. Dad wired our house in the 40s when electrical gadgets were not all that common. Now, in the 60s, the fuse box was really struggling to keep up with the needs of our growing family and modern technology.

Moments later, Dad appeared, towel wrapped around his waist. Still dripping, he padded into the kitchen on bare feet to inspect the fuse box.

"Louis, you're wet! Don't stick your hand in that fuse box!" Mom cautioned.

Dad went through the motions of drying his hands on the towel around his waist, then reached into the box with a bare finger. I braced myself to witness his near certain electrocution and his bare, wet naked body and towel flying across the room.

"Ouch!" he said, quickly extracting his hand. My heart skipped, but he didn't fall jerkily to the floor or collapse against the nearest wall as I expected. Instead, he blew on his fingers and said in mock surprise, "Why, honey, it's hot." The fake out left me feeling both relieved and disgusted. I picked up my copy of *Black Beauty* from the coffee table and dug out a flashlight from under the couch. I refused to watch "The Daddy Show," as I'd come to think of it, any longer. Even I knew a blown fuse would be as hot as a firecracker.

Often at dinner, Dad would relate a self-deprecating story as proof he didn't know what he was doing. "Your dumb father passed on buying that property." He'd shake his head at the evidence he related to us before taking another bite of beans or mashed potatoes.

"Now, Weinstein bought it, and he made 200K in six weeks. All he did was mow it, stick a sign on it and turned it around for a huge profit. Not me!"

His list of self-criticisms ran long some days and did nothing to instill our confidence in him. Yet, if anyone offered him advice about how to handle the situation better, he would spend hours tearing apart alternative theories.

"That man can make you feel pretty low," Mom said. And I agreed. Did Dad know what he was doing? Or didn't he? I found the whole thing confusing, so mostly I kept quiet.

An acrid smell of burning wire filled the den. I coughed and turned a page of the book I was reading while Dad worked on the fuse box. I tried to look disinterested in what he was doing.

"I plugged in the mixer to beat the potatoes for dinner," Mom said, "and I guess the water heater cut on at the same time. It blew a fuse, again. Louis, we need a bigger electric box. Not a fuse box but a breaker box." She waved the fingers of one hand hopelessly toward the cabinet that held the fuse box.

We blew fuses several times a day. Plug in a hair dryer or a radio at the wrong moment, and the whole house went dark. Constantly overloaded, the fuse box frequently sent up distressing smoke signals. Mom stood in front of the cabinet waving a cup towel to disburse the smoke when that happened. It seemed a bit like what Mr. Douglas had to deal with on television show "Green Acres"! We did have a working phone inside the house, but our electricity supplies were similar.

"Louis, you can't wire a house out of scrap wire from a hotel that burned down and expect it to work right," Mom whispered.

"I didn't take wire from the part that burned, honey. I only got the *good* wire. Wasn't even the wire that caused the fire," Dad retaliated.

"How do you know that? If the wire caused the fire how could there possibly be any good wire in the hotel. They would have used the same wire all the way through, right?" Mom rolled her eyes and waved the towel harder.

"Well, it looked good to me!" Dad said and continued to poke around in the fuse box.

My brother and I looked at each other and simultaneously rolled our eyes.

Our fuse box had four small blue fuses and one big red one. "This house isn't equipped for so many electrical gadgets," Dad said as he rustled around in several drawers looking for new fuses. "We got by without all that when I was a boy. My Mom did laundry once a week and did it outside over a fire in a pot. Each week we'd get a towel and a washcloth and that was it. We didn't need a clothes dryer then, because we had sunshine! And we used the sun and wind to dry our hair and our clothes—everything really. Blenders, toasters, hair dryers AND a hot water heater for a bath? You don't need all that!"

Mom sank into the chair beside me, placed her face in her cup towel for a moment, then looked up and leaned over to me and whispered, "One washcloth—all week! That's what your father had. Same one for his face and his butt! Do you think he kept track of what he washed first?" she pursed her lips and looked at me. That was more information than I ever wanted to know about Dad. At our house, Mom washed and bleached all towels and wash-clothes every time we used them. She washed them so often Dad said she wore them out washing them.

She responded, "When we were kids, we didn't have a lot, but we were clean. All the appliances make a wife's work easier, and it makes it possible for me to have time to do things for you, Louis Hinkle. And I really think we need a new breaker box so I can keep doing those things for you. I don't know anyone boiling their clothes in a pot anymore!" she finished with a flourish stretching out the word a-n-y-m-o-r-e.

After shuffling around in several boxes, Dad found a fuse that fit and screwed it into the socket. The lights came back on, and the television flared to life in time for us to see the credits roll on.

"Louis, we can't go on like this. We need to hire an electrician to come in and rewire. You've added on to this house three times since you put that fuse box in! It's hopelessly out of date and overloaded!"

"I'm not going to pay an electrician to do what I can do myself," Dad drawled, loudly, sounding like a stubborn motorboat someone was trying to start.

"But you aren't an electrician!" Mom stood up from the sofa and put her fist on her hips.

"That doesn't matter. I've wired many a house. I wired your parents' house if you remember correctly! And I can wire this one again."

"You'll going to kill yourself someday!" Mom declared. Walking back into the kitchen, she pulled the hand masher out of the silverware drawer with a clatter, and started pounding the potatoes in the bowl into a white pulp. "We are all going to burn alive in this house," she muttered, between vigorous smashes. "—that or you're going to fry yourself—or one of the children with one of your do-it-yourself wiring jobs. I don't know which is most likely to happen first."

Smashed potatoes exploded out of the bowl onto the red-marble-patterned Formica counter onto the front of Mom's apron. Some flew onto the tip of her nose and some even went into her hair, but she just kept pounding away, as if she wished the bowl contained Dad's head.

"I'm not going to kill myself." Dad, still dripping from bathwater, stomped off to the bathroom to finish drying and to dress. Barefooted, as he was, the stomping lost a bit of its psychological impact on us. In fact, my brother and I smiled at each other. This was a routine scene in our household, and most of the time neither of us took it very seriously.

None of us thought Dad would really rewire the house. He hadn't fixed the drippy faucet in the bathroom, had he? It had dripped all my life. Each time the faucet started a new leak, he threaded the old nozzle and shoved another cut-off valve into the existing opening. We were up to three cut-off valves on the tub alone and the most recent faucet still dripped. He hadn't fixed the French doors in the hallway either. In cold weather wind whipped under the doors until the asparagus ferns in the hall turned mushy with frostbite on the side closest to the door. We all lived with bronchitis all winter because of the draft, but he had yet to fix the doors. So why would he decide to fix the fuse box now?

Still, the burned-out hotel wire thing haunted me. Would we be burned alive in our sleep? A few days later, I crawled up into the attic to check for myself. Sure enough, the fabric coated wires looked old enough to be from a different century. In places they looked charred and discolored by smoke. The fact that Mom spoke the truth didn't make me sleep any better. Often, I'd lay awake at night staring at the outlet in my room half expecting it to burst into flame and burn a path up the wall and into the attic at any moment. I didn't feel at all confident I could open the wooden-framed windows, which had been painted shut for as long as I could remember, in time to escape—especially in damp weather. Finally, I moved a sturdy dining chair into my room so I could use it to break a window to get out if the house caught fire.

A week or so later I heard Dad whistle calling for us to meet him at the back door. Dad sometimes did this when he wanted to talk to us, much like you'd summon a dog. And, like dogs, we responded.

"What's up?" Franky asked after we'd gathered round. He looked glad for a break from his homework. His math class had just started algebra. Normally a steady A or B student, he had come to accept the C+ recently in math and thank God for it.

"Franky, come help me unload the truck."

Mom put down the blouse she was sewing on the black Singer sewing machine she kept in the large foyer and headed outside behind Dad and my brother. I trailed behind. Dad climbed up into the bed of the rusty, white Ford truck and rolled a huge spool of what looked like industrial electrical wire to the end of the truck bed. Between himself and my brother, they lowered the spool to the ground. It looked like what I'd seen draping from telephone pole to telephone pole alongside the road on the drive to school. Not what I'd pictured inside the walls of the house. I recognized the metal cabinet in the truck as the circuit breaker box since I'd seen them in several of the new houses Dad built. Next, he handed that down together with a long wide silver pipe. And following that he off-loaded enough spools of interior house wire to wire our house and then some.

"What's that wire for?" Mom asked, pointing to the giant wire.

"We have to run a new line from the pole at the street to the house to upgrade the service," Dad told her.

"Are you planning to do that?"

Dad whistled again. He often whistled when he felt stressed or got angry at our questions. "Why, sure, my Great Big Beautiful Doll! I'm.... going to do it." He fixed a rebellious stare on her over the top of his glasses as if daring her to say more.

"That requires changing the wires out. Louis you aren't a licensed electrician, not to mention that wire belongs to the electric company. You are not supposed to touch that at all. Touching the commercial lines is even more dangerous, and probably illegal! You'll be fined if you're caught—if you aren't killed first! You know my sister-in-law's sister's husband worked for the utility company, and he touched the wrong wire, and it killed him! And he knew what he was doing!"

"Well...apparently not!" Dad said with a grin. "Don't worry you're pretty little head over it, Mother. I'm going to do it. And it will all work out." He continued to look over his glasses at her like a wolf about to eat a chicken.

"Louis, don't do this! You'll wind up in jail, dead, or worse...burned to a crisp in front of your children! It would ruin their lives to see their father electrocuted. Do you want that on your conscience?"

"Well, it wouldn't do much for me either! But, no I don't, and no it won't happen! And I don't want to hear any more about it! You are the one who wanted the house rewired. Well, I'm going to rewire it." Dad jumped down from the bed of the truck and dusted off his hands on a white hankie he pulled from his pocket. Then he picked up the breaker box and started toward the house with it.

"What do you want me to do with the wire?" Franky asked. He seemed oblivious to the tension between parents. Maybe algebra still weighed on his mind, and he'd missed the part about Dad burning to a crisp before our eyes. He'd had 5 more years than me with Mom and Dad. Maybe their arguing didn't upset him quite so much anymore. Most of the time I was used to it too, but the mental image of Dad spontaneously combusting atop a telephone pole…well…it gave me pause.

"Roll it around to the front of the house. We'll start first thing in the morning."

"You aren't going to ask my son to help you! It's too dangerous!"

"He's OUR son! And I need his help. He doesn't have to touch the wires," Dad said over his shoulder.

Clearly Dad DID plan to change out the commercial line as well as install the breaker box. I didn't understand all the ins and outs of an electrical license thing, but from Mom's reaction I understood wiring without the proper papers was a bit crazy and very hazardous. I pictured Dad in all types of contorted death positions like cartoons on television. I could see his eyes like black coals, hollow and vacant, his fingers charred black, and his hair standing on end trailing off into tendrils of smoke!

I pictured the headlines in the newspaper; "Father of two electrocutes self while illegally rewiring home," and "Stubborn man killed by fuse box mishap!" Maybe our house would explode. We'd have no place to live! What if it happened fast and we couldn't get out? My stomach started to quiver, and I felt sick. That night I couldn't sleep. The next day might be our last as a family. Thinking about the loss, suddenly my house seemed lovely to me. The possibility of losing my brother almost made me like him. Almost.

If Dad got killed, Mom would go crazy, and I'd have to go to an orphanage—if I even survived. Or maybe I'd die, too. In a wiring accident, who knew how fast the house would burn up. I slid out of bed and started cleaning my room by the light of my angel night light, feeling each little thing as if it might be the last time. I loved my black plastic horse more than anything—and my teddy bear. I hugged him close. Clearly, I needed to get my mind off all the possible catastrophes tomorrow might bring.

I took all my clothes out of my chest of drawers, folded each item, and put it back perfectly. Then I lined up all my shoes. I put all my books in my bookcase, lining up the edges so they looked nice. I prayed to God and asked him to forgive me for letting my brother take my spanking for the tack I'd put, pointy end up, in Dad's chair. I also asked God to forgive me because I had not been nice to my cousin Lilly during summer vacation when she'd visited our family. Mom always made me let her sleep with me even though she had sand between her toes and refused to wash them before she got into bed with me—which drove me crazy!

Finally, I prayed God would forgive me for peeing inside the podium at church when I was 5. Back when all the kids, including me, played hide and seek after church each Sunday. On this Sunday, it caught me by surprise. I'd had no idea that I needed to go until I heard whomever was "It", say, "Ready or not, here I come." And I went. I never told anyone about it, but Mom told me that

God knows everything. I prayed on my knees in my room for a long time that God would forgive me all these things and welcome me into his arms if Dad set the house on fire the next day and killed us.

Once my room was spotless, and I was exhausted from praying, I crawled back into bed and read a chapter in *Bally the Blue Whale*. It felt good to read about life under water when your home might be destroyed any minute by fire. When I reached the point of exhaustion where I didn't care if I lived or died, I drifted off into sleep.

The next morning, I walked into the kitchen and through the front window I could see Dad already had the truck backed up to the utility pole and a ladder set up in the truck bed. My throat grew tight as I slid into my chair and tucked my napkin into the collar of my shirt.

"Hungry?" Mom asked.

I nodded. I gazed through the kitchen window where I could see Dad climbing up the ladder with heavy work gloves stuck in the back pocket of his overalls. My brother stood on the ground ready to hand him tools. As I watched, I felt my throat constrict until I could hardly breathe. Swallowing felt out of the question.

Mom spooned eggs onto my plate. It seemed like she was making a point of not letting her eyes stray toward the window. I didn't want to watch either, but I couldn't help myself. I picked up my fork and started moving the eggs around on my plate trying to act normal, but all the while stealing glances outside. The old circuit box clung to its spot inside the kitchen cabinet with the door hanging ajar like a silent witness, as if sensing that soon it would be torn remorselessly from the wall where it had rested for decades. Sawdust sprinkled the kitchen floor and cabinets where, earlier, I'd heard Dad sawing to make a larger space to insert the new circuit box into position. By leaning down a little, I could see up through the top into a low corner of the attic. If I sank still further down in my chair and craned my neck, I could just make out the blue sky beyond through the hole Dad had cut in the roof so he could run the tube and wires. Hopefully, Dad planned to patch that hole. We already had rainwater leaking down through the kitchen light fixture when it rained ever since his last remodeling venture, and Dad already needed to patch that again.

When I glanced out the window again, I could see Dad hard at work. He'd gone up and down the ladder several times. The ladder seemed to stretch endlessly up toward the blue sky. My hand started to perspire just watching. It made me think of the Tower of Babel I read about in the Bible. So high they hoped to talk face-to-face with God. As I watched, scarcely breathing, I saw him switching wires and things back and forth. I was unsure what he was doing, and I wondered if HE knew what he was doing. Then he unhooked the old utility line that ran to our house from the pole. Then, with my brother's help at the bottom, he unrolled the new wire from the spool. Dad, tugging hard, hefted the end of the new line, up the ladder. The ladder shook with his efforts. I could see the wire pull taunt as Dad tried to attach it to the pole. He tried several times but apparently didn't quite make it.

Why what he was doing didn't result in his immediate electrocution, I'm not sure. Dad once tried to explain the rules of electricity to me, but it wasn't much use. I'd asked because I frequently saw squirrels using the electric wires to cross the road from our aunt's yard to ours. So why didn't it kill them? Dad said it was because they didn't touch the wire and the ground at the same time.

My heart pounded so hard I saw spots. I'd mashed the eggs in my plate until they looked like a small yellow puddle. If they had been boiled and Franky had been at the table, we would have swapped parts, he would eat the whites, and I'd eat the yokes. But Franky was not at the table he was outside helping Dad. The eggs were scrambled, and now I'd mashed them into an unappetizing paste.

Mom sat with her back to the window and stirred her coffee and stared straight ahead at the goldfish bowl on top of the television across the room, in the opposite direction of the window. Even the fish seemed nervous swimming back and forth, back and forth as if sensing the tension.

Dad apparently found some way to make the end of the wire stay on the roof for a bit. He crawled down the ladder from the pole, and moved the truck directly in front of the kitchen window on our side of the road, I took a bite of cold cinnamon toast. Thank God, he wasn't dead yet. My heart curled around a tiny nugget of hope. I chewed. The toast felt sandy on my dry tongue. I couldn't swallow it.

Now Dad was back up on the roof. I could hear scraping and shuffling sounds right over our heads. I heard Dad's heavy work boots clomp clomp clomping around. Periodically, he shouted down to my brother, "Hand me that saw! No! No! The hammer, that's what I need! Give me the wire clips! Hurry! I can't hold this position all day!"

Off and on, I'd hear him grunt, like he was straining to pull the ends of the wire to meet up with something. At the top of the window, I could see the thick wire sway, and I could picture Dad pulling it into place over our heads, his big arm muscles bulging like a wrestler's.

His voice sounded tense, which made me think he wasn't so certain after all that he could do the job without burning the house down. Mom continued staring at the fish and unconsciously stirring her coffee in the same direction the fish swam until I thought maybe her spoon might melt. Her eyes looked as blue as Arctic ice I'd once seen on a postcard.

Unable to swallow the endlessly dry toast, I discretely spat it out into my napkin.

The first sign that all was not well began when I heard a slithering-like clatter, like Dad dropped something.

"I—Yeow!" he screamed.

Then I heard a huge thump and multiple clatters overhead. It sounded like he'd fallen on the roof right over us.

"Louis!" Mom jumped up and tried to see up through the hole Dad had cut through the cabinet. I saw tools randomly rain down in front of the kitchen window outside. My brother jumped backward to avoid the falling items. The hammer, saw, wire grips, tool chest all hit the ground. At that moment, the thing I dreaded most happened. I saw the wire stretching across the yard to the pole at the road go slack and land on the road. Dad must have lost his grip.

"No!" I screamed. "Daddy!"

"Watch out below!" Dad cried.

As I watched, the wire snaked down from the roof of the house as the tension caused it to retract like a cobra back toward the pole 100 yards away. The end of the wire Dad had tried to attach to the breaker box hit the ladder in the truck and knocked it toward my brother. He plunged down like a man diving into first base and hit the ground on his hands and knees beside the truck to avoid the falling ladder that crashed down within inches of him.

The wire popped back and forth striking on both sides of him narrowly missing him. The end made contact with the ladder, and a thunderstorm of sparks flew. They showered the truck and all around my brother who ducked his head under his hands. Then the naked wire hit the saw and sent even more sparks flying. In scant seconds, the wire hit the ground a dozen times all around my brother.

"Stay back, son stay back!" Dad screamed from the roof. My brother turned over and pulled his legs toward his chest as the heavy wire, pulled by its own weight skittered further back across the yard and away from him.

Then a lot of things happened at once. My brother raised his head climbed to his knees and started crawling toward the wire as if he intended to retrieve it.

"Stop!" Dad screamed.

"Don't!" Mom pounded on the kitchen window frame. "Don't touch the wire. Please don't touch the wire. It's live!"

At that moment from my place at the window, I saw Dad appear feet first, then the rest of him somersaulting through the air like a circus acrobat. I marveled that what I'd often heard was true. Terrible things do happen in slow motion. Dad seemed poised like a bug in amber, framed against the sky, first this way, then that way. My mind took endless snapshots of him as he fell, in a variety of odd positions with looks of amazement and surprise on his face. His arms and legs first up like a diver, then down like a grasshopper as he tried to right himself in mid-air. A laugh bubbled up inside me as I saw the ridiculous look on his face. I started laughing and could not stop. Right before he landed in Mom's freshly planted petunias under the maple in our front yard, he looked just like Wile E. Coyote from Saturday morning television as he first plunged off the cliff.

The sight of him, sprawled in the flowerbed caused me to burst into even more hysterical laughter. I laughed and laughed and laughed. I could not stop laughing.

"Jane!" Mom shouted at me. "Your father may be dead! Stop it!"

I laughed harder and tears came out of my eyes.

She grabbed me by the arms and shook me for a moment, then released me. She ran outside. Somehow, I managed to suck it up and stop laughing and follow her, brushing back the tears as I went. But I couldn't quite shake the cadaverous smile on my face as we both leaned over Dad who lay motionless on the ground looking just like ol' Wile E. Coyote, after the Roadrunner outsmarted him and he went off the cliff. A giggle escaped me, and I quickly slapped my own hand over my mouth.

Mom, still holding the cup towel, cried, "Louis! Are you okay? Louis?" She bent down and placed her hand on Dad's shoulder, prodding him gently.

"Ugh," he groaned and shook his head.

"Dad! Dad!" I called.

"Dad, are you alright?" My brother got to his feet. He looked dazed. He had grass stains on his knees, and his shirt had streaks of dirt; but otherwise, he appeared unharmed. Over his shoulder, I could see the wire had stopped moving some distance from us, the end coiled in the air like a cobra ready to strike.

"I think so!" Dad sat up slowly amid the scrambled petunias. Dirt fell all around him, from his head and his shoulders. He looked down at his legs as if the sight of them still attached surprised him. He felt one leg with his hands, then the other and winced. Mom felt his arms and neck.

"Do you think you've broken any ribs?" Mom asked.

"I don't think so." He had scratches on his arms and a few bedraggled flowers on his head. But otherwise, he appeared largely unharmed. However, Mom's flowers looked to be a total loss.

"Don't go near that wire, son. It's not safe." Dad plucked some grass from his head then slowly stood. A bit of belated safety precautions, I thought considering our circumstances.

"What do we do, Dad?" my brother asked.

"I thought I'd cut the electricity off, but apparently I didn't. I'll need to try again. I'll cut the electricity off at the main pole, and then we'll try to re-attach the wire. And the wire is too heavy for me to pull it tight by myself. I'll need someone to help me pull it up on the roof or a way to leverage it."

"You aren't going to use MY son to do that!" Mom screamed. "Not now! Not ever!" Mom swung the wet cup towel at Dad's head. Back and forth she flogged him about the head and shoulders with the wet cup towel.

"What! Stop! What do you think you're doing?" Dad backed up several steps to position himself, so the trunk of the maple stood between him and Mom. Mom swung the towel around the tree wrapping it around his neck with a snap. Dad dodged.

Glaring at him, eyes dark with anger, "Louis Hinkle, you are a crazy man! You can do the wiring yourself if you like. But you won't use my son to do your craziness! You've nearly killed him!" she shrieked.

"Okay, Okay! I'll call Herman, and he'll help me finish."

"Herman! *Her...man!*"

Herman was an old friend of the family who sometimes worked for Dad doing painting and odd jobs. Most of the time he smelled like apple juice to me—Mom said he drank a lot of it.

"If you could get *Herman*, to do this, why didn't you?" She threw the cup towel down. And, grabbing first my hand, then my brother's, she dragged us both back inside the house.

"Go to your rooms and don't come out until I say so."

Within the hour, Herman came over, shut the electricity off at the pole and helped Dad hook the wires up to the house. By that evening, the new breaker box replaced the old fuse box, looking somehow ordinary after all the drama. Dad and Herman rewired the entire house and added several new outlets. It was a small house and did not take them long once they got started. The house did not burn down as I feared. No one died, though Dad did have to sit on a pillow to eat his supper. He told us proudly that we had enough electricity to run every appliance we had, now all at the same time if we wanted to, which sounded like heaven to me.

After we were all in bed that night, I heard Mom in the next room ask Dad again, "If Herman could shut off the electricity at the pole, why didn't you call him in the first place?"

* * *

2006

Auschwitz Prison convicts probably had more comfortable bathroom facilities than Dad's master bath. His new house is modern and large. It's well furnished with things Mom, my younger sister, and I pooled our money to buy. We decorated Mom's bathroom in pale green with tiny printed floral wallpaper and placed tranquil bird prints on the wall. But when I walk into Dad's bathroom that evening to take a second look and more pictures of Dad's "Jacuzzi" I feel like I've stepped back to the Dark Ages. Everything is brown and rough and dirty.

Inside the shower I find an unfinished board stretched across the top of the tub for him to sit on to bathe. In the tub is a toilet brush, presumably for him to use as a "body brush"? Also, in the tub I find a cattle trough warmer, to which is attached a cord that runs to an outlet he's installed next to the tub, against code of course.

I've only seen such a thing once, back when we still had the farm. Yes... Dad is using a cattle trough warmer to try to construct his own Jacuzzi. As usual there is no electric plug at the end of the wire, instead he's cut off the plug, split the cord in two, stripped the wire ends and inserted each one into the plug on the wall next to the tub. I take pictures and just sit for a while and look and consider my future.

The next week we gather in court to decide if Dad will be going home, or if he will be going to assisted living. The courtroom is quiet when we arrive. Dad sits with his lawyer on one side of the room. My sister and I sit on the other side. My husband, Hock, is there for moral support. He sits at the back, perhaps to catch any of us if we try to escape.

As the judge walks in, before the bailiff can say, "All rise," Daddy rises on his toes and yells, "Your Honor! Why am I being persecuted!" Not prosecuted, persecuted. His lawyer pulls him down and court resumes.

Our case is first on the docket.

The judge asks Dad, "Mr. Hinkle, do you know why you are here today?" Dad stands up again from his seat, totters on his toes with earnest outrage and said, "NO your honor! Why?"

His attorney stands beside him. My father is unsteady on his feet, but the attorney does nothing to steady him. I am on the other side of the room unable to put my arm around Dad to reassure him. I have been ordered to sit where I do. All I can do is watch as Dad rocks back and forth from heel to toe and asks why he is in court today. My heart…breaks.

There is a brief attempt made by my soon-to-be-ex-brother-in-law to become Dad's Conservator. I believe his heart is in the right place and in many ways I wish it could be so. My Dad loves this man. He's been like a son to him for many years. However, the judge quickly dismisses this request feeling it will not be in Dad's best interest. Taking care of Dad is not a job I would wish on my worst enemy.

We present letters from Dad's doctors and his psychiatrist that relate information about Dad's poor health and his deteriorating mental condition. In these assessments both doctors state Dad is not competent to manage his own life and healthcare. My sister and I both tell the judge about all the previous steps we've taken to try to take care of Dad and how the results are far from good. We explain all the close calls with heavy equipment and vehicles. We explain how Dad is not paying his bills or looking after his other financial interests. Finally, we present the pictures of the condition of Dad's house and his person, and this seems to have the greatest impact on the judge.

I recall the conversation with Dad about the trough warmer/Jacuzzi that took place the week before, but now felt like it happened a lifetime ago. It really is the deciding factor. I know we've made the right decision. But I can't help wondering if Dad will ever forgive us.

The judge exits to his chambers to consider all the information and review the pictures more closely and decide our fate.

The next thing I know, after a brief consultation with our attorney, my husband and sister, I am thrust forward before the judge who decides to make me Conservator of Dad's financial interests and my sister Conservator of his health interests. The order says I must sell my house in Texas and move to Tennessee where I am to organize Dad's affairs, property, tools and all his hoarded assets and sell all of it to pay for his care. The judge agrees that we should divide personal items that Dad does not want and need and distribute them fairly among family members. Then, once Dad is deceased, it is my job to dispose of the remainder of the estate and divide it equally among family members including my two nieces, the daughters of my deceased brother.

And so, the hammer falls...on me... and I feel like someone has shoved me off a high cliff into a rapidly flowing river. I can almost hear the water rushing by my ears and the current flooding over my head.

◇

"Even to your old age I am he, and to gray hairs I will carry you. I have made, and I will bear; I will carry and will save." (Isaiah 46:4)

◇

Barbecue Pork Sandwiches

Place one pork shoulder in an oven-safe glass baking dish.
Mix 1 cup of brown sugar, ½ cup apple cider vinegar, 2 tablespoons of honey, 6 oz. can of crushed pineapple with syrup along with ¼ cup ketchup.
Pour mixture over the pork shoulder.
Cook at 375 degrees until done enough to fall apart when fork is inserted.

Slaw

Grate 2-parts cabbage to 1-part carrots in separate bowl.
Add dill pickle juice to moisten (not too wet).
Sprinkle with celery seed, salt, and pepper.

Once pork is done, let cool, then place strips of barbecue pork shoulder on bun of choice.
Top with slaw mixture and eat with side of dill pickle and potato chips.

Chapter 10 – Don't Badger Me
"Louis, do not fire that gun! You never clean it! It's rusty! You could blow your own hands or head off!" — Velma

2006
"Conservatorship for Louis Hinkle is granted to his daughter, Jane Eden. You are hereby ordered to sell your house in Texas and move to Tennessee to manage your father's financial affairs and see after his care. This court orders you to put your father's business and finances in order, organize his assets, sell those assets, and bank the funds to provide for him. You are further ordered to file regular updates with this court."

The judge strikes his podium with the hammer. "This case is concluded."

I stand. Numb. My sister stands next to me, not looking at me. During a brief intermission only 30 minutes earlier our attorney came out from the judge's chambers to tell us the judge was leaning toward giving my soon-to-be-ex-brother-in-law conservatorship. For some reason, the judge was unwilling to accept my sister as Conservator. Perhaps he felt she had already done enough caring for Mom, and currently her life is complicated with the pending divorce. She also has two young daughters to raise. My children are grown. Our attorney mentioned that if I was willing to move to Tennessee, they would consider me as Conservator. And I told him I would.

When he heard the judge was considering the brother-in-law, my husband virtually shoved me forward and said, "Here's your girl."

Never did I think I'd be Conservator, but in face of the alternatives, I reluctantly nodded.

It appears the judge took me at my word. Apparently, he prefers a family member over someone who would soon to be ex-family.

Unsure how my sister will feel about these developments, and unsure how I feel about them myself, we file out of the courtroom. My life, in a matter of moments, has turned upside down. So has Dad's. What about our Texas-based business, our Texas house, kids, granddaughters, our life? What about my husband's travel schedule? When we entered the courtroom, I thought my sister would be appointed Conservator and I would play a supporting role. Now the roles are reversed.

After the judge's decision Dad's attorney says goodbye to Dad and leaves him with my sister. Feeling numb myself, somehow we all wander out of the courthouse and load Dad into my car. We take him to Autumn Manor, the assisted living facility my sister and I selected. My sister follows us to the facility in her car to help with paperwork, then she goes to Dad's house and picks up some things he will need for the night while I help him get acquainted with his room and we meet the staff.

We decide to have some of his furniture and other belongings transferred the next day. That evening we get him settled, putting away a suitcase of his clothing and toiletries. I feel as if I've entered a time warp. It reminds me of when he and Mom settled me at church summer camp and then drove away leaving me in unfamiliar surroundings with people I did not know. I sit with him a while on the edge of his bed trying to comfort him with my presence and ease the pain of transition. He is not happy, but he is at least speaking to me. As we sit a very pretty nurse comes in to take his blood pressure. As a joke we ask her to take mine too. My blood pressure is higher than Dad's.

Dad says, "Why Jane, assisted living does not appear to agree with you!"

"Apparently not," I tell him, shocked at the amount of stress I feel and, at that moment, I am apparently more stressed than Dad!

As we walk the halls to get familiar with the place old friends come up to Dad and speak to him. We run into members from his old church. It was a church he helped build and played an active role in for most of his life. For many years he even served on the board. They tell him about how they gather around the piano on Friday nights at Autumn Manor to sing hymns like in the old days. Dad loves to sing. He does not want to like this place, but I can see him begin to visibly relax in the company of people he's known for so long. Eventually we find our way back to his room where he can gaze out the window at lovely, tall pine and oak trees and an expanse of green grass. Occasionally, we spot a squirrel hopping across the lawn. It is a beautiful room with a nice view. For a man who has spent little time away from home, I realize even a pretty room, friends and a view are not enough to prevent the whole process from feeling incredibly unsettling. He must feel entirely lost, and I am bit lost myself. It is difficult for me to comprehend that I won't be going home to the house my parents lived in for so long to see Dad anymore. In fact, I'm going to have to sell it…and everything else. But first, I must get the horrendous, hoarding mess cleaned up so it's even fit to sell. This thought is overwhelming beyond description.

The next day movers bring Dad's favorite furniture, and we set up his room. He has space for his bed, small couch, end tables, dresser and small craft table and chair. We bring some photos from the house and paintings and hang them on the walls. My sister and I buy a shower curtain, towels, and other things he will need to personalize his bathroom. We also buy several different crafts for him to work on using the craft table we set up. Little bird houses and paints to paint them. We think maybe he might decide to work on them or maybe guests will when they visit. We also buy him a television set. Dad has not had a working television for more than 5 years and, even then, he rarely watched it.

"I don't need one of those things. They are the work of the devil. I won't watch it. You can take it away," he says.

"Dad, they have cable here. There are nature shows, religious shows you may enjoy watching. Give it a chance," I tell him.

I flip the channels several times and show him how the remote works. I demonstrate how to find the Home and Garden Network and a nature show, and he begins to get interested in a sports show on fishing.

As I leave, he is watching TV and eating a snack that one of the pretty aids brings him. He looks comfortable sitting on the couch with a throw over his lap made of a rich dark animal faux fur. I am beginning to feel a bit relieved that things are settling in. Still horrified about the abrupt and painful process that made it all possible, but also resolved that we did the right thing. I hope someday he will feel the same way, and maybe even forgive me. The sight of the animal throw tossed over Dad's lap causes the years to roll back in my mind to another shimmering sight of animal fur.

* * *

1969
"Louis! Look, look, look! What IS that?" Mom cried as she stands, coffee pot in hand, looking out the kitchen window. The rest of us are seated around the kitchen table enjoying our typical breakfast of scrambled eggs, pancakes, and home-made syrup.

We all pushed our chairs back from the kitchen table simultaneously with loud scraping noises on the floor. Soon, all four of us stood lined up in front of our long row of kitchen windows scanning the maple trees.

"It looks like a mink coat crawling across the yard, doesn't it?" Mom whispered excitedly. She pointed to a mass of rippling, sable-like fur making its way across our front lawn headed swiftly toward the expansive juniper bushes in front of our living room windows. Her voice held the awe of a woman who had never hoped to see, let alone own, a mink coat. Now a furry coat appears to literally be crawling across her yard on a bright early morning.

"It's not a mink. Too big. Must be a badger. But I've never seen one so large. Must be close to 30 pounds," Dad said.

Nudging between Dad and my brother, fighting for a better corner of window to see through, I watched the rippling mass of glossy brownish-black fur traveling at a fast clip across grass still wet with morning dew.

About that moment, our dogs, Scoop and Rusty, must have seen the badger too, because they let out what could only be described as blood-curdling yowls, followed by thundering feet and vicious barking and snarls, the likes of which I'd never heard. Who knew our mongrels, part collie, part hound dog, could make such hideous noises? The primal noise sent shivers down my spine. It sounded like a dog cartoon fight from Saturday TV complete with the large cloud of dust where dogs are thrown out of the fight and scramble to get back in.

"We've got to get him before he kills one of the dogs or crawls under the house," Dad said. Pushing through the abandoned dining chairs, he headed for the hall closet where he stored the shotgun, and shells in a dusty red box. My thoughts flew to the access door that led under our house. Once a month Mom would say, "Louis, have you fixed the access door so it will stay shut? It's opened all the time, and anything can crawl under the house! One of the cats will crawl under there and die if you don't get that fixed."

Dad would say, "I know it, but I haven't had time." And that would be the end of the discussion until the next time. Mom, the family prophet, I thought.

"No Dad," I hung onto his sleeve. "You can't kill a badger! It's not going to hurt anything. Please, it's so pretty! Please don't kill it."

He jerked out of my grasp and reached to lace his boots. I didn't get a good look at the badger, but I could already tell it was probably the most beautiful thing I'd ever seen in my entire life! I couldn't stand the thought of it…dead! Yet, I could hear a serious dogfight beginning under the junipers. I shivered. I heard yelps and growls and dirt splashing up against the side of the house from under the bushes. Even at my age I instinctively recognized the sounds of mortal combat.

"We have to kill it, Jane."

Dad threw shells from the box on the hall shelf into the chambers of the rusty shotgun.

"Louis, do not fire that gun," Mom said. "You never clean it! It's rusty! You could blow your own hands or head off!"

I hoped her prophecies were wrong. For a moment I pictured Dad's head separating from his body in a bloody gush. Or his hands flying off left and right. I shivered. Then cartoon versions minus the blood replaced the image. Versions where he stooped down, collected his head and asked me please to set it back on his shoulders, which I did in my imagination with shaky hands. None of these imaginings provided any comfort. My knees shook at the responsibility of screwing my father's head back on. Best if his head never left his shoulders, I decided. I'd heard about a neighbor who came in from hunting, set the shotgun, butt first, in the corner, and blew his brains right into the attic.

"Someone had to clean that up, you know," Mom said after we heard about it. A grizzly imagining there too.

I prayed if Dad blew his brains out it would not be me that had to clean it up. I'd seen Mom scramble beef brains with eggs, and the sight made me want to throw up.

My thoughts leapt from brains to other breakfast talk of all the neighborhood accidents. Lost thumbs, lost fingers. Accidental hangings. Suddenly, any one of these accidents seemed possible. In his heavy boots, my father could run fast, but he was not what you would consider fleet-of-foot, or graceful. He might trip while running with the shotgun. *Was I having a premonition?* I wondered.

Mom had premonitions all the time.

Daddy, don't go! My mind screamed, but I stood silent, unable to utter a sound. After all, I was just a kid. He wasn't going to listen to me!

"I'm going too! I want to see what happens!" Franky yanked on his Ked sneakers. Now pictures of my brother on the ground dead, blood trickling out of the corner of his mouth filled my mind! Neighbors would congregate over his small coffin at the local funeral home and say things like, "How tragic. He died so young."

Stop! I screamed silently to myself to make the pictures go away!

"No, you aren't!" Mom grabbed Franky by his shirttail as he headed toward the door, her voice unusually firm. "Badgers are dangerous, and your father's out there with a gun!"

"Ah, man, you never let me have any fun!" Franky flung himself down on the leather sofa in the den with a thud that sent it several inches backward toward the foyer. He crossed his arms and stuck out his lower lip with a pout.

Bang! We heard the shotgun fire! ...more yelping from the dogs. Had one been hit? More tearing and wrestling of shrubbery! Chaos followed.

"Did you get him?" Mom screamed loud enough Dad could hear her through the closed kitchen windows.

"No! He's run under the house…!" Dad moved out of sight around the corner of the house, gun under his arm.

Soon we heard kicking and dogs yelping as Dad cleared the dogs away from the two-foot-high crawl space that ran under the floor.

"I'm going in!" Dad hollered.

"Louis," Mom yelled. "Don't you dare go under the floor after that badger!" The walls vibrated from the force of her voice. Suddenly our home felt like a Civil War battlefield.

Too late—we all heard Dad kick the permanently ajar trap door that led under the floor so hard that it left its hinges and flew out into the yard. Through the bedroom window where we'd run to observe, we saw it catapult end over end until it came to rest against the pool fence. We looked at each other, and then, in unison, we rushed outside.

A highly tense scene awaited us. I could see Dad's legs encased in blue overalls and his brown work boots fast disappearing through the crawl-space doorway, or hatch, or whatever you called it. The dogs tried to fit through the hole with him but every other move, a huge tan work boot made contact kicking them backward onto their tails. I assumed he had the shotgun with him because it was nowhere in sight.

"Quick, get the dogs," Mom ordered.

Franky and I stood frozen. What only that morning had been tame pets had turned into mad dogs slobbering like wild, rabid animals as they tried to get to the badger. Neither of us wanted to go near them, let alone collar one. They appeared frenzied, their eyes looked glazed and unfocused. Rusty bled from multiple gashes on her shoulder. Blood ran into Scoop's eyes from a large gash that ran along his face and around his chin.

"What happened to them?" I asked. "Are they gonna die?"

"Badgers have huge claws for digging," Mom said. "Few dogs can get the best of a badger. In fact, a badger can kill a dog with one good swipe. They're kind of like small bears."

"Here, Rusty! Here, Scoop." Franky and I both called, clicking our tongues in our most appealing dog calls. After several calls, the sap seemed to run out of the dogs and they sat down on either side of the crawlspace access, breathing heavily, bleeding and slobbering. Their fur was wet from blood, and saliva.

For several moments we heard nothing from underneath the house except subtle rustling noises as if Dad were crawling around first one direction, then another. Even the dogs seemed to hold their breath, listening.

Thump! Thump! I heard what I thought was Dad adjusting his position and maybe hitting his head on the floor over his head.

"Louis, you come out from under that house this instant! You are going to get yourself killed with your children standing here watching!" Mom said as she paced in front of the broken door.

Silence.

"Louis?" No response.

Sweat trickled down the back of my neck. It felt cold. My mind raced to the imagined funeral where everyone stands around at the reception speaking in low tones.

"Yes, sir, killed by a badger he chased under the house. And in his prime. Two young children. So sad," someone would say, and they would look at Franky and me with pity. Franky would wear his white Sunday coat, red tie, and black trousers. I would wear my yellow smocked Easter dress with white lace socks and black patent-leather shoes.

After the funeral we would go home, and people would come over and hang out at the house to offer more sympathy. Our Mom would cry, her nose red and swollen and she would pour everyone coffee as she dabbed her nose with a lace-edged handkerchief, and afterward she would rush to the bathroom to sob uncontrollably into a towel to muffle the sounds. Neighbors would look at each other with brows furrowed and mouths turned down at the corners. They would listen and shake their heads and look at Franky and me. "What will become of them now?" someone would ask.

"Daddy!" I cried unable to stand the silence or my wild imaginings any longer. "Please, Daddy! Come out!"

Intense rustling and scuffing noises ensued, with my father yelling, "Get back you!" and pounding noises rattled the floor from underneath. Then more scuffling noises like Dad was dragging himself across the uneven ground underneath the house.

Bang! Bang! The shotgun sounded. To me it appeared as if the blast magically lifted the house off its foundation for a moment. Smoke curled out several of the ventilation holes. My brother, Mom and I stood in shocked silence. I didn't know what to think or do. Surely if enough time passed, one of us would have to crawl underneath the house and remove Dad's body for no doubt that rusty gun had blown apart and killed him.

Slowly, after about a lifetime passed, we heard rustling. For a moment, we thought maybe the badger was coming out. We all took a few steps backward in unison, and Mom grabbed a lawn chair to use as a shield. The dogs moved behind us with their tails tucked between their legs, heads low, seeking protection from this fierce bear-like animal and they looked at the crawl space from a safer vantage point somewhere behind our legs. Surely these humans had everything under control now, their little eyes pleaded, looking up at us with furrowed brows. They sucked their lolling tongues back in, licked their lips and swallowed audibly almost in unison.

Then we saw the barrel of the gun, followed by Dad, his dirty, balding head, and then the rest of him in, filthy, as he crawled out from under the house. Once out, he reached back into the crawl space and heaved out a large, very dead badger. It was as big as a Labrador retriever, but much prettier, or at least it had been before he shot it half to bits and dragged it across the ground under the house. My heart ached for the limp animal.

"Dad, are you alright?"

"Louis? What happened?"

Dad smiled. "Why, I shot him, dear. That's what happened?"

He pulled out his handkerchief and began to rub the dirt and perspiration from his ears and face. "Man alive! My ears are still ringing!"

"It's a miracle you aren't deaf!" Mom said. "You could have been killed."

"What are we going to do with it?" Franky asked.

"Why, we're going to eat it!" Dad said.

"Ew-w-w!" I said.

"And I'm going to nail the pelt to the side of the garage to dry. When it's dry, we'll take it to a furrier and have a collar made for your mother to wear with her wool coat on Sundays."

"Would you like that, Velma?"

* * *

2006
The next day I contact a local realtor and get a recommendation from her for a foreman to manage the cleanup of Dad's property. She recommends someone, and once I engage him, he hires a crew of six men. They will work in groups, one group will clean out Dad's old house, paint and prepare it for sale. One group will clean out Dad's current house—along with the garage and an exterior

shop building—and prepare it for sale. There is also a large shop to be dealt with, about a quarter mile away. Next to it is the old family cabin and then a quarter of a mile further around the horseshoe-shaped subdivision is our old barn, and then the old house, now a rental, but empty. Next to that is yet another exterior garage. Behind both sits a tractor trailer full of who knows what. Every place and structure is piled high with every type of thing Dad's saved over the years.

Dad had saved old lumber, bathroom fixtures, tools, cars, trucks, tires, leftover items from major construction sites and more, and piled it all over the property. It will take a huge effort to clean everything up. I decide to have a local metal recycling company come out and pick up whole cars and buses and haul them away for scrap. In general, it's an overwhelming, dirty, and nearly impossible project. I imagine it is much like cleaning up a massive junkyard mixed up with an auto salvage lot, mixed up with numerous wrecked businesses.

The next week we begin the work. I say "we" because I must be there to organize and help wherever I can and make countless decisions. I go to the job site each day and work alongside the men. Each morning when I arrive the cleanup operation is in full swing with Harold, the foreman, supervising. Loaders and dozers buzz, throttle, and strain all over the property making large animalistic prints in the mud as the men sort metal from debris and load what's sellable onto trucks to either transport out, or to group for later auction. Brush, undergrowth, and damaged trees are scraped up and burned. Items we unearth must be sorted. I operate a loader myself, something I have not done since my teens, helping with the overall project. My muscles ache, my back hurts, and periodically I crawl down from the machine, wade through knee-deep mud and load things by hand into the loader bucket.

I long for easier work inside the shop sorting through tools and other items organizing them for sale. It's good to be in the shop out of the weather, but I reserve that work for early in the morning or for rainy days. At first it's hot during the day but soon winter sets in and along with it cold weather. The large shop is constructed of a wooden frame on a concrete floor, and it's enclosed with only a thin layer of tin with many holes in the walls and roof. It has a huge 1000-gallon underground gas tank that's been re-purposed as a wood-burning stove to heat with. Dad added a door to the front so we can load wood into it and a huge fire grill inside to place the wood on so air can circulate underneath. The stove pipe runs out the top of the tank and out the shop roof to carry smoke away. With a fire built in it, the tank walls glow red, and you can see the fire through the holes in the sides of the tank. It is an almost demonic sight. I worry that it will get hot enough to melt or might catch the shop on fire.

Outside with the loader I dig up old tires, bits of housing construction waste and every type of metal imaginable sorting it in the loader bucket. Part of it I take to an industrial dumpster I have rented for that purpose, other parts go into piles of similar items. The machine vibrates under me like a large, purring animal as I move it around the area working in one spot until it's relatively clean, then moving on to the next spot. A few months earlier I would not have pictured myself atop this large machine, but soon I feel like my teen-age-self working for Dad again. After a while, the machine feels like a mechanical extension of my arms and legs and I realize why Dad enjoyed this work so much. You feel powerful operating it.

After many hours working one day, I park the loader and throw the lever into neutral to let it idle outside the old garage behind our old house. I grab the steering wheel and step over the seat and slide to the ground where I adjust my hat and gloves for warmth.

One of the two garage doors hangs open, half on, half off its hinges. It's been like that for decades. I push down the dried Johnson grass that's obstructing the door from moving and push it further back so I can enter and allow some light into the very large garage. Down the right side is a crude apartment with three rooms that Dad and Mom rented for extra income when they first got married. How anyone could live there I'm unsure, but it has the remnants of wallpaper, a sink, counter, presumably they had an outhouse out back that's long gone. The left side is strictly storage and workbenches. A tree has grown up beside the other door making it impossible to close. I sweep the cobwebs aside as I walk in.

I look back at the entrance and think about how this is the exact spot where my brother was mowing the yard at age 10 and disturbed a rattlesnake. The snake bit through the end of his tennis shoe narrowly missing his big toe. For a moment he shook his foot, then quickly realized it would be best to abandon the shoe. So he pried it off with lightning reflexes and ran away. We never found the snake, but when he came back to collect his shoe that displayed two ominous holes where it narrowly missing his toe.

I look at the doors remembering where Dad nailed the badger pelt to this very door to allow it to dry. I half expect to see it there now! But it is long gone. The pelt was stolen by some neighborhood boys. However, leaning in and looking closer, peering through the moist fog my breath makes on my glasses, I can see the holes where the nails once held the pelt. So, it was not a dream. It really did happen. I touch the holes to confirm my memory. I wonder, *what finally happened to the pelt? What did they do with it?* The very thought of the crawling badger hunt makes me smile. As my eyes adjust, I look around inside the shop at the rubble of broken canning jars, stacks of worm-eaten lumber and an old tablesaw abandoned in this ramshackle edifice. Rough shelving lines the walls, hammered into place along the sides to hold lumber Dad needed during his house-building days.

Overhead on high shelves, rest broken discarded storm windows stacked at odd angles and threatening to fall and decapitate anyone reckless enough to bump into them. I inch through the debris making my way deeper into the shop.

A ragged workbench, once a kitchen counter, runs lengthwise along a center wall. It's filled with discarded machine parts and cardboard boxes. In the shadows I find what's left of my very old and favorite friend, my 12" high black, plastic horse with flowing mane and tail that I played with as a child. One leg is broken and missing. The tail is missing too. I pick it up and clutch it to my chest, a reminder of how I first came to love horses. Maybe there are other relics of my childhood here? I collect a broom, bucket, shovel and plastic bags from out of my truck parked behind the house and begin sweeping and shoveling through the debris.

The work is hard, dirty, heavy. I wear a bandana as a mask over my face to keep from choking on the dust. Soon I have piles of recyclable metal, trash, and personal items heaped at the door. I collect all the unbroken, empty canning jars. I find a 25th wedding anniversary drinking glass that belonged to my parents that I bought for them on their anniversary. In the dirt on the floor, I find the reins to my old pony cart. Then I find the bridle, both are rigid and flaking with age. Nearby I find the collar to my first dog along with a leash made from shoestrings tied together. I finger the weathered, cracked and dried leash considering how poor we really were when I was a child, so poor we could not afford a real leash. Yet I never felt poor. As a child I recall having freedom, a vivid imagination, lots of space; and, despite all Dad craziness, I recalled feeling loved.

Eventually I work my way back to the center of the shop where I spot my paternal grandmother's trunk. At one time, it contained her fine linens from my ancestors, and all the things my grandmother felt were too special to use. So fine in fact that even though Dad brought the trunk home with him after his mother's death, he didn't want Mom to use the contents. And so, it sat from my grandmother's death until today.

When I open the trunk lid a dusty, abandoned rat nests, once stuck inside the lid, fall into the truck itself like dirty snow and tumbleweeds. At one time the trunk contained my grandmother's wedding dress, old thin, inexpensive wedding rings worn nearly in two, and tablecloths made for her trousseau. I believe it contained old quilts made from shirt and pant fabric that had been pieced together as well over the years, representative of their worn-out wardrobe. But none of this is in the trunk now. Long ago someone else has divested the trunk of its contents. I have no idea who or when. Now there is almost nothing left inside except fabric shavings, old rat nests, and dust. Even the rings are gone.

Cleaning the dirt out of the trunk, I close it, and scoot it out of the way. Then I sweep the dirt from the rooms in the shop until my arms feel like they will drop off my body. I carry trash to the loader and put it in the front bucket until it is full. I drive it to the industrial dumpster we rented and dump it. Then return for more.

Again and again, I go back inside the shop and clean. Eventually, while sweeping my thumb catches on a nail under an overhang and I rip half of the fingernail right off my finger inside my glove! Soon my glove fills with blood from cuts and scrapes on my hands, and blisters form despite the gloves. I go to my truck for paper towels to wrap my hand in to squeeze off the bleeding.

On the way home that evening, after dark, I stop at Autumn Manor to see Dad. My clothes are covered in mud, dirt, and diesel stains. The on-duty nurse looks at my finger and insists on washing and bandaging it.

"How did your day go?" Dad asks as we sit at the dining table for his evening meal. He pushes a bowl of cottage cheese and pear slices toward me attempting to share his food. I manage a smile, grateful for his generosity and eat the pears and cottage cheese savoring the sweet fruit.

"It's hard work, but we're making progress," I tell him. I think about how many times we've had this conversation...but in reverse...over the years. Once he was the one who smelled of smoke and diesel. Now it's me. Once he came dragging in, now he's rested, and I am the one who is exhausted. Life has a way of turning the tables on us if we live long enough.

After the drive home I pull boots off at the door, step inside and remove my clothes before walking farther into the house. I go straight to the bathroom throwing the clothes in the laundry and then run a bath. After I'm clean I go to bed in Mom's old bed, where I lie down and look up at the ceiling. I close my eyes. I dream of Mom. "Let's go for a walk," she says. And I reach out and take her hand in my dreams and we go for that walk. We will go see Suzie the deer at the state park below the house. Mother takes apples to feed her.

◇

"I clothed you in embroidered cloth and gave you sandals of badger skin; I clothed you with fine linen and covered you with silk." (Ezekiel 16:9-10)

◇

Homemade Syrup
Add one cup of sugar and 1 tablespoon of butter to 1-quart saucepan.
Heat at low temperature.
Cook sugar stirring until brown.
When it begins to caramelize, add 1 cup of water, slowly.
(Mixture will splash and bubble; so be careful.)
Continue stirring until it thickens.
Serve over pancakes while hot.

Chapter 11 – Wine and Kitty Valium
"If I catch the no-good rascal who stole my skill saws, he'll wish he was dead!"
— Louis

2006
My days cleaning up Dad's property preparing for the sale begin to unfold one after the other without rest. They are long, exhausting days of lifting, carrying, sorting, decisions, more sorting; and in the process I often encounter places or things that flood me with memories. At first, I thought I could stay at Dad's house during the cleanup. But it soon becomes clear, I can't.

I began to notice curious people driving by Dad's house staring at the property watching all the work underway. Some pull up in the driveway to gawk. When they see me, they turn around and drive away, but still looking. Pointing. Word gets around about the cleanup and pending auction, and that Dad is not living there anymore; and I realize they are looking for information to share on the local grapevine—and for opportunity.

There are crazy rumors circulating that Dad has a mattress stuffed with money. Or that he has a safe in the shop or at the house with stacks of valuable coins inside. Maybe he buried money under the house? Or down the well? They wonder. They talk. They look. I start to suspect some may want to see what they can grab and haul off to sell later.

It isn't long before my fears are confirmed. Once or twice, I think I hear gunshots in the late evening, which scares me. I wonder if the shots are at something in particular; or designed to just frighten us away. I want to believe the shots are from hunters, but it occurs to me that people may be fighting over Dad's stuff! Then, things start to go missing. I remind myself, not everyone is a "good person" as Dad would say. At one time I would have argued with him about this. Aren't all people basically good inside? Now, noticing item after item simply evaporate overnight, I'm not so sure.

Only one bedroom in the house is habitable for me to sleep in. It is the room where Mom died. A long, white tassel I bought for her long ago still hangs from the pull on the ceiling fan. I spent a lot of time in this room sleeping on cushions on the floor, holding the button to the morphine pump for Mom, pressing it to help relieve her pain when she could no longer press it herself. So did my sister. It is the room where we bathed her, fed her, changed her sheets in the last months of her life. It is the room where she had her last meal, looked out of the window at the tall trees and longed to go outside. It is in this room she confessed her sins to her Lord in low murmurs with us by her side, some of which I could not quite hear. When I asked her to repeat what she said she only smiled a smug smile. Only God needs to hear and know everything about a person. I felt guilty for eavesdropping on her private conversation with him.

During the first days of the cleanup, at night I find myself lying in bed in the exact position Mom was in when she died, in the exact same spot in her room. I know it's morbid, but I cannot pull my mind away from the memories. It is only a room, after all, I reassure myself. Like it was before, like it has been since she died. I clean, dust, vacuum the room and polish the furniture. I bring in my clothes and hang them in the closet. Everything looks normal. But it's not. I can feel it.

All rooms have a history, I tell myself. I install my laptop and printer on a small desk next to the bed. There…that's all I need. I lie down between clean sheets under a soft blanket I've just washed, and I try to read. I finally fall asleep. I wake up in the middle of the night and look at the ceiling without my glasses and see a small green light on the ceiling.

"Mom?" I say under my breath. No answer. "Mom, is that you?" Still no answer. Sleepy, dreamy, heart pounding, I prop myself up on my elbows, put on my glasses and look again and see the light on my computer is casting the green light on the ceiling. I sigh in relief, but also feel a little sad. I like to think Mom is still with me. We had an agreement that when my time comes, hers will be the first face I see. I guess that's not going to be tonight, I tell myself. Finally…exhaustion overtakes me. Much like when I was a child, even if the devil himself is under the bed, I no longer care. I must sleep.

Cleaning up "Hoadersville" is the most physically challenging work I've ever done.

I write letters to the neighbors to keep them informed of the progress of our cleanup hoping to discourage lookie-loos. I believe in my heart when we are finished they will be happy with the results.

Dad's property and all that he's hoarded has been a source of contention and an eyesore for years. The cleanup will improve their property values. I promised to do our best to work swiftly; but the fact is, there's no way to unearth 50 years of collecting and haul it away without some noise and mess.

Dad's main shop is 10 thousand square feet in size, filled nearly to the rafters with more things than I can possibly describe. The rafters themselves are rotted and near to falling in on us as we work. It and the surrounding area make up the largest portion of our work.

We park huge dumpsters on the property and sort through what we unearth. Much disappears into the dumpsters. Hand tools and materials are sorted within the confines of the shop where we've reinforced the walls and covered the windows with plywood to provide a modicum of security for more valuable items.

It's still a paper tiger of a shop, and we know it. On good days the men and I crawl onto Dad's heavy equipment and unearth the larger items, discarded equipment, tools, tires by the hundreds (maybe thousands) and more. Sometimes we pause to consider if there's a market to sell an item or if it's only good for scrap. If there's a possible market, we keep it and organize it with other, similar items.

There is everything on the property including a vintage printing press and a machine that molds plastic signs with heat and suction. There are huge crates of television tubes from days gone by. There are Indian artifacts discovered by Dad over the years and simply thrown into his tool chests and forgotten. There are worktables from sewing mills and cabinets from ancient grocery stores. There are vintage Coke machines and a life-size policeman statue used at school crossings to slow traffic. And so much more, but all of it is piled into huge piles alongside things of no value. Most of what we find has no value to us, but maybe it will be of value to someone. The tools, equipment and large collection of oddities Dad gathered will be sold and the funds banked. There are dozens of sets of hand tools, some complete sets, some incomplete. We find two dozen skill-saws, and tools Dad used when he ran a sawmill. We find the actual sawmill stored in the log cabin. Oddities include the log cabin Mom and her family bought for their parents to live in back in the 30s. It will remain in the original location until the auction. Then the buyer will disassemble it and move it to a new site and reassemble.

In addition to the houses and shop Dad has piles of scrap and stored goods in the old barn and even more items and material covered in plastic and stacked around the acres of property behind the house. All must be inventoried and sorted, and decisions made about what to do with it all. There are an impossible number of items to be grouped and priced; so, in many cases we group them in lots to be sold in bulk—buyer takes all. In one tractor trailer alongside herbs from my aunt sent to Mom wrapped in plastic in the 80s we also find love letters written between my parents from the 40s. I find them only because a workman brings them to me to see if I will give him the stamps!

"No!" I tell him. And I take and keep the letters to explore later and share with family members.

And there's more. There's also scrapped hospital equipment including several X-ray machines. The discarded X-ray machines were from a hospital Dad tore down. These worry the nosy neighbors the most. Salvaged medical equipment in all shapes and sizes might present a bio-hazard. As a result of my "trying to be nice" progress letters, a neighbor calls the EPA. An EPA case is filed! We are served with papers to stop the project. I take to my computer keyboard again and create a countersuit filling out endless forms with mountains of explanations, and we fight to reverse the court order to stop the cleanup. The EPA begins to fly overhead in helicopters to observe the cleanup. The clock is ticking to get everything cleaned up and sold. There's a very real concern we will soon run out of money and time and have to file for bankruptcy. Bad winter weather could shut down the cleanup until spring. Dad could die before spring. The EPA analyzes everything, find nothing wrong, and allow us to start up again. The government helicopters containing inspectors continue to circle overhead so they can report any new developments. Neighbors continue to drive by and whisper their concerns to their local authorities.

Another complaint is filed! We are shut down again. An EPA representative comes to test the soil and the runoff. I move the crew down the street to work on Dad's rent house, old garage and barn while the EPA makes up its mind about the large shop and surrounding property. All the neighbors either stay carefully indoors or avoid looking at us when they drive by while the EPA is there. I know the cleanup looks messy, but we really are creating order out of chaos. And this is not Chernobyl!

In a few days we find we've passed the EPA tests again. The cleanup continues, but this time I'm feeling less charitable toward the neighbors. I continue to keep them advised of our activities via mail, but I no longer have any hope they will demonstrate any form of gratitude, neighborly support, or love us for our efforts.

Things lay exposed on the ground as we dig through masses of items, and now theft becomes a serious problem. I am in the sheriff's office frequently filing theft reports. Soon I know the sheriff by his first name and have him on speed-dial. And he knows me.

Haunted by memories, fearing burglars and thieves, I can't stay in the house any longer, so I move into a rented apartment in a nearby town. Our house in Texas is for sale, but has not sold. Hock stays there when he can. He flies in for the weekend with me as often as possible. After I rent the apartment he flies in and in 2 hours at Sam's Club we outfit the apartment with nearly everything we need. I pull the bed from Dad's house, Hock promises to ship one of our couches and a television from home, and we buy towels, washcloths, dish towels, dishes, silverware and everything else for $250. I bring the desk and chair from Dad's house so we won't have to buy these things. It is amazing, really, how little you need to live. We finish our shopping, set everything up and Hock is gone back to Texas by evening. While I miss him, I'm grateful for a nest away from the chaos and to not have to sleep in the same room in the same position my mother died in at her house.

Each morning, in jeans, tee shirt and jacket, packing a pistol on my hip, I leave the apartment before daylight and drive to Dad's property where I work alongside the day laborers. They are a mixed bunch of guys, with a plethora of personal and health problems, but each one becomes dear to my heart in a short period of time. The foreman, Harold, especially, is a resourceful and kind man. He is a Godsend, creative and trustworthy. We bond as soldiers bond on the battlefield, only our battlefield is a bunch of ramshackle buildings and an odd junkyard of heavy equipment odds and ends that we must somehow turn into money. All the men on his crew are game to do anything I ask and generally smile at me shyly whenever I talk to them. One blushes continually yet never says a word, he only nods and does his work quietly.

They use Dad's dozers and loaders to clear the property and unearth things long buried. For the largest items, like tractor trailer trucks and old non-working dozer parts, a large scrap company comes and picks those up with special equipment that looks like giant dinosaurs with jaws like claws. In one giant claw they pick up an entire truck or car and put it on a tractor trailer to haul it away. The hauling trucks line up alongside the road to the house waiting their turn to be loaded. Once loaded they take the broken-down equipment away to the scrapyard where it is weighed and sold, and the money put in Dad's bank account. Fortunately, the scrapyard is only about 6 miles away. The scrapper pays us by the pound. Different metal. Different price. Copper wire brings the most.

We discover the copper is highly coveted by thieves in the area. We are hit several times. One weekend, these garbage pirates decide it is too much trouble to pull off the rubber coating on the wire, so they pile a huge pyramid of it in a far corner of one field and light it on fire, thinking to burn the rubber coating off and then haul away just the wire that remains. The ground is dry, and the fire quickly spreads. Someone calls the fire department, and they extinguish the blaze, but not before a good section of ground is scorched and the neighborhood is filled with the caustic fumes. By the time I arrive, the thieves have disappeared with much of the wire still smoldering. They are never caught.

I'm beginning to understand why Dad complained so much about people stealing his stuff. Until then I thought he imagined most of it or he simply misplaced things a lot. I realize now theft in rural areas is common. Sometimes we forget that humans can behave like animals. Sometimes they rationalize their theft thinking they will only borrow something and then forget to return it. Others take because they think their victims have more than they need, and it won't be missed. Some are truly in need. Many enjoy the "high" from the "get-over" or "the take". The reasons are countless.

I recall Dad telling me the Bible story of Ruth gleaning in the fields of Boaz and think…maybe thieves are partially right.

Maybe the "theft" is the tax people who have property pay to those who do not. So, I post warning signs and file crime reports and lock up what I can of my father's belongings. And I pray. Every morning on the way to work I listen to Christian rock and pray for my family, myself, for the workers, for extended family, for Dad, that we will all survive this and succeed in our mission; and that no one will get hurt. We work as quickly as we can to minimize financial loss and try to avoid on-the-job injuries.

One evening when my husband is in town and we are eating at a Waffle House I am so tired I put my head down on the table. For a minute I cry, overcome with exhaustion.

"You know you don't have to do this. We could tell the judge you can't do it and pack up and go home right now," he says.

I think about this for a moment with my forehead pressed against the cool Formica tabletop. I can smell the waffles cooking and the bacon. Smells of home, and yet not. I can also smell my sweat, and I can feel the dirt in my hair from working all day at the cleanup. No, I think. No. I'm not a quitter.

"No," I say aloud. I lift my head. I brush the tears back, then I stare into his cool blue eyes. "No, I won't quit. I'm not a coward. Dad deserves better than a quitter. He is no quitter. And I am not going to let a few unscrupulous, mean people scare me out of doing what I know I need to do. He deserves my best effort. My family deserves my best. They deserve for me to do a good job and make sure that what we sell provides for Dad, if possible, and then after he's gone that what's left is equally distributed to remaining family. No, I can't quit…even if it kills me. I won't quit!"

He looks at me for a moment, takes my hand in his and kisses it. I feel that priceless connection that makes us—we. His faith in me sustains and encourages me.

And then…I feel better. And we eat our cheese and eggs for dinner and go back to the apartment and fall into bed exhausted.

I never manage to catch anyone in the actual act of stealing, though some neighbors do see them and tell me about it. We do catch some people selling things for scrap that do not belong to them. The scrapyard has it on film, but we decide not to prosecute those people. It simply is not worth the time, cost, effort and bad will it will cause. Really, in the end, there is little we can do except try to get the cleanup finished as soon as possible. Eventually, I do learn the names of a few of the thieves. I don't stop the rampant theft entirely, but I do slow the losses. Sometimes human law can make things right. Sometimes only God can make things right. As I work, I come to realize that God has a big job separating the guilty from the innocent, and I can't be second-guessing the way he works when it comes to thieves and their reckoning. All I can do is my best to not expose weak souls to temptation if I can avoid it.

As weather cools, we learn to feed and operate the giant, wood-burning, tank heater in the shop to keep us warm. Though my thumb has recovered nicely from thumb joint reconstruction I had shortly before I became conservator, I am now having serious back problems. The problems are significant enough that I'm having trouble lifting my right foot, and hot pain shoots down the front of my shin when I walk.

Every day I work from daylight until dark. I limp to my vehicle and drive to Autumn Manor to visit Dad. Sometimes I have dinner with him. Sometimes I eat nothing and simply go back to the apartment and drink my dinner while soaking in the bathtub. I've lost 20 pounds since the cleanup started, yet my face is swollen from the cortisone the doctors give me for my back pain.

When I arrive home at the apartment I undress under a towel at the door before I go inside because my clothes are so dirty. Mexicans watch me do this from the other end of the outside hallway and mutter *"chica loco"* but they don't come near because they see the pistol at my side.

As soon as I am inside the apartment, I chunk my clothes in the washing machine, pour myself a giant glass of wine, and sit at my desk in my underwear for a few hours to do computer work related to project tracking and management. I track our financial activities on spread sheets and handle other work related to our own personal business by remoting in on my computer in Texas from my laptop in Tennessee. That business goes on largely without me for now, thanks to my husband. He has shouldered as many responsibilities as he can to keep our business afloat. Often this means he must stay in Texas while I remain in Tennessee.

Hock tells me sometimes when he's in Texas working late at night he will look up and he can see what I am doing on my computer in Tennessee, displayed on the desktop computer sitting on the desk next to his. He says it feels like my ghost is sitting next to him in that room more than 700 miles away. It is an eerie and sad feeling for him. He travels nearly every weekend to teach. He joins me in Tennessee when he can.

On one of my trips home to Texas for a few days I notice Opal, our cat, is losing weight. She remains in Texas with Hock who must be there to work and to see about selling our house; and when he is not there a friend looks in on her. While home, I take her to the vet, and he tells me she is in kidney failure. I don't want to put her to sleep. She isn't quite bad enough yet for that. I've had her nearly 18 years, and at this point she is my longest lasting relationship! I love her like my child.

So, the vet loads me up with cans of special diet foods, fluids to inject under her skin, and kitty Valium, and I take her and all her gear back to Tennessee with me. We fly this time. In the airport waiting for the plane, I take her out of her carrier and place her on my lap to watch the people go by. Some stop and comment on how pretty she is, a small tri-color calico with lots of confidence but weighing less than 7 pounds. She doesn't look sick, only thin. She is calm because she is with me.

Back in Tennessee I take her everywhere with me that I can. She is, after all, a Tennessee cat since I got her from my parents 18 years ago. I believe Tennessee smells like home to her. She adapts well to the small apartment. All it seems to take to make her feel at home are her food bowls, litter box, and bedding…and me. She is wonderful company. The thought of losing her breaks my heart. At night, I give her a kitty Valium, and I take one too as I settle back into a bathtub of hot water with my glass of wine. I know it's wrong to do this, but in the total scheme of things I consider it a minor sin and one hopefully God will forgive.

As I sip the wine, she walks the side of the bathtub and watches my hair float. A habit of hers. I listen to myself breathe in…out…in…out and watch her watch me. (Just breathe, I tell myself. Breathe.) Opal purrs, in and out in time to my own breath. She studies her own reflection in the water and pats at herself. I relax. I pray. Somehow together we've made it through another day.

Finally, I crawl out, dry off, braid my hair, and together we crawl into bed underneath one of Mom's old comforters lying on well-worn sheets I carried to the apartment from the house. I lay there and think about Texas, my kids, grandkids, husband. I miss them. Then Opal curls up on the pillow next to my head and we drift off into sleep in a tiny apartment nestled among Bradford pear trees in a small town in Tennessee.

Walking into Dad's house the next morning I am intensely aware that he is no longer there. Each morning when I walk in, I remember a hundred different scenarios I've walked in on before… some not so long ago. This particular morning, I remember a visit where Dad greeted me at the door and declared "I've been robbed!" His voice sounded hoarse. He pointed to deep gouge marks on the doorframe that lead to the garage attached to the house.

I look there today and can still see the marks. I run my fingers along them and remember.

* * *

2004
"Looks like someone forced the door with a claw hammer or a crowbar," I said. I touched the deep grooves with my fingertips and then turned the knob to test it. It feels fragile in my hand, as if someone's broken the inner workings.

"Are you missing anything?"

"I think a checkbook. And some cash I kept in the coffee can is gone." He lifted the dirty ball cap and scratched his head in wonder.

"Dad, we need to call the bank and flag the account for those checks; do you know the numbers?"

"Honey, I don't even know the bank." He shook his head.

"Dad, who's been here lately?"

"What do you mean, who's been here? The usual, friends, family—you!" He looked at me accusing.

I tucked my chin back in surprise, "Don't look at me, I have a key. I don't need to pry your door open!" I pulled the key out of the flap of my purse and showed it to him.

"What about those guys you get from the employment office—the ones on parole? Any of them been hanging around here lately?"

"A few weeks ago, I hired one to wash the windows and rake leaves; but he was a good man, just down on his luck. He wouldn't do this."

A shiver worked its way down my spine. I'd seen some of the people Dad liked to bring home because they are down on their luck. "Did you pay him?"

"Yes, I paid him. I paid him what he was worth—which wasn't much." He laughed a dry laugh that ended in a hacking cough. He took out an ancient, striped handkerchief and wiped his mouth and nose. He blew his nose into the handkerchief with the efficiency only 80 years of experience can perfect, working his calloused fingers up and down like he was playing a clarinet.

"People nowadays, have no idea how hard money is to come by," he continued. "They want 15 or 20 dollars an hour. I remember Mom and Dad paying men 25-cents a day to haul hay—that, and Mom cooked them lunch, and that was plenty."

"Most likely the guy came back to get what he thought you owed him. Dad, you've had four robberies in five years. When are you going to stop hiring convicts to work for you?"

He didn't answer. Instead, he ripped open his cell phone bill using the sharp blade of his pocketknife with surgical precision. He took the bill out of the envelope and spread it on the desk to read, adjusting his glasses better to see around the paint spots and speckles on the lenses where welding sparks have left their mark.

He made a low whistling noise between his teeth. "Do you know anybody in the Bahamas?" he asked.

"No. Do you?"

"No. But my cell phone has five hundred plus dollars in charges for calls to someone in the Bahamas."

"Where's your cell phone?"

"I haven't seen it in a couple of weeks. Guess I lost it. It's a piece of junk anyway. Those devils, they just sell you a worthless piece of plastic with an antenna and take your money. I can't even hear it ring, anyway. Now how am I supposed to use a phone like that, I ask you?" He glared at me, waiting for enlightenment.

* * *

2006

Back in the present, I think, one thing is for sure, there will be no more conversations like that with Dad. At least not at his house. He's in a safe place being cared for by professionals now. My sister and I both check on him regularly. He is "adjusting". I pause and look at those grooves on the door one more time.

Then I pass through the interior garage door and into the house where the workmen are waiting to discuss our goals for the day. As we have our morning meeting, I wonder if these guys are stealing from Dad? And looking at those grooves I begin to understand a bit more every day why Dad was as paranoid as he was. It's not paranoia if it's really happening, right? Or is it?

My mind flashed back to a story that happened when I was a child before Dad took us to collect nails on the highway. A memory about how Dad bought the powerful Ford truck that landed us out on that highway in the middle of the night.

* * *

1968

"If I catch the no-good rascal who stole my skill saws, he'll wish he was dead!" Dad shouted.

"Louis!" Mom scolded. Her piercing voice made me jump. She reached over and clapped her white, Sunday-gloved hands over my 10-year-old ears. I tried to pry her hands away, but she resisted with fingers strong as steel bands from weeding, pot scrubbing and hanging out laundry. Through the soft, white cotton I heard her whisper between clenched teeth, "Louis! Don't swear in front of the children. It's Sunday. Easter Sunday at that!"

We were on our way home from church, but Dad wanted to stop by the shop to check on things so there we went. Mom and I were sitting in the car in front of the large shop with the doors open to keep the car cool while Dad and Franky walked around to make sure everything was in order.

When they came back, Dad stood outside the car and ignored her, his face red. His dark brown eyes looked black and sparkled with anger. When they settled on me, they made me shiver. Mom said he got that look from his mother whose maiden name was "Looney".

"Gives me the shivers, I tell you," Mom told me once. "There's something to last names. Mr. Shoemaker's great-grandfather likely made shoes. Mr. Fillpot's ancestors likely made pots."

Made me wonder if Dad's mother's family name, Looney, came about in the same way. "Loons?" Did they live near a lake with loons, or did they just behave like loons! How much Looney blood ran through my veins? I wondered. Would I eventually start looking at people like a "Looney Tunes" character and make them shiver too?

As I watched, Dad picked up the biggest rock he could find from the gravel driveway in front of his shop. He weighed it in his hand, then hauled back and threw it as far as he could toward the old, gray, log house nearby where Mom lived before, she married him. The house stood next door to what we call Dad's new shop, about a quarter of a mile away from our own house, but still within sight. The old log cabin naturally leaned toward the south pasture, likely pushed that direction from long years of wind and rain. It looked like what it was, a deserted pile of horizontal logs standing precariously on an island of overgrown weeds surrounded by a bed of ancient, yellow daffodils and giant oak trees. On the south side there were also some very badly broken-down apple trees and an outhouse.

Through Mom's gloves I heard a windowpane break. Goose bumps duck-walked from my wrist up to my elbows. Dad seemed bent on destroying any sign that Mom's family had once owned the property we now lived on. I'd heard that people often married to expand family holdings. Mom's family had bought property down and across the road about a mile from Dad's people. Both lived about a 5 mile walk from town. It took a little over an hour to walk it or 15 minutes to drive it. Mom said Dad proposed to her after he found out his old girlfriend, whose property adjoined his along the backside, stuffed her bra with socks to impress him. How he found out remained a mystery to me as did the reason for it. I asked, but Mom only pressed her lips together in that firm-line-way she had and refused to say any more about it. Apparently desire to own more property had its limits and accepting a bra-stuffing, flat-chested woman as a bride was one of them.

Mom sighed and dropped her hands from around my ears to her sides. She didn't say anything about the attack on her old home place. She'd told me often enough that fussing didn't do any good. Long ago Dad had made her old home place a storage pit for rough-sawed lumber, worn out woodworking tools and saws. For a while he had a tractor parked under the collapsing front porch roof of her old home. He'd shoved lumber into windows until it completely filled all the bedrooms, "to keep it dry." I knew Mom hated seeing her former home destroyed like that, it was the final place she lived with both her parents, the last place she and her siblings lived when they were still all together. She cared for her father in that very house for many years after his stroke until he died. Once she told me that the night her Dad died, she'd stood under the 100-year-old oak trees next to the well and screamed and screamed at God asking him why. She never mentioned if she felt God answered, and I felt it inappropriate to ask. But the fact that God took my grandfather away before I had a chance to meet him made me wonder about God. How could he hurt my Mom and her sisters like that? My grandmother? I gave God the benefit of the doubt, for now. But it was one of the first questions I intended to ask him when I saw him.

"We didn't have much, but we had love," she always said with a faraway soft look in her eyes. "And we had each other."

"Kids! Let's go home, and let your father cool off," Mom called.

"Louis, before we go, I want to check the old apple tree to see if any apples are ready to pick before we go," Mom said. And she and Dad walked a little way around the house to check on the tree.

Franky came running from behind the shop where I knew he'd been secretly checking on Uncle Dave's tobacco crop that grew in the field behind it. He ran over to the car with a torn green leaf in his hand and held it out to me.

"As soon as it gets ripe, I'm going to pull some leaves, dry them and roll them into cigarettes and smoke them," he whispered in my ear. "I'll smoke a few and sell the others to the guys at school." He smiled happily, thinking of all the money he'd make.

"You better not, I whispered. God sees everything! The tobacco belongs to Uncle Dave. It's stealing if you take it and sell or smoke it! You'll go straight to hell for doing that even if Uncle Dave doesn't catch you!"

"No, I won't!" He hissed back. He kicked a hole in the dirt with the toe of his shoe and stuffed a piece of the leaf in his pocket. "He wouldn't care. And besides, he's my uncle. Taking something from family isn't real stealing," he said. "It's borrowing. They want you to take things. Makes them feel like they're needed."

"No, it doesn't! It's stealing, if you don't ask, even with relatives," I retorted. "Besides, it'll probably make you sick anyway."

"No, it won't. I've smoked lots of cigarettes!" Franky bragged.

"Only a puff or two off the butts people drop in the driveway. Phew! Haven't you seen those big fat worms that use the bathroom on the tobacco leaves—the ones Dad showed us? How can you even think about putting that mess in your mouth! Turns my stomach."

"I pick the worms off!" he muttered defensively. "There aren't that many!" I cast a meaningful glance in his direction as he crawled into the back seat of the car, just to let him know, I planned to tell Mom at the first opportunity.

Franky reached in his pocket. "Want a peppermint? I saved the ones they gave me in Sunday school last Sunday. I'll share if you want."

I accepted the ransom peppermint and popped it into my mouth still looking him in the eye, knowing eventually I'd tell, but I really didn't see anything wrong with the peppermint buying my brother a little time. It would be best if he'd come clean without my help, I reasoned. I settled back into the seat careful not to wrinkle my dress. Mom would want me to hang it up when I got home so it could be worn again before washing. Washing clothes wore them out, Mom said. So, we tried to get more than one wearing from every outfit if we could. Still, Mom insisted that we smell "fresh", so nothing went so long that it smelled. We were country but not smelly country.

Dad and Mom came back and got into the car, and Dad started the engine of the white '59 Oldsmobile that we drove to church twice on Sunday and once each Wednesday night for prayer meeting. It was the same car Mom drove to buy groceries on Friday's now that Dad would let her drive. Same car she washed in her bathing suit and me in mine. Mom closed the door on her side, and Dad hopped in on the driver's side and drove us the short distance home. It was the only car my parents bought new. Dad had purchased it when the old green Ford had blown a head gasket the day before they planned to drive to Michigan to visit Mom's sister who was in the hospital.

When Mom heard about her sister, she begged Dad to take her for a visit afraid she might die before they got there. When Dad said he had to work, the car wouldn't make the trip, and we couldn't go, she threw herself across the foot of the bed and howled like a grieving wolf mother. Dad stood for a long time with his hands in his pockets stirring his change and didn't say anything. After a while, when she hadn't stopped, he went outside and drove off in the old Dodge truck. That evening he brought back a brand-new car so we could make the trip. After that, when Dad grouched at Mom, I'd think about what he did and considered that maybe he really did love her, underneath it all. That, or he couldn't stand to hear crying anymore and just caved in for once.

Off and on, Dad had trouble with vandals at the shop. In the last few months his shop had been burglarized several times by what he thought were local teen boys. Dad thought the Taylor boys were behind it all. Their parents owned a sawmill several miles away, and everyone said they were a wild bunch. Each time Dad claimed they got away with hundreds of dollars of tools, equipment, truck batteries and sometimes even tires and radios out of the trucks. What they didn't steal, they tended to trash. This time, just for sport it seemed, they'd busted out the windshield on one of Dad's newer trucks. A 1966 2-ton Ford. This really ticked Dad off. He considered that truck a real find. When it was almost new someone had accidentally driven it off a cliff. Dad quickly snapped it up at auction and brought it home.

"I can fix that good as new," he said. And he did.

The broken windshield really bothered him the most. He'd just put a brand new one in. The old one had been totally crunched out from the sudden impact of a 20-foot drop straight down a bluff. We never heard for certain what happened to the driver. Whether or not he died or was just really messed up. Franky and I assumed the driver had gone to live with Jesus after we found a huge slab of hair with the scalp still attached to it under the dashboard behind the brake pedal. I was pretty sure no one could live with that much scalp missing. It looked all dried out and stuck together with what Franky said was probably blood. It reminded me of our music teacher's toupee and smelled sickly sweet. Franky threw it at the dog after pushing it around with a stick on the ground for a while. The dog snapped it up, trotted off with it, and we never saw it again.

We didn't like going to the shop after dark once Dad bought the truck. We thought the dead driver's spirit might hang around somewhere waiting to get us or, at the very least, scare the living daylights out of us for playing with his hair with a stick. But during the day, when the sun was shining, we figured we were safe enough. Franky said he read in a book somewhere that ghosts couldn't come out in the daylight. Since I figured he was older and wiser, sometimes, I took his word for it. Sometimes, but not always. For instance, I knew tobacco was disgusting. He didn't.

The truck was a lovely sky blue. While Dad worked on it, I'd sit in the driver's seat and pretend to drive. It was the only truck Dad had with upholstery still covering the seat springs. —That is until the thieves sliced the seats and pulled the stuffing out. That was just mean, Dad said. No wonder he got mad.

That night, Dad came home depressed from his final shop check. "This time they've taken all the radios out of all the trucks. I don't have much, but I sure did like having a working radio. But now I guess I'll have to do without that too. They stole most of my good Stanley tools, and even took the brand-new set of tires I put on the pickup only last week. Hundreds of dollars' worth of building supplies are gone too."

"How did they get in?" Mom asked. We were sitting in the den on the brown faux-leather sectional sofa Mom liked so much because she could wash it with a damp cloth, and it never tore and wore like "pig-iron". Dad sat in his green cloth recliner, in front of the stacked-stone fireplace, the corners of his mouth turned down, his lips white the way they got when Mom said his blood sugar was low. Mom had dished us all up a piece of pineapple upside-down cake on pretty Churchill Willow Blue dinnerware that she saved for special occasions—and sometimes Sunday nights, if she felt like washing them after.

"The thieves broke a window in the door. I patched it up with plywood, but I'm going to need a new door, one without a window. That will cost a good 20 dollars, money I don't have!"

"Do you think they'll come back?" Franky asked.

"I'm pretty sure they will. Once they find a place to pick over, they usually come back until they have everything worth having. Next time, they will likely get the welder."

Dad loved his welder. It allowed him to make all kinds of parts for his equipment that would otherwise cost him an arm and a leg.

"Yes, they saw the welder for sure. Probably didn't have the time or truck big enough to take it; but they'll be back. Something like this can put me completely out of business," Dad scowled. "Tools cost money. So do batteries. I can't afford to supply the whole neighborhood."

"What are you going to do, Dad?" Franky asked.

"I'll have to file a police report." Dad shook his head tossed his hat on the coffee table and went off to take a bath before bed. "And I'm going to concrete a great big ring into the floor of the shop and chain the welder to it so they will be less likely to take it," he said, his mouth set with determination.

The next day detectives from the sheriff's office came out to fingerprint the truck. They dusted it all over with black powder and found lots of fingerprints, even some of mine, which were easy to make out because they were smaller than all the rest. I wondered if my fingerprints were now on record. If I committed a crime when I grew up, would they be able to trace it back to me? What if someone else's fingerprints matched mine? Would they come and get me for a crime I didn't even do? I pictured myself falsely accused, standing trial—perhaps receiving a death sentence, oh so young, for something I didn't even know about. I imagined myself begging for mercy before a jury filled with people who had angry, wrinkled, uncaring faces. My knees wobbled at the thought. When the detective wasn't looking, I took my finger and smeared over all the small fingerprints so they wouldn't make good copies; then I washed my hands in the rain barrel beside the shop, quick before anyone caught me.

We didn't hear back from the detective for several weeks. And when he did get back to Dad, he said none of the prints matched any they had on file. I felt greatly relieved that mine didn't match anyone else's and started to sleep better again at night. However, it didn't help Dad any to know that whoever was robbing him wasn't a known criminal.

"I asked them to patrol the shop on their regular route, but they wouldn't do it," Dad said. "Our tax dollars at work! Where's the law when you really need them? I tell you!" He spat at a rock on the ground in disgust.

For weeks, Dad fretted about his tools. He installed chains around the bay doors at the back of the shop. He boarded up the windows in areas that you couldn't see from the road. He chained the welder to the floor. Each night after dinner he'd go back to the shop and sit inside in a straight chair with his shotgun laying across his lap waiting for someone to break in. He even bought a Doberman pinscher and kept her inside the shop at night. She had a dark red coat and pointy ears that made her look like Satan. Her long, lean body ended in a fiercely bobbed tail. However, as I got to know her, I realized she was really a pussycat in a dog suit—at least most of the time and especially with me. When I called, she'd bound up to me and would lick my hand. Probably she wasn't much of a crime deterrent. In fact, she was lonely at the shop and so friendly to anyone who came to visit, that I decided to call her Rose. She was so sweet and loving she greeted you as if she were giving you a bouquet of flowers.

Franky didn't like the dog's new name. "We need to call her Spike or Killer so she knows her job." He tossed a leftover pork rib from dinner at Rose one evening. She jumped amazingly high in the air and caught it mid-air then settled down on her stomach, bone between front paws and began to chew the meat off.

"We need to feed her gunpowder. That would make her mean," Franky told me. He was cutting open shotgun shells to get the gunpowder to add to her regular food. Whenever he turned away, I took the opportunity to throw bits of it away.

"Darn, it takes a long time to get this stuff out, and it doesn't amount to nothing," he looked at the small pile in a cup he'd been collecting, and I'd been dumping into the trash when he wasn't looking. Finally, he gave up in disgust. Rose continued to eat her Gravy Train dog food and table snacks with relish, *sans* gunpowder.

Sometimes Dad took Franky with him to the shop in the evenings, and they waited together. While they waited Rose prowled around trying to flush out some of the stray cats that lived there to keep mice away. She'd whine softly, scratch at a box, and Dad would say, "Shush Rose. You'll scare the burglars."

This completely puzzled me. Wasn't that what she was supposed to do?

Rose would lie down under the table-saw and lick the dust off her feet. Clearly, she wondered what all the fuss was about and why we kept her locked up in the shop all the time.

Franky had his .22 rifle.

"Can I shoot them if they try to break in?" he asked Dad.

"No, let me shoot them. You fire over their head to scare them," Dad told him.

"Shooting someone at your age could ruin your life."

He didn't say what would happen to him if he shot someone. Did you have to be 21 to shoot someone?

Shop sitting went on for a couple of weeks. Finally, Dad got tired of sitting in a chair after a hard day's work. "What we need is a crow's nest," he declared one evening. He leaned back in his easy chair and pulled off his work boots so he could go and take his bath before dinner.

"What do you mean, a crow's nest?"

"We'll build a kind of tree house in the top of the shop. With a floor and a peephole and a place to stick the guns out and shoot someone coming up from the front. We can sleep up there at night. And when we hear something, we'll grab our guns and shoot the sorry no good scoundrels!"

"Louis, watch your language in front of the children," Mom shouted from the kitchen where she worked, cutting biscuits with a cutter made from the sauce can out of a Chef Boyardee pizza kit.

"I apologize, honey."

"A crow's nest! That sounds like a great idea! Let's do it!" Franky said.

That Saturday, Franky and Dad built a big, nice crow's nest in the corner of the shop. The ceiling was about 20 feet from the floor so Dad could store large equipment, lumber, pipe and other things in shelves along the sides. They picked the northeastern-most corner and knocked together a scaffold to climb up to the ceiling.

By the end of the day, they finished the crow's nest, complete with retractable ladder. It looked just like Dad described. A mini fort of wood, but it blended in with the roof until you really could not tell exactly what it was. Dad had cleverly sawed out two 12-inch sections of wood in the exterior wall. He'd attached these sections to hinges on the inside so they would fold out and allow Dad and Franky to stick guns through the holes and fire at would-be robbers at the front of the shop outside.

Unlike the tin sides, the front of the building was horizontal overlapped boarding at the top, brick at the bottom, so you really could not see the hinged peep hole up toward the top from the outside. Personally, I wondered what would happen if the criminals decided to fire back. If so, my brother and father would have nowhere to go, and I was unsure if guns would penetrate the overlapped siding on the front. I suspected they would, but Dad had spent so much time building his crow's nest and was so proud of it, I felt it best not to bring it up. They did have enough room in the crow's nest for two sleeping bags, and even a small Coleman stove to keep them warm in winter. It really looked very comfy.

"So, this is what it's come to," Mom said, surveying their work one day, her arms folded over her chest. "You are crazy, you know that!"

"Crazy, like a fox." Dad grinned.

As I looked at it, I just kept hoping Franky and Dad were good enough shots that no one would have the chance to fire back.

That night Dad and Franky moved into the crow's nest. From such height, they could survey nearly the entire shop, which was piled full of all kinds of junk and supplies. Many piles were stacked so precariously that a good sneeze might send it all tumbling. If one pile fell, then others could potentially domino. Dad seldom threw anything away. He kept every old tire he'd ever worn out. The dust that accumulated on all the junk generally set me into a sneezing fit whenever I walked into the shop.

Dad and Franky stayed, every night for two weeks. I noticed Dad looked bent over in the mornings when he came home for breakfast.

"Anything happen last night?" Mom would ask.

"Not a thing. Sorry scoundrels!" Dad said.

"Louis!"

"Dad, if nothing's happening, then can I sleep in the crow's nest one night?" I asked.

"Might as well, if it's okay with your Mom. Doesn't look like it's good for much else other than a hideout for you kids to play in."

I looked at Mom, questioning?

"If your Dad stays with you, then it's okay with me."

"Yea!"

That night, I packed up my favorite quilt and pajamas and went with Dad and Franky to spend the night in the crow's nest. Gingerly, I climbed the ladder to their hiding place. I moved over their sleeping bags and found enough room to put mine in alongside. I placed my flashlight under my pillow. I brought it so I could read a book until I got sleepy. Soon Dad and Franky joined me.

"How much longer are we going to do this, Dad?" Franky asked. "My back feels out of whack."

Dad scratched his beard stubble. "Don't know. Maybe the robbers got everything they wanted the first time. No point in us killing ourselves trying to catch them if they aren't coming back."

"What happens if they come tonight, Dad? How will you see them in the dark to shoot them?"

"Your ol' Dad's smart," Dad said with a smile. "I wired a light switch up here so I can turn on the flood lights real quick outside and inside to catch them in the act. It will be like shooting fish in a bucket," he sighed with a smile. "The light will blind them, and before they know what's hit them, I'll fill their sorry hind-ends with buckshot."

"Yeah! They're sure going to be sorry. I bet they won't be able to sit down for a week!" I echoed Dad's tone. But then I felt worried when I thought maybe the light might blind Dad too.

The two of them settled into their sleeping bags and after about 5 minutes of reading we agreed it was time for sleep. I yawned as I peeked out into the shop. Below, I saw Rose pacing back and forth along the aisles of stored lumber and plumbing supplies. She went to the table-saw and turned several times underneath making a bed out of the sawdust. Then she lay down with a soft groan, put her head on her front paws, signed, and closed her eyes. Then she sneezed. She sighed again and closed her eyes once more.

I settled back into my sleeping bag.

"Turn your flashlights off, kids. Say your prayers—but to yourself," Dad mumbled.

In the dark, the crow's nest felt cramped. Through his sleeping bag, Franky's knees poked me in the back. I tried to adjust my position to ease some of the pressure. This must be the way puppies felt when they were inside their mother, I thought. We'd just had the class in school that explained how animals grew inside their mother; and I felt older and filled with knowledge on the subject.

My eyelids had just touched down with sleep when I heard light, little scuffling noises.

I held my breath.

There it was again.

I wondered if Dad and Franky heard it. I listened harder, but all I could hear was Dad's nose whistling as he slept. I strained more. There it was again.

Rose jumped to her feet and barked—one deep bark.

"What was that?" Franky whispered.

"Probably a mouse," Dad mumbled.

"I heard it," I told Dad. "It's not a mouse. It's outside. It sounded like someone at the window on the other side of the shop."

Dad sat straight up in his sleeping bag and hit his head on the low roof of the crow's nest. He swore under his breath. I heard him rub his head, then reach for his shotgun he'd put next to him, opposite of where I lay.

I crawled to the peephole and opened it to look out. Below us outside everything was cloaked in pitch black. No moonlight tonight to show us what lay below.

We took turns watching through the peephole until sunlight streaked the night sky with a pale haze of orange. Nothing happened. No one was there.

"Probably a raccoon," Franky said.

One Friday about two weeks after that last night in the crow's nest, Mom went to the grocery store.

"Isn't that Mrs. Taylor?" Mom asked me, as we were selecting bananas from a table in the center aisle.

I looked in the direction she glanced.

"I think so."

Mom placed her bananas in our shopping cart and wheeled the cart toward Mrs. Taylor.

"Evelyn? I thought that was you!" Mom's voice sounded warm, like Mrs. Taylor was her best friend. "Why, we haven't seen you at church in ages!" She grasped Mrs. Taylor's hand and shook it warmly. Mrs. Taylor's mouth dropped a little, and her gaze darted this way and that as if considering dashing down another aisle. A small woman with tightly permed, salt and pepper hair, Mrs. Taylor looked like a woman who'd worked so hard all her life that she no longer had time for warmth or humor.

"Well, hello, Mrs. Hinkle," she greeted Mom. "No, I haven't been to church in a while. Just never seem to get around to it. Between the dishes and the laundry, I hardly have time to read my Bible anymore."

"So how is Mr. Taylor?" Mom asked.

"Still drinking! Always drinking! He doesn't even go to the sawmill anymore, I'm afraid. Thank goodness I'm going to have a good garden this year, and the fruit trees look like they will bear, so at least we won't starve." Mrs. Taylor dropped her head as if searching the floor for something.

"Mrs. Hinkle," she confided. "Walt's not good at all. I've prayed and prayed, but I guess God's just not listening. I think it's his liver. He just doesn't look right to me. Probably the drinking..." Her voice trailed off.

Mom furrowed her brows in genuine concern. Everyone knew Walt Taylor was an alcoholic, but usually he managed to stagger down to the sawmill occasionally to cut enough lumber to sell to keep his family supplied with beans and rice.

"What about the boys, aren't they old enough to work?"

"Mrs. Hinkle, that's the blessing and the curse of it. Both William and Dale got their draft papers a few weeks ago. It's off to Vietnam with them as soon as they finish basic training. They left today. If they don't get killed, they've promised to send money home as soon as they can." Mrs. Taylor looked both worried and relieved. "I'm sure going to miss them though, those rascals!" Her voice cracked, and her face wrinkled up as she struggled not to cry showing an amazing number of rotten teeth.

"Well, I'm sure your prayers will protect them, and God will send them home safe," Mom offered. "Now I would love to see you in church some time, okay?"

Mrs. Taylor smiled a tiny smile. "Okay!"
"Good to see you!"
"And you!"

That night as Dad gathered his thermos of coffee, Mom said, "You don't need to go tonight."

"Sure, I need to go tonight. Why wouldn't I go tonight? We haven't caught the scoundrels yet!"

"You won't catch them!"

"Why not?" Dad asked in disbelief.

"I ran into Mrs. Taylor in the grocery store today. William and Dale were drafted a few weeks ago. They left for basic training this week, and after that they are headed for Vietnam. Most likely they robbed the shop to sell the stuff and give their mother money to tide her over until they get paid. Mr. Taylor's not able to work. His liver, she thinks."

"Oh!" Dad said. He sat his thermos down on the table with a tiny click.

No one said anything for a long time.

"I guess I need to go over and see if he needs help with the haying this year. Maybe with enough hay he can fatten up one of those skinny cows enough to have beef through the winter," Dad said. Then he poured the coffee from his thermos down the kitchen sink drain and sat down in his recliner to watch "Lawrence Welk".

Six months later, we heard William Taylor was killed in Vietnam, and Dale went missing in action shortly after. The water heater exploded in their house a year later killing both their parents and burned the house down, and the rest of their brothers and sisters were killed in the fireball caused by the explosion. I'd like to say the thieving stopped entirely. But over the years, off and on, Dad continued to have trouble with people stealing from his shop.

* * *

2006

I place my fingers in the grooves on the door one more time, and at that moment I understand the way Dad felt about the Taylors. Then my mind shifts to a time closer to the present yet still a memory that had to do with skill saws.

* * *

2004

Dad had decided to build a rent house to give him some extra income "for retirement". He set up his saws in the garage, ordered lumber and sawed out the two-by fours for walls and all the rafters himself. He nailed each section together in the driveway of his house. Then he loaded them onto the back of his truck with a loader, carried them over to the work site and set them up with a second loader. He'd put the wall in place, brace it with the loader, set up a ladder, climb up and nail the walls together. He finished in about a year. A nice couple bought it, and Dad self-financed the note for them and they made payments to him in a "toting the note" arrangement.

Right before he completed the house, Dad drove up one Sunday afternoon to find a long-lost relative stealing his tools and loading them into the back of a car from a bucket he'd found at the job site. Dad gave him the tools and the bucket and took him to lunch. After lunch Dad gave him all the money he had left in his wallet and told him he loved him and to "not steal anymore to just ask if he needed something."

Truly, the more things change, the more things stay the same.

* * *

2006
That night when I get home to the apartment, I can tell Opal is not doing well at all. She has not eaten well in weeks. I've exhausted all culinary options in the cat food aisle to tempt her to eat; but she just won't. She barely drinks any water. I've been giving her under-the-skin-fluids three times a week as the vet prescribed for months now, but I can tell she's really failing. The kitty Valium helps her with pain, but it constipates her, and increasingly she finds it difficult to go to the litter box. She prowls at night walking aimlessly around the walls of the strange apartment. Clearly, she misses home too. As I work on paperwork for an upcoming court hearing to account for Dad's assets and funds, I see her squat repeatedly, first here, then there, trying to go to the bathroom, but can't. I can tell she's in pain. I pick her up, unbutton my shirt and stuff her inside with only her head sticking out like an infant. Never a large cat, she has dropped to half her normal weight and now only weighs 4 pounds. She likes this position and soon goes to sleep inside my shirt next to my heart. I continue to work preparing for the court hearing until late in the night. When finished I take a sleeping Opal from my shirt and tuck her into bed beside me on a pillow. She feels like a kitten in my hands, she is so thin.

The next day is Saturday, Opal is again up and circling the rooms, squatting here and there as I fix breakfast. I try to tempt her to eat some egg, then some leftover chicken. She is not interested in food. She cannot get comfortable. My heart is breaking as I watch her angular figure stagger around the rooms. She knows me better than I know myself and I know her better than I know any human. And I can tell, it is time to say goodbye. I pull out my phone and search for a vet and make the appointment.

On the way to the vet, she sits beside me in the animal carrier. As I drive, I insert the index finger of my free hand into the cracks of the carrier and stroke her fur. She rubs her whiskers against my finger and purrs. She seems content to be in the carrier not questioning where we are going, only happy to be with me.

My resolve weakens; maybe it's not time yet? Maybe she's not as bad as I think? Then I think of her endless circling, endless straining and know, now is the time. Before she knows herself she is dying. I can at least save her that. And I must admit to myself as well, I'm no longer able to care for her. I leave her for endless hours in the apartment alone. There is no view of trees, birds or squirrels from the window to engage her; and I know I am leaving her alone with her suffering much of the time. This is no life for my dear companion and friend.

The vet is gentle. He gives her something to make her drowsy, and I hold her and stroke her face. She purrs.

The vet tells me it will not hurt, that I am welcome to hold and talk to her if I like and to call him when I am ready. I hold her and tell her how much I love her. I talk to her about all the adventures we've had and how grateful I am to have had her company for so many years. I tell her how glad I am my daughter picked her from all others in her litter when she was a tiny kitten, and how glad I am that she's always been our cat.

When we got her, I privately hoped for a beautiful black cat, an elegant cat not this waif of a tri-color calico, barnyard cat who always looked a little undernourished with odd patterns on her face. Now as I look at her, I realize, as I have for some time, that she is the perfect cat. She is beautiful. She has her own elegance, and she's pretty inside and out. Even now, sick and about to die, she is beautiful still.

She has loved me, and I have loved her. She has weathered most of my life's most critical events with me. She was with me when I left my second husband, and she was with me when my daughter left home. She was with me when I met Hock and when we got married. She has moved many, many times with me. She was there when my first grandchild was born and when my mother died. She has been with me for more than a third of my life. Now she's been with me for a good part of taking care of Dad and the cleanup of his estate; but I can tell, she does not have the strength to stay with me to the end.

I stroke her little head one more time and consider what a companion she has been, what a comfort, how much company and how much love she has offered. I place my fingers on her shoulder and can hear the soft motor inside her chest. She is relaxed, she seems happy. I whisper "I love you FOREVER" in her ear. Then I call the vet. He comes into the room. He strokes her fur, then he inserts a needle in an IV in her front leg. She goes even more limp than before. We wait three minutes. He takes his stethoscope and listens.

"She is gone," he says.

I pay the fee and go outside and sit in my car and cry with my head down on the steering wheel. Tears fall onto my jeans until my knees are soaked. Somehow, I get myself together enough to drive home where I fall onto the couch and cry even more. I cry until my eyes feel like sandpaper. I cry for Opal. I cry for my own sorry circumstances. I cry for the situation with Dad. I cry for loneliness of my husband and kids. I cry over this stinking apartment I'm living in which is really a pit compared to the house in Texas that I actually love. I cry because there is a mountain of impossible work and no end in sight, and I don't know what to do about any of it. I cry about the upcoming court hearing where my work will be examined and criticized from all sides from people who cannot or will not help.

I cry until my eyes are so swollen I can no longer see out of them. Then I cry more. When there is no moisture left in me and I know if I don't stop, I may lose my sanity, I make myself stop. My chest hurts from the effort. My very heart hurts. The apartment is more silent than I can ever remember any place on earth being. I think for a moment of the saying "silent as a tomb" and find that fitting. I wonder if the neighbors have heard my sobbing and consider what on earth they must think. I lay there for a while in the silence, alone, and then my thoughts wander to Dad. I think about him buying lunch for a thief and giving him spending money. I think he deserves a strong advocate, not one that cries and feels sorry for herself. With all his faults, Dad has always seen I had food and clothes and a warm place to sleep. I wonder sometimes how often he felt like crying and how often he actually did. He and my mother taught me about God, and hope, and gave me morals, and values, and I can't and won't abandon him now.

I feel gratitude in my heart for him as my father and for Opal my companion for 18 years; and I consider myself a fortunate woman to have had both. I have a husband who loves me, kids and grandkids who also love me. How blessed I've been to have the life that I have. Hard work will not kill me. Nor will critical voices second guessing me. I simply will not let them.

Finally, I get up, shower, put ice on my eyes hoping to shrink the swelling, and when I feel some relief in my heart from it all I go to bed. The pillows feel cool and soft on my face. Opal's pillow still has tiny little Opal hairs on it and is dented from where she spent her last night. I put my hand on the indentation and fall asleep. I dream that she is in the upper corner of the room looking down on me as I sleep. She asks me why I put her to sleep? She tells me she could have gone a little longer down the road with me. I feel guilty that I was not stronger. That I did not have enough faith in her and enough patience to see the situation through longer. I try to find the words to tell her, but she disappears into a red glow before I can say the words. The glow startles me, and I wake up. I look around the room and don't see her. I lay back in bed and look at the ceiling of my room through the slits in my swollen eyes and wonder if I will live to see the end of this job. Will I be able to take care of Dad until he no longer needs me? Or is it all really going to kill me. And I resolve that if that is the case, then I will simply die trying.

◇

"The thief comes only to steal and kill and destroy; I have come that they may have life, and have it to the full." (John 10:10)

◇

Fried Egg Sandwiches

In stainless steel skillet fry bacon until crisp.
Drain on dish lined with paper towels and place in microwave covered by a plate to keep warm.
Retain grease from bacon in skillet.
Break eggs into skillet on top of remaining grease.
Fry until done on one side. Add salt and pepper to taste.
Then flip and cook to desired level.
(Some like yolks runny, others like them hard. I like mine DONE.)
Butter bread (2 slices per sandwich) on one side, place on baking sheet, lined with foil buttered side up, and place in oven on broil for 3 minutes or until bread browns and butter melts.
Remove toasted bread from oven, add fried eggs, bacon, and a slice of American cheese singles. Some people like mayonnaise. I substitute vanilla yogurt for mayonnaise and heap it on thickly.
Eat promptly.

Chapter 12 – Betrayal

"You are trying to kill me! I'm taking that meat loaf to Dr. White. He will bear witness to what I'm have to live with, so help me God!" — Louis

2006
The wind in the driveway of Dad's house blows cool on my arms and floats my hair around my face until it's difficult to see. I take off my husband's Victoria, Australian police ball cap that they gave him when he trained police there, and I pull my hair into a ponytail. Then I put the cap back on, pulling the ponytail through the hole in the back to keep it out of my eyes. I slide into my rental truck to drive to Dad's shop to check on how the cleanup is progressing. Then I plan to go to town to run errands. I have on my heavy jeans, Dad's flannel shirt and black Roper work boots that have become my uniform over the last month. For four weeks now the crew and I have worked like people possessed, to clean up Dad's property in a race against time.

Huge semi-trucks rumble and groan past the house all day taking D-9s, old tandem trucks, mounds of scrap left from old buildings to the recycle center. So far, the scrapping fees have paid for the cleanup and more. But I can't expect my good fortune to hold out. We have scraped so much metal off Dad's property we've glutted the market in our area. If we haul continuously, they will give us the same price. But if we stop and start again, the price will drop.

When I get to the site, I see several men standing around a truck from the water company.

"What's up guys?" I ask getting out of my truck. Easy, the head equipment operator, smiles. He looks smaller on the ground than when he runs his giant machine with claws. The tractor has wheels as tall as a double-decker tour bus, and likely weighs more. With it he bounds around the property picking up entire dozers and setting them on flatbed trucks to be hauled away. He operates the giant claw machine like an extension of his hand, like a surgeon uses a scalpel.

"Well, Miss Jane," he says scratching his head. "Looks like we found the water tap." He points to where a guy wearing a utility company uniform squats. "Ran over it this morning. I called the utility company soon as it happened. This fella just came out to fix it."

"Are you Mr. Hinkle's daughter?" the man asks. "My name is William Jenkins." He stands and reaches to shake my hand. "I know your father real well. I used to work for him. He's a good man, your father. Works harder than anyone I know. I really respect that."

"Thanks, I'll tell him you said so."

"I need to go see him. Just haven't had time. How is he?"

"He's good. They take good care of him at Autumn Manor. He likes it now, but at first it was like trying to cage a lion."

The men laugh. "I hear you."

"I'll have this fixed in a minute and marked so your men can see it," William says.

"Appreciate that." I smile.

"You guys having a good day?" I ask the ground crew. There are three other men that make up the ground crew on this site. They nod, smile. I notice Harold, the foreman is absent. I wonder where he is, but don't ask. The others are a haggard lot, wearing old clothes, their hands rough, the knees of their jeans worn threadbare. They spend their days combing through dirt, mud and underbrush sorting the metal on the ground and loading it into loader buckets so it can be placed into huge open-topped tractor trailers for the trip to the recycle center. Looking around the property I see it now looks more like "War of the Worlds" or a nuclear attack zone than a shop and farmland. These days, that's progress.

William excuses himself and goes back to his work.

"Looks like you guys are working our plan."

"We hauled off 16 tons yesterday, Miss Jane," Raymond announces.

"That's great. How much longer do you think this will take?" I ask.

"Two weeks."

I laugh. Ever since we started, the answer has always been—two weeks.

"Miss Jane. Can I talk to you a minute in private?" Raymond asks.

"Sure." We move to the other side of the truck from the men.

Raymond clears his throat, "Remember last week you said that no one was to sell anything but you? That the court ordered you to be responsible?" He clears his throat, looks out over the pasture across from the shop.

"Yes. I've been telling you guys that every Monday when we have our meetings. Just so no one gets confused about that and so I can file accurate reports with the court."

"Well does that include that fella, that family friend of you all?" he asks.

"Yes, of course."

"Well, I hate to be the one to tell you this—but whenever you're gone, he hauls stuff out of here like mad. And when you were in Texas arranging things there, he made double loads. He hauls off the expensive stuff like aluminum and copper."

I feel a cold rush—the kind of rush you get when you stand up too quick.

"Are you sure?"

"Positive."

"Maybe he's just stacking it over at the house to keep it safe?"

"Maybe," Raymond shakes his head, "but I don't think so. You see, I was at the recycle center the other day to take some of my own stuff, and he was in line in front of me. He had doors that belonged to one of your dad's trucks—the one he had lettered for advertisement with his name on it—he was selling those. Your Dad's name, big as brass, painted on them."

"Sounds like a hard thing to make a mistake about," I say. I lean back against the side of my vehicle for support, cross my arms against the chill.

"No, Miss Jane. No mistake. Did he give you the money from the sale?" Raymond asks hopefully.

"No…not yet," I tell him gazing over at the log cabin near where we are talking. Behind the cabin I can still see the remains of the stone fence my grandfather built by stacking the stones out of the field behind the house as he prepared to plow it. Many stones. Many hours. How many hours did my family have invested in this property? I wondered. Many lifetimes. Now part of my lifetime is invested here too.

Raymond shakes his head. "I'd think he would have told you or given you the money by now if he planned to. I sure am sorry to have to be the one to tell you this."

"Well, that's okay. It's—" I search for the right word, "unfortunate," is the only word that comes to mind. "Raymond, it's okay. Thanks for letting me know." I say.

My head spins a little.

"Does anyone else know?"

Raymond shifts from one foot to the other, folds his arms, leans against his giant tractor, and looks out across the field with me. "I'd say so, Miss Jane. But maybe they think you have an arrangement and had it worked out. Him being a friend of the family and all."

"No arrangement," I tell Raymond. "Thanks for letting me know."

"Sorry I had to be the one." He waits a moment more, "Well, guess I better get started. This stuff ain't going to move itself. Have a good day."

"You too."

He climbs up on his mammoth piece of equipment and starts it up with a rumble.

I climb back into my truck and look out at the road. So much history here.

After Raymond goes back to work, I get out of the truck again and walk down the old road and up to the old family cabin. I can almost feel my Mom's arms embrace me as the wind stirs around me causing the leaves of the old oak to rustle. We used to take our walks and come here and pick honeysuckle from the bush to make flower arrangements. Sometimes we would pull off the base of the blossom and suck the nectar. I could still remember how it tasted.

What should I do? I wonder. What can I do? If I turn him in it's sure to cause problems in our family. If I don't, I'm legally liable for what he's taken.

During the War, Mom and Dad saw each other for the first time from this very spot near the oak tree. Mom and her sisters came home from church, dressed in cotton-print dresses, white gloves, and Sunday hats. Dad and his brother were cutting corn in the field across the road. She said the first time she saw him she knew he was the one. His wide smile, angular face and tanned muscles caught her attention immediately. Later, he won her heart. "He's all mine, girls," she told her sisters. "Hands off."

They dated for five years, writing long love letters to each other, and attending church nearly every service. They took piano and violin lessons from the same teacher. They dreamed of a Christian marriage and of raising Christian children who knew God.

His parents did not want them to marry. They thought Mom was too "citified" for Dad. They wanted him to marry a good "farm girl" who would help him in the fields. But Dad had different taste. He had good taste. So, they carried on a secret love affair by writing letters and meeting whenever they could, hiding their relationship from his parents. It took Dad a while to save money to marry, and he hoped he could win over his parents in time. But he never did. Eventually, they eloped.

Mom and her sisters had brought their aging parents to this rambling cabin to escape the city life. They thought the country life would do their father good. Papa Hickson had had several strokes and was dying of advanced heart disease. The grown kids pooled their money and bought the cabin and the 26 acres that now made up a subdivision my father developed and the property where his farm, house, and shop still stand. Shortly after they married Mom and Dad built a small house on the southeast side of the property that her parents planned to give her. Dad's family had more than 300 acres across from Mom's parents and down a side road. Land that was later divided between Dad and his brother and sister, largely farmland.

During her Dad's life, Mom's family set the example that if family all pulled together, they could move mountains. However, after his death the sisters sold their property, all except Mom, and they all moved away. Mama Hickson, my grandmother, would live with first one, then another, sometimes with us, for the rest of her life.

Over the years I poured over family pictures of Mama Hickson, and various family members standing in the yard of this same cabin under the same oak. Mom told me her mother boiled clothes in a pot under this very tree. The well is still here where they drew water. I've seen pictures of family gathered under this oak tree smiling with their arms wrapped around each other.

Mama Hickson, when she lived with us, would walk the road to the cabin and back to our house each evening. She would stand in front of it, as I stand now, her hands clasped behind her back, remembering. Rusty, our cocker spaniel, would walk behind her, then sit alongside her as she relived many memories looking at the cabin.

No matter how far I've wandered, this place has meant family and home to me. Despite all the chaos and individual shortcomings we all have, underneath it all, I felt loved here and I loved my family deeply despite everything that's happened.

During my life I've traveled the world. I've never lived in one spot, other than this farm, for more than a handful of years. My daughter has told me many times that home is where I am. But to me, home has always been here. Everything else was temporary. This place had always been, and I always thought it would always be—forever. But it's temporary as all things are.

As I've cleaned up Dad's property, I've often thought about what my daughter said. How fortunate I have been to have a physical place to call home as well as family there. She moved with me, so she has not known that feeling—much to my regret.

Nothing lasts forever, except love. Most people don't have a special place. I realize the days of this place are numbered. But I'd always thought the people that made up the family and our extended friends would go on even without the place. I have no choice about having to sell everything, but I want to keep the family together even if the place is gone. Having a friend of the family who is close to family members yet is taking advantage is creating a delicate issue to resolve and keep family intact. But resolve it I must. First, I must find out if what Raymond told me is true.

I drive into town to the recycle center and talk to the manager. He promises to check the videotape and let me know if he can confirm what Raymond told me. He tells me I must not wait; I must go to the police. I hesitate to do this because once the accusations become public, there is no turning back. Whether I am right or wrong, my relationship with this person, and perhaps affiliated family members by association, will be damaged perhaps beyond repair. I decide to sleep on it and see what the new day brings.

The next day the manager at the recycle center calls me.

"We have your man," he says. "You must call the police."

I can't speak for a moment. What do you say to news like that? Call the police on a friend of the family? Absently I say, "Thank you" and hang up the phone.

There is no more time. If I wait, I will have betrayed Dad's best interest, and the responsibility placed on me by the court. The family friend is stealing from Dad. I must protect Dad and the rest of the family. So, with the heaviest of hearts, I make the call and take the scrap weigh tickets and videotape to the sheriff's office and file a report.

Within a week I receive an email from an unknown email address. The message is clearly from the "friend of the family". It reads: "If you don't withdraw your complaint and stop the legal process, I'll find someone who will make you stop."

This person has had a colorful past that includes assault with a baseball bat.

He has dealt drugs in the past, and he has had dealers for friends. We all felt he'd left this dark life behind him, but now it's clear he has not. I think about the brave badger so long ago, with rich fur, sharp claws, and how the dogs attacked it, and how Dad shot it. I think about Dad now, his own worries about theft when I was growing up. I think about how sometimes he thought maybe his life was being threatened. I think about how I am firmly caught between honoring my promise to Dad and fear for my own safety now. And as I think, a story comes to mind from our past that reminds me how things can get completely out of control in our heads when we are tired, sick or stressed.

* * *

1969

One morning Franky and I were shaken from our beds by the sound of Dad priming his four-ton diesel, dump-truck engine with ether. The shotgun-like explosions caused smiles to spread across our faces like sunshine as we cried, "Daddy's home!" We jumped from our beds and ran outside across the gravel driveway on bare feet wearing our pajamas to offer him a hug.

"Stay back," he yelled, and motioned impatiently from his perch on top of the large front bumper. We both stopped short. He leaned into the motor at a precarious angle to pull the choke, gunning the engine into a regular stroke. Mother often told us ether was highly flammable and Dad took his life in his hands every time he did this. Like TV cartoons, I sometimes pictured Dad with his Acme truck, spraying ether into it until an explosion would launch him across the sky, arm and legs spread out like a starfish. However, no such thing happened on this clear crisp morning. Soon he had the engine running like a large kitten, and he hopped down from the bumper and walked right past us cleaning his hands on a cloth. We followed him in to breakfast.

Dad had been traveling a lot for jobs recently, sometimes gone for as long as weeks at times. When he was gone, we missed him. But now that he was back it felt like he'd never been gone. Each morning, as was his way, Dad started before daylight. First he'd feed and milk the cows. Then he'd load his equipment on one of the trucks and fuel it up. Mother would sometimes serve him breakfast before she woke us so he could get an early start. Other times, we'd have breakfast together.

On Mondays mother trussed up her apron a bit more tightly to cinch in her waist. Then she'd fluff the bow in back for added assurance. With special care, she applied Brick Red Cover Girl lipstick to her full, well-shaped lips in preparation to ask Dad for grocery money.

After pouring a second cup of steaming coffee for Dad, Mom would sit down at the breakfast table, shoulders back a notch to accentuate her curves and, crossing her hands, under her chin prettily, she'd smile and say, "Louis, I need grocery money for this week."

To which Dad would reply, "Well, sweetheart, what did you do with the money I gave you last week?" This would, of course, make her angry. But she would smile still wider flashing her white teeth. Her clear, blue eyes would turn arctic blue, and the battle of wits would begin.

For a while they would go back and forth in verbal swordplay—counter, parry, thrust, counter parry, thrust. Franky and I would cut glances at one another as we ate our eggs and toast and drank our milk, much like we watched a live game of tennis at the park. Why she needed the money, what she spent the money on last week, how poor he was and how little money there was to go round all were fair game for discussion. He would provide a full list of all the places the money needed to go. She would furnish him an equally long list of parallel necessities. The only thing they could agree on was how expensive everything was.

Most encounters ended with Dad offering to write her a check. When she refused—she always refused because about half the time they bounced and embarrassed her—a few more minutes of sparring would follow at which time he would finally open up a hugely-stuffed, very worn, dusty, brown wallet that crackled like an old dried-up onion. From it he would extract a few bills and toss them on the table in mock defeat. Good weeks, he tossed $35 dollars, bad weeks $25. He'd put on his cap, collect his thermos and walk out the door. When it slammed on his heels Mother would collect the bills from the table with shaky fingers, fold them double and hold them to her chest. Afterward, she'd sit for 10 minutes and sip her coffee and stare out the kitchen window at the squirrels playing in Aunt Gretta's orchard across the street. In his stormy wake, a blissful peace would descend over the house. Mother often said it was her favorite time of day.

Mom abandoned the idea of a joint checking account with Dad after several embarrassing bounced checks at Hills Grocery where she shopped each week. Dad never had time to balance the checkbook, so he kept three bank accounts instead. He'd write checks on one until they started to bounce. Then he'd let it sit and write on another until they started to bounce, "and on and on and on" Mom would say, rolling her eyes heavenward when she opened the bank statements when they arrived in the mail. It seemed no wonder that he never quite knew how much money he had.

With so many bank accounts, tax time always proved to be a complete nightmare. Dad had difficulty with the concept of filing, and really with all things abstract in concept. He was a man who liked to put his hands on things to figure them out. Working hands-on he was a genius. But in order to calculate anything he had to literally hold it in his hand. Had he not owned a business, perhaps this would not have been such a problem, merely leading to a life as an eccentric clutter bug. However, Dad owned a large business that involved lots of purchases and lots of people.

To calculate his taxes Dad would bring into the house several pieces of eight-by-10 plywood and place them across sawhorses spreading them down the entire length of our den and hallway and into the small kitchen. Then he would begin to sort the checks by expense type, date and vendor, and stack them in neat piles on the improvised plywood tables he'd constructed. This process would take at least six weeks since he only worked on it at night and weekends. The timetable also depended heavily on the back door remaining closed to avoid stray gusts of spring wind. Such a wind would, and often did, send a snowstorm of checks swirling across the kitchen where they would pile in snow-like drifts against the windows and at the foot of the stove. If that happened, we would all sigh knowing an additional six weeks of check sorting could well follow.

Mom usually avoided causing such a catastrophe by entering and leaving the house through the living room during tax season, which could stretch, from January to July if things went really bad. Franky and I were not always so mindful. Causing checks to fly across the house was a spanking offense for certain if we were caught. Dad would withdraw the homemade paddle from his desk with ceremony effectively designed to make us shiver and our knees to become disjointed. Dad would call the guilty party forward to his office behind folding doors located in the corner of the den, and there he would issue a terse and lengthy verbal warning with the paddle dangling conspicuously from his fingers. It was a foot long, made from the fallen limb of a steely-hard 200-year-old oak that grew right out of the grave of some French Canadian who remained in our town after the Civil War and was later buried in Hinkle cemetery beside Dad's family home. Sometimes I thought that paddle took on mean and bitter human facial characteristics in a manner indicative of how anxious it was to punish little children. Franky and I hated and feared it. At night we plotted how to make it disappear, but the opportunity had not yet presented itself.

The paddle had seven—I counted—seven roughly drilled holes in the center complete with dangling splinters that Dad had not sanded on purpose. He claimed the holes eliminated much of the wind resistance on the downward thrust allowing it to pick up double speed on the way to its intended target. For me, it was a terror to behold for it could meet out such pain that I cannot accurately describe it.

Dad would perform what he considered his duty as our father with set jaw and red face. Mother would beg him to mind his blood pressure and give us another chance. Then she'd rush around collecting the checks from their various hiding places. Each time she found one she tucked it behind her ear for safe keeping while she searched out the next. Months later we usually found a stray check in a flowerpot, or behind a chair. When that happened Mom disposed of them by striking a kitchen match and burning them over the sink then washing the ashes down the drain so no trace remained.

The banks didn't seem to hold Dad's inability to balance a checkbook against him. They loaned him money whenever he wanted, as long as he brought Mom in to co-sign the note. Mom, all dressed up in her heels and blue Sunday shirtwaist dress, made a fine impression on the bank officers. They took a long and lingering, mouth-watering, gaze at her and deduced that there must be more to Dad than met the eye for him to win the heart of one of the most attractive women in town.

That spring Dad came away with a check for the amount he requested made out to him alone, as he always specified. These checks were for investment, not for family expenses, he told us. The next day he purchased a piece of property that included a small lake east of town ripe for investment. He congratulated himself at dinner that night in front of all of us. Thank goodness he snapped it up before anyone else recognized its true value. The next morning he went whistling off to work.

That night when he came home, he was not whistling. The downside to gaining sole custody of thousands of dollars to do with what you will is the pressure to make it perform. That pressure over the next few weeks began to eat a hole in Dad's stomach. A few months into the loan repayment Dad started looking really pale. Mom told us Dad had confided to her that the property he bought was the old dumping ground for the town's shoe factory. They'd been dumping shoe sole trimmings and chemicals there for years.

One Saturday mother drove us out to the property to take a look for herself. Just as she had heard, blue, black and red shoe-sole trimmings spread for acres and acres across the landscape and choked the small lake into a multi-colored oily looking puddle. I racked my brain trying to think of a use for so many trimmings that would make us millionaires, but none came to mind. Apparently, Dad couldn't think of any either. He had intended to clear the material away by hauling it to the dump, but had not known how toxic it was. Newly passed environmental laws made it unacceptable to any dump. Dad feared all the money was lost because the lake and surrounding property were listed as an environmental hazard.

Over the next few weeks the pallor in Dad's face intensified until the skin around his mouth started to match the shade of his sky-blue pajamas. He lost weight and every week it seemed he needed to punch another hole in his belt to keep his pants up. At breakfast he'd complain of lack of sleep and tossing and turning all night. Worried, Mother fed him peppermint sticks at night after dinner, and in general fussed over him a lot.

"Louis do you feel, alright?" Mom would ask him.

To which he would respond with a complete list of every unfortunate event he'd encountered all day that would last through dinner and continue on in their bedroom in dark murmuring tones until long after I went to sleep at night. After several months of this, Dad grew weak and staggery and ghost-like in appearance. Frantic Mom might become a widow and heir to a mountain of debt, one afternoon she packed Dad in the white '59 Olds and hauled him off to see Dr. White, leaving my brother and me across the street with Aunt Gretta.

While Franky and I sat happily munching on tea cakes and sipping milk, in town Dr. White diagnosed Dad with bleeding ulcers. He admitted Dad to the hospital and gave him several pints of blood over the next 24 hours. Days later when Dad was feeling more himself, Dr. White dismissed him and sent him home with pills to take before each meal and instructions for him to "take it easy". He gave Mom a list of food preparation instructions, which Dad read out loud to us that night in place of our Bible story.

Over the next few weeks, we watched helplessly as normal concern for his diet turned into a full-blown obsession with Dad. Long past the IRS deadline, all check sorting had come to an abrupt halt. Mother threw a tablecloth over the plywood table's full of checks, and they started doing double duty as surfaces to sort clothes and stack books with no protest from Dad. Underneath, we suspected that checks drifted intermittently between piles unnoticed as Dad took up a new post hovering over simmering pots on the stove bird-dogging Mom's every culinary decision. In the evening he would come home early to watch her cook. He'd question her about how she planned to prepare the fish, the roast, the chicken. Suddenly, instead of fried chicken and mashed potatoes with butter we were eating boiled chicken, boiled potatoes and boiled squash—boiled everything—with no salt, no bacon, no butter, NO FLAVOR!

All the watching and second-guessing began to take its toll on Mom. Between having to weave her way around the saw horses and plywood during the day to do her work and dad bird-dogging her cooking in the evenings, mother began to forget to change her clothes some days and to brush her hair on others. In no time the back of her hair began to stick up like the backside of a turkey and dark circles formed under her eyes. For weeks she'd been unable to remember where she left her lipstick and no longer even seemed to care.

Arguments about food preparation lasted all evening with Mom saying, "Louis, I'm cooking, go sit in your chair and watch the news. Or, read the newspaper!"

And Dad saying, "It's my stomach, I have a right to know what you are putting in my food!"

"Louis, just go on!" she'd shake the cup towel at him to shoo him away. But he wouldn't go.

One day after lunch, mother apparently determined she'd had enough. She bathed, washed her hair and put on a clean dress and lipstick. Then she started dinner early. She prepared a nice meat loaf in the oven with real French fries to go with it. She fried them in Crisco on top of the stove and prepared steamed, fresh green beans. She hummed about happily to herself as she worked. The house began to smell almost normal. Then the phone rang and between answering it, and helping me find my lost crayons, she completely forgot about the meat loaf until circles of smoke came spiraling down the hallway and into my bedroom.

"Mother!" I called, "Meat loaf burning!"

Mother raced to the oven, threw open the door and, using a cup towel, removed the meat loaf from the oven. In her haste, the edge of the cup towel touched the burner on the stove and ignited.

"Mom!" I cried.

"Yes, I see it!" Mother cried, and set the meat loaf on the counter with a thud and proceeded to beat the flaming material out on the counter top, then tossed the smoldering mass into the sink and ran water on it to quench the flames.

At that moment, Dad walked through the door.

"That's it! I've had it! Louis! I can't live in a house full of plywood and saw horses and checks scattered everywhere eating only boiled meat and potatoes! Get those saw horses out of this house, or I'm going to my brother's house and taking the children until you do."

Dad tossed his notebook and cap in the corner of the hall with a thud, and went into the kitchen. For the next 30 minutes my parents argued.

"Is this what you fixed for dinner?" Dad asked picking up one end of the rapidly cooling, blackened meat loaf.

"That's it, and if you want something to eat, you'll eat it, Louis! I'm not fixing anything else, until you get this mess cleaned up."

"I can't eat it."

"There's nothing on the list that says everything has to be boiled, Louis. It's only a meat loaf."

"You are trying to kill me!"

"I'm not trying to kill you—yet! It was an accident!"

But Dad was no longer listening. With the bit between his teeth, he professed, "No man should have to live under these conditions!"

"No woman should have to live under these conditions!"

"You are trying to kill me! I'm taking that meat loaf to Dr. White. He will bear witness to what I'm have to live with, so help me God! It's no wonder my stomach's a mass of holes." Dad looked heavenward and cried, "Lord move upon the scene. No man should have to endure so much! Help me Lord!" he prayed, loudly.

His dramatics did not move Mom, even in light of potential public humiliation. "You will not take that meat loaf to Dr. White's! What will he think? What will everyone think! Louis, that's crazy!"

"I'm taking it, give it to me, woman! Get the behind me Satan!" he shoved her aside, scavenged the kitchen drawers until he found her new red and white checked oven mitts. More for effect than necessity now, he picked up the meat loaf and headed out the door with it clutched in mitted hands.

Mother sat down in a nearby kitchen chair and cried when she heard the truck engine start.

"Mother where did Dad go with the meat loaf?" I asked.

"He's taking it to Dr. White's to prove I'm trying to kill him!" Mother dabbed her eyes with the edge of her apron. Suddenly, she started to laugh and cry at the same time. Briefly, I wondered if she'd lost her mind, but her eyes still seemed wide and intelligent to me. I put my arms around her neck and gave her a hug. So did Franky. For a while the three of us sat together in a group hug. Then Franky and I started to laugh.

There was nothing else to do but laugh; so that's what we did. Mother laughed too and hugged us both. I imagined Dad rumbling up to Dr. White's office in his battered and dusty dump truck, still wearing the checked oven mitts, the smoldering, blackened meat loaf in the passenger seat. What would Dr. White do, we wondered?

"I guess I better call Jan and warn her that he's coming," Mom said, dabbing her eyes. Jan was Dr. White's receptionist. Mom had known her for years; she lived just down the road from us, and they were good friends.

She dialed the phone. "Jan. I've thought I ought to prepare you. Louis is on his way in..."

Jan told Mom later that Dad stormed into the small waiting room of the doctor's office crowded with patients. Still dressed in his dirt-covered uniform and large muddy boots and cap that said Hinkle Construction, Dad carried the meat loaf clutched in front of him. The red and white checked oven mitts seemed seriously at odds with the rest of his outfit. Everyone in the room turned to see Mr. Hinkle. The only sound came from the light classical jazz music piped in through the sound system as he walked across the waiting room. Suddenly, everyone seemed to be holding their breath. He held the meat loaf in front of him like an priceless human relic and approached the glass-partitioned counter.

Jan didn't bat a single, dark, thick, false eyelash, "Why, Mr. Hinkle. It's good to see you! Did you bring us lunch?" She nodded her head. Her dark, shortly bobbed hair glistened under the lights as did her white nurse's uniform. Any other day her attractive smile would have coaxed an equally pleasant one from Dad. But not today.

Dad's face turned the color of a ripe beet. "I want to see Dr. White. Right now!"

"He's with patients now, Mr. Hinkle. But if you'd like to sit a moment?" Dad had no intention of sitting in the waiting room clutching the meat loaf with oven mitts for an hour while Dr. White saw everyone ahead of him. A sixth sense likely told him Mom had warned Jan.

"I need to see him now." He headed toward the door that led to the treatment rooms. Jan jumped from her chair and headed around the counter through the back doorway to the hall, intending to intercept him.

"Mr. Hinkle, I'm afraid you can't see him right now, he's with patients." She motioned out of Dad's sight and hearing for one of the nurses to get Dr. White. When Dad opened the door between the waiting room and the hall for the treatment rooms, Jan was waiting. She took his arm, "Mr. Hinkle, I'm afraid, I must insist. You will have to take a seat and wait your turn."

Shockingly enough, Dad began to struggle with her and shout! "I'll see him now, I tell you! My wife is trying to kill me. I've brought the evidence!" At the sound of his shouts, treatment room doors began to open. Patients and nurses stuck their heads out to see what the fuss was about. Jan tugged Dad's arm and tried to gently herd him back into the waiting room, but he would not have it.

"I want to see Dr. White. Now!"

Outside in the waiting room heads began to turn, one to the other. People began to whisper.

"Who is that crazy man with the meat loaf?"
"Was that Mr. Hinkle, from the church?"
"I think it was Mr. Hinkle."
"Do you think he's dangerous?"
"I do think he's dangerous!"
"Surely not!"
Pause....
Looks....

One lady took her young son's hand and dragged him out the front door.

"Mr. Hinkle!" Dr. White came out of one of the treatment rooms with a smile on his face, as if every day he had an angry patient standing in his hallway holding a burnt meat loaf with oven mitts. Taller and more physically fit than Dad, Dr. White put his arm around Dad's shoulders and steered him into an empty treatment room. He motioned for everyone to go back to what they were doing.

Jan, said, "Dr. White, I tried to get him to wait!"

Dr. White, held his finger to his lips so she could see it, but Dad could not, then turned back to Dad and shut the door behind them.

Jan told Mom that after that, she did not know what happened. Dad and Dr. White were in the treatment room for a while. When Dad came out, he seemed calmer. Apparently, Dr. White was successful at convincing Dad that Mom was not trying to kill him. Dr. White patted him affectionately on the back as he was leaving, and told him to take care of himself, and to give his love to Mrs. Hinkle.

We know all this because Jan called Mom the next day to give her the scoop. Mother attributed Dad's behavior to his low blood count from the bleeding ulcers, but I never was quite sure.

Dad came home sometime after dark that evening without the meat loaf, the pan or the oven mitts. We never knew what happened to the pan and meat loaf. I always wanted to ask Jan if maybe Dad left it there. But I never got around to it. Dad did not return the oven mitts, and mother never asked about them. I saw them later under the seat of Dad's truck. When I asked him about them he said he wore them to spray ether into the engine. He said they worked really well to protect his hands.

Somehow, Dad eventually sold the property and repaid the note. He never mentioned the lake property again.

* * *

2006
Even after the threat from our "family friend", the cleanup continues but now it's a little different when I go to the job site. I wear a pistol on my belt all day as I work, and I have a folding knife hooked to my pocket. Inside the car I carry a change of clothing in a bag, along with pictures of my daughter, grandkids and husband in happier times. I plan how to respond to different scenarios in case the "family friend" comes to the job site and creates a "disturbance" or makes threats. I do my job. I do not fear death. I am doing my best to do the right thing.

I think about Dad and what stress over the lake property did to him. After he sold the property, the buyer paid someone so they could dispose of the waste and now it's a lovely subdivision with a lake in the center. Dad got nearly all his money back and started to feel better and went on to undertake many other business ventures. I am glad Dad managed to recover his health after that incident. It gives me some hope now that I may live through my current circumstances and someday recover myself. We are, after all, made of strong stuff, Dad and me.

◇

"Therefore do not worry about tomorrow, for tomorrow will worry about itself. Each day has enough trouble of its own." (Matthew 6:34)

◇

Meat Loaf
1 pound of ground chuck.
Handful of crackers smashed, either in your hand, or in a plastic bag with a rolling pin until they are fine.
½ cup ketchup.
Salt and pepper to taste.
¾ cup chopped onions.
½ cup chopped red or green peppers.
1 egg (beaten).
In large mixing bowl combine all ingredients.
Take one bread loaf pan and mash the mixture in the pan.
Pour more ketchup on top.
Bake in oven at 375 degrees until done.
Let set for 10 minutes.
Slice and serve with French green beans topped with sliced almonds and baked potatoes with sour crème, butter and fresh chives.

Chapter 13 – Nut Hunt
"I can make a living off a flat rock." — Louis

2006
Today I spend the better part of my day picking up trash and sorting things to either keep or sell. I start at the barn, where when I open the door to the stalls, I automatically run my hand over the low rafter next to me just a little higher than my head. I do not know what I'm reaching for, but my fingers find hardened strips of leather and I pull the object down to look at it closer. It is a leather halter my brother made in a leather works class for my pony Bupp. The leather is rough and brittle, but it is still in reasonably good condition right where I left it at about 14 years of age. I look at it for a few moments, then tuck it under my arm and take it to the truck with me. I'm unsure why, I just know it's going home with me forever now. If it's waited for me for 40 years in this spot, I won't turn it loose again.

In these stalls I learned how to milk a cow. This is where Dad would sit on a stool milking and would ask me to go and get a bowl and he would milk some for the cats which would all come running to drink. Sometimes he would spray the milk right into the cat's mouths and they would line up, sit back on their back legs with front paws in the air waving him on. A few sprays were all they could take, and they would race off to wash the milk off their faces. It became a game, and it always made Dad and me laugh to watch them try to catch the milk in their mouths.

Outside the barn in the barn lot, I pause for a moment considering that this is the place where I first learned to jump a horse. First, I would put rails on top of a concrete block, then on top of two until I worked up to a rail on the top of 3 concrete blocks. Misty was my jumper, and she took to it eagerly. I never put her to a jump that she declined. Soon we were able to jump over any fence on the farm. Many times, we jumped the fence and rode into town, or down to the lake where I would swim her across an inlet, then lay in the sun to dry while she cropped grass. The sense of freedom that comes with being able to jump a fence is impossible to describe. For hours I would take Misty over the jumps I created in different locations around the barn lot until we were both tired, sweaty and exhausted. It felt like flying to jump those rails. I look at the side of the barn and the stack of concrete blocks are still there, broken and crumbling now. The wooden rails are long since rotted away. For a few moments I consider picking up a piece of the block and putting it into my pocket too, but reluctantly I do not. I cannot save everything attached to a memory. In fact, I can barely save anything at all.

This is also the barn lot where I found Lady, our 3-year-old filly, dead one morning in early spring when I was 14. I had come to the barn that morning to saddle Misty, and ride. It had been raining, and the grass had grown quickly. We did not think how eager a young horse would be for spring grass after wintering on hay, and we did not limit her access to it. We had never had a horse founder or get sick on green grass before; yet she did, and we did not know until it was too late. I still remember standing over her lovely, well-muscled Palomino body in this very lot wondering why she was so still as I walked up. Perhaps she was sleeping, enjoying the sun? But it was muddy. She would not lay down in mud. Then I noticed that her top ear was filled with water, and that's how I knew she was dead. A young life snuffed out from too much grass.

Two years before I'd saved her in the field right below the barn when she became entangled in an abandoned roll of barbed wire leftover from fencing. I came across her when I was headed to the pond to fish. She was down on the ground with the barbed wire entangled around her back legs. She had been struggling for some time and was bleeding from her feet and her sides. That time I'd run to the barn, collected some wire cutters and went back talking soothingly to her until she stopped kicking. Carefully I clipped the wire in different places and pulled it loose from her feet until she could stand. How she did not kick me to death or entangle me too in the barbed wire I do not know, but somehow, I got her clear, I saved her that time. But I could not save her from eating too much green grass.

During the cleanup, now, there are literally thousands if not millions of decisions to make, and I must make them all quickly. I finish cleaning the small sections of stalls and the barnyard, then I go back to the main house to clean more. Quickly I fill several dozen trash bags from Dad's yard, then I take up a rake and rake up the leaves into giant piles of fluffy brown. Under the leaves millions of acorns settle to the bottom of the pile. In collections they are heavy. Too heavy to rake. I find buckets to shovel them up with and then wonder what to do with them when the buckets are all filled. Finally, I carry the buckets of acorns to the back of Dad's yard where there's a ditch, and I throw them in to fill in the ditch. Perhaps the squirrels or the deer will find and eat them through the winter.

All afternoon I work on the yard. As I rake, I think about a time before the house was built here. At one time it was a little glen that I visited by riding Misty down a winding deer path to a clearing in the center of the property. Dappled light would filter through the trees onto the mossy clearing making it look like a moving carpet. It is one of my happiest memories just sitting there in that clearing. Often, I would ride to the glen, unsaddle Misty and she would crop grass while I leaned back against a tree and read a book. The wind would stir in the treetops from time to time making them roar like the ocean. Now, most of the trees are gone. The glen is overgrown with tall grass, thorns and thickets.

That evening, with aching shoulders and back I stop by Autumn Manor to see Dad on my way home. I'm tired. I have dust in my hair that itches, and my nails have grime underneath them. They are stained with the effort of my day. I long for a bath and a glass of wine; but I want to see Dad first.

As I walk into his room, I find him sitting in his recliner leaning back and looking out the window at the oak trees behind the center. He appears lost in thought and does not notice that I've entered the room for a moment.

"How are you doing, Dad?" I ask him.

"I'm okay. You?" he asks. He does not turn.

"Tired, but okay," I say. "You looked like you were lost in thought."

He nods.

"What are you thinking about?"

"I was thinking about when I was still living at the house, you know. A few months ago."

"What about it?" I asked.

"Well, I was thinking about that day that I thought I still hadn't turned up my heels yet, and was glad about that," he responded.

"Do you mean turned up your toes?" I asked thinking he'd got his metaphors mixed. Kicking up heels as in lively, turning up toes as in dead.

"No, I mean heels. As in when I fall, my face usually hits the ground, and my heels turn up. That's what happened a few months ago at home in the yard." He laughs a raspy laugh.

"What do you mean?" I picture Dad sprawled on the lawn, looking like a discarded sack of old clothes.

"There were acorns on the ground. I decided I'd gather some to fix for supper. I was bent over gathering them up and putting them in a bag when I just fell."

"You fell! Were you hurt?" I pictured Dad bent down at the waist like a drinking bird toy, his head on level with his knees as he gathered acorns. It's an oddly limber position for a man his age, but one he assumes often to spare his knees. He had knee replacement surgery several years ago, but the habit lingers on even after the repair healed, making knee bending possible once more. It is a posture that I wonder might cause a strain on his heart or maybe even a stroke, another reason I feel better now that he's in assisted living. He no longer needs to reach down from this position to weed the garden or hunt acorns.

"Yes, I fell right there in the front yard. Soft like. Just thumped over. It didn't hurt." He laughs again making his shoulders shake. "I laid there for a while looking at the grass, kind of checking to see if I'd damaged anything."

"So really, nothing hurt?"

"Mostly my pride. Two neighbor ladies went by on a walk around the subdivision. I thought they might stop. Help me. But they walked right on just yacking their heads off."

I pictured it, two little white-haired ladies—the only kind left in Dad's community—walking by his house. Walking right by him! The ladies must have been so lost in conversation they didn't even see Dad.

"They must not have seen you!"

"I think they did, but I think they might have been a little afraid to stop. A little afraid of your dear old Dad," he says with a smile.

"Did you call to them?"

"No, I wanted to see what they'd do."

"And they didn't even call to you?"

"No."

"So, what did you do?"

"Well, I lay there for a while until they were good and gone, then I rolled over easy and got up. I finished picking up a mess of acorns, took them in and ground them up in the blender. I browned some hamburger, threw in the acorn meal, added water and made some acorn stew."

"Acorn stew!" I said. "I didn't know you could eat acorns," I said.

"Well, honey, you haven't eaten until you've had acorn stew," Dad said with a smile.

While this is not the first experience Dad has shared with me about foraging for food, I've never known him to cook acorns; so, this activity must date back to a time even before I was born. I wonder how Dad learned to cook acorn stew and why he had the urge to cook it that day. But somehow now did not seem the right time to ask. I am tired and I can tell from his face he'd like me to leave him to his memories. So, after a few light exchanges I leave to go home, and he returns to staring out the window at the encroaching darkness. Night is falling on the land. As the sun sets, light filters through the leaves on the oaks in shades of orange and black.

Maybe it's true, I thought as I walk to my car, we do revert to our childhood ways as we age. I wondered how many times in his childhood Dad had acorn stew for dinner. I wondered how many times acorns were all that he had. That night I looked up acorn stew on the Internet and came up with some wonderful recipes. I discovered acorn stew is served in fine restaurants in famous locations. It made me wonder how many of Dad's humble meals that we thought we were too good to eat were actually *haute* cuisine? How much of what he'd tried to teach us of value had we turned up our nose and rejected out of hand?

* * *

1969

As a child, behind our original house in an open pasture stood a lone black walnut tree that during storms frequently became a giant lightning rod. Every year it seemed lightening would strike that tree. When it happened it would produce an earthshaking rumble, and sharp missiles of flaming bark would shoot sparks that lit up the field in the darkness. They would smolder for a while before burning out. The tree's trunk bore the charred and jagged markings of numerous life and death encounters with nature's original electricity. Many of its branches had jagged tears, others were broken, blackened and dead; yet portions of the tree lived on, forever altered and arthritic looking, yet hardy. Sometimes I'd risk falling branches to stand under that tree on a sunny day and trace the paths made by lightning with my fingertips. I learned to shoot a bow and arrow by stacking bails of hay at the foot of the tree and shooting them while my horse, Misty, grazed nearby. I'd wonder why lightning kept striking the tree and how it lived on in its unique twisted form of beauty in spite of being half-fried to a crisp. Gnarled and stooped, it didn't produce a lot of walnuts, but the ones it did make were mammoth in size, hard to crack, yet they tasted juicy-sweet if you could somehow manage to extract the kernel without smashing your fingers. Looking back I wondered if the tree made sweeter fruit than the rest of the walnut trees because of its suffering, or perhaps in spite of it.

Some years the tree would go dormant and Mom would tell Dad, "Louis, we need to pull down that walnut tree before one of the limbs falls out and hits one of the kids in the head and kills them."

Dad would say, "I'll do it when I have time." Which we all knew meant never. It also meant if we wanted to live, we needed to look to our own safety, because Dad didn't have time, really, ever. As a result, I frequently plotted how a 9-year-old girl could safely remove dead branches from a tree without getting bonked on the head and killed. About the time I was ready to try my luck with a tall ladder and cut it down the tree would give some indication of life. One day I noticed it had pushed out scraggly, green shoots and curly leaves from darkened branches, proving it wasn't dead and really not a danger after all. It would indeed produce another crop of large black walnuts that year that the horses would nose out of the way so they could graze under the tree, seemingly oblivious to the danger of falling limbs.

We had 17 black walnut trees on our place in addition to the aged tree in the middle of the field, and an unidentified number of hickory and pecans. They supplied our family with nuts for baking or just eating if we had the patience to harvest, dry and crack them. Walnut gathering usually took place on Saturday. To prepare for walnut gathering we pulled out our oldest clothing and shoes knowing soon we'd be covered with walnut stain. Before daylight, Dad emptied the tools out of the 65 Dodge van and removed the two bench seats to "make room" for the nut harvest. We had a supply of cardboard boxes on hand, that we used to carry collected walnuts to the van and dump them through the open windows. We kept the boxes stacked in the shed between walnut hunts. It was my job to collect the boxes in preparation for the work. Occasionally I'd find the dusty remains of a deceased former inhabitant—a mouse, or squirrel who perhaps ate himself to death in the excess of nuts we did not use. This happened frequently enough to make me alert when I collected the boxes.

Once I had them safely in the van, Dad shouted, "All aboard!"

Franky, my friend Kate, along with Dad, and myself, would all get in the van and then we would putter down to the barn gate. There Dad hopped out to open the gate, and Franky would drive the van through the opening. Then Dad would shut the gate behind him and take over driving again.

Cows raised their heads from grazing to stare at our noisy intrusion into their pastures. They'd sidle away chewing, wary ears perked toward us in watchfulness, tail raised in salute as if the mere sight of us gave them gas. They swung their heads and rolled their eyes our way as we motored to the back of the property, scattering cow pies and turf behind us and bending down dried milkweed and brambles in front of the rumbling van with a swish and crackle.

Eventually we coasted to a stop near the tree line at the back of the farm. Among the fragrant cedar trees and leafy oaks stood some fine black walnut trees – their green, fertile orbs scattered with thoughtless abandon on the ground in shiny, soft grass. Wasps and bees settled on the broken flesh of the outer hulls of the nuts, so we tried to proceed carefully to avoid their sharp stings.

"A dollar per box," Dad said. "A dollar bonus to the one who gathers the most boxes."

"Ah, Dad, is that all?" Franky belly ached. He was used to getting 10 cents per bale of hay during hay season. The boxes were huge and it took a long time to gather enough walnuts to fill them, if you wanted to successfully avoid angering the wasps.

"That's it! Take it, or leave it!" Dad always drove a hard bargain.

Being second on the totem pole, it never occurred to me to bicker over wages. I was just glad to get any money at all. I had never held more than 5 dollars in my hand at one time, and didn't even own a wallet. I grabbed a box and headed for the tree intent on making at least 10 dollars before the day was out. Plunk! Plunk! The first walnuts sounded small against the empty box as I tossed them in.

For several hours we picked walnuts like maniacs, driving from tree to tree until we covered most of the pasture fence rows. We dumped boxes full of black and green, shedding walnuts in through the open windows until the van was full completely up to the bottom of the foldout windows in back. We kept the hickory nuts separate in boxes which we sat on the front floor of the van. No room for people inside in the back. Wasps buzzed angrily all around. They darted up in the sky and dive-bombed us. Once in a while we had to rush around the base of the tree to put it between our attackers and ourselves. But still, we kept picking. Using a scrap of chalk from my pocket, I tallied on my favorite box how many I loaded into the truck.

"Twenty-five cases: Twenty cases of walnuts and five of hickory nuts." I announced.

We really should get paid more for hickory nuts, I decided. They were smaller and more difficult to find. A lot of the hickory nuts had squirrel teeth marks already in them or worms had gotten to them first, some were cracked and even more turned out to be empty casings where the squirrels had finished them off entirely. Still, dollar signs danced around my head making me dizzy. I'd earned 15 dollars even without the bonus! More than enough to purchase that rainbow stripped Navaho saddle blanket I'd had my eye on for a year at Riddles Feed Store.

Glancing down, I noticed my black-walnut-stained hands. The sap from the walnuts had seeped through the gloves where there were holes worn in the fingers. Yuck! What took walnut stain off? I wondered.

"Are we ready to go? Looks like the van's full," Dad said.

"Shotgun," Franky cried out the slang word for sitting in the front seat. He scrambled into the van's front seat elbowing me out. "You've got to ride in back with all the nuts." He jerked a thumb toward the back where the green, fragrant mountain of walnuts filled the back of the van up to the windows. Bees and wasps buzzed in and out of the windows angry at having their food source removed. I shuddered. If I rode in back, I'd be black speckled for a week, unfit to appear at either church, or in town for Friday grocery shopping. What if I saw a boy from school I liked, and he saw my hands all black.

"Dad! He rode shotgun on the way down!" I cried, dancing in place.

"Kids, I don't want any squabbling! Jane, get in the van! I've got to go to work."

"When do I get to ride shotgun?" I asked.

"When you've got these." My brother made a muscle. It really wasn't a very big muscle. His arms emerged from his plaid shirt sleeve long and thin after what Mom called his "recent growth spurt". But his tan, brown arms were far larger and more muscular than mine. A definite bicep bump had resulted from the many long hours spent working with Dad. I reached out a finger and poked it with envy. Not to be out done, I pulled up my shirtsleeve, bent my arm and tried to emulate his demonstration. I focused. Mentally strained, even. Nothing visible appeared. I concentrated again, and tried harder. A tiny twitch of my arm resulted. Franky laughed! Oh, to only be born a boy!

I elbowed my way into the van, and Kate and I sat on the engine compartment between my Dad and brother on top of an old bathroom rug so the heat from the motor wouldn't burn us. Dad stepped into the already squatting van and slammed the door shut. There were no seat belts. Dad had cut them out long ago calling them a nuisance. So we balanced precariously by hanging onto the sides of the warm compartment.

Dad started whistling a song he'd heard on WJIG Radio, as we bounced and jostled over the hills and through the valleys of our farm, the van following the cow path toward the house. Walnuts bounced and rocked behind me in the van, I could hear the swish of the grass as it wiped down the underside of the vehicle, leaving a trail behind us like the wake of a ship on the ocean. Once I glanced around and thought how easy it would be going downhill for the walnuts to simply wash over us in a wave and suffocate us inside the van. The van smelled like a walnut-pie factory.

Perhaps the stampede of walnut flesh would catch us by surprise as we started downhill toward the pond in the front field. It was a craggy narrow path with lots of deep ruts. Yes, I could see it clearly in my mind, the walnuts would spill over onto us making Dad unable to steer the van. He would lose control as he was driving. We would slide into the pond leaving only faint, expanding ripples of murky water and bubbles for a few moments to indicate our whereabouts for anyone who cared to look, and then nothing. It would be as if we had disappeared off the face of the earth! No one would find us there until maybe walnut stain turned the pond black and perhaps someone would wonder why.

I knew my imagination was likely running away with me and I tried to get a grip on it. But the panicked feeling persisted.

"Dad, can we drive by the barn rather than the pond?" I asked.

"What's the matter with you?" Franky elbowed me.

"Nothing!" I wasn't about to tell him I was afraid. "I just want to go by the barn."

"Okay," Dad, smiling, happy at the size of our harvest, easily obliged me. He turned the van and circled around the field before starting up the even steeper hill by the barn. But this time the slope was uphill. Safer. No worries about all the walnuts rolling forward.

Hearing us approach, Mom came out of the house and opened the gate so we could pull out of the field and into the driveway. "Did you get any?" she asked.

"Did we get any what?" Dad teased with a smile. "Kids, show your Mom what we got."

Franky hopped out of the van with me and Kate close behind. He unlatched the back door and opened it. With the roar of a million hail stones on a tin roof, an avalanche of walnuts spilled into the driveway. When they came to a standstill a pile of walnuts approximately 3 feet high in some places and 10 feet wide pooled beside the van. And there were still walnuts to be shoveled out and boxes of walnuts to be removed, as well as all the hickory nuts.

"Yeah!" my brother jumped up and down, stirring the walnuts outward from the van door. When the avalanche completely stopped, he crawled up in the van, pulled out the remaining boxes of nuts and then began shoveling the last few pockets of remaining walnuts out with his hands. Then he unloaded the boxes of hickory nuts from the front of the truck and stacked them on the screened-in porch.

"You've got to be kidding," Mom said! "What will we do with all these nuts?"

"Eat them," Dad said with a smile.

"But how will we get them hulled?" Mom's eyes widened with shock.

"We'll leave them in the driveway for a while and run over them with the car for a couple of weeks. That should get most of the outer hulls off," Dad told her.

"We can't do that!" Mom said. "How will we get in and out of the cars? They'll roll under our feet. What about our Sunday shoes? We'll get walnut stain on them. We'll be tracking it in and out of the house."

"I've got to go to work. Got all the walnuts out of the van, Franky?"

"Yes, sir," Franky threw the last one out into the field toward the grazing horses.

They raised their heads and shied away from the nut, then waited heads high for a few moments to see if he would repeat the assault. When he didn't, they again dropped their noses into the grass, and returned to grazing, but kept their gaze locked on him—just in case.

Dad collected Mom into his arms and pulled her toward him for a swift kiss. She grimaced and drew back from his embrace, her eyes remained fixed on the mountain of walnuts now piled in her driveway.

"Goodbye, you Great Big Beautiful Doll," Dad said, oblivious to her horror. With a stolen kiss on her cheek, he released her and hopped back into the van.

Mr. Hinkle, can you take me home? Kate asked.

"Sure, jump in," Dad told her. He reached into his wallet and paid Kate for the boxes she had collected.

She looked really happy when she saw the amount and said, "Thank you, Mr. Hinkle.

"You are welcome," he said. "You worked hard."

Dad started the van, waved at all of us as he backed down the driveway. Kate waved too. We could hear him whistling "Moonlight Becomes You" as he drove off down the road.

Mom said. "What am I going to do with all these walnuts?"

"Eat them," I smiled echoing Dad's words.

"We can't eat them until we hull them, and shell them," Mom said. Her eyes roamed in disbelief over the huge pile of nuts. "I have dishes to do, and dinner to fix. There's so many, and their shells are so hard. How on earth will we hull them all?"

"Franky and I will do it!" I said.

"Speak for yourself, I've got fishing to do," Franky said.

Seeing Mom's shocked face, I knew she was right. The walnuts would stain our clothes and be a terrible nuisance when we tried to get in and out of the car with them underfoot.

"Franky you can't go fishing and leave us here with all this work!" Mom said.

"We can hull them, Mom!" I reassured her.

Franky's gaze strayed back toward the shed where the fishing poles were, but duty called and he gave up the notion for now.

"Don't worry Mom," I sounded more confident than I felt.

Reluctantly, Franky said, "Yeah, we'll hull some this afternoon."

"If you could just hull enough for us to make some walnut bread for dinner that would be terrific," Mom said. "And then rake the rest of them out on the far driveway so the trucks will run over them when your Dad comes in and out. In a few days, the outer hulls will dry out and fall off. Then we can gather them back up and shell them as we need them."

After she went inside, I collected two 5 gallon buckets and a steel brush. I filled one of the buckets with water and hefted it over to the pile of walnuts. Then I put on a pair of old work gloves and pulled up an old stool we kept outside.

Gingerly, I took a black walnut and plunged it into the water and began to scrub. Franky pulled over another stool and the work began.

After an hour we had only filled half of a 5 gallon bucket with walnuts ready to crack. Even with the gloves, our arms were deeply stained with walnut stain all the way up to our elbows. Franky and I looked at each other and at the pile of walnuts. We laughed at one another.

"You look like a real Indian now!" I said. "At least from the fingers to your shoulders!"

"Well you look like an Oreo cookie," he laughed back. "White in the middle with two black sides!" We both fell over laughing looking at our arms in wonder. Would they ever be normal again?

"Think there's enough for a loaf of bread?" I asked after we finally stopped laughing.

"I'm not sure. I don't think bread has a lot of nuts."

"They are really hard. Have you ever tried to crack one?"

He shook his head.

"Let's try."

I ran to the shop to get the hammer and returned. We looked around for something to crack the nut on. I picked up a nut and took it to the edge of the concrete patio and placed it at the corner. As swift as I could, I brought the hammer down on the nut. Nothing happened, not even a dent. I tried again. Nothing.

"Let me try," said Franky. He ran to the shop and got Dad's 10-pound sledgehammer. He came back, grabbed a nut and set it on the edge of the patio. Then he raised the hammer high and brought it down with full force on the nut. The nut shot across the yard intact and a 6-inch piece of the corner of the patio broke apart and skittered into the yard. We looked at each other for a moment in surprise.

Then Franky got up and got another nut. Nut after nut, the results were about the same. Each one shot out into the yard and each attempt dented the patio. Thinking the concrete patio too soft, we moved over to the corner of the well house made of concrete blocks. The blocks cracked on the first blow. The nut remained undamaged. We moved on trying to crush one between two bricks. A brick broke. Then we took a nut to the old garage near the garden and put it in the vise and cranked it up as tight as we could (after both of us put on safety glasses—of course), but could not crack the nut. Franky hammered away at the nut on the anvil with a hammer. Nothing. We tried lots of nuts. All with the same result. Looking at the nut I suddenly found an entirely new appreciation for the persistence of squirrels everywhere and for the sharpness of their teeth.

Exhausted and sweating, with walnut stain all the way up our arms, we sat down on a log in our backyard to rest. Franky stirred dust up from the worn spot in the grass with his tennis shoe.

"What are we going to do?" I asked. "We aren't ever going to be able to crack all those nuts."

"I know," said Franky, looking over at the huge pile in the driveway. "Maybe Dad can crack some of them when he comes home."

"Maybe." But I doubted it. If we couldn't crack a nut with a vice, I didn't think even Dad could crack those nuts.

After we rested, we raked the nuts across the driveway where Dad parked the trucks in the evening. It took us the rest of the afternoon to complete this task. The nuts settled into their new home among the limestone rocks, pea gravel and Tennessee soil like another kind of rock. Already they looked dryer and less likely to stain bare feet or shoes. However, they were very round and difficult to walk on. Even when mixed into the gravel, they tended to slide this way and that as the softer outer hulls gave way to the hard nut in the center. Both of us knew Mom was right. Until the outer hulls rotted away, and the shells dried out, the driveway was going to be tricky to navigate on foot.

Exhausted, we dragged ourselves into the house. One look at us, and Mom knew the score. Taking in our disheveled, dusty hair, walnut stained arms and hangdog expressions, she didn't even ask. "Wash up," she said. I have tuna sandwiches with chopped eggs and pickles, and chips for you when you're ready.

Dad came home that night to find us depressed, lying on the couch watching "The Andy Griffith Show" on television our arms washed but still very brown.

"What's the matter here? Did you not get enough walnut bread to make you happy?"

"There isn't any walnut bread," Franky said.

"We couldn't crack any of the nuts," I told him.

"We'll let's see if I can crack some. Let me go to the shop and make something really quick." Dad grabbed a flashlight to guide his steps down to his shop.

"Do you want to go?" he asked.

"No thanks." I shook my head. My back ached from stooping to pick up nuts and loading them in the van. My eyes felt like I needed to prop them open with my pencil.

The evening was warm and through the open windows of our house we could see the reflection of the light from the garage spread across the back lawn when Dad had the shop light on. Then we heard him fire up the table saw. For the next few minutes we heard sawing and the professional tap, tap, tap of nailing. Then the light went off, and we could see Dad following the flashlight beam back up the path to the house.

When he came in the door he was carrying a stand he'd made from a sawed off 2-by-four. It was made in the shape of an upside down T reinforced with cross pieces of wood. It stood about knee-high on a platform to keep it stable. The top of the upside down T was covered with metal that he'd hammered out in the middle making a soft depression so a walnut would fit neatly into the hollow, half buried. He also carried a hammer and a sharp metal punch. Dad sat down in his recliner and placed his nut stand in front of him with his feet on either side of the base to keep it steady.

"Jane, bring me a nut and let's see if this works."

I ran outside to the back porch where we'd placed a bucket of nuts that already lacked the outer soft hull, and brought back a handful to try.

"I don't think it will work," Franky said. "We tried everything. We even knocked a corner off the concrete patio."

Dad's eyebrows raised a fraction on his forehead, but he didn't comment.

"Let's see." Dad placed the punch on top of the nut along the seam, then raised his hammer and brought it down on the top of the punch. He changed the orientation of the punch and struck it with the hammer again. The nut cracked neatly in two equal parts perfectly exposing the interior, which fell out into Dad's hand when he picked the shell up and shook it.

Franky and I stood there with our chins hanging down. "How did you do that?" Franky asked. "You make it look so easy?"

Franky picked up the shell and looked at the even cut along the edges.

"Remember, my father was a blacksmith, he knew all kinds of tricks for putting things together …and taking them apart," Dad said. He cracked another nut and picked the kernel of the nut out of the shell with his finger, and popped it into his mouth and chewed.

"That's good! Want a bite?" he asked me.

"Yes!"

"Franky get a bowl."

In half an hour Dad had cracked and shelled enough walnuts for Mom to bake several loaves of bread. Mom collected the bowl from him, and stirred a measured quantity of nuts into the batter she'd prepared. Then she placed the pans of batter into the warm oven. Whenever she opened the oven door a cloud of fragrant, salty, slightly yeasty scent billowed through our house.

That night, in bed, my stomach full of warm, tasty, black-walnut bread, I thought about the big walnut tree out in the pasture. How hard it fought to stay alive so it could produce the biggest sweetest walnuts on the farm. How hard Franky and I worked to gather the walnuts and how Dad had cleverly figured out a way to separate the sweet inside from the hard outside. I decided that maybe to get the best of something in life, you had to be smart, willing to work hard, and maybe get a little dirty. But it sure was worth it. I reached under my pillow with clean, walnut-stained hands to make sure the money I earned collecting the nuts was still there. Tomorrow I'd get Dad to take me to the feed store and buy the Navaho blanket.

* * *

2006

The next morning I go back to Dad's house to finish cleaning up the yard. As I rake more acorns I reflect on Dad's story and about my own nut-filled memories. Lost in thought I don't at first hear my name being called from a distance. Then it gets louder.

"Jane," my foreman, Harold, interrupts the memories flowing through my head. "What do you want us to do with the contents of the attached garage?" he asks.

I set aside my rake and follow him to the garage attached to Dad's main house and look at the overwhelming piles and more piles of stuff discarded there. Dad's always saving for a rainy day. Something catches my eye and I pull out several small pieces of sheetrock, some insulation, a few leftover chunks of wood discarded from something Dad had been making. There underneath it all I find the walnut cracker Dad used so long ago. Wobbly now, the wood dark with age. The metal piece at the top is missing, but I would know it anywhere. A relic from the past come to life again. It is like seeing an old friend. A useful tool created out of nothing by Dad to help feed us. The sight validates my memories of long ago. Proof that I'm not as crazy as I feel sometimes. It did all happen. Looking at it, I feel a bit of comfort that somehow Dad, over the years, always managed somehow to take care of us. He could take something as hard as a black walnut and as bitter as an acorn and turn them into something warm and nourishing. Often he made it look easy, but I know for a fact it was not.

"I can make a living off a flat rock," Dad once said. I laughed at him in disbelief then. But today I'm not laughing as I look at the nutcracker. Today I realize not only could he make a living on a flat rock, but that he often actually did make something out of nearly nothing in order to provide for us. If he could do that all his life, I can clean up the mess.

◇

"We work hard with our own hands. When we are cursed, we bless; when we are persecuted, we endure it." (1 Corinthians 4:10)

Black Walnut and Banana Bread

2-3 ripe bananas, peeled.
(You can use over-ripe bananas that you keep in the freezer until you are ready to make bread.)
1/3 cup Land of Lakes salted sweet butter (melt slightly in cup in microwave).
1 teaspoon baking soda.
¼ teaspoon salt.
¾ cup brown sugar.
1 large egg beaten.
1 teaspoon vanilla.
1 ½ cup flour.
1 cup black walnuts.
Preheat oven to 350 degrees.
Smash bananas in bowl with a fork.
Add melted butter and mash together.
Add dry ingredients and egg and stir.
Bake in standard bread pan for 50 minutes at 325 degrees or until done (insert toothpick in center to test).
If bread sticks to toothpick when inserted, cook an additional 10 minutes.
Slice. Serve with whipped topping.

Chapter 14 – Poor Man's Lobster
"Something gave in my back." — Jane

2006
As the days pass and the cleanup continues my back increasingly becomes a problem. It hurts—a lot. The pain limits my motion and wears on my psyche. It is a weight I carry around constantly in addition to the responsibilities and physical work required during the cleanup. Not only does it hurt non-stop, but it grows increasingly difficult for me to pick up my right foot. My toes simply will not lift up when my brain tells them to. By the end of the day working inside the shop and lifting and sorting things I develop a strange gait. My back muscles draw me backward, and my legs feel stiff so I walk a little like a lobster. Sometimes I walk sideways or squat rather than bending over to spare my back. I need to see my back doctor in Texas, but don't have time to make the trip. So instead I soak in hot bathes at night, take pain meds, and steroids and try to tough it out.

One evening I walk into the assisted living facility and, when the nurse sees me, she says, "Jane, you are walking all bent, honey. Are you okay?"

"Yes, it's my back. It's really stiff from all this work."

"Seriously, you need to see a doctor about that," she cautions.

"I know. I will. Just as soon as I can." Slowly, with shoulders drawn back I walk down the hall to Dad's room trying to relax my gait. Dad and I visit for a while. He tells me he's joined an exercise program and is now peddling 20 minutes on a stationary bicycle. That they have a group that meets in the mornings to work out with flex-bands while sitting in chairs. He tells me they have singing on Wednesday night. There is a woman down the hall from him that's 98 years old and she makes clothing for premature babies. On the other side is a woman in her 30s that's disabled from a stroke, but she is able to knit. I see Dad has been working on his bird houses and he tells me he's started watching a television show about fishing off the coast of Alaska that he enjoys. All of this is new for Dad. He's been a lone wolf for so long. Talking to and interacting with people is progress. He is neat and clean when I come to see him, and his room is tidy. He says he feels better on his new medications and can tell his legs are getting stronger. I am glad for all the good news, and when I head home I feel like the world is coming right again in many ways. While the cleanup on the property is long and tiring we are making progress and the conclusion to the hard work is within reach. I cannot wait to get home and lie horizontal with an ice pack on my back.

A few days later, still stiff but better, I pick Dad up to take him to Nashville for a visit with his psychiatrist. The doctor thinks we need to tweak Dad's meds to better control his bi-polar episodes. He's much better than when I first became his Conservator, but we still have a way to go. When he moved to assisted living he refused to bathe and argued and ranted about nearly everything. His room, his food, the way the nurses put away his things where he couldn't find them made him very angry. Now that we actually have him on more appropriate meds for his various health conditions he has grown more pleasant and cooperative. Some days when I see him he actually smiles and tells me a joke or two.

At first he refused to watch television at all. He claimed he had better things to do. As a child he'd tell me how many shows on television were the work of the devil and would not allow me to watch them. But now, with little else to do, he does watch television. When I arrive to pick him up, I find him watching "Jaws". He sits in the center of the couch, head thrown back a little, arms pressed down and back on the seat of the couch. He grips the sides of the cushions tightly, and I believe his hair stands up a little as he watches the giant shark attack the fishing boat. For a moment he is lost in the movie, and I revel in our success getting his thoughts off himself and onto something else—anything else. The sight makes me smile.

"Hi Dad," I say. My voice makes him jump. I think he looks relieved to see me. He quickly reaches for the remote and turns off the television.

Two successes I think, when I see him do this. He's lost himself for a few moments in a movie, and he's learned to work the remote. All good.

"Ready to take a quick trip to Nashville?" I ask him. "We need to go see your doctor."

"Well, I could skip the doctor part, but I'm game for anything that gets me out of this place for a while," he says. "Let me get my hat."

Taking him on a trip means a slow walk to the car, me with a very stiff and painful back, him slowly pushing his walker. Gently, I use the method the home health nurses have shown me to lower him into the car using a wide cloth belt we buckle around his waist. Once settled, I help him lift each of his legs into the car, making sure all his clothing, fingers, toes etc. are inside the vehicle. Then I carefully shut the door. After I have him loaded I roll his walker to the trunk, fold and load it. Today I brought along a straw hat for Dad to wear because the sun is shining brightly, and I think he'll enjoy it if we roll back the sun roof in the car. The hat will help shade his eyes.

The drive to Nashville takes about an hour. It is a pleasant sunny, warm day and the drive goes well. Dad and I talk about the many trips he's taken to Nashville over the years. Pastures with Angus cattle grazing draw our attention, and he comments on how the landscape has changed since his boyhood days.

We arrive at the doctor's office and after a brief wait in the lobby they call us back. Dad had known this doctor for several years. He has a psychological profile on Dad that indicates he is bi-polar and obsessive compulsive with violent tendencies (he screams and throws things). The list goes on. I wonder sometimes how well a psychiatrist can diagnose another person. There's the Dad on paper, and then the more complex Dad that I know. He has empathy for others, and sometimes for animals. He believes in God and he tries always to do the right thing as he sees it. Life and people are never simple. Trying to commit a three-dimensional person to a one-dimensional sheet of paper seems a bit like trying to bottle the wind. I wonder as the doctor talks to Dad how we came to this point where I'm more his parent than child? At what fork in the road did we all zig when we should have zagged? And are we here as a result of any one thing someone did or didn't do; or is it simply our path in life; our destiny?

There remains some mystery about whether Dad sustained brain damage to his frontal lobe when he was born. Dad's mom worked a long day in the garden that day. She labored a long time. She was quite old to birth a first child, and she was what Dad called "heavy set". According to relatives who knew the details, the birth had not gone well. It took place at home with a midwife in attendance as was common for the time. My grandfather only called the doctor after it became clear my grandmother was in trouble. When the doctor finally came he took one look and reached for his forceps. After quite a lot of tugging, baby Louis arrived, but his head was smashed somewhat flat from the birthing process. Seeing this, the doctor took Dad's soft baby head in his hands and gently remolded it rounding it out.

Whether this explains some of the strange operation of Dad's overall thinking process, I can't know. Dad can be quite brilliant in many respects at times, but he's also what Mom calls "odd". One of his oddities is that if something is not where he can see it, he cannot conceive of where it is. He spends a lot of time hunting for things and then ranting about it when he can't find them. Often we can follow along behind him, pull open a drawer, and find exactly what he's looking for with hardly any effort. Our success where he has failed does not make him happy.

Due to this tendency, Dad never puts anything away if he can help it. All things must remain in view. He also finds it challenging to conceive of a person having a life outside the life they share with him. At some point he might ask you about your day, and you could tell him; but at the point the information does not involve him, his attention wanders as if you are reading to him from a book that holds little interest for him. This makes light conversation with Dad difficult. It is the manifestation of an odd sort of egocentric existence that we struggle to work around in order to connect. His actions are geared only toward his own immediate needs. In the face of these challenges Dad has many gifts as well. He can do advanced math in his head, is excellent at calculating angles when building a house. He can visually calculate distance and provide accurate timelines for work. He's articulate when he writes and persuasive when he speaks. He's also an excellent singer.

As an independent adult his challenges may not be so apparent, but as a parent during my childhood they sometimes spelled disaster. His challenges have not diminished as he ages. In fact, they have gotten worse. Meds do help Dad deal with the mood swings if not the root of his issues. At this time in his life, if we can find a way, any way, to make Dad a little more content maybe even a little happier and cooperative, we consider it a huge success.

"Mr. Hinkle, how are you doing, sir?" the doctor asks after we make ourselves comfortable in his office.

Dad smiles, takes off his hat and rubs his head, "About as good as you'd expect for a man forced out of his home and taken prisoner by his overbearing children," Dad answers. But he smiles when he says it.

The doctor pats Dad's knee, nods as if he understands and says, "Quite an adjustment living in assisted living after living alone for so long, isn't it?"

Dad rubs his hair into place with one hand, then places the hat on the table with the other hand, before he says, "Oh, it's not too bad. They feed me pretty well."

"I know how much you like to eat!" the doctor says.

Both men laugh and it breaks the ice. The examination continues. I can tell the doctor thinks Dad looks well. This makes me happy.

The discussion is short. The doctor's questions are direct. Dad responds equally direct. The doctor writes out new prescriptions, and we leave by the same door we came in. Again, I help Dad into the car, fold his walker and load it into the trunk. As I reach to close the trunk something in my back pops. I feel it give. My knees almost buckle. Hot pain bolts down my right leg, and I must hold onto the back of the car to support myself for a moment to keep from falling. Eventually, I lobster-walk, inch by inch around the car and manage somehow to open the door and get in on the driver's side. This is not good.

"What took you so long?" Dad asks.

"Something gave in my back," I say. I rub the lower part of my back with my fingertips. It feels like something is out of place. I reach around for something to place between the car seat and the small of my back to press on the spot while I drive. I find my red clutch purse and place it behind my back. The pressure helps some but it doesn't make the pain go away. Dad watches as I do this.

"Honey, this is not good," he says.

"I know," I respond. I try not to betray the fear I feel. He is counting on me. I feel like I am all he has.

"Let's get you home," I tell him and start the engine.

We enjoy the drive home too, but we don't talk quite as much. Both of us are, no doubt, thinking about my back. As for me I am wondering if I'll be able to get out of the car once we reach Autumn Manor. I wonder if I'll be moving "lobster-like" to the door walking sideways holding onto things, or if I'll even be able to walk at all. As we drive I keep shifting the clutch purse behind my back hoping for a better position. It helps some, but the pain persists. On the way we pass a fork in the road. One fork goes back to our hometown, the other goes to Kentucky. For a moment I think back to another trip I once took with Dad. A trip taken long ago. A fun trip when life was fresh and new and felt hopeful and filled with possibilities. An adventure. It was the day I saw my first lobster-like creature and did a little lobster-like walk myself then too, but for very different reasons.

* * *

1969

I was perhaps 12 when I went into the kitchen that morning and found Mom wrapping sandwiches in plastic wrap then handing them to Dad who carefully packed them into a red and white Coleman cooler. My friend Tess was with us. It was summer and she'd spent the night the night before, and we had a weekend adventure planned. Tess and I were the same age and, in many ways, thought and looked enough alike to be sisters. Her hair was longer and her face a bit rounder, but otherwise we could pass for twins.

My younger sister, now four, played in the living room with a small Winnie the Pooh stuffed animal watching cartoons on television and humming a Bible song she'd learned at church.

"Kids, get your stuff and get in the car! Time's a wasting!" Dad finished packing the cooler, put the lid on it tight and picked it up heading outside to load it into the trunk of the car. As he walked I could hear the ice shifting around inside. Mom and I followed him out. Once outside, Mom ran ahead and opened the trunk of the car so he could place the cooler inside. She had already loaded a quilt and some pillows in the trunk in preparation for a picnic.

"Louis, do be careful. Those containers in the cooler could pop open. Do you want the potato salad to dump out onto the sandwiches?"

"And what about the chicken and the pineapple upside down cake? You did pack that, didn't you?" I asked. I ran and grabbed my shoes from the edge of the patio and then leapt into the back seat of the car holding them in one hand and a pair of oversized purple sunglasses in the other.

"Don't worry. I've got it," Dad said.

Mom ran back into the house to collect my sister, her toys and things she needed for her day, then they both came back to the car and joined us. My sister and Mom sat up front with Dad.

As a baby, my sister had a child safety seat, but after she outgrew it my parents did not buy another. Dad didn't believe in them. So Mom kept her in the front seat between her and Dad so she could hold onto her if there was an accident.

"Come on Tess, or Dad's going to leave you!" I patted the seat next to me, and my friend slid in beside me. We both wore tee shirts and frayed cutoff jeans.

She wore white Converse tennis shoes with a red stripe on the sole, I wore white Keds. The wind blew her waist-length brown hair across my face. I brushed it aside and spat a few strands out of my mouth.

"Keep your hair out of my face." I slapped her shoulder lightly more in fun than seriousness.

"You watch your mouth, or I'm going to deck you!" Tess drew back her fist, but she was smiling too. We both tried to look mean, and then both laughed, relaxed, and settled back into the warm, green-upholstery seat. We were excited to be going anywhere. It was summer and a beautiful day awaited us.

Tess was my best friend since I started school in 4th grade. We were now enjoying our summer before we started 7th grade in the fall. A different world. During the summer we always spent a week or more at a time living first at her house in town, then my house in the country. Mom said it made for a well-rounded summer vacation experience. Mostly, Tess and I figured it gave our parents a break from us. We didn't care one way or the other. We just loved hanging out together.

When we were together, Mom thought we encouraged each other to get into mischief. And maybe she was right. It had been Tess's idea to take our pony Bupp into the pool for an afternoon swim, and then into the house for iced tea out of a bucket to cool him off. Bupp was game for almost anything—but Mom wasn't. We were both grounded for two weeks when she caught us in the kitchen with the pony. And again when we took a 10 mile bike ride without telling her we were leaving the house. But we'd served our time, and we were excited to be back together again about to go on a new adventure.

That morning, Dad must have thought Mom looked like she needed a break, so when he announced, "I'm going to Kentucky for the day to check out a job, would you, and the girls like to come?"
Mom said "Yes," eager for the diversion for herself and for us.

"Want me to pack us a lunch?"

"Great!" Dad smiled.

Dad liked to look at jobs. His work reminded me of a kid playing in the dirt in a sandbox. Pushing trees down, leveling the dirt. Dad always got excited at the possibilities of what he could create with the dozer. Looking at possible jobs was one of the more fun things he did.

Franky had gone to Scout camp in Georgia that week, it was his last year and they were doing increasingly advanced skill training. So it was just us girls and Dad today.

As Dad backed the car down the driveway, Tess started to tickle me, and I screamed.

"Girls!" Dad said. He stopped the car abruptly resulting in a slide on the gravel drive, then turned and looked over his shoulder at us sternly. "Now you will have to behave, or we won't go anywhere."

"Yes, sir!" I piped up immediately.

"Yes, Mr. Hinkle!" Tess added for good measure.

"That's better!" Dad turned and put the car in drive and we were off. I stuck my tongue out at Tess and she crossed her eyes at me. We laughed again and settled back for the ride.

The trip to Kentucky took a couple of hours. On the way we all played games counting license plates from different counties. We started out counting from different states, but it got too boring. Most of the people who came to Tennessee came to see The Grand Ole Opry, or Gatlinburg. Few lingered in rural areas like ours for long.

Dad listened to the local radio station as we drove out of town until it faded, which only took about 30 minutes. Then as he fiddled to tune in another station, and we were forced to listen to painful intermittent blasts of static. Each time we drove under a power line the radio roared louder. Asking him to turn the radio off was not something I had the courage to do; so we toughed it out for a while and hoped he'd find another station. He didn't, and finally he just shut the radio off much to our relief. The quiet felt blissful on our ears.

For a while I think both Tess and I fell asleep because when I sat up and looked out the window again we were no longer on the highway but were following a smaller curving two-lane road with farm houses separated by long stretches of woods.

"Are we nearly there?" I asked. "I've got to go to the bathroom."
"You should have gone before we left home!" Dad said. "There aren't any bathrooms where we are going."
"I did, but that was hours ago. Mom!"
"Just another few minutes," Mom said. "We're almost there. I brought some toilet paper, you can go in the woods."

That put a new light on things. I was owner of the world's smallest bladder, and I was terrified that a snake might bite me if I walked into the woods by myself. I'd heard of people getting poison ivy on their private parts after bathroom breaks in the woods where they made an unfortunate selection of leaves to conclude the process. So news that Mom brought paper was somewhat of a relief.

Tess motioned with her fingers like she planned to tickle me.
"Don't you dare!" I gave her my darkest glare.

Finally, Dad pulled off the road to the right and stopped in front of a gate. On the gate was a sign that said, Private Property. TRESPASSERS WILL BE PROSECUTED!

"Is this it?" I asked.
"Yep!" Dad said. He put the car in park, but left the engine running and opened the car door. "I'll open the gate. Velma, slide over and drive the car through. I'll close it behind us."

"Are you sure this is the right place?" I asked again. "What does 'Prosecute' mean?"

"It means they will shoot you're ass, if they catch you," Tess whispered.

"Tess!" Mom scolded her at the language.

"I'm sorry, Mrs. Hinkle. It just slipped out!" Tess said.

But behind Mom's back she poked me once in the rib. I almost wet the car seat.

"Stop it!" I whispered, then grabbed her finger and bent it backward.

"Girls stop fighting!" Mom put my still-sleeping sister down on a blanket on the passenger seat, then slipped into the driver's seat and drove the car through the gate opening. Dad closed the gate behind us, and Mom returned to the passenger side and picked up my still-sleeping sister. We pulled forward down a winding road between tall oaks and silvery maples, their leaves shimmering in the light breeze. The sun was now high in the sky, but it felt cool and peaceful underneath the trees on the little dirt and grass path. I expected to see a deer grazing, but I only saw the white-tailed rabbits bouncing up and down as they hopped away fast in front of the car, before darting off into the woods on either side. Finally, we came to a small creek winding its way through a bank of moss and blackberry bushes with patches of sun alongside. Dad stopped the car and turned the engine off.

"Louis, this is lovely. You say they are going to build a house here?"

"Yes, a huge house. More than 5000 square feet of house, not including the garage. There'll be a lot of groundwork here…and over there." He pointed.

"They plan to put in stone terraces starting at the top, then winding down to the creek. You see it? So when the creek floods the house site will stay dry, but they'll have access to the creek whenever they like from the house."

"You girls entertain yourselves for a few minutes. I'm going to go look for the surveyor stakes and see where the property boundaries are. The builder is supposed to have marked where we should start digging." He climbed out of the car, "But I still want to see what he has in mind." Dad headed off through the trees in the direction of some small red flags fluttering just above the high grass like butterflies.

"Girls, help me set out lunch."

"Can we play first, Mrs. Hinkle?" Tess begged.

"I've got to go," I piped up dancing nervously beside the car.

"Get the blankets and the cooler out of the trunk for me. Then you can go play in the creek for a few minutes while I get things ready."

"I've got to go now!" I told her again!

"The paper's in the trunk," Mom whispered.

I ran around to the trunk and found the toilet paper, then paused. "Where do I go?" I asked her.

Mom peered around. "There's no one around for miles. Why don't you just find a place right over there behind a tree? The grass is short and you can crouch there. No one will see you."

"Don't let that bear get you," Tess said with a smirk and pointed off toward the woods!

"What if I get lost?" I could find my way around the farms near my home like a hunting dog. I never worried about getting lost there. But we were in a different state—anything could happen. I could see the headlines, "Girl Lost in Kentucky Foothills!" Or maybe they would read, "Girl Mauled by Kentucky Bear, Narrowly Escapes," or maybe "Girl Killed by Bear!"

As I picked my way through the bushes and splotches of tall grass, I could hear Tess singing loudly, "The bear went over the mountain, the bear went over the mountain, the bear went over the moooounnnntain! To see what he could see!"

Sometimes Tess was a real pain in the neck; but I was really glad she was singing. That way I could follow her voice back to the car if I got lost.

Then... I would slowly kill her.

It didn't take me long to "take care of business" as Dad liked to call it.

When I was back within sight, Tess said, "So you made it out alive," smirking. She was helping Mom make a place to set the cooler down beside the blankets which were already spread out beneath some trees.

My sister was awake now, and she stood in a little clearing holding the stuffed Pooh in one hand and plucking at her shirt collar with the other as she looked around her as if she didn't quite know where she was or how she got there, and she wasn't sure she liked it. Mom patted a blanket for her by the cooler and she wandered over to it and sat down, still gazing around with her hand clutched tightly around Pooh's neck.

"I made it back...barely." I said to Tess.

"Let's go down to the creek!" she said. And when she said it, I forgot all about being mad.

"Okay," I said, and started walking the direction Dad pointed earlier.

"Be back in 30 minutes," Mom called after us.

We picked our way down to the tree-lined creek. Fluffy green moss and wild flowers grew on the bank. Among the flowers I could see Black-Eyed Susans, Butterweed and among the rocks some tiny little blue violets that I was not able to name but which I found incredibly fragile and beautiful. It looked like a place fairies would live, and I half expected to see one sitting on the bank looking into the water. Not that I still believed in fairies at my age—but you just never knew. The world was filled with stranger things. The trees overhead rustled gently in the breeze almost like they were trying to start a conversation with us.

Soon we were at the water's edge. A babbling creek with a smooth flat bottom and stones of every size and description worn smooth by the constantly rushing clear water cut through the landscape bordered by trees. It was less than a foot deep in many places perhaps 12-15 feet wide, and water quickly, yet gently, bubbled over the rocks. The sight of the water flowing was so beautiful and looked so cool and inviting, it made me eager to take my shoes off and stick my feet in it.

"Let's go wading," Tess suggested.

We both shucked our shoes, and rolled up our shorts to keep them from getting wet. I waded in first.

"Gosh, it's cold!" I told Tess. I crossed my arms over my chest, and waded in a little deeper. The smooth stones rolled under my feet and underneath them I felt the fine silt-like sand. You could see straight to the bottom of the creek. The water remained almost completely transparent even after I stepped in. Wading didn't churn up dirt; there didn't even seem to be any. Mostly there were smooth moss-covered surfaces in different colors. I flipped a few stones over with my toe and a number of tubular-shaped rocks about half an inch wide and round on the sides rolled under my toes.

"Look at this," I called to Tess.

She waded over to examine the tubular rocks I held.

"It looks like the bones you find in a can of salmon," I told her. "But they are very hard. I think it's the vertebra of a small fish."

As we examined the fossilized bones, out of the corner of my eye, I saw several of what I thought might be crayfish hovering near the edge of the creek. I moved quickly to catch one, but missed.

"You missed it," Tess chortled.

I ignored her and came back to look at the tubular rocks some more.

"I bet you're right! Those do look like a fish backbone. Wonder if there are any more?" Tess asked.

"Maybe," I responded. "Wonder if we can catch a crayfish?"

"We can try," she answered. "Do you see another one?"

"Over there." I pointed. We watched for a few minutes, and then we saw several crayfish in a deeper area of the creek. We walked slowly over to get a closer look yet not disturb them.

In the sunlight I saw one close and picked it up. The crayfish wiggled between my fingers. It felt creepy, and I wasn't sure whether or not it could hurt me; so I put it down. It crawled away with its claws held up and its little legs carrying it sideways more than forward. We watched them wiggle their tails as they moved through the water.

"Look at how strange they move, from side to side like that," I said. I wiggled my backside and did my best to imitate the crayfish taking small steps. This made Tess laugh.

For a while we crouched down on our haunches looking a bit like giant lobster creatures ourselves and watched the crayfish go about their lives there in the clear, rippling creek water. We demonstrated how we would move if we were crayfish and soon we had each other in stitches. A couple of times we nearly fell headlong into the water. That made us laugh even more. The crayfish didn't like all the noise we made and soon they disappeared into hiding. If they found a rock and remained still it was nearly impossible to find them even if you were looking right at them. They were the exact color of many of the rocks in the water.

"I wonder if you could eat them?" I asked Tess.

"Probably could, but there wouldn't be much meat on them. They are pretty small," she answered.

Since the crayfish all seemed hidden now, we turned over rocks looking for fossilized fish vertebra and put them in our pockets.

"Wow we found a bunch!" we both said at once. "Let's find all we can and pretend they are money!"

"Okay!"

For the next few minutes we searched the area by walking lobster-like through the creek overturning various rocks that looked like a place you'd find lost backbones of fish. We found enough to fill our shorts pockets. Just as I was reaching down along the edge of the bank to pick another one up, something large moved in the shallows.

"Yikes!" I jumped up and back from where I'd been lobster-walking through the stream with a splash and almost dropped my handful of fish bones.

"What?" Tess screamed. She jumped back as well.

"I don't know! Something with a lot of legs and claws moved over there in the water."

"Where?"

"Right there!"

We both crept closer, bent over, we gazed all along the creek bed-searching! Tess leaned in closer than me, and in a flash, she picked something up off the bottom. "Got it!"

At that moment, my opinion of Tess skyrocketed.

"What is it?"

"It's a really BIG crayfish! More like a fresh water lobster. Look!" She held it out so I could see it. What she held really did look like a medium-sized lobster, about 8 inches long with good-sized claws. Its tail moved back and forth, and she held it behind the pinchers. Probably the other crayfish were the babies of this one.

"What are you girls doing?" Dad asked, coming to the edge of the creek.

"Mr. Hinkle, we found a giant crayfish…ah lobster." Tess held up her catch so Dad could examine it.

"You did? Let me see."

Tess walked over and placed the wiggling creature in his hand. As he held it we could clearly see its head and eyes looking around taking us in.

"Well, that's some mighty good eatin'," Dad exclaimed. "If you can find four or five more this size, we'll cook them, up right now!"

"Ugh! You've got to be kidding," I said!

"No, I'm not kidding. Haven't you watched the "Beverly Hillbillies" on television? That's what they call crawdads! They're a poor man's lobster!"

"I'll see if I can find more," Tess said.

"You can find all you want to; that thing looks like a giant bug, and I'm not eating a bug," I told them both. I shivered at the thought.

"Come on, be a sport, help me find more," Tess called to me from the creek.

"…Okay." I responded, reluctantly. "I'll help you catch them, but I'm not going to eat that thing."

We hunted around and found six more good-sized crayfish. We tossed them into a bucket that Dad had brought down from the back of the car to keep them from getting away. They were all fairly large, but I still couldn't understand how we could eat them. They had hard shells and long legs, and they looked really mad!

"Come and get it!" Mom called.

"Mom, look what we have!" I shouted. I showed her the bucket full of giant crayfish.

"Wow. I don't think I've ever seen any that large," Mom said, looking at them, but she did not seem inclined to touch them.

"Very nice. Now put them down, wipe your hands off with these." She handed us moistened wash clothes she'd brought in a zip-lock bag, "and come and eat your tuna sandwich before it gets hot."

"We're going to cook them Mrs. Hinkle," Tess said. "Mr. Hinkle is going to show us how."

"For lunch? We already have lunch!" Mom said, shaking her head. She pointed out the spread of sandwiches, potato salad, chips, and cups full of tea she'd brought with us in a gallon thermos that matched the cooler.

"We'll fix them for dessert," Dad said with a smile, and he took a big bite out of his sandwich.

We finished lunch and cleaned up, putting all the used paper plates in a bag Mom brought for trash. While we did that, Dad looked around and picked up lots of twigs and leaves and rocks. In no time he had cleared a circle of grass and placed rocks in the circle around the pile of wood and twigs. Taking matches from the glove compartment of the car, he started a fire. Then he placed three rocks in the center of the fire. He took the empty Tupperware container from our tuna sandwiches and, fishing in the bucket he placed each crayfish in the Tupperware and closed the lid on them leaving only a crack for air so they could not get away but could still breathe. Then he took the empty bucket to the creek, filled it with water, brought it back and placed it on the rocks in the center of the fire.

"What are you going to do?" The suspense got the better of me. Tess sat on the blanket with my sister and together they watched his preparations.

"We're going to boil some giant crawdads!" Dad said.

To the water, he added some of the Lawry's Seasoning Salt Mom always brought on picnics.

While we waited for the water to boil, we listened to the birds and took turns guessing which ones made what calls. Dad knew all of them. And I recognized the dove, the owl and the mockingbird right off.

Mom sat in the front seat of the car with the door open and her feet extended onto the grass. The car was well shaded and a nice breeze blew through the trees around all of us. Mom pulled her knitting out of a bag she brought with her and began to knit. Her current project was a cap for winter for me. It was almost done. We could hear the crayfish trying to escape the Tupperware, and the flies buzzing looking for tuna that was all gone.

Finally the water in the pot started to bubble.

"Get ready, girls. You are about to experience a gourmet delight!"

Dad dropped all the crayfish into the bubbling pot all at once.

"You've got to be kidding!" I screamed, horrified. We both jumped up.

"You mean you cook them alive?"

"They aren't alive anymore!" Dad said.

It was true. The giant lobster-like creatures struggled for only a few seconds emitting tiny little death squeals, and then they stopped. Before I could cover my eyes, I saw them turn up limp and lifeless as the water began to boil again.

I started to cry. "You killed them! They are God's creatures, and you killed them!"

"Oh, shut up! You big, baby, you!" Tess said. "What do you think happened to that tuna you just ate! It didn't just wander into the supermarket and jump out of its skin and into the can all by itself!"

"Yes, but I didn't see it killed, either. I didn't have to think about it!" I struggled not to cry. I was too old to cry in front of my friend, but I could feel the tears pressing on the back of my eyes wanting to escape. I looked up at the sky hoping to keep them from falling.

Dad looked at me as if I'd completely lost my mind. He patted me on the shoulder, rough hard pats that were meant to be kind but that felt like a bear claw on my shoulder. "Now, now! It's a swift death. And you'll forget all about their tragic end once you taste one."

"I'm not eating that! It looks like a bug!"

Several minutes passed and the water bubbled along and turned foamy. Finally, Dad pulled out his Swiss Army knife. It had a fork on the end of it. He cleaned it off with his hanky, then stuck it into the pot and pulled out a crayfish. He blew on it for a minute.

"Jane, are you sure you wouldn't like to try one?"

I put my hand over my mouth and shook my head back and forth.

"How about you, Tess?"

Tess glanced first at me, then Dad. "Don't mind if I do."

I jerked my hand away from my mouth. "Are you crazy?" I asked. Dad handed her the speared crayfish.

"How do you eat it?"

"You break off the claws first, pull the meat out and eat with your fingers, then we'll snip the body with these little scissors on the knife and you can eat the tail."

At that moment, I knew I lived among aliens! I longed for a bear to just walk right out of the woods and eat me so I wouldn't have to watch this unholy scene. My best friend, eating the claws and tail of a bug! Yikes!

I ran to the car, threw myself into the back seat, and slammed the door. Mom looked up calmly from her knitting? "Are you okay?"

"No! I'm not okay!"

Even in the back seat, I could hear Tess and Dad crunching up the claws and tails and digging out the crayfish meat. They were laughing!

"Hey, Jane. These are great," Tess called after me. "You ought to try one!"

"No way!" I screamed. "You're both nuts!"

Finally, all the crayfish were gone. Dad dumped out the water, and threw dirt on the campfire.

"Go get your shoes, Jane. It's time to go," Mom told me.

I wandered back to the creek and picked up our shoes. Only a couple hours earlier it had all seemed like such a beautiful place. Only a couple of hours ago, the giant crayfish were alive taking care of their children. Now the little ones would have to take care of themselves. The parent crayfish were in someone's stomach. Still, I realized it was the cycle of life. Things live, they die. Parents leave, children become parents, then they get sick and die and on and on to infinity.

On the way home, I could smell crayfish on Tess's breath! I put a pillow over my head and pretended to sleep. In my pocket I felt the fish vertebrae I'd picked up from the creek. They felt smooth and innocent in my hand, yet they were in fact what was left of something that had died. I thought about that for a moment. Then the moment passed and a wish replaced it. I wished they really were money. If they were, I could take myself far from a place where you had to actually kill something yourself to eat.

* * *

2006

I remind Dad about the crayfish hunt on the drive home from the doctor's office. He doesn't remember a lot about it. He does remember the 1966 green Oldsmobile that had a 371 cubic inch V-8 engine and was fast as lightning. The thought of that makes him smile. The old car was stored on his place when he left it. Sadly, though he doesn't know it yet, I had it crushed and hauled off for scrap last month. I do not share this particular bit of knowledge with Dad though.

When we get back to Autumn Manor I somehow manage to get out of the car, and get Dad out as well. We walk slowly inside and down the hall to his room. By the time I get back into my car my back is screaming for relief. My thought is that something is way out of place. If I can only make it home and roll on the floor maybe I could put it back.

By the time I get home I am so stiff I can hardly walk, and I have flames of pain shooting down my right leg. Clearly something is horribly wrong. I slowly make it up the outside stairs to my apartment door, go inside and collapse on the floor in the living room. I lie on my back rolling my hips, first to one side, then to the other, hoping for a click that will mean my back is back in place. No click comes. I crawl on hands and knees to the kitchen, pull an ice pack from the freezer and lay in the floor in the kitchen with the ice pack on my back. Maybe if I can get the inflammation down the disc will go back in place. I lie on the pack until it is soggy and warm. I crawl back into the living room across the soft carpet and roll back and forth again. No relief. Finally I take some of the kitty Valium. Opal is gone now. She no longer needs it.

I somehow crawl up into bed that night and finally fall into a fitful sleep.

The next morning I can barely move. The only way I can make it from room to room is to hang onto things to try to relieve some of the pressure on my back. A chair, a table, a counter top help me propel myself along to do what must be done for the day. I start rolling my office chair around to support me so I can walk. This is not good. I call Hock in Texas and tell him what has happened.

"You need to see a back specialist," he says.

"I know, but I can't fly on a plane like this. I can hardly walk around the house. I'm not even sure I can make it to the car. And I'm 13 hours away from Texas by car," I tell him. I lie on the floor in the living room with another ice pack on my back.

"Can you sit up?" he asks.

"I sat up to drive Dad home yesterday. I think if I can get to the car and put something at my back I can drive home," I tell him. "But I can't carry anything down to the car. I can barely carry me."

We talk some more, and we finally agree I'll carry only my wallet and keys to the car and some water. I'll take a rolled up towel to put behind my back, and I'll drive back to Texas to get medical attention.

I call Autumn Manor and tell them there has been an emergency, and I need to go home for a week. They understand and promise to take good care of Dad. I also call an adult sitter I know and ask her to check in on Dad every day to keep him company while I'm gone. The sitter agrees. My sister will be checking on Dad as well. I call Dad and tell him I need to go home but don't tell him why. I call Harold, the job foreman, and tell him I will be away for a few days but don't tell him how long I will be gone or the reason for my absence. I don't want the crew goofing off or stealing while I'm out of town. If they don't know when I am coming back they will be less likely to slack off.

Then, without a shower, a change of clothes or anything else, I slowly inch out the apartment door and lock it. Holding heavily to the outside railing I go downstairs and, somehow, I get into my car; and drive the 13 hours to Texas only stopping once for gas and to go to the bathroom.

When I get there Hock helps me from the car, takes me into the house and I crawl into bed. He calls the doctor and makes an appointment for the next day. I can no longer lift the foot on my right leg and my entire leg feels like its on fire. The next morning Hock lays me down in the back seat of his truck and takes me to an orthopedic clinic in North Dallas to see a back specialist. The news is not good.

◇

"Do all things without grumbling or questioning, that you may be blameless and innocent, children of God without blemish in the midst of a crooked and twisted generation, among whom you shine as lights in the world."
(Philippians 2:14-15)

◇

Crayfish Boil

Wash crayfish making sure all are still alive. Discard dead crayfish.
Fill 5-quart pot with water.
Add ½ cup chopped onions, bay leaf, teaspoon garlic.
Bring to a boil. Let boil 5 minutes.
Add crayfish to pot and boil five minutes longer.
Drain.
Discard water.
Dip crayfish in favorite sauce, (cocktail, ketchup, Tabasco).
Peel, dip and eat.

Chapter 15 – Rattlesnake Sandwiches

"What's wrong with the pressure cooker, Louis?" — Velma

"Nothing's wrong with it. I just got tired of the pressure valve popping out all the time and releasing all the pressure from the pot, so I welded it in." — Louis

2006

"Ms. Eden, you've ruptured disc L4 in your back. That disc is placing extreme pressure on the nerve that runs down your right leg. It's the nerve that controls your ability to lift your foot, especially the big toe. If we don't operate to relieve the pressure you may permanently lose the use of your right foot," the doctor tells me. We are sitting in his office on the 7th floor of a North Dallas orthopedic clinic. He hands me the photocopies of the scan of my back. Hock and I study them. It is easy to tell the disc has ruptured. In the picture it looks like a smashed jelly donut with the insides melting out and down the back of my spine.

    I look at the images and a lot goes through my mind. I wonder how I did such damage. No doubt years of abusing my back have come down to what I see. And then I wonder how something so damaged can ever possibly be fixed. Then I wonder when they can do the surgery? And what is the risk? Will they be able to stop my pain? Will I be able to walk again? And if so, how long will it take?

    Hock looks at the image, then reaches for my hand and squeezes it in his own. I can tell by the look on his face he is seriously concerned. I look out the window. No tears fall. It is raining outside and even through the window I can hear the traffic swishing by on wet pavement. For a moment I feel like I'm in someone else's body living someone else's life.

    After a few moments, I ask the doctor all my questions and he does his best to answer them. Possible results of the surgery, much like all life, are uncertain. Soon we move from talking about "if" to "when" without my actually saying "yes".

    "We call this an emergency," the doctor tells us. "If I move some things around on my schedule, I think I can fit you in tomorrow."

    "Tomorrow," I say. "So quickly?"

    "The longer you wait the more damage will be done. The sooner we do it the better your chances are to avoid permanent disability," the doctor says.

    "Okay...then let's do it." My brain screams for me to slow down, but facts indicate speed is necessary. I find some comfort in the knowledge that this doctor is a real pro. He's put rodeo riders back together after bulls have mauled them. He's the back surgeon for numerous NFL players. If anyone can fix me, he can.

The next day we go in, they put me under anesthesia, and the doctor removes the bulging portion of the disc from my back in a procedure called a laminectomy. It is same-day surgery, and they let me go home a few hours after I wake up. The pain is reduced almost immediately, but my back feels weak. Between the medication and the surgery, the burning pain I felt in my leg before the operation has largely subsided. But I cannot lift even the weight of a sheet with my right foot once I'm tucked into bed. And my leg will barely support me when I try to walk. I must lean on Hock to get back and forth to the bathroom. I wonder if this is a temporary or permanent situation. In a follow-up call the next day the doctor reminds me I need to rest for 6 weeks. This is–of—course–impossible. I cannot leave Dad for 6 weeks.

Three days later I go for a follow-up in the doctor's office. I can walk, but I still can't lift my big toe off the floor with thought alone; so I walk with my foot turned sideways, mostly on the heel in kind of a shuffle. Still, the doctor seems encouraged by my progress.

"Why can't I lift my toe?" I ask him.

"Because the nerves running from your back down to your big toe have been damaged," the doctor tells me.

"How long until I can lift it?" I ask.

"Hard to say," he tells me. "You need to begin gentle physical therapy now. With rehab you may regain most of your mobility."

"Most?" The word involuntarily rolls past my lips. "How long will that take?" I ask.

"Depends. If you work hard, maybe 3-6 months. The mobility you have after 18 months will likely be what you'll have for the rest of your life," he tells me. He is cupping my foot in his warm hands when he tells me this. Hock is standing by the window, leaning back against the casing with his arms crossed over his chest just looking back and forth from the doctor to me.

"I see," I say. My gaze meets Hock's. There really is nothing else to say.

"I need to get back to Tennessee to take care of Dad," I tell the doctor.

"How soon can I travel?"

"You need to avoid over exerting yourself for at least 6 weeks," the doctor tells me slightly revising his first directive. "Don't lift anything over 5 pounds."

"I can avoid lifting more than that, but I have to go back to Tennessee," I tell him.

"Suit yourself," he says, "but it may impact the final outcome of your recovery."

"I'll be careful," I tell him. "I'll fly back, and I'll do the rehab there."

Both Hock and the doctor look at me. Neither look happy. But I can't think of any other solution. Dad is my responsibility. I need to get back.

Two weeks later I board a flight to Nashville. We make plans for Hock to bring my car to me later. Until my car is back in Tennessee I plan to rent vehicles for trips to see Dad and to continue my oversight of the cleanup and sale of the property. I locate a physical therapist in Tennessee near our apartment and begin simple exercises to speed my recovery.

Recovery starts slow. Even going to the grocery store presents a challenge. It takes me a long time to walk anywhere. It's physically exhausting to focus intently on just lifting my foot; and I shuffle when I walk. People in stores get impatient with me because I walk slow and they make a fuss if they are behind me and I don't move fast enough. Suddenly I feel like I'm in everyone's way. I realize how older people or people with disabilities feel marginalized in subtle ways that I never imagined before my injury. I can feel how impatient people are with me as I make my way through duties I must complete each day. I feel impatient with myself that everything takes longer now. Often I have to remind myself to just BREATHE! Hopefully this will pass. However, it gives me insight into what Dad must feel every day. Once a strong, action-packed man, now he too shuffles. He is slower mentally and physically, but he is sharp enough to sense if people are impatient with him or not. It is not a pleasant way to live. It makes you feel "less than" what you once were.

The apartment is lonely without Opal. As soon as I am back I call Dad to see how he is and tell him I plan to come and see him.

He sounds overjoyed that I am coming. "Jane, it is so good to hear your voice! Are you calling me from Texas?" he asks.

"No, Dad, I'm back in Tennessee," I reassure him. I do not tell him about the ruptured disc or the surgery because I do not want to worry him.

"When are you coming to see me?" he asks.

"Tomorrow, Dad. I'm coming tomorrow."

The next day I slowly walk into his room. Dad is sitting on his couch. He is wearing clean clothes and the sitter is with him. She is putting fresh socks on his feet, and I can tell she's recently combed his hair. His nails look clean and clipped. Together they are watching television. He looks happy to see me. His hair smells fresh and his clothes look crisp from the cleaners. I can tell he likes this sitter. She is a large woman, but she has a ready smile; and she is kind.

I visit with the sitter for a few moments before she leaves.

"So how did the trip go?" Dad asks me. "How is your back?"

"They did a little surgery on my back, Dad, and it's better now."

He scowls, "Surgery?"

"Yes, surgery, but I'm better, really."

"Well that's quick," he says. "Looks like you are still walking a little slow to me. A lot like your old man!"

"Yes, slow, but I will improve," I tell him. I sound more self-assured than I feel.

"I remember when Dad got down in his back one time," Dad tells me. "A cow who had just calved got mad at him and threw him up against the barn wall when he got in the way. Nearly killed him. Took him months to recover." He half smiles at me. "He walked about like you are walking now." He points an arthritic finger at me.

"Didn't you ever have a bad back, Dad?" I ask him.

"Many times, but I never let it stop me," he says proudly. "Once I fell off the roof of the house, do you remember? I lost my balance carrying a bundle of shingles up the ladder and fell right there on the hard driveway. Nearly scared your mother to death."

"Nearly scared us all to death!" I suddenly remember. "And I believe you were back up on that roof the next day."

"Yes, I guess I was." He inserts a toothpick into his mouth and thoughtfully chews the end. "Hurt like the dickens, but I kept working. No choice," he says. "I had a leaky roof and a family to keep dry."

Most of my life I've thought I was very different from Dad, but as I listen to him tell about his own back I realize just how alike we really are. Responsibility and love and concern for family propel us forward when perhaps others would sit down and take a break. Whether this is good or bad, I no longer know.

We talk a while longer. Dad shares memories of life on the farm he grew up on filled with hard work but also with happy, funny moments too. I have brought photo albums I've put together from family pictures that show his life in chronological order from elementary school to marriage and many of the jobs he's undertaken. We leaf through them for a while remembering.

"Your old man was once a handsome man, wasn't he?" he says and points to a picture where he has his arms looped through the arms of two friends and they are striding down a street confidently with large smiles on their faces. His teeth are even and white, and his expression says he feels he can do anything.

"He is still a handsome man," I tell him and kiss him on the ear. He smiles and even blushes a little. He turns the pages with arthritic fingers and pauses over each one with interest. He identifies old friends in the pictures by name and tells me a little about each. As he talks Dad reveals a lifelong interest in learning, in being a good person, and in doing the right thing. He has worked hard. Harder than anyone I've ever known. Despite that confident expression on that young man's face, it's apparent Dad has at times not felt equal to what life dished out. He no longer sees himself as a success. But I do.

Dad has been subject to what we are all subject to, rationalization; in some cases, anger and acts of self-preservation; decisions made out of desperation and fear. Sometimes life doesn't give us good choices. We must choose from what is available to us. Dad has lead a moral, productive, good and upright life. He's made the most of what God and life gave him. He has faith in his maker and he loves his family, though sometimes it has been hard for us to understand and accept the sometimes tough-love he offered.

Sometimes we've felt mutual disappointment in unmet expectation we held for ourselves and him—and in life in general. As I age I am coming to realize life is a crazy, mixed up mess at best. And we are all just doing the best we can. The core values that have made Dad who he is have been passed on to me. They are as natural to the two of us as breathing. It is a good moment. I regret when it is time for me to go.

After our visit I drive to the job site while considering how glad I am for these quiet talks with Dad. These conversations never happened before he got sick. Always too busy. Somehow we seemed always at odds when we did talk. Now, his illness gives us time—perhaps for the first time—to really get to know each other. Life gets in the way of really knowing someone—even parents. We can live with them all our lives yet not really understand what makes them tick.

Good progress has been made on the cleanup and prep for the auction while I have been gone. All the scrap metal and junk are gone, the dirt around the shop and across the front of the farm has been cleaned, smoothed, and leveled. All the brush has been burned and the ashes have been scattered. The driveway to the shop has been graveled. The equipment and tools in the shop have been partially sorted and organized for the sale. It all looks much better. Yet there is still much to do. I do not know if we can be ready for the sale in time. Looking at it, I am grateful that my back did not give out before this point in our progress or I do not think we could have completed it all. Clearly my days on a bulldozer and loader are over. I can't stand for long or my back begins to feel like a wet noodle. I will have to find other ways to keep the project moving on schedule.

There are fliers to create, ads on the web to set up, and sale announcements for the newspaper to construct, and schedule and there are people to call and tell about the sale. We still face more inspections by the EPA that we must pass in order to sell the land. We must have perk tests done on lots we plan to sell for future development. I must decide how to divide up the land in lots, and how it will be sold in order to maximize what we take in. I must organize the items that go to family members and arrange a system so they can claim sentimental items they want before the balance of the estate is sold.

Over the next two weeks I spend my days sorting through things and creating an inventory of potential items family members might want. Items that will not be included in the sale unless they go unspoken for. I photograph everything, add all the pictures to a photo file and create a master list of everything in Excel. It's determined that family members may request any item. If more than one family member requests the same item, the first time it happens the item will go to the youngest. Next time the same two people request something it will go to the next person in age. And this will continue in rotation until the selection process is complete. Once this is done, I will combine all the items each family member selected into individual groups, and workers will place them into a rental storage unit where the family member may pick up their property at their convenience.

I also create a complete inventory of items to be sold and work with a local auction company to determine how we should arrange everything for sale. There are houses to sell, property, tools and equipment. There's the log cabin that belonged to my grandparents that will also be auctioned off and later relocated. This is perhaps the most difficult thing of all to part with. But no one in our family has the ability or place to store a log cabin. And there are literally thousands, if not millions, of things big and small that must be sold, so many small things will be grouped and sold in bulk.

My days fall into a new normal. In the mornings I go to physical therapy, then to the job site, then to visit Dad. Then I go back to the apartment to work well into the night on inventories, finances and creating plans for the auction. I consult with financial advisors, bankers. I lie down when I can, which is not often. Gradually my leg regains strength. I begin doing what I call barcalounger exercises, lifting weights with my toes while sitting in a lounge chair at night. At first I start with the weight of a towel. Then I buy Velcro ankle weights that I can remove weighted sections from pockets in the fabric and start with the lightest weight in each pocket. Still, I drag my foot when I walk, and if I try to carry more than 5 pounds I can't lift my toes on my right foot off the ground at all and must drag it.

One day I am cleaning behind the shop and I come across some iron railroad tracks that Dad has salvaged from a job and has worked to cut into sections to sell as scrap. The sight of them makes me recall a conversation I had with my sister sometime back while I still lived in Texas and before I became Conservator.

"Daddy's lost his mind," my sister told me that day over the phone. It was a frequent conversation starter.

"Tell me something I don't know," I said, only half joking.

"I'm not kidding. You need to come home!" Her voice sounded tense. I pictured her in her nursing uniform, just arriving home from work, her stethoscope still looped around her neck. I could almost picture her hand gripping the phone, my father's old wedding ring flashing on her thumb.

"I can't deal with this by myself."

We both knew what she meant then. I had moved home long enough to help her care for Mom until she passed away. That time was approaching again for me to go home to help with Dad. We could both feel it. We also knew we could not do for Dad what we did for Mom. Even if he were willing, neither of us had the strength or the resources to care for him at home.

I looked at my desk, piled high with phone messages and paperwork, and wondered, as I often did, what gives a child the right to tell a parent what to do? What defining moment is it that makes the role reversal complete between parent and child?

"What's he doing now?" I asked, not sure I wanted to know.

"He's standing out in the field cutting up railroad tracks on the back of the property with a cutting torch, loading them by himself with the loader into the truck, and hauling them off to the recycle center."

"That's good news. We've always wanted all that old stuff hauled off. At least he's not on the roof of the rent house, telling the roofers what to do, like he was last month."

"Jane, he's 79-years-old. It's 95 degrees. He's going to die of heatstroke, if he doesn't get snake-bit first; or maybe he'll set himself on fire with the cuttin' torch! He's committing suicide via work!"

"You can't stop him! We can't stop him! We've already tried. If he wants to die, there's nothing we can do about it!"

Right after Mom's death we made the mistake of trying to persuade Dad to stop driving after he had a minor stroke. When he wouldn't listen to reason, my sister took the truck keys away. He pulled a gun on her and made her give them back. The very next day he was driving again. At another point we tried a group intervention that included his doctor. We sat him down and talked to him about all of it. The dozer, the trucks—we told him it was all too dangerous. But he would not listen. Instead, he went right back to working.

"Jane, there are snakes up there. Copperheads. Rattlesnakes. They're all over the place."

I sighed, feeling helpless.

That day, I decided not to go home after all. Somehow we worked through an intervention plan that she could implement that didn't require me to be there. Somehow Dad had not gone back to cutting up the iron railroad tracks for scrap after that day. Maybe he'd found an easier job. Maybe my sister had talked him out of it after all.

But as I'm looking at the cut rails scattered in the thick weeds where he stopped working I realize anew just how precarious and how dangerous Dad has always lived his life. It was very snaky-looking in that area and it was truly a miracle he had not been bitten or otherwise injured himself. It really was as if he's had a death wish; I ponder it all as I look around. It is not the first time that I've thought Dad had a death wish or that snakebite has been a very real threat in our life.

* * *

1972
Sometime in the early 70s Dad decided that he needed to stop building houses

and instead do building-site preparation. So he got a loan and bought his first piece of heavy equipment—a John Deere 350 track dozer.

Within a couple of years he'd added a loader with a backhoe. And just like that he abandoned house building for site preparation, building demolition, and earth moving. During slow times of year he hauled creek gravel and topsoil to make ends meet.

Meanwhile I grew up, married and went off to college and his business expanded. Some weekends I would come home and once in a while I would attend church with my parents when we were in town while my first husband would visit his parents.

One such Sunday on our drive home from church Dad said, "I won the bid to the job in Tellico where the Tennessee Valley Authority plans to build dams on the Tennessee River to make lakes and use them to generate electricity."

"Are you going to take it?" Mom asked. She sat up straight in the passenger side of the car staring out the window at the rows of corn tassels blowing in the wind in the fields we drove past. My younger sister sat next to me combing her Barbie's hair and singing, "Jesus Loves Me" quietly.

"We need the money. They've offered me more than I could ever make around here. And, it's steady work," Dad said.

"But it's so far away, nearly three hours away…near Knoxville, isn't it?"

"I'll come home on weekends," Dad said, as if that settled the matter. "And maybe sometimes I can go see my beautiful daughter and her husband at the great University of Tennessee." He laughed a little.

Dad had seen the apartment my husband and I were living in. In fact he'd helped haul our furniture to Knoxville and moved us in; but he had never visited overnight. As we rode I thought about this with a mixture of excitement and also with no small degree of skepticism and anxiety. Dad rarely traveled very far from home; and when he did he didn't stay long. It was hard for me to picture him coming for a visit or working so far from home for long.

"You are welcome to come and stay with us," I offered, despite my misgivings. "We do have a spare bedroom."

"Okay, my beautiful daughter. It's a deal," Dad said. He smiled.

That Monday Dad rumbled a couple of truck engines to life and fine-tuned them, testing clutches and brakes. Then he loaded the dozer and the loader with the backhoe onto their respective hauling vehicles using huge tree-trunk stumps instead of trailer ramps because he couldn't afford real ramps. He packed his camper, waved goodbye to us, and he and the hired help headed off on their long trip to Tellico. With questionable brakes on both trucks they would make the climb up and then the scary ride down the other side of Monteagle Mountain as they carried themselves and all the equipment to the new job site. There he planned to do his part for the historic remodeling of nature's waterways making them safe for recreation and also helping to set up a reliable electric system for future generations of Tennesseans—or so TVA told us. When he arrived, his job was to tear down and burn or haul away buildings and trees that might float and break off fishing boat propellers once the area was flooded.

Dad left, and my husband and I followed him in our car for a while to make sure his small convoy got over the mountain. Then we waved goodbye and headed back to our apartment at the University of Tennessee and he went on to Tellico.

Many of the homes and barns had housed families for generations in that area. Prior to the work Dad was scheduled to do, all the farms had been bought by the government and families ordered to move. Some families left their property willingly. Others packed up their homes on huge trucks and moved them to different property out of the flood zone reluctantly. The amount of work involved to purchase the property and move out all the families was truly mind boggling. And what Dad had scheduled to do himself appeared nearly impossible. Relocating whole comminutes was no small thing. And moving didn't involve just the living. Some of the moves also involved the dead as well.

For families who did not want their ancestors eternal resting place to be under as much as 30 feet of water, Dad would dig up the bodies and the local undertaker would move them to higher ground. Some families chose to do this, others did not. Those who did not would discover some time later that dead bodies do rise out of graves from the bottom of the lake and can float down river for quite a while. Some may even have made it all the way to the ocean, or nearly, much to the displeasure of folks all along the way.

And there were a few living residential holdouts who did not want to sell the property that had belonged to them for generations. Many remained on their property arguing with TVA until Dad and his workers showed up with their bulldozers to level their barns and houses. Sometimes local authorities had to be called and negotiations made on the spot before Dad could do his job. The situation was often tense and from time to time involved gunfire. Dad carried his shotgun on the dozer for just such cases and kept a rifle in his camper. And he persisted in doing his job under the orders of TVA authorities. Ultimately TVA won—as we knew it would. It's impossible, really, to hold back progress. Many families had no choice but to take the money offered them and find another place to live and move out quick, often with bulldozers idling right outside their doors. The situations were sad for almost everyone. It was tense and dangerous work for Dad. It was one of those scenarios where the needs of the many trample the rights of the few. Dad found himself stuck in the middle of all of it, contracted to do a job that he soon lost taste for but was obligated to complete.

Tellico, in the 70s, was not the vacation paradise it is today. In fact, it probably contained some of the roughest terrain and most backward and dangerous people imaginable. The gun racks in the back window of most trucks were there to be useful, not decorative. Less than a week after Dad arrived he realized that coming to my apartment every night to sleep really was not an option. Instead he found that to protect his equipment from theft and vandalism he needed to stay most of the time in the camper and sleep with the gun pressed close to his side under the sheets.

After a few weeks Mom and I drove up to see Dad and investigate how he'd settled into this new lifestyle. We knew he was lonely and wanted to cheer him up. There were still some loose plans for him to come and stay with me once in a while at the apartment. For many years my brother worked with Dad in the heavy equipment business; and if he still had been with him, he too would have been on the job in Tellico. But in recent years he'd started his own industrial painting company and that kept him very busy. He also had a wife and a daughter with another child on the way. So he did not join us on this trip.

So, I drove home, picked up Mom. She left my sister with our aunt because the drive promised to be long and hot. After a few hours drive we arrived at the location where Dad was working and found Dad there at his campsite. Everything looked neatly arranged with all the trucks and the camper pulled into a circle around an open campfire. It reminded me of the "Wagon Train" show on television.

"Well, here's my family," Dad said. He hugged me and kissed Mom on the cheek she offered.

"Hello Jim," Mom said to one of the guys that worked for Dad. "How's Mr. Hinkle treating you?"

"Fine, Mrs. Hinkle," Jim said. But he didn't look fine. He looked thin and dirty. After nodding to Mom, he headed toward the creek, shirtless with a towel and a bar of Zest soap and a razor to clean up.

"Is he going to take a bath in the creek?" I asked Dad.

"Well, yes. That's the way it's done out here," Dad said. "We're roughing it."

"Where's the rest of the help?" Mother asked.

"I gave them the day off to go into town and pick up what they needed. Jim wanted to stay and earn some overtime. Want to see inside my camper?" he offered.

I nodded.

Dad gave me the tour. "Here's where I sleep. Jim and the others share the tent over there." He gestured to a tent set up not far from the camper. Everything inside Dad's camper looked neat. His clothes were stacked in shelves next to the tiny bed that ran the width of the truck. Dad would have to sleep curled up, but otherwise the bed looked fairly comfortable. In addition to a bed, the camper contained a small gas stove and cooking utensils.

"Is this where you cook?" I asked Dad.

"Most of the time we cook outside unless it's raining," Dad told me. "It's too hot to cook in the camper, so we avoid it if we can. I'll show you." Dad took

Mom and me to the campfire where a spit had been set up over a wire stove rack that rested on large rocks. It was easy to see the rack could be raised and lowered based on needed cooking temperature by placing different size rocks under it. On the rack were several pots including a small pressure cooker.

"What's wrong with the pressure cooker, Louis?" Mom asked picking up the pot. The little plug that was designed to pop out during emergencies looked melted and damaged. She rubbed her finger over the plug several times examining the melted texture

"Nothing's wrong with it," he said taking the lid out of her hands. "I just got tired of the pressure valve popping out all the time and releasing all the pressure from the pot, so I welded it in." Dad set the pot back on the wire rack over the fire.

"Louis, you can't do that. That's like creating a bomb," Mom cautioned.

"There has to be a pressure valve on the pot or it might explode when you pick it up. It could blind you or maybe blow your arm off!"

"Woman, that's the least of my worries," Dad said.

"Ready to go to work?" Dad asked Jim who was walking up the hill. His hair still glistened with creek water, and he looked refreshed. Dressed in clean clothes he walked with his towel slung over one shoulder, his face cleanly shaved.

"You aren't going to work today, are you?" Mom asked. "We drove all this way to visit."

"If I want to fulfill the contract on time and get paid, we've got to work, even if it is Sunday," Dad said. "The Good Lord is just going to have to understand, I need to feed my family! Stay here and enjoy the view for a few hours. We'll be back before you know it. Jim and I'll cook dinner for you when we get back tonight."

Mother looked doubtful. She'd put on her Sunday dress, done her hair and applied lipstick for this trip as she always did. She wasn't exactly dressed to sit under the trees near a campfire all day. But it was Sunday, after all, a day when families should be together.

"Okay. What can I do while you're gone?"

"If you'd go through the recipe book I brought and mark the recipes you think might work in a Dutch oven, I'd really appreciate that," Dad told her. I looked at Dad, amazed. Dad liked to eat, but I never really knew he liked to cook.

However, Mother seemed pleased. "How about if I make a peach cobbler for you while you're gone," she offered.

"Sounds great! Jim, let's go," Dad said. Dad went to the pickup, reached in behind the seat and pulled out a shotgun and a rifle.

"What's that for?" Mother asked.

"People around here are none too friendly. You'll be okay here in sight of the road. But where we're going I like having a gun with me. This is wild country; you can't be too careful," he cautioned. He left the rifle on the bunk in the camper and took the shotgun with him.

Mother was still looking into the camper as Dad and the workers headed out. They both climbed onto their dozers, started the engines with deafening blasts and slowly tracked up through the hills at a distance cutting wide paths into the underbrush until we could no longer see them, but we could still hear the engines roar as they worked.

Mother found a lawn chair. She set it up under the shade of a large oak nearby. Then she went to the camper and got the cookbook. When she came back she sat down in the lawn chair, careful so as not to wrinkle her dress, and began going through the book. She removed her shoes and propped her feet up on a nearby rock so her legs would get some sun through her stockings as she studied the recipes. She turned down the edge of some of the pages and made notes in the margins with a pen from her handbag.

Taking her cue, I found something to do as well to pass the time. I was just learning to crochet and was working on squares to make a crocheted handbag. I brought it with me planning to work on it in the car on the drive while Mother took her turn driving. I collected it and found a place near her to settle down in another lawn chair.

We stayed like this for most of the day. The dozer engines ebbed and roared in the background keeping us aware of Dad's location. Once in a while a mockingbird would settle on a branch and mock the sound of a chain saw or the dozer before flying down to the creek for a drink of water. Clearly they were learning a new vocabulary based on recent activities in their area. Squirrels came out to gaze at us then, when they decided we were not going to move, they would explore the campground for leftover apple cores and watermelon seeds Dad left out for them. The trees bent and rustled in the afternoon breeze and all seemed tranquil except for the constant hum of heavy equipment in the distance.

"Guess I should start the cobbler," Mom said. "I believe he has the ingredients here." She rose and went to the camper to search for what she needed. Through the door of the camper I could see her locate the pie pan, peaches, flour, sugar, water. She washed her hands from a bucket Dad kept by the stove for that purpose. With deft fingers she patted out a piecrust and placed it in the pan she greased with butter from the little camping fridge. Then she added the peaches and put on a lattice crust. When she finished she ignited the gas oven and put the pie inside to bake.

"Whew, your Dad's right. It's too hot to cook in there," she said. "We'll have to stay out here until it's done, then air out the camper so he'll be able to sleep tonight."

Just as she sat back down, we heard the shotgun fire.

"Wonder what that's about?" Mom said. She stood up and shaded her eyes with her hand and looked in the direction of the dozers.

From the engine sound I could tell both dozers were now idling rather than working.

Another shotgun blast echoed down the valley. I gazed up toward where the sound seemed to come from, but couldn't see anything except a cloud of dust drifting our direction.

Six more shots were fired in only a few moments.

"Jane, I'm worried," Mom said. "Maybe we should walk that direction and see what's happening."

"Don't you think we should just stay here? Dad told us it's rough country. You don't have any boots. He's probably just shooting at some rabbits, don't you think?"

"Probably." Mom folded her arms across her chest and paced slowly in front of the campfire ashes, looking nervously in the direction of the gunfire sounds.

"Pie smells good," I commented.

"I'll check and see if it's done." She walked to the camper and, finding an oven mitt, removed the pie from the camper oven. She sat it on the camp table to cool, then opened the windows in the camper wider to allow more air to circulate.

The heavy equipment engines roared up again, and we could tell they were moving back in our direction. Mother seemed to relax a little.

"Well, I guess they are coming back this way. Must have been rabbits."

Some time later, Dad and Jim came back into camp on their dozers. Even from a distance I could see Dad had a big smile on his face. When they pulled up below I saw something that looked like half a dozen thick ropes looped around the bar hitch on the back of the dozer. They swung limply as he stopped.

"Jane, you and your Mom need to come see this," Jim yelled from atop his dozer. He and Dad killed the engines and jumped down from the dozers.

"See what?" Mom asked. She set the cookbook aside, and we both walked toward the dozers.

"Dinner, that's what!" Dad said. He wiped his hands on a hankie he pulled from his pocket standing beside his dozer.

"Did you shoot some rabbits?" I asked.

"No. Not rabbits!"

"Look here!" Jim said. He walked around to the back of Dad's dozer and untied something from the hitch.

"Oh my, goodness!" I said. "Isn't that a rattlesnake?"

"You bet that's a rattlesnake," Dad said. "I flipped a large bolder over up there on the hill and underneath it was a whole nest of them. They were laying under the boulder to keep cool. There were hundreds of them in that nest. There are a lot of them around here too. We've seen quite a few in camp just when it's getting dark. Most of the time if you don't bother them…they won't bother you." He smiled.

"When your Dad saw those rattlesnakes, he slammed on the brakes on the dozer, pulled out his shotgun and started firing just like an ol' time cowboy," Jim said with amazement. "Scared me to death, I got to tell you. Your Dad, he's quick on the trigger. A real cowboy! That's what your Dad looked like up on that dozer, like a man atop a horse! Firing away!"

"Dad, you must be some shot to shoot so many."

"I can't take too much credit. I think the vibration from the engine confused them. They were all huddled in one area."

Jim said, " He shot six of them, see?" He unlooped two more snakes from the hitch and held them up. All with their heads blown off.

"How did you blow their heads off so neat with a shotgun?" I asked.

"A snake senses heat, and he'll strike at the buckshot. These snakes literally bit the buckshot and blew their own heads off," Dad explained.

"Would you ladies like to try a rattlesnake sandwich?" Dad said with a smile!

"And Velma, maybe we can find a way to make a few of these into belts." Mom visibly shivered.

* * *

2006

"Dad, how are you?" I ask him when I walk into his room at assisted living that evening.

"Pretty good, how about you?" he asked me.

I settle onto the couch in his room next to the recliner where he's sitting. "Pretty good. Tired." We sit in easy silence for a few moments. I look around the room. It is a pleasant room containing his bed, a couch and also a recliner facing a wide-screen television. There is a large window beside his bed that faces west overlooking a grove of tall pine trees. When the sun sets it is an especially beautiful scene out the window. It reminds me of a studio apartment. On the craft table set up in one corner of the room are the bird houses that I bought for Dad to work on. There are paints for Dad to use to paint them if and when he wants. This also provides something for his visitors to do when they come to see him. They can work on the bird houses as they talk. If they want, they can take their work home. I see several of the houses are in the process of being painted. Even though Dad has aged, he takes pride in his work. His painting skills are still pretty good.

"Dad, do your remember the railroad iron you were cutting up for scrap on the back of the place?" I ask him.

"Yes, I never got around to finishing that. Got too hot. And I got called to do a dozer job for Preston that paid more; so I just never finished it."

"Well, I came up on that job today and Dad, it looked pretty snaky in there. I'm glad you didn't get bit or die from heat exhaustion running a cutting torch and cutting all that up. That was really hard work for you to try to do at your age."

He smiles, "Yes, it was pretty hot. Your sister was worried about me too. She bought me some, what she called, "do rags" to go on my head to keep the sweat out of my eyes. One had skulls on it and the other had flames." He laughed at the memory.

"How did you avoid the snakes?" I asked.

"Well honey, snakes won't bother you unless you bother them," Dad says.

"Besides it was too hot out there in the middle of the day. They were all under a rock somewhere in the shade. Smarter than your old man you know." He laughs again more grimace than laugh, really.

"Dad, do you remember the job at Tellico when you took the crew up there and did the clearing for the lake?"

Dad looks thoughtful, then the memory dawns. "Why yes I do. I remember having to eat my own cooking and it wasn't very good," he says. "I remember your Mom and you coming up and she cooked a fine peach pie. That was the best pie I think I ever ate. We let your Mom and you have a piece, and then I think Jim and I split the whole rest of the pie after you left."

"Dad, do you remember coming off that mountain with all those rattlesnakes?"

"Why, yes I do. We killed a good bunch of them that day. I think we killed more than 100 rattlesnakes during that job. Wish I'd kept some to make some boots or a belt out of. However, I don't think your Mom was too keen on that idea." He ponders the memory for a few moments, perhaps thinking about what rattlesnake boots would have looked like on his feet.

"Dad weren't you afraid up there working on those steep hills, surrounded by rattlesnakes? Didn't you ever get scared?"

He seemed to think for a few moments. "Well, I guess I did get scared once in a while, but not really that much while I was working. Too busy to really think about it. And we were careful enough."

"Yes, I remember just how careful you were. You welded the plug into your pressure cooker. It's a wonder you didn't blow your head off."

Dad laughs again, "Yes, as I recall that did worry your Mom. But it really wasn't all that dangerous. Especially compared to everything else we were doing. The seal on the pot would have given out before it really blew up," he said.

"So why did you do it? Why did you take that job?" I ask him again.

"Well, it was a good job. It was something I thought I could do to make some real money. And there weren't many jobs then. And, it gave me a chance to come and see you in Knoxville a time or two. That was good. Not often but once in a while I got to come and see my beautiful daughter where she was attending college. It was the most money I ever made too. Best paying job I ever had. I made 16K on that job. It helped provide for your Mom, me, your sister. I think I even helped you a little with college tuition from that job."

At that moment I can feel his mind as well as mine turn to what happened after he completed his work. Only a short time after he finished, Franky fell from the scaffold while painting the Wilson plant and smashed his head on a steel I-beam and died on the way to the hospital in Nashville. I remember getting the call that Franky had fallen. I'd been staying with my first husband's parents that night. We were in for Thanksgiving break and had just had dinner with my family and Franky only the day before. Dad called my in-laws, and when I came to the phone he said, "Your bother has fallen, it's bad, please come to the hospital to be with your mother."

We drove to the local hospital where I saw my brother as they loaded him into an ambulance to take him to Nashville where there were specialists capable of performing brain surgery to relieve the pressure so he might live. As they loaded him into the ambulance I saw blood running from his ears. My husband and I went to Franky's house to pick up my sister-in-law to take her with us to Nashville; but Franky died on the way to the hospital. We received the call from Dad who, along with my mother, had been following the ambulance to Nashville in their car. Dad stopped at a gas station to call us. He told me the ambulance had pulled over at Bell Buckle because Franky had died. He'd died before my sister-in-law could dress and we could follow. We had just called a neighbor to come and stay with his children so we could go. My brother had a 2-year-old daughter and also a daughter only 6 weeks old. After the call I noticed the clock in his bedroom stopped. The clocks on the wall of the kitchen and the stove clock stopped as well. They all stopped at the same time 12:58 a.m. I remember my sister-in-law saying "Is he gone? Is he gone, Jane?" I could only nod as I hung up the phone. And then she started to scream. Her screams hit my brain in a way I could not describe, and I went outside to be sick at the edge of the patio in the darkness.

Two days later we buried my brother. It sleeted on the way to the cemetery, and I did not have appropriate clothing to stand beside the grave with sleet pouring down. I shivered uncontrollably as the minister said final prayers over the coffin. My Dad took pictures both at the funeral home and at the cemetery. Then he locked himself in his office for days afterward and did nothing but look at those pictures and cry. Finally, the third morning he came out, eyes red, lips bleeding with dryness. He walked out of the room wearing the same clothes he'd worn for days, his unshaven face looking haggard. He put on his hat and went back to work as Mom begged him not to go. He didn't look at her. Instead he walked out the door. Something fractured between them that morning that could never be fixed.

Neither of us mention my brother by name, but we can almost feel and see his presence in the room.
Eventually, Dad clears his throat and says, "I used a good part of that money to pay for your brother's funeral you know." Even after all these years I can hear the catch in his voice.

"I know. You did a good job. It was a dangerous job and I appreciate that you were willing to take the risk for us more than you know." I reach out and take his arthritic, grizzled, rough hand in mine. It is a hand that has done countless things. It is a hand made stronger and calloused with hard work through time. There are twists and places where it has been mauled and broken over the years, but somehow it continues to work, and now still has the strength and the flexibility to paint a delicate bird house.

His hand is unresponsive to my grasp, but I hold it anyway. We both look up as the sun begins to filter into his room through the pine trees. It is a lovely view. A lump rises in my throat, but I resolve not to cry. If Dad can manage not to cry, I'm not going to cry in front of him.

After a few moments Dad gently squeezes my hand and then he lets go. A tear rolls down my cheek, and I turn and look at the bird houses again so I can brush it away before he sees it. He turns his face to look out into the setting sun.

We sit like this for a while. He watches the sun set out the window. I look at the color on the wall until it fades.

Finally, one of the assisted living nurses sticks her head in the door and says, "Hello Jane. Mr. Hinkle? They are making some peach cobbler in the kitchen. Would you like some?"

We both look at her for an extra long moment. Then Dad chuckles and smiles a little, "Why yes. Some peach cobbler sounds nice." His voice cracks as he says it. I wonder if he's thinking of the peach cobbler Mom made so many years ago in a camper at Tellico too?

<>

"Blessed are those who mourn, for they shall be comforted." (Matthew 5:4)

<>

Rattlesnake Sandwiches
Cut the head off the rattlesnake and discard in a safe place.
Preferably use an axe or a machete to do this to avoid contact with the head as a dead snake can still bite you.
Do not touch the head itself or risk contact with venom.
Wear gloves to handle the snake as they carry salmonella.
Use cooking scissors to open up the skin on the snake belly starting at the head and cutting on the underbelly all the way to the tail.
Use a sharp knife to peel back the skin and remove the rattles.
Grasp the snake firmly in one hand and begin peeling the skin off from head to tail.
It should peel off much like peeling a banana.

If you want to keep the skin, sprinkle borax on it thoroughly and place in a plastic bag in the freezer until you tan or mount it.

Remove the entrails by grasping the snake firmly and beginning at the head strip them out. They should peel out in one long piece. Discard.

Cut snake into 3-4 inch segments.

The meat should peel away from the backbone leaving bone-free tender meat.

Batter or bread as you would chicken in flour, cornmeal and egg mixture.

Fry in cast iron skillet and Crisco to 165 degrees (to kill potential salmonella).

Rattlesnake tastes like a cross between frog legs and turtle.

Serve on Po Boy bread with mayonnaise spread and pickle relish.

Serve potato chips and coleslaw on the side.

Chapter 16 – Squirrel, the Other White Meat
"The life cycle has come full circle now. Now, he's the child, and I'm the adult."
— Jane

2006
I've been back in Tennessee only two weeks when Dad's assisted living facility manager calls me late one night. "Jane, your Dad has fallen. We sent him by ambulance to the local hospital. We think maybe he broke his hip."

I hang up the phone and throw on some clothes then drive the 20 minutes to the hospital. I can barely walk myself, and I am dragging my leg a bit as I hobble through the lobby and follow directions to Emergency where they tell me Dad is waiting for his scan results. I find him propped up on a rolling gurney-bed braced with thin pillows looking pale and slightly blue around his lips.

"Dad? What happened?" I set my handbag on a nearby chair and take his hand in mine.

He avoids my question for the moment. "Well, Jane, how are you?" he asks politely as if he's not stiffly propped up in a bed surrounded by ugly green cloth partitions at the end of a row of partitioned enclosures just like it, each one containing people dealing with their own crisis.

"Well, Dad I was better before they called and told me you fell! Are you hurting?" I ask him placing my hand on his shoulder so I can lean in to kiss his cheek.

"A little," he says, but his face tells me different. He's hurting more than a little. He literally looks rigid with pain.

"Jane, I've been here a while. Mostly I need to go to the bathroom," he says looking embarrassed. The color rises in his white face.

"Have you tapped the button?" I ask.

"I've been tapping it. I've been holding it down, but no one comes."

I look around the emergency room and several units down I find a portable urinal, bring it back and hand it to him. It looks like half a plastic milk carton with a handle. He takes it from me, tries to turn on his side to use it. Groans. Tries again. He just cannot hold himself up on his side in a position to do what needs to be done. The terrific pain makes it impossible. I hesitate only a second, then I take the next leap in our relationship. I get him into position by putting pillows at his back, and then help him use the urinal. It takes…a while. Dad, of course, has prostate cancer as well as many other challenges. He looks embarrassed as we wait, but all I can think about is that he's hurt and I don't know what else to do. Modesty…the last sacrifice of old age and last barrier between us topples.

Eventually he finishes, and I take the urinal from him and set it on a nearby cart for pickup later.

I know part of him wants to die right there on that gurney, but I am not ready for him to go. I hope for brighter days—even now. Even if our roles are reversed, I still need my Dad.

"So, tell me what happened," I say. "Did they do X-rays too? And what did they find?"

"I fell. I don't remember much about it," he says. He wipes his wrist across his brow to remove sweat that's formed. "They did a scan of some sort too. They brought me here in an ambulance. I've never been in an ambulance before," he says. "I've followed them. But I've never ridden in one."

I can feel my own mind gravitating to the last "ambulance" experience we had. That one involved the last ride my brother took. He's probably remembering too.

Then we hear footsteps, and the doctor turns the corner and stops at the doorway of our green-curtained room making the fabric walls billow out slightly.

"Hi! Are you his daughter?" he asks?

"Yes, I'm Jane." I tell him. "Can you tell me what's wrong?"

"It appears your Dad took a nasty spill, but we don't see any serious damage."

"He cannot even roll over, it's got to be more than just a little spill," I say in disbelief.

"No, just a little spill," the doctor says. "Why don't you just leave him here with us for a few days. He can rest. Soon he'll be as good as new." He smiles. I don't like that smile. It makes me feel cold inside.

I look around. The hospital has an unkempt feel about it. It's old, and small in a small town. The people in the other green curtained rooms look like people who don't have options. They look like they don't have hope. They look like people who have never really had good care. I look back at the doctor and notice that his tie is stained and his nails are dirty. The waiting room I walked through had dirt in the corners and the ashtrays were overflowing. The garbage cans needed to be emptied. The receptionist was on her phone and punched buttons with artificial nails that looked filthy. Her eyes looked dull when I asked her where to find Dad. The lighting is dim. I don't like anything I see here. I cannot leave Dad in their care. There is nothing that gives me an ounce of hope or confidence in this place.

"I want a second opinion," I tell the doctor. "I want to take him to Nashville where they can get a better scan of his hip."

"You don't need to do that, we can take care of him here!" the doctor assures me.

"I know you can, but I'd just feel better," I insist.

"You'll need to sign paperwork that says we aren't responsible if you take him," the doctor persists. There is urgency in his voice. The urgency convinces me even more that this is not the place for Dad. I can tell…now it's personal with this doctor. I wonder if he's a part owner of the facility.

"That's okay," I say. My voice sounds falsely casual. "Bring me the paper work. I'll sign it." As I say this I wonder what makes me so certain. A little God voice inside is whispering they are wrong. That little voice is telling me if I leave Dad here he will die. I can't let that happen. I wonder at my own ability to stand there, only two weeks out of surgery myself, and argue with a doctor —an authority figure. At one time I could have physically rolled Dad out of the hospital myself, but I'm not able to do that tonight. I can hardly walk myself. There's a powerful, silent struggle of wills going on between myself and this doctor. I feel threatened by him, but all kinds of alarms ring, loudly enough in my head, to make me over ride my own fear. I have to get Dad out of here. Don't people Dad's age get blood clots from broken bones?

"We are leaving—with or without the paperwork," I tell the doctor. "So if you want me to sign a release, you need to get it here in the next 5 minutes."

It takes more than 30 minutes to get the paperwork. I sign it without reading it. I figure all the responsibility is on me regardless. I wonder for a moment if anyone will sue me for this decision if Dad dies. But I can't think about that now. I can't make a decision based on fear for myself. I need to think about Dad and what's best for him. What happens, later, happens.

The ambulance arrives to load Dad up 5 minutes later. Dad is amazingly quiet during all this negotiation and activity, uncharacteristically surrendering himself to my decisions. It's 10:30 p.m. before he's settled in the ambulance and it pulls out of the hospital parking lot turning west toward Nashville. I follow the ambulance in my rental car. On the way I listen to the WOW CD my daughter gave me of Christian inspirational music and tears roll down my cheeks. I feel relief at leaving the doctor and hospital behind. Something just felt wrong, and I acted on that feeling. I was not willing to take a chance.

It's 12:00 a.m. before they check Dad into Centennial Hospital in Nashville. It's not St. Thomas where Mom went and where a painted mural of her and her doctor is still on the wall; but it's a good place and it's better than where he was. It will have to do.

Immediately upon his arrival they take Dad to X-ray and to do another scan. The nurse shows me the room where they will bring him after his tests, and I wait for him there. I do not know how long I wait standing at the window, looking out at the lights on the street and the occasional lone car drifting past. I pray reaching out to God more often than ever before asking for his support and guidance. I recall my grandmother's absolute faith in him and my confidence in her judgment and that memory deepens my trust in him now. I pray silently that Dad will get well and that my back will get better so I can take good care of him and find a path forward in our new life.

The new doctor finds me waiting in the room looking out the window still wearing my coat and holding my car keys.

"Are you his daughter, Jane?" he asks. But this time it's with a kind voice. I turn and see a gentle, caring face. His hands and tie are clean, and his hair is combed.

"Yes I am," I tell him. I like his eyes. His handshake feels firm, dry and warm. His clothing looks clean. I restrain an impulse to hug him with relief.

"Well, it's a good thing you brought your Dad to us. His pelvis is fractured. It's a bad break. This is not something that would have gotten better in a few days. Your Dad needs constant care for the next few weeks, and it's going to take a while for him to recover. How well he recovers will depend on the care he gets and how still we can keep him. It's not something we can operate on and fix. It must heal on its own. But we don't want him too still because he is at risk for blood clots. So someone will need to turn him carefully and regularly." He takes my hand in his and pats it.

"Okay," I say. I exhale with relief. What he tells me Dad needs is possible for me to make happen. I will find a way. I feel instinctively the diagnosis is accurate. Now that I have the facts, I can make a plan.

"I don't think where he lives now is prepared to give him the care you describe. Is there a place here in Nashville that might be able to do it?" I ask.

"There are several that would do a good job," the doctor tells me. "A lot depends on your budget."

"What's the best facility," I ask him. Budget is the least of my worries right now.

He recommends one, and I tell him I'll call tomorrow—which is actually today now.

They roll Dad into his room. He looks tired and a bit white-faced, but he seems cheerful.

"Well, Jane, so we meet again!" he says with a smile.

I kiss his cheek.

"How you feeling, Dad?" I ask.

"Pretty good for an old man with a fractured pelvis," he tells me. He reaches out his arms to hug me and I gently embrace him.

"Well, the important thing is we know now what's wrong, and we are going to take care of it," I tell him.

"I believe it!" he says and smiles. "At this point I think you can take care of anything," he says.

High praise from Dad.

"Now your old man needs some rest."

"Are you hungry?" I ask.

"A little," he says.

The nurse who rolled him in asks, "Do you want me to bring you some ice cream?"

"Would you?" Dad asks. I can tell they've given him some pain meds and he's slurring his words a bit, but he doesn't look as rigid as before. I gather the pain is not quite as bad.

"I'd be happy to do that, Mr. Hinkle. I'll run right now and get it," she says. And out the door she goes to get some ice cream for Dad. She also brings one back for me.

The next day I check out several nursing homes. It is storming and I must pull over frequently because I cannot see through the rain; but I persist and get to as many as possible before closing at 5:00 p.m. The ones I want don't have a room. The ones I don't want do. I check out the facility the doctor recommended. They are nearly full but after talking to the administrator I find a room has just opened up. The most expensive room—of course—at the top of the five-story facility. It overlooks beautiful mature trees. I negotiate hard to get the price down, and they do give me a break on the cost. A corner room with a view over the lovely entrance lined with thick maples. Dad is not expecting this luxury. For once in his life I want him to feel special. I sign the papers.

"The captain who lived here died two days ago," the administrator tells me as she shows me the room. "He was here for many years and enjoyed it."

I can see why. It has a beautiful view and feels more like a luxury suite at a hotel than a nursing home. It's a big, airy, single room with floor-to-ceiling windows and a private bath. Dad has never in his life experienced such luxury. I walk the facility and see the timeless wood furnishings, the well-kept residents, and review a menu with the administrator. Meals includes poached salmon, shrimp and all the foods Dad has always wanted to eat but never felt he could afford. I decide whatever it costs it's worth it. For once in his life I want Dad to feel spoiled. Back in his room I take a last look at the view out the window as I wait for the administrator to bring me a copy of the final paperwork. As I look outside I see squirrels bounding from tree limb to tree limb. That tree must be their home. Dad will enjoy watching the squirrel while he heals I think. The sight of the squirrel takes my mind back.

* * *

1966

Sammy came into our lives on a Sunday. The day started out like so many others—with Dad sitting in a recliner reading his Sunday devotional while Mom ran around like a mad woman trying to feed, dress, and herd us out the door before Dad beat her outside and started to pound the car horn to speed us up.

Most Sundays Mother carried her nylons and shoes to the car, shooing the rest of us ahead of her like unruly chickens. On the way loose curlers would fall from her hair and she'd have to double back to collect them. As Dad started the car, she would pull any remaining curlers out (sometimes a good deal of hair with them) and tuck them into the glove compartment for collection later. Then she'd brush her thick hair into place and spray the whole mass into firm submission with Aqua Net hair spray as we drove to church.

With hair done she'd slide her legs into the nylons she carried to the car and pull them up to her knees, but no further. She'd point her toes and slide her pretty feet into her shoes. After she had her shoes on she'd say, "Franky turn your head."

Once he turned away, she drew the hose up over her shapely thighs and hooked them to her garter belt. Dad would let out a catcall, which made Mom and me laugh. Lipstick, she applied like an artist, completing her preparations to face God with her best and brightest face.

But this Sunday didn't go quite as planned. As she herded us out the back door toward the car, my nose detected an offensive smell, "What's that?" I planted my shiny, black Mary Jane's firmly on the ground and sniffed the air.

"Ugh!" Franky grasped his nose with his fingers and tugged his shirt up over it to act as a shield. "It's Scoop. He's been chasing a skunk—again!"

"Kids, get in the car, quick before the scent settles on your clothes," Mom warned.

Scoop was a German shepherd mix that had come to our place a few months before. Presumably he'd been chasing something and got lost. He looked half starved when he arrived, but he was a sweet dog; so we soon fed him enough until he filled out and decided to stay. And now he sat in the backyard next to the driveway panting, a big doggy smile spread across his face. He always smiled when he'd been out all night—Scoop was a good dog in most respects, but he loved to run after things. Cars, trucks, skunks, squirrels, Scoop didn't care. He'd chased rabbits through briar patches so often his ears had long cuts up the middle where briars had torn them nearly in two. Once he'd even chased a skunk under our house. A terrible battle ensued, which Scoop lost. We had to live with Aunt Gretta across the street for three days until the scent died down.

Franky opened the car door for us to get in, but Scoop excitedly jumped in ahead of us and sat down on the back seat, tongue lolling.

"Oh, no! Franky don't let him in the car!" Mom pleaded.

"Get him out, right now!" Dad shouted.

"I didn't mean for him to jump in!" Franky pulled on Scoop's collar. But he wouldn't budge. He loved car rides almost as much as chasing skunks and rabbits.

"Phew, he smells!" Mom covered her mouth and nose with her hand. "Get him out!"

Franky tugged and tugged, but he and Scoop weighed about the same and, of the two, Scoop wanted in the car more than Franky wanted him out. The waves of skunk odor radiated off the dog's warm fur. It penetrated every surface.

Finally after vigorous tugging, Scoop jumped out of the car, casually, as if part of his master plan was to stink up the car before he relinquished it.

"Franky, take him to the pig shed and lock him in with some water so he won't stink up anything else until we get back." Dad motioned toward the shed.

"Yes, sir!" Franky grabbed for Scoop's collar. But Scoop quickly dodged Franky and dashed off.

"Corner him, quick!" Dad threw out his arms as if to herd the dog like he herded cows. Scoop darted toward Mom, sensing now a new game was afoot. She danced around. "Louis! Get him away!"

Scoop tried to dive between her legs then swerved around her at the last second. Mom threw curlers into the air, and jumped into Dad's arms! "He's going to ruin my dress!" she wailed, throwing her arms around Dad's neck as he struggled to catch her.

Franky chased after Scoop who raced across the yard with his back arched and his tail tucked, thrilled at the attention.

"Franky, you come back here this instant! We don't have time for you to chase that dog!"

But Franky was into the chase now. Most Sundays, church bored him, and this was way more fun. The two rounded the far corner of our house and disappeared from sight.

Dad placed Mom feet first on the ground. She leaned her head inside the car and sniffed. "Oh, Louis, we can't go anywhere in this! We'll have to wash it out, maybe spray some air freshener in it and let it set a day or two with the windows down."

In the distance I heard Scoop making the special cry that said he'd hit the trail of something important. "Bar-oh, Ba-oh!" Part normal bark, part howling bay.

"Franky'll never catch him now," I said.

"Ba-oh!"

"Well, we might as well go back inside and change our clothes. We can't go to church smelling like skunk and dog." Mom stooped to pick up her rollers from the driveway.

"Yippee!—I mean, okay." I wasn't particularly sad to miss church. We went 3 or 4 times a week, so missing once would not hurt.

An hour later, I lay on my bed happily reading a Nancy Drew Mystery. Suddenly I heard scratching on my window screen. I went to the window and pulled back the drapes. Franky stood at my window with his finger pressed to his lips.

"Shh!"

"What are you doing?"

"I've got something. Come out and see."

"What is it?" I whispered back.

"I'll show you, but be quiet when you come out. I don't want Dad to know."

The mystery in his voice hooked me. I pulled on my tennis shoes and slunk unnoticed from the house. Franky beckoned me from the garage door near the garden. I ran down the small hill to where he stood.

"What happened with Scoop?"

"I don't know. The last time I saw him, he was running after a rabbit headed toward Uncle Dave's briar patch."

"Promise not to say anything?"

"I'm not promising anything—the last time I promised..."

"I know, last time you promised I'd nearly shot you in the eye with a BB gun and then asked you not to tell; but this is different, I don't even have the BB gun anymore!"

"It hit me in the temple, and it really hurt! I still have a scar!" I told him.

"I know. I'm sorry. Okay, fine. I'll just tell Dad, and he'll kill it then."

"Okay, okay, I promise."

I followed him into the detached garage, and he led me over to a cardboard box. Inside was a beautiful, gray squirrel—a big one. It looked like it was asleep.

"Is it dead?"

"No, just knocked out—see, you can see its sides moving."

"Where did you get it?" I whispered. I couldn't resist putting my hand into the box to stroke the squirrel's soft fur. It didn't stir when I touched it. The fur felt finer than Scoop's. It felt even softer than our cat. I touched its tiny ears with my finger. Softer still.

"Scoop was chasing a rabbit and I was chasing Scoop when this squirrel came running down the trunk of a tree. He ran right smack into my leg—hurt like the dickens. I think it knocked him out, and I stepped on him. I think I broke his leg. He just fell over, and he's been like this ever since. I couldn't just leave him there—Scoop would eat him. So I brought him here."

"You know if Dad finds him, he'll kill him and put him in the cook pot."

"I know. That's why you can't tell him."

"You can't keep him!"

"Well, I can't let him go like this. Something else will eat him before dark. Scoop, or maybe a fox."

"What are you going to do?" I asked.

Franky looked around the garage for a few seconds. His gaze came to rest on an old birdcage. It was the birdcage that had once held his parakeet, Jo-Jo... another Sunday story. That Sunday when we left for church our two parakeets were fine. When we came home we found my green parakeet had escaped his cage but then drowned trying to drink from the fish bowl. Franky's parakeet Jo-Jo hung by his neck from the top bars of his cage—an escape-artist attempt sadly gone wrong.

"We just don't have a lot of luck with pets," Mom said, blowing her nose on a dishtowel as she cried over the birds. We buried them on the hill behind the swimming pool, and mother had stored the cages in the garage—in case we ever wanted to get another bird.

"The cage would work for the squirrel, don't you think?" Franky asked.

I shrugged. "I guess." It pretty much depended on what you considered working—it didn't work all that well for the parakeets, but the squirrel's head was larger, maybe it would be okay. "If we are going to keep him, don't you think we ought to name him?"

"I guess." Franky thought a minute. "How about Sammy?"

"Sammy? Why Sammy?"

"Well, he kind of looks like Sammy Davis. Don't you think? He's got his arms curled up, and he has a white chest, kind of like he's wearing a tuxedo. I've never seen a squirrel that had a white stripe that wide," Franky commented. With his little paws drawn up toward his chest I decided he did look like Sammy Davis. I nodded. "Okay by me. Sammy."

Franky got a ladder and climbed up to get the cage off the shelf and handed it down to me. We looked around and found some old newspaper and lined the bottom of the cage.

"Doesn't that look uncomfortable to you? Maybe we should put a towel in the bottom, or maybe some grass?" I suggested.

"Yeah!" We scrounged around in the garage some more until I found some old towels that mother was saving to tear into strips to tie up tomato vines.

"How about this?"

"That'll do."

We lined the cage, and we put Sammy inside.

"What are we going to feed him?" I asked.

"I don't know. I guess seeds and nuts."

"Mom's got some mixed nuts in the pantry—I'll go get them."

"What about water? We'll have to find a bowl or something."

"I'll see what I can find." I dashed off to the house to collect the nuts and a bowl.

"What are you doing?" Mom asked when she walked into the kitchen and found me taking the nuts from the pantry.

"Nothing?"

She gave me that look.

"Franky and I are hungry. I thought we'd eat some nuts, like a picnic, out in the backyard."

"A whole can? No. You can't take a whole can outside! You'll get sick if you eat all those nuts. Give me that."

I surrendered the nuts with regret.

"How about a few? And maybe a sandwich?" Mom suggested.

I wasn't really hungry, but I nodded like I was. "Thanks, Mom."

How many nuts could a squirrel eat anyway?

Mother packed up an entire lunch complete with brown bags and Tupperware glasses of cherry Kool-Aid. When she wasn't looking, I grabbed a couple of mayonnaise lids from empty jars I thought we could use to give the squirrel water—and out the back door I went.

Back at the garage, Franky sat with his nose pressed to the bars of the cage gently blowing on the squirrel.

"What are you doing?"

"I'm trying to wake him up?"

"Is it working?"

"I think so—look!"

Sure enough, Sammy's eyes fluttered open. He looked at the two of us like we were part of a dream. Then he suddenly startled awake. He sprang to his feet and tried to run the sides of the cage, but it was clear that his leg was injured. After only a few half-hearted circles he cowered back into the corner of the cage and just looked at us.

"Let's try feeding him. Maybe it will heal if he just rests for a while."

We inserted some nuts through the bars of the cage, but the squirrel didn't touch them. I filled the mayonnaise lid from the hose at the corner of the garage, and Franky set it in the cage with the squirrel. It watched us closely, little sides heaving.

"Let's leave him alone for a while. Maybe he'll eat if we aren't watching."

We covered the cage with a light blanket, then left the squirrel and went back to the house, with plans for Franky to check on it again that night and for me the next morning. We mainly used the garage for storage, and it was unlikely either of our parents would go there anytime soon.

Over the next few days, the squirrel ate Mom's entire tin of nuts. He wasn't happy being in a cage, and he scolded us whenever we got near him, but he ate and drank from the lid, which we filled every morning and night. Once he finished off all the nuts I started gathering wheat kernels from the field across from our house. A week passed and each day he put a little more weight on his paw. Things were going really well until one morning when Dad unexpectedly walked into the garage while we were feeding Sammy.

"What's this?" he asked.

Franky and I both jumped and turned to face him.

"It's a squirrel. I found him," Franky said. "He was hurt. We are helping him get well."

"We've been taking care of him," I chimed in.

Dad stooped down to look into the cage. "Can I hold him?" Dad asked.

"He's kind of skittish," Franky said. But he pulled Sammy out of the cage and handed him to Dad. Dad grasped Sammy in his huge hand and, with one work-roughened finger, stroked his head. Sammy closed his eyes when Dad patted and talked to him. As I watched I wondered if the next minute he'd grab Sammy by the tail and bust his brains out against the garage door frame like I'd once seen him do to kill a rabbit that a shotgun had not quite killed. That time the rabbit didn't die with the first blow, so he bashed him again. But this time he just stroked the squirrels head and made cooing noises at him.

"We named him Sammy, after Sammy Davis Jr.," Franky told him.

"He looks like Sammy when he's entertaining. He holds his front paws up and he looks like he's wearing a tuxedo," I added.

Dad studied the squirrel for a moment, then put him back in the cage. Sammy ran around and around the cage looking out at Dad after he closed the door. "Well, he looks fine now. You kids need to let him go."

"I don't think he's quite ready yet, Dad," Franky said. "He can run, but he can't climb yet. Maybe we need to keep him another couple of weeks?"

"Well, if you think so," Dad said. He picked up a nut and stuck it through the bars to Sammy who promptly took it and began to eat. Dad smiled.

Over the next two weeks we would often find Dad morning and evening down in the garage with Sammy. He would gently insert nuts through the bars, and Sammy would take and eat them watching Dad carefully all the time he chewed. Dad would even clean Sammy's cage from time to time, and that wasn't easy. Dad took to carrying a tiny little bucket of nuts down to Sammy to feed him. It looked like a little toy milk bucket. Dad would feed Sammy and then watch him as he ate.

Finally, one morning we were all standing in the garage and Dad said, "Franky, you've got to let this squirrel go. I'm sure he's completely healed by now."

"I guess you are right," Franky said. My heart sank. I knew we would all miss Sammy, but he needed to be back in the wild with other squirrels. We all knew it.

"If you don't let him go soon he's going to be completely tame and won't be able to survive on his own," Dad said. "How about we let him go after breakfast?"

"Okay Dad," I said, sad but in agreement. "Right after breakfast."

"That sounds like a plan," Dad agreed, and he walked slowly out of the garage carrying the little toy bucket. Franky and I smiled at each other. Looked like Sammy would be okay; but we all felt sad, I could tell by the long faces on Dad and Franky

Right after breakfast Franky and I took Sammy over to the shop where there were oak trees and lots of nuts. It was a long way from the house. We didn't want Sammy to hang around the house because, if he did, we would feed him. And then he might become tame. We didn't want that because at some point he and Scoop's paths might cross again, and Sammy would be the loser in that. Besides the shop was where the fattest nuts were, Franky thought. We sat the cage on the ground, backed away and within a few seconds Sammy scampered to freedom, tail high in the air. "Bye Sammy!" We both waved. "See you around." A few weeks later, Dad was talking at dinner, "...seems like something's carrying off the nuts we gathered last summer from the boxes we stored in the shop," he mentioned in passing.

Franky and I stopped eating and looked at Dad.

"Really?" I asked, thinking of Sammy. Had he found a way into the shop?

"Really!" Dad said. I think it's the squirrels. I'm going to have to do a little hunting over there. Thin them out. Over several months Dad reinforced places in the walls of the shop where he thought squirrels might be coming in. He went hunting several times and brought home numerous squirrels. Thankfully, none had markings like Sammy. Eventually, Dad got busy with other things. The nuts slowly continued to disappear—all 2 cases from the shop over the next few years. We never saw Sammy again. The little milk can that Dad used to carry nuts to Sammy was converted into a pencil holder and it stood on Dad's workbench. And every time I went to the shop and saw a squirrel, I wondered if it was Sammy.

* * *

2007

About a week after the accident Dad is able to leave the hospital. The ambulance takes him to the nursing home I picked out, and I follow behind the ambulance in my car. I am feeling hopeful now, rather than scared. This is not scary like the long ride to the hospital behind the ambulance only a week before.

It's not a long drive, and by the time I park my car and make my slow way through the lobby and up in the elevator to Dad's room the nurses are in the room getting Dad settled. They make a fuss over him and I think he likes it. I look at his face. He's uncomfortable from the ride, but I can tell by the way he is glancing around at the comfortable bed, the big windows with the lovely view of the treetops, the warm greeting, he is amazed and pleased.

"So how do you like it?" I ask Dad.

"What does it cost?" Dad asks me.

"Don't worry about that. Not as much as you might think. You need good care and your insurance is picking up the tab for a lot of it," I tell him.

"How much do we have to pay?" he asks me.

"I'm not saying, and don't ask me again," I tell him. I'm firm with him as he used to be with me. I smile and kiss his head, then rub the lipstick print off the bald spot. He smiles.

"How are you feeling?" I ask him.

"Hurting, but better. Not that bad, actually. They gave me something to ease the pain for the trip. Thought for sure I was going to die, you know. But I didn't. I guess God still has a mission for me," Dad says, looking out the window.

A dietitian comes in and asks Dad to fill out a menu. There are some very nice things on that menu. Dad points to the salmon listed and asks, "How much extra for the salmon?"

"It's included in the basic price," the dietitian says.

"Jane, you are paying too much for this place," Dad looks at me sideways. "You are going to break your old man."

"I'm not going to break you. You have more money than you can ever spend, and it's time some of it got spent on you and not on a piece of heavy equipment or some loser coming to the house begging for money," I tell him. I look at Dad half wondering how he's going to respond to this bold statement on my part, but he's looking out the window at the squirrels playing in the trees.

"Look Dad, you have squirrels for neighbors!"

He nods. Smiles.

The squirrels bound and race from branch to branch circling round and round the trunk of the tree climbing up and down like acrobats. It's a miracle they don't fall, and I find myself holding my breath as I watch. They are truly amazing. So alive. So happy-looking.

"Well, look at that," Dad said. "Jane, you'll have to bring me my little bucket of nuts! I think that one of those squirrels looks a little like Sammy! Don't you?"

I am surprised Dad remembers Sammy. For a moment I am silent. Then I choke out, "Dad, I have that very bucket. I found it in the garage on your workbench. I'll bring it to you with some peanuts next time I come, okay?"

And I do. And together on pretty days we go outside and feed the squirrels.

◇

"Above all, keep loving one another earnestly, since love covers a multitude of sins." (1 Peter 4:8)

◇

French Squirrel

Cut head off squirrel, and remove skin, feet and tail.
Remove guts, toss over pasture fence for dogs.
Cut the remaining squirrel into quarters.
Check squirrel for wolves (small worm-like creatures in meat) and other parasites. Remove those with knife.
Put freshly dressed squirrel in pot of boiling water with salt, pepper, parsley and 2 cloves of garlic.
Cook uncovered on medium heat until flesh falls away from bones.
Carefully remove bones, and add dumplings.
Cook until done.
Serve with fresh cornbread and turnip greens.

Chapter 17 – Black Beauty
"Do you want to go inside?" — Jane
"No. I think I want to remember it like it was." — Louis

2006
Gradually Dad's pelvis heals and so does my back. I take a new apartment within walking distance of where he is staying in Nashville, and every day I walk down to see him. This becomes part of our mutual mental and physical recovery. It is a pretty walk down a tree-lined street gradually sloping downhill. On the way I pass through large iron gates and then circle around a fountain on the way to the door. I think it looks a bit like heaven with the ancient trees and stately pillars surrounding the entrance. It is so much nicer than so many places I visited. But still, it is not heaven. Home is really the happiest place on earth. And home is where loved one's are. Yet even though the facility is nice, if I am not here, it probably doesn't feel like home to Dad. So I come every day.

As soon as Dad's able, I put him in a wheelchair and take him outside for a roll around the grounds. In the beginning it is difficult for me to make this walk pushing his chair with the additional weight added to my own physical challenges. My foot is slow to lift due to nerve damage in my back; so I must try to focus on every step to make it actually happen. But eventually we both get stronger and better. Gradually, I can make the walk without stopping to rest several times along the way.

Almost as soon as I settle into the apartment, another health crisis arises for me. I am doing yoga in the apartment one morning lying face down on my chest. When I get up I notice spots of blood on my shirt. A quick doctor visit reveals I am bleeding from my breast and the doctor recommends removing a portion of my breast. Feeling this is a bit drastic I seek a second opinion from a specialist. She decides to do an exploratory to see where the blood is coming from. Within a week they have me in the hospital, draped, on the table ready for surgery and then...after prayer...the bleeding miraculously stops. The doctor had intended to follow the path of the bleeding to locate the source. Since nothing shows up on images she tells me surgery is no longer necessary and to go home and live my life. If the bleeding comes back then I'll come back and see her, but otherwise I'm to followup with annual mammograms as usual. It is nothing short of a miracle to me. *(Note: To date, the bleeding has not returned.)*

After a few weeks, Dad graduates to a walker, and we walk the halls at the facility stopping at the window seat at the end of the hall to rest and to enjoy the view. On pretty days we walk outside. Sometimes I arrive at dinnertime, and find him sitting at a table in the dining room with a collection of very pretty widows. There are lovely paintings on the wall that Dad says remind him of farm life back home. It is a nice dining room with subdued lighting. One widow with silver hair and a pleasant face develops the habit of holding Dad's hand while they wait for their food. Dad looks embarrassed, but he allows her to hold his hand anyway.

"She misses her husband," he tells me when we are alone. "It makes her feel better. And I really don't mind."

I wonder if it makes him feel better too. I cannot recall my father and mother holding hands.

The food is good at the facility, but I also notice things are not quite right there either. The portions of salmon I see in the kitchen are not what end up on the plates of the residents, in some cases. And often residents are supplemented with canned protein drinks to up their calorie intake if the food on their plates is not sufficient. Perhaps this is necessary at times if someone doesn't eat. But in other cases I think the food does not make the trip out of the kitchen to the resident. I suspect that there's a collection of workers stealing food. So I make it a point to arrive at mealtime to make sure Dad gets his designated portions.

One morning I arrive to visit Dad, and he is still waiting on his breakfast.

"Jane, my stomach is telling me my throat's been cut," he says when I walk into his room.

I try to make light of this strange, but telling, comment, "Oh…you are always hungry, Dad!" I partially kid him.

"Yes! Breakfast is late! Can you hear my stomach rumbling?"

I offer a nervous laugh, "Well, I don't hear it right now, but give me a minute. What did it say it wanted?"

We both laugh.

"It wants food!" Dad says.

I go to see what's keeping breakfast. In the kitchen they tell me the cook burned the muffins, but I don't smell anything burned. I ask for cereal, fruit, milk, and coffee and take it back to Dad to keep his stomach from talking back. I set the food on the small table in Dad's room in front of the window and then sit down across from him. We look out the window at the trees with squirrels looking right back at us. As I glance at Dad I am pleased to see his skin looks rosy despite the challenges with the staff and food distribution. It confirms my belief that a strong advocate is very important for a person living in assisted living or a nursing home. The patients that have regular visitors are treated better than those who have no one to check on them. It is…unfortunately…a fact of life.

"How is your pelvis feeling?"

"Better," he says. "Not as good as new, but I can get to the bathroom by myself now and not call for a nurse. That's a big step for an ol' man like me." He laughs again.

"I'm in as good a condition as a man in my condition can be in," he adds with a smile and eats his cereal finishing it off by drinking the milk from the bowl, then scraping it dry with a spoon.

"So how's the work going?" he asks me. He stares straight ahead out the window, not looking at me. It's unusual for us to talk about the cleanup. Dad generally avoids the subject entirely. It's difficult to have a conversation with someone about how you are completely dismantling their life. The subject is so overwhelming to think about, so vast, truly so terrible, in many respects, that finding a way to talk about it is next to impossible.

"Pretty good," I tell him cautiously. "Would you like to go and see it?" I ask him on impulse. I almost immediately regret the offer. I look at him out of the corner of my eye to see how he will react.

He continues to stare straight ahead. After a moment he reaches and takes a toothpick from the little vase shaped like a milk can on the table, unwraps it and inserts the end into his mouth. He chews on it. "Yes. I think I would."

"Okay, finish your coffee, get your shoes on, and I'll take you to the work site. You can meet all the guys that are cleaning things up."

We drive slowly to Dad's house. It starts to rain as we drive. By the time we pull up in the driveway to the house it is raining hard enough Dad decides he does not want to get out of the car. We pause there staring through the rain at the house with the windshield wipers going back and forth across our line of vision. Huge puddling drops hit the windshield blurring our vision. Richard Harris sings "MacArthur Park" on the radio as we sit there. At first it's a pleasant background sound. Then I realize how horrifyingly appropriate it really is, and I can't believe the terrible timing. I want to reach and turn off the song, but my arms feel frozen. So we sit and listen as the rain comes down and the windshield wipers click and clack.

"MacArthur Park is melting in the dark, all the sweet green icing flowing down; someone left the cake out in the rain....and I can't take it because it took so long to bake it, and I'll never have the recipe again. Oh No!..There will be another song for me for I will sing it. There will be another dream for me, someone will bring it."

Only there will be no more songs, no more dreams for Dad. This was it. This was the stage on which all his life's dreams and dramas unfolded. And the show is over. I am folding up the sound stage and all the equipment in Dad's MacArthur Park in his life. I nearly choke to keep from crying, but somehow I manage not to. Later. I will cry, a lot. But not now.

It all looks vastly different than when he left. All the junk is gone. Everything unnecessary has been hauled away, the brush cut, the trees have been trimmed, the shop behind the house has been emptied and its contents have been taken to his big shop for sorting and sale. I've planted the flowerbeds with yellow pansies. It all looks nice. It looks nothing at all like he had it. It looks like an ordinary upper-class house in a nice upper-class subdivision in Tennessee! The house has a new coat of gray paint with fresh white paint on the gingerbread trim. The whole place looks virtually new. The only thing that betrays its former condition are brown spots in the yard that show where the junk once set.

Dad looks at it for a long time. He chews thoughtfully on a toothpick he brought with him. I can tell he no longer feels connected with this place. His home looks different. It feels different. He is different. Nothing is the same.

When we took him to live in assisted living he looked like a street person, dirty, unkempt, skinny with sores, and he was raving nearly out of his mind. Now he is dressed in clean clothes, hair combed, nice hat and shoes, lucid. He is even wearing cologne that gives me flashbacks of our Sunday mornings when I was a child and he was getting ready for church. He looks like the person I've always known him to be inside but life's tragedies just sucked it all out of him along the way. He looks like someone cares about him and like he cares about himself. The angry, bitter, resentful, fearful person that went into assisted living has been replaced with this gentle man. *But is he happy?* I wonder. *Is it possible to be happy at this stage of life?* I wonder more.

As I sit there I consider why we did not take control sooner and make him take better care of himself? But even as I wonder I know, we could not. Free will is important. Self-determination…is vital for as long as possible. As we sit here I almost don't recognize him. But I also almost don't recognize myself. Never would I have dreamed I could accomplish what I've accomplished. Without God's help and guidance I could never have done it. I've also had support from many of my relatives, huge support from my husband, kids and many friends and even total strangers who came into my life at the right moment. Never did I want to take on this task. Had I felt that anyone else would or could, I wouldn't have taken it on myself. It felt like a leap into a raging river. It was an act of love, of faith, and of duty.

I don't know how long my days will be. But at this moment I think what I've done has shortened them considerably. But I love Dad. Despite everything, I love him. With all our strange and twisted memories, our up and down life together—that love remains solid. I have been mad enough to kill him at times. Mad enough to move off and for years avoid him. But I never disrespected him. We have never had cross words between us, ever. And love remains steadfast across time and space. And I know, even if he doesn't show it, he loves me too. He loves all of us. He does. In his imperfect way, he loves us with all that he has and is. We are all broken, just doing the best we can.

Dad doesn't say anything for a long time, he just looks at the house. The windshield wipers swing back and forth making a squeaking noise on the windshield. And I realize in that moment that with all the order, with all that was necessary to do that I've done to take care of him, I have also very neatly erased all his dreams from the landscape. It is generic now. It is no longer representative of him. The realization breaks my heart. Yet there is nothing else I can do.

"I will be thinking of you and wondering why..." the song goes on. *Why, is life like this?* I wonder. I will add this to my list of things to ask God when I see him face to face.

"Jane, it looks good. You've done a wonderful job," Dad finally says. His words bring tears to my eyes again. "Do you want to wait until the rain stops so you can go inside?" I ask.

"No. I think I want to remember it like it was. Let's go see the shop," he says.

We drive a little way around the subdivision and come to the shop. The rain stops. The men have been working with the equipment piling up brush and there are several brush fires smoldering in the rain. The shop has been completely cleaned and organized, the drive graveled, equipment not in use has been lined up along the side in preparation for the sale. The windows have been secured with plywood to keep theft at a minimum.

We pull up alongside the road and as we do, the half-dozen workers see us and stop what they are doing and walk over to the car. I do not need to tell them this is Mr. Hinkle. Somehow they just seem to know. I get out and shake hands with all of them. Dad rolls down his window and they file by and shake his hand by turns. He smiles and compliments them on their work.

"You men have done an incredible job," he tells them. "I do not know how you have done it. I never could have done what you have done," he continues. His praise is shockingly complimentary, almost effusive. It is not what I expected. I really expected him to pitch a fit. But he doesn't. One of the workers reaches through the window and hugs Dad around the shoulders.

"It was a pleasure to do it for you, sir!" he says. He pats Dad on the shoulder again and moves on so the next man can shake his hand.

Harold, the foreman, shakes Dad's hand and points to me, "You know, sir, she's been out here on the equipment herself, knee-deep in mud right alongside us helping in the cleanup!" He laughs. "You should have seen her!" He shakes his head.

"I have no doubt," Dad says with pride. "She is quite a girl," he tells Harold.

"Yes she is," Harold says.

I am embarrassed by Harold's praise, and amazed that this is Dad's response. I half expected Dad to jump out of the car and start cursing the men and demanding that they stop immediately and put all his stuff back. But somehow it appears he's come to terms with the necessary changes in his life. It is, still, the end of an era. But now it seems right. It seems appropriate. If it must end, then let it end on a conciliatory note.

The men stand around for a few moments and answer questions that Dad has about what happened to some of the more expensive items. He nods in agreement with the decisions made. Rain starts to patter down again, and I don't want to keep the men standing out in it, so we say goodbye.

We drive on around the subdivision to the old house where my parents lived when I was born, and where I grew up. It is the house Dad built laying every single concrete block that he made himself. He built it, roofed it and every part of it represents his sweat, hope and dreams. We pull into the driveway there and stop. It has been many years since Dad and Mom lived here. It's been rented and relatively uncared for, and we had much to do to prepare it for sale. Our cleanup efforts are also apparent here as everywhere. Dad looks at it. He says nothing. Just looks. I wonder what he's thinking?

As I look, I see the place where I stepped on a nail and my brother helped me to the house so Mom could tend my wound. I see the road where I crashed my bicycle and broke my arm. And where Beauty bucked me off and broke my other arm. I see where I used to lie in the field after the rain where the runoff would make a stream down the hill. In the distance I see the poplar tree I used to climb and sleep in as a child. Beyond that I see the walnut and hickory trees where we gathered nuts. I see the pond where we fished. I see the old shop behind this house where I found the "Peace Not War" signs my brother painted to protest Vietnam. I see the window to my parent's bedroom where they would lie at night and have long conversations about our future and theirs.

These conversations lulled me to sleep countless nights during my childhood. I see where we swam in the pool, and where frog kingdom once existed and has long since been concreted over. This is where we had pony cart rides with Beauty hitched to the cart, where we made homemade ice cream in the summer and where a million other happy and sad events of childhood lives unfolded. I see the old chicken house that we converted to a tack shed for the horses once the chickens were gone. I see where I once sat on the roof of the car and experimented with painting what I saw many a summer afternoon. There is beauty here and ugliness, joy, tragedy, heartbreak and living that links us forever unto death and beyond. We may have to sell all of it, but those memories will live on in us, long after the home belongs to someone else.

There's the rose bush still at the corner of the patio where we took pictures for Mother's Day and Father's Day before heading off to church on countless Sunday mornings dressed in our finest. It is the rose bush my grandmother brought from the old home place and gave to Mom when she and Dad got married. The maple tree by the driveway still stands. It's where I had my first kiss under it's branches. Soon it will all belong to someone else.

"What do you see?" I ask Dad as we are sitting there.

"I see a lot I didn't get to," he says. "And now I'll never get to it. What do you see?" he asks.

"I see a place my Dad built out of next to nothing except lots of dreams and a whole lot of love," I tell him.

He says nothing, then after a moment he turns to me. "Well, Jane, I'm ready to go home."

Home is now somewhere else. It is where we spend our time together—wherever that may be.

Slowly I back out of the driveway for the last time. I put the car in forward, we drive by the forsythia bush and the bridal wreathe bush Mom planted when she came here as a young bride. They are the last things Dad sees of his old home as we turn onto the main road.

We are silent until we get to town. Then I take a chance and ask, "Are you hungry?"

"Your Dad is always hungry," he tells me.

"Milkshake at Dairy Queen?"

"Sure."

"Maybe we can fatten you up," I tell him.

"I can remember you being a little puggy at one time."

In 15 minutes we are at Dairy Queen and have our orders. He's sitting with his elbow on the armrest of the car, arm pointed up, and I notice how crooked his arm is just behind his wrist. It's crooked because he broke it and didn't leave the cast on long enough for it to heal correctly. That seems like a lifetime ago.

* * *

1966

"Mmm…good!" I licked my lips and pushed my chair back from the table where I'd eaten my after-school snack. "Thanks for the milkshake, Mom. Can I go play?"

"Put your plate in the sink before you go!" Mom folded the dishtowel she had in her hand and placed it on the counter.

"Jane. Come here." She motioned for me to turn around with my back to her. I felt her hands go around my waist and tug the waistband of my shorts. She could barely insert a finger.

"What?" I pulled away. "You're pinching me."

"Are you gaining weight?"

Never in my 9 years had I ever considered my weight. But at that moment I felt the eyes of both Mom and Franky sizing up my waistline. I sucked in my stomach and gulped, "No Mama!" Feeling guilty—but not sure about what.

"Janie's gettin' fat! Janie's gettin' fat! Ha, Ha, Ha!" Franky chanted.

"I am not!" I yelled.

He gulped down the last chunk of chocolate-chip cookie from his plate and in three gulps downed the last of his shake. Sitting at the table with his shirt unbuttoned, I could count his ribs. Absently I ran my hand up and down my side but only felt soft flesh. No ribs poking out anywhere.

Mom looked at Franky and said, "Now, go play!"

"Okay, but I'm not playing with fat girls," Franky said. He put his plate in the sink, then turned and swelled out his cheeks and crossed his eyes at me from where Mom couldn't see him.

"Franky!"

"I'm going! I'm going!"

"Can I go to my room?" I asked. "I want to read."

Mom's cool, blue gaze sized me up. "Sure!"

In my room I looked at myself in the mirror. Maybe I had gained weight. I'd noticed my dresses felt tight lately, but I thought it just meant I had grown and needed new dresses. Turning sideways I noticed my stomach stuck out further than my chest. That didn't make me feel any better. Any girl knows it should go the other way. I sucked in, but couldn't make the distance equal out the way I wanted.

No one in our class at school was fat, except Rebekah. She had black-rimmed glasses and the old-fashioned, white, Peter Pan collars on her small floral-printed dress. She wore black shoes and white fold-down socks that always looked too small and tight. Yuck! I was on my way to looking like Rebekah! I resolved right then to go on a diet. No more second helpings of pineapple-up-side-down cake for me. No more second helpings of Mom's mashed potatoes. And absolutely no more green beans—I hated these anyway, so it was easy to give them up. Crackers. I would eat crackers three times a day—nothing else. Just then I heard Dad's whistle. "Jane! Franky!" he called. "Come here! Velma, you too!"

Dad always called for us to meet in the family room when he had an announcement to make. *He's home early,* I thought—*so it must be important.*

We all gathered around Dad. Sitting on the brown vinyl couch we waited to find out what was up. Once Mom sat down, Dad began, "Jane, I know how much you want a pony."

"Did you get us a pony?" I gasped.

"Now hear me out!" Dad interrupted. "There's a man in town who has one for sale. I saw it tied to a tree in his front yard with a sign."

"Dad, can we buy it, can we, can we?" I started hopping up and down on the couch!

"Jane, sit down!" Mom cautioned. I plopped down to sit at attention, hands at my sides. But inside, my heart raced.

Dad continued, "Now I'm not saying we will buy it, but I thought you might like to look at it."

"Yes, please! Yes! Yes!" I nodded my head up and down vigorously.

"Ah, we don't need a pony!" Franky said. "What we need is a horse!"

"Franky, I know you think you need a horse, but have you ever ridden one?"

"No, but I know I could handle a horse if I got the chance."

"Well maybe a horse next year, but a pony this year would be a good, safe way for you to get used to riding—then we could get a horse."

"Ah, Dad! People are going to laugh at me on a pony!"

"That's enough."

Franky sat back on the couch and folded his arms across his chest. "Some news."

"I haven't decided to buy it yet, but don't you at least want to go see it?"

"Oh, alright!"

Within 30 minutes, we all stood on a tree-lined driveway of a house on Jackson Street southwest and three houses down from the viaduct in town in front of a dark red brick house with wide, deep porches. Hay lay scattered around the yard. In the center, tied to an ancient oak tree, stood the blackest, shiniest, and most beautiful pony I'd ever seen. Her coat, iridescent in its blackness, looked nearly blue. Her mane hung all the way down to her withers and her tail dragged on the ground behind her even when she raised it to trot away at the end of her tether—as she did now. Nervously, she rolled an eye at Franky and me as we stood gaping at her until I could see the white part.

"She's a circus pony," the owner's son told us with pride. "My Dad bought her because he wanted me to ride in the Christmas parade last year."

"Did you ride her in the parade?" I asked.

"Shucks no! That pony threw me off and broke my collarbone—I ain't riding her anywhere. She's mean!"

"She doesn't look mean." I inched forward and stretched out my hand to the pony. Her black eyes glittered with mischief. Gently she stretched out her nose and wiggled it across the palm of my hand—searching for food. Instantly, I fell in love. I simply had to have her. She was round and plucky looking. So round that I wasn't sure a saddle would even stay on her back. But she didn't look fat to me. She looked beautiful. Maybe being fat didn't mean you had to be ugly. The pony was the prettiest thing I'd ever seen.

"Well, kids, let's go home," Dad said. He'd been standing over in the corner of the yard talking to another grownup, presumably the owner. But now they moved apart as Dad called to us.

"Are we taking the pony?" Franky asked.

"We'll talk about it on the way home," Dad said gruffly.

We both knew better than to stand in the driveway and argue. That was a sure way to get a spanking when we got home. Instead, we got back in the car and waited to see what Dad would do.

"Jane, we have a decision to make as a family and everyone gets a vote. You first. What did you think of the pony?" Dad asked, after we'd driven away from the house.

"I liked her. Can we get her?"

"Franky what did you think?"

"I think ponies are for babies. Fat ones!" He poked me in the ribs to make sure I knew he meant me.

"Then I guess you wouldn't be interested in driving a pony hitched to a cart would you?"

That took Franky by surprise. Several of his friends took their girls on rides in carts around our neighborhood. It had become a "cool" thing to do after one of the richer families had bought a cart and started riding the back roads on Sunday afternoons. Soon there were half-a-dozen or more people that bought carts and gathered to do the same. It quickly became an excuse to bring your favorite girl home after church on Sunday, and go for a cart ride. I could almost see the wheels inside Franky's head turning. Maybe if he had a cart, Dinora, the girl he liked at church, would come home with him some Sunday for a cart ride.

"Well, I guess a cart would be okay," he offered grudgingly.

"In that case, I'll call Mr. Wilkerson when we get home and tell him we have a deal."

"Yeah! We're gettin' a pony. We're gettin' a pony!" I bounced up and down on the seat! Not only was I getting a pony—something I'd dreamed of nearly my whole life—but I knew riding was good exercise. Soon I'd be thin again. No one would call me fat anymore. I wouldn't have to worry about looking like Rebekah!

"So what are we going to call her?" Dad asked.

"Franky?"

"I don't care. Call her whatever you want."

"Jane?"

"I want to call her Black Beauty cause she's a beauty and she's black."

And I had just read the book.

"Okay with you Franky?"

"Whatever."

Beauty arrived two days later. Mr. Wilkerson brought her out in his stock truck. He had a blue and white pony cart strapped to the side of the truck and a nice leather saddle resting on the passenger seat. Carefully they unloaded everything, and he gave Dad instructions on how to hook the pony to the cart. After that, they stored both the cart and saddle in the garage below the house. I ran my hand over the white leather upholstery of the cart and thought surely I dreamed the entire thing up. I pinched my own arm. "Ouch!" I closed my eyes. When I opened them, the cart was still there. I couldn't believe it.

That evening we hooked Beauty to the cart to take it for a spin. Dad drove her around the yard at a quick trot to make sure everything worked. Then he called, "Velma, come take a ride."

"Louis, are you sure it's safe?"

"Sure it's safe—jump in."

Delicately, Mom stepped into the cart still wearing her plaid everyday shirtdress and apron. Her hair gleamed dark blonde in the fading sunlight. Dad flicked the reins over Beauty's back, and off they went. After that, we each took a ride. Dad even let me drive—but not alone.

"Can I ride her?" I asked Dad after the last circle?

"Sure you can ride her."

Dad unhitched Beauty, then put the saddle on her back and helped me up into the saddle. Beauty peered around at me and nibbled on the stirrup while Dad adjusted them on each side. Suddenly she nipped my ankle!

"Ouch! Dad, she bit me!"

"I'm sure she's just playing! Just push her nose away."

Suddenly, I didn't feel good about Beauty. Images of falling and breaking my collarbone, like my friend Kate or the little boy who owned Beauty, zoomed through my head. Didn't the little boy say she threw him? I thought he was just trying to keep us from buying her, but now I wondered. Maybe Dad didn't hear that part.

Dad put a rein in each of my hands and showed me how to hold them. "Use just enough tension so you can feel her mouth, but not so much as to make her chew the bit. Pull back to stop her, and kick her in the sides and tell her to 'Get-up' to go forward."

"Dad, I'm scared!"

"You'll be fine. I'll lead you the first couple of times around the field, okay?"

"Okay!"

Off we went. Dad led the pony around the field behind our house several times. As he lead, Franky grew bored watching and went inside the house.

"I'm going to check dinner," Mom said, and she went inside as well. The newness of the pony had already rubbed off for them.

"How you doing, Janie?" Dad asked.

"Okay, but don't let go!"

Just then my Uncle Rex rumbled into the driveway in his truck followed by a swirl of dust. Uncle Rex was my father's younger brother. He often dropped by in the evenings to talk business with Dad.

"Jane, you go around a couple times by yourself while I talk to Rex. I'll be right back."

"Dad!"

"Don't be nervous! Just go! You'll be fine."

Suddenly, I was alone with Beauty. She turned her head and nibbled at my foot in the stirrup. I kicked her mouth away.

Jiggling the reins, I said, "get-up!" Nothing happened. She laid back her ears and started chewing and side-stepping. Then she danced a little and did a bit of a crow hop. My heart began to beat hard. "Dad?" I called. But he was busy talking to Rex in the driveway and didn't hear me. "Get-up!" I shouted again. Beauty started to move forward, more or less in the direction I wanted her to go—but partly sideways. We went a few yards, and then I noticed that she was drifting toward the center of the field where the old, black walnut tree stood. I started pulling the reins to guide her in the other direction, but she kept heading for the tree! I pulled back on the reins. She kept going. Quicker than I could have imagined, we reached the tree. Beauty passed so close to it, that I had to lift my leg out of the stirrup and swing it over the saddle horn to keep from scraping my leg on the tree. She made several attempts at scrubbing me off, first one side, and then the other.

"Dad!" I screamed. He waved, as if to say, don't bother me and did not look. Instead he pulled at his pants leg and hiked his foot up on the bumper of Uncle Rex's truck to settle in for a long talk. I could hear words, but couldn't make out what he said.

Feeling like a girl all alone on the prairie I decided it was time to teach Beauty who was boss. I pulled up on the reins with all the strength I could find and guided her away from the tree. Whew! I thought, as she moved away. I wiped the back of my hand across my forehead to clear the sweat away.

"Get up!" I said, trying to guide Beauty back toward the edge of the field away from the tree. But Beauty had other plans. Suddenly, it felt like she was folding up underneath me. Before I knew it, she lay down, right next to the tree. Quickly, I hopped off—just in time! Beauty rolled over on her back—right on top of the saddle! I would have been crushed if I'd remained in it.

"No, don't!" I shouted, and jerked the reins trying to make her get up! Beauty rolled back and forth on the saddle with satisfied grunts and several loud farts!

"Ugh!" I covered my nose with my fingers. "That's terrible! Get up!" I pleaded. At this point I was about to cry. She was destroying the saddle and most likely Dad would spank me when he saw it.

Finally Beauty rose, front end first, then back. She shook herself vigorously and dust swirled around making me cough. She looked at me contentedly as if nothing was wrong and began to chew the bit happily. Suddenly Beauty didn't look so beautiful anymore. She had grass in her mane and was all dusty with dirt on the saddle.

I stroked her nose and talked to her for a minute and pulled some of the grass out of her mane and tried to smooth it back in place. Maybe she'd gotten whatever it was out of her system. Maybe she would behave now. If I only could get back on her, everything would be fine. I'd make Dad proud of me that I'd learned to ride the pony so fast. I'd never gotten on a pony alone before, but I'd seen cowboys do it in movies so I gave it a try.

I collected the reins in my left hand and grabbed hold of the saddle with the same hand. With my right hand I steered my left foot into the stirrup. Then I gave a hop and swung my leg over Beauty. Beauty started to walk before I settled into the saddle.

"Whoa!" I called. Beauty didn't listen. "Stop!" I shouted. Beauty broke into a trot. I'd seen cowboys trot on horses on TV, but it felt different than I thought. Instead of bouncing gently in the saddle, with every step, I bounced awkwardly from side to side. Each step I bounced higher and higher until it seemed I almost didn't touch the saddle. As I bounced, the reins got looser in my hand. Beauty headed for the front fence. She went faster and faster with me bouncing on top of her. She went right past where Dad stood talking to my uncle.

"Stop Beauty! Daddy!" I yelled. Dad turned just in time to see Beauty break into a full canter! It seemed like forever, but I'm sure it only took us seconds to reach the fence. I knew for certain we would crash. Then, at the last second, Beauty plowed to a stop. She threw her head down and I went sailing off over her head into the fence post right at my father's feet! Everything went dark.

"Jane? Janie? Are you okay?"
Uncle Rex knelt down and patted me on the cheek.
"Where's, Dad?" I asked.
"He's over there," he pointed.
Gradually my vision cleared from cloudy to normal, and I could see Dad across the field, chasing after Beauty. As I watched, he caught her, and with his heavy work boot, he kicked her repeatedly in the ribs. I could hear him yelling at her, but couldn't hear what he said.

"He's likely to kill that pony," Rex murmured under his breath, hand rolled, bent cigarette dangling from his mouth.

"No, it was my fault," I told him. But he didn't listen. Instead he took a deep puff and absently created smoke rings as he exhaled.

"Do you think you can sit up?" he asked me.
"I'll try." Turning on my side, I started to pull myself up on my knees.
"Ah!" I screamed, and collapsed down again.
"What's wrong?" my uncle asked.
I cradled my left arm with my right. "My arm, I can't put weight on it."
My uncle took my arm and pressed several places between my elbows and wrist. As he did I felt a sick, weak feeling. For a minute I thought I might vomit from the pain. The ground swam up toward me. Through the haze, I saw Mom running from the house toward us.

"What's wrong? What happened?" she called
My uncle picked me up in his arms. I leaned my head against his shoulder which smelled like the tobacco pouch he had in his pocket, that and Wrigley gum. He headed toward her and the house with me in his arms.

"The pony threw her. I think her arm's broken."
Over his shoulder, I could hear Dad yelling at the pony and the pony neighing in pain.

Then the world turned fuzzy. Some time later I woke up in my bed. Mom sat on the edge of the bed beside me. With the tips of her fingers she gently brushed my bangs back from my forehead, which felt cold with sweat.

"How do you feel?" she asked me.
I felt my arm with my good hand. It felt weak and swollen. I tried to lift it

off the bed. "Ouch!"

"Does it hurt much?"

"Yes. I can't move it. It hurts—bad." I took my good arm and gently lifted the sore arm. Mom placed a pillow next to me to rest it on.

"Let me see!" She examined the arm, pausing in the center between my elbow and wrist. "I feel a knot here. I think it might be broken, Jane. Do you remember if you hit it when you fell?"

I shook my head.

"I'm going to call your father. We need to take you to see Dr. White."

"—broken arm? Not a broken arm, Kate broke her collarbone and had to stay in a body cast for 2 months! I've already had one broken arm from a bicycle fall! You can't get two broken arms, can you? Who can be unlucky enough to get two broken arms?" I started to sniffle. I could feel the corners of my mouth turn down to make my cry face. The sensation embarrassed me. I didn't want to cry. I wanted to be brave. But my face seemed to have its own ideas.

"What's up?" Franky asked from the doorway. He still held a book he'd been reading in his room while I was outside on the pony. He must have heard the ruckus when I fell.

"I think Jane may have a broken arm. We need to take her to the doctor."

"Wow! That's pretty rough. Want me to make you a sling? I've learned how in Boy Scouts."

"If you want." I didn't know what a sling was, but if it made my arm feel better I was all for that.

"Can I have an old pillowcase, Mom?"

"There are some old ones in the hall closet."

"You lay real still, Jane. I'm going to get your Dad," Mom said.

"Where's Uncle Rex?" I asked.

"He had to go pick his kids up from choir practice. He said he hoped you got back on that pony really soon."

Mom left the room. A moment later I could see her through the bedroom window as she walked to the edge of the patio and called Dad up from the barn. He must have taken Beauty there to unsaddle her.

"Louis!" she called into the distance."Loooouuuuuiiiiis!"

A little while later Dad came to my room and sat on the side of my bed.

"Let me see you bend your elbow," Dad said.

"I can't. It hurts."

"It doesn't look broken," he said, patting the arm up and down. He tried to bend it for me.

"Yow!" I cried out. "Don't touch it—please don't touch it."

"Stop crying. You just took a little spill. You'll feel fine in an hour."

"No I won't! It's broken," I called to his retreating back as he left the room after patting me on the head.

For most of the afternoon I lay in my bedroom and cried. Each time I looked at my arm it looked more swollen and began to turn black. I had no idea how a broken arm was supposed to mend, but I knew for sure that it wouldn't mend on its own like this. Through the walls, I could hear the murmur of my mother's voice as she talked and reasoned with Dad. Listening, I finally drifted off into a fitful sleep.

Franky shook me awake. "Sit up. I got something for you." He unfolded a pillowcase that he had carefully torn in several places.

"What do I do with it?"

"Here, I'll show you." With a twist and a turn, he cradled my arm in the sling, then crossed the torn ends over my chest and pulled them behind my head. There he carefully adjusted the height of the pillowcase so it would hold my arm evenly across my chest. When he was satisfied, he tied it securely around my neck.

"There. How does that feel?"

"Much better." It really did. Now I could see how I could get around, even though the arm felt useless. It felt much better in the sling than it had hanging by my side or even resting on the pillow.

"Okay, kids. Let's go." Dad came into the bedroom rattling the car keys in his hand.

"Go where?" Franky asked.

"We're going to take your sister to the doctor to see if her arm's really broken or if she's just making a big deal out of nothing."

At that moment I truly hated Dad.

Franky helped me out to the car. Mom came out a few minutes later. She had hastily changed into a white-eyelet shirtwaist dress and held her shoes and purse in her hands. She gingerly walked barefoot to the car and slid into the front seat after Franky and I climbed into the back seat.

At Dr. White's office a nurse helped me climb onto a large cold table and told me to lie still. This was not my first X-ray experience. Only the year before I'd broken my other arm riding my bicycle down the road when I hit a ditch created by runoff and I fell sideways. That time my grandmother was living with us. She didn't drive, and had to call Aunt Gretta to take me to the doctor because Mom was away attending a first-aid training course. The irony of this did not escape us. And for the rest of the course Mom made me go with her, and the group used me to practice their first-aid.

So once again, they took pictures of my arm with the huge X-ray machine as I lay on the table shivering. Then they sat me on an exam table in the room where I'd been only the year before, and I heard Dr. White talking to my parents out in the hall. Mom started crying. Dr. White spoke encouraging words. I liked him because he always gave me candy and told me knock-knock jokes.

"Well, little lady, I guess you know you've broken another arm," he said coming into the room a short while later.

"Yes, sir!"

"Not your first rodeo. But we're going to fix it right up."

"How?"

"First we're going to set the bones, like we did the last time. Remember?"

Yes, I remembered that part. Not fun. I nodded.

"However, this one is broken so high up toward the shoulder that we can't put a cast on it. If we put you in a cast we'd have to put you in an upper body cast, and we don't want to do that."

I nodded remembering how Kate broke her collarbone and had to have a body cast for 8 weeks.

"That means after we set it, you just have to keep very still," the doctor said. "Can you do that?"

I nodded. "Okay!" I sniffled. I wanted to run away, but didn't want to appear chicken. Franky would never let me live it down if Dr. White had to chase me down in the lobby. I braced myself for the pain and prayed I wouldn't faint! Only sissies fainted. God, don't let me be a sissy. Isn't it enough that I am fat? Dr. White carefully felt around on my arm, turning it first one way, then another. His fingers probed and prodded. Suddenly, he grabbed the shoulder and elbow and turned carefully, pulling out at the same time. I heard a loud click. Flashes of light seemed to explode in my head. Then—honestly—it didn't hurt all that bad anymore. Dr. White must have heard the click too. He smiled a satisfied smile.

"There," he said, rubbing his hand up and down my arm feeling and testing it. He started humming to himself—Frank Sinatra I think. Dr. White opened a drawer and pulled out a sling. It was a nice sling made for the specific purpose of holding arms in place. But I held onto the one Franky made for me anyway. Probably I would need a spare, I thought.

Dr. White carefully put my arm into the sling and then tied it first around my neck, then around my waist to keep my arm firmly in place.

"There," he said. He looked at me and smiled. "How does that feel?"

"Much better, thanks!"

"Let's go show your parents."

Mom, Dad, and Franky were waiting for me in the lobby to take me home.

The next six weeks taught me a lot about how much I needed both hands. I wrote with my left hand, ate with my left hand. But I needed both hands to comb my hair, button my blouses and fasten my pants. I even needed both to go to the bathroom. Without one, I had to ask for help. Mom often fed me when I got frustrated. Sometimes, without thinking, I'd try to scratch my nose and I'd hit myself in the face because the sling would jerk my hand back. After the first couple of days, my arm felt itchy inside the sling, but I didn't scratch and was careful not to move it. I didn't want a body cast.

After about a week, I started to go outside to visit Beauty. She stuck her nose through the fence and sniffed my arm. I told her all about how she'd broken it, but she just looked at me with innocent, shiny black eyes. It almost looked like she wanted to say, "I was only playing; what's the big deal?" She didn't seem to feel a bit bad about throwing me. In fact, she seemed cocky, like she'd won the first round. I fed her potato peelings and the ends of carrots Mom cut off our dinner and pictured myself back in the saddle. I could see myself riding her around the field, directing her where I wanted to go. She'd dance sideways, but I'd know just what to do to make her behave.

I remembered how the boy who used to own Beauty told me she came from the circus. Now I believed him. Beauty knew lots of tricks. But I knew a few tricks myself. Right then I resolved to show Beauty that I planned to be a ringmaster, not a clown.

Six weeks later, Dr. White checked my arm and declared it mended.
"You going to ride that pony again?" he asked.
"Yes, sir! Can't let Beauty think she's won!"
"Are you nervous?"
"A little—maybe."
"How soon can I ride?"
"I'd take it easy for a couple weeks until your arm feels stronger." He patted me on the hand, like a grownup lady. I looked up at Dr. White. He had dark brown eyes. Kind eyes. He had tended me when I was sick ever since I could remember. Mom said doctors were smart. That it took a long time to get through medical school. Dr. White looked like he knew almost everything there was to know. I bit my lip, then plunged ahead.
"Dr. White?"
"Yes?"
"Do you think I'm fat?"
"Do you think your fat?" he asked me.
"Maybe. Franky teases me—says I'm fat. I don't feel fat. But I don't know what size a girl like me should be?"
"Stand up!" He motioned me to stand in front of him.
"Turn around." He crossed his arms and rubbed his chin with one hand.

I turned slowly all the way around, conscious of his eyes looking closely at me. I could feel my face grow red under his gaze.

When I finished turning and looked at him again, he placed his hands on my shoulders.
"Jane, I think you are just the right size for a girl your age?"
"Are you sure?"
"I'm sure. Just keep doing what you're doing. Eat lots of fruit and vegetables; drink milk so your bones will grow strong. And keep riding that pony."

Show her who's boss."

"I'll do it!"

"And Jane, don't take your brother's teasing too seriously."

"I won't."

"How about we go show your Mom and brother how well your arm's healed?"

We walked down the hall to where Franky and Mom waited.

"Dr. White, I saw your new corvette in the parking lot," Franky said. His face lit up with excitement. Franky loved cars as much as girls.

"Yes, sir. I just got that last week! Newest model."

"Blue. My favorite." Franky said. "Someday, I'd like a corvette like that." He shoved his hands in his pants pockets and stood with his feet spread wide apart in his guy stance. He was tall for his age, with shiny black hair. He wore a white shirt and black pants. Even though I was nearly 5 years younger, I could see why girls were crazy for him. Even a sister had to respect that.

Dr. White reached into his pants pocket underneath his white doctor's coat. I heard a key jingle.

"Would you like to go for a ride?"

"Could I, really?" Franky gushed.

"If it's okay with your mother?"

"Can I, Mom?" Franky asked.

Mom smiled, nodded.

"Let's go!" Dr. White said.

He and Franky went out the door into the sunshine.

"So what did the doctor say?" Mom asked while we waited. I knew she wanted to know about my arm, but that felt like old news now. I rushed to tell her what I thought was really important.

"He says I'm not fat. I'm just right for my age."

Mom looked shocked for a minute at the quick change of subject. Then she smiled and hugged me.

"Don't you know? You're perfect," she said. And keeping her arm wrapped around my shoulders, we sat down to wait for Franky to return from his Stingray joyride.

Later, we drove into our driveway at the same time Dad arrived home from work.

"Well, hello kids! Jane, how does your arm feel?"

"Weak, but good!"

"Let me see?"

I walked over and extended my arm so he could have a look. He bent down and considered it closely. Then looked at me.

"I want you to know I'm real sorry you broke your arm. I just couldn't believe it was broken."

"I know."

"I hope you'll forgive me for not believing you."

I thought for a moment, I was still mad at him. And I didn't feel safe with him, like I did Dr. White. But he was my Dad. Slowly, I walked into the arms he extended and wrapped my own around his neck. He smelled like sunshine and the outdoors. "Yes," I sighed.

Dad patted me on the back. His hands were so big that when he patted it hurt but I held my breath and tried to enjoy it. Really I didn't mind that it hurt a little.

A few weeks later we came home from town where Mom had taken us to pick out new tennis shoes. Dad was sitting in the kitchen with a glass of tea. He had been cleaning out the swimming pool, getting ready to fill it for swim season. He was holding his arm and looking pale.

"Louis, what on earth is wrong?" Mom asked as we came in the house. Dad sitting, doing nothing was not something anyone was used to seeing.

"Well, my Great Big Beautiful Doll, I think I've broken my arm. I was cleaning the pool, leaning over the empty pool in the deep end. I was trying to fix the automatic skimmer that's attached to the side there. I was twisting the pipe to tighten it, and I lost my balance and fell into the deep end of the pool with no water in it. Nine feet deep. On the way down my arm caught on the hook of the pipe and it yanked my arm. I think it's broken."

Mom looked at the area located just up from Dad's wrist, and so did I. It was bent in an unnatural shape and had already started to turn black. It looked pretty terrible.

"Are you sure it's broken?" Mom asked. She reached out and felt the wrist. I smiled and looked at first Mom and then Dad. "It's broken alright," I said with confidence. "Dad, better get in the car. Mom and I will take you to see Dr. White."

* * *

2006

Dad still functions pretty well even though his arm remains somewhat crooked from his long-ago accident. After he and I finish our snack at Dairy Queen, I take him home. As I drive I think about that broken arm that happened so long ago. Mom and I did take Dad to see the doctor, and Dr. White put a cast on it, but Dad couldn't work with it very well. He waited about 2 weeks then sawed it off himself. While it did heal so he could use it, a noticeable lump remains, and his arm is permanently disfigured. Now as we drive he seems content, if not even happy. He does not bring up the cleanup on the way home, and I'm happy that we have peace between us for now. We are both glad to be walking again, to have had ice cream and for the cleanup to be nearly finished. Things seem to be looking up in a lot of ways.

Over the next few days I return to the garage behind the old house and there I find the ancient, blue pony cart. The white seat is long since ripped and half eaten by mice. Digging around in the dirt at the garage I find all the tack necessary to hook the pony cart up to a pony, but it is too old and brittle to use. I cut off a piece of the leather as a keepsake, dust off the cart and tell the workers to put it in the sale with all the rest. However, I never see it at the sale. Somehow along the way it disappears. I like to think that whoever got it really needed it. And that somewhere, another beautiful, black pony is pulling that cart making kids happy. I think Dad would like that.

◇

"I have fought the good fight, I have finished the race, I have kept the faith."
(2 Timothy 4:7)

◇

After-School Homemade Milkshake
Combine 1 quart of milk with
¾ cup sugar,
1 teaspoon vanilla,
and raw egg and place in blender.
Add 1 cup of ice.
Blend until smooth.
Pour into tall glasses.
Serve with fresh-baked cookies.
(There is a risk of salmonella, but at the time we did not worry about this and never got sick. I believe Mom wanted to add more protein and calcium to our diet.)

Chapter 18 – Chipmunks and Peanuts
"We paid for your mother's cemetery plot with that money." — Louis

2006
When I'm not with Dad, I'm at the new apartment in Nashville right down the street from his nursing home trying to help Hock keep our business afloat. We have developed a portable office of sorts, three white folding tables, one for him, one for me and one for the postal machine and a DVD burner. We use the burners to create DVDs to fill customer orders for our business. When I'm not with Dad or overseeing the final cleanup preparing for the sale, I spend my time in the living room at the apartment handling all things needed to keep everything moving forward. In addition, there's the paperwork and court filings for the estate cleanup which continue to take a lot of time as we satisfy EPA requirements, file court reports, appease angry neighbors and answer questions from all involved parties and relatives.

In the evenings when Hock is with me we take our wine out onto the balcony patio and enjoy the trees as they sway in the wind and watch the sun set. Sometimes we see chipmunks prowling the bushes below looking for food. Soon we start throwing them peanuts in the shell. After only a few throws the chipmunks begin to stand on their hind legs and signal to us to throw another peanut which they are quick to catch. They stuff the peanut in their roomy cheeks, then signal for another until they have stuffed all the peanuts in that their cheeks will hold. Once full, they scamper off to hide their collection.

In Texas we do not have chipmunks where we live, so this provides a lot of diversion and entertainment for us in the evening. Occasionally we miss the chipmunk's paws and the peanut hit them, but they take it in good spirits, only fussing at us a little for our bad aim then signaling again for more. I wish I could take the chipmunks back to Texas with me but know they probably wouldn't survive the hot climate. Probably there's a law against it as well. So, we do our best to enjoy them all we can now. There is something so innocent and beautiful about a chipmunk.

At the nursing home one day I mention to Dad that we are feeding the chipmunks at our apartment and how much I enjoy watching them.

"Do you remember the chipmunks that lived at the foot of the tree where we built the tree house for you and your brother? The one at the south end of the garden?" he asks.

"I had forgotten all about that!" I tell him.

"They lived and played at the bottom of the tree while you played at the top," Dad said.

"Yes, I think I recall it now. I used to imagine putting a little sign above their door that said 'Home Sweet Home' when I was a kid. Mainly I remember you and Franky building that tree house. The tree was a large twin oak tree, and you nailed steps between the two tree halves that lead up to the top. Then you put up a huge platform and railing where we could sit, have lunch or even nap. The rail around it was sturdy to keep us from falling out. It was a lovely tree house," I tell him.

"It was until the neighbor's son decided it was on his property and fenced around it, and his Dad forbid you kids from using it," he said.

"Yes, I remembered that part too. Not very neighborly," I responded.

"We told the neighbor he could use the tree house anytime he wanted after we found out the tree was on his property, but he decided it was his anyway, and legally I guess it was. But it wasn't very neighborly. He even posted a sign at the base of the tree that said, 'Private Property' and 'Keep Out', remember?"

"Yes, I remember," I tell Dad.

My mind drifts back to other chipmunk encounters as I help Dad paint bird houses. We had several chipmunk experiences when I was growing up. Some happy, some not so much.

***

1969

The scratching in the attic over my head gradually nudged me from sleep when I was perhaps 12 years old. It wasn't the first time the noise had awakened me. In fact, I'd had difficulty sleeping for months, off and on. I lay on my back, wrapped in the velvet blackness of my bedroom, and waited, trying to imagine what was making the sounds. There, it came again. I heard quick, tiny footsteps coming and going. Sometimes I heard noises like someone dropping marbles on the ceiling. They seemed to bounce and roll. Other times there came high pitched fast squeaking noises, like dwarves arguing far away. I wondered if a ghost lived in our attic. The thought made me shiver, and I pulled the covers over my shoulders until only the tip of my nose stuck out. I opened my eyes wider to see into the blackness trying to take in the darkest corners of my room—searching until they hurt. It was a long time before I fell back to sleep.

Dad built the house we lived in before I was born. He liked to talk about how he mixed the mortar and poured the concrete blocks for the foundations himself.

"There's no place I'd rather be than in this house in a tornado," Mom told me over breakfast the next morning as I told her about the noise and my sleepless night. "Your father mixed the blocks heavy on cement, and it would likely withstand anything the weather has to offer—maybe even a nuclear blast." She poured more coffee in her cup and dipped the edge of her toast into it thoughtfully before taking a tiny bite. Dad had already left to milk the cows and she enjoyed a rare, second cup of coffee before she started making beds and doing laundry.

"Maybe it would survive a tornado, but it's not keeping the rain out." I told her.

We both looked up at the water dripping off the end of the light fixture over the table where we sat. A steady rain had fallen all morning; and as usual, some of it found its way inside. Every couple of years, Dad had to go up on the roof and repair where the water was coming in around the gable, then inside he'd take the sheetrock off the kitchen ceiling, cut out a bigger hole and patch the ceiling with a new piece of sheetrock and paint it to repair the leak.

"It's because he didn't build the gable right," Mom acknowledged, dipping her toast in her coffee again and taking another bite. With one hand she moved a pot on the table a tad to the left to better catch the rain and keep it from splashing into my oatmeal.

The gable was right over the center of the kitchen, and when the wind blew exactly right, rain seeped in and ran down the electrical wire through the ceiling and dripped onto the kitchen table. The gable was vented which allowed water to blow in.

"So, what's making the sounds in my room at night? Do you think it's a ghost?" I asked her. We'd been watching the series, "The Ghost and Mrs. Muir" on TV, and it seemed so real. I liked the thought of a friendly ghost in the attic. One that would watch over me and scare away bad people. "Maybe it's Grandpa come back from the dead to ask me why we don't come to the cemetery to visit him more often."

Mom smiled. "A chipmunk more likely. I've seen them on the roof a time or two. The trees have grown limbs close to the house. Close enough now for squirrels and chipmunks to jump onto the roof and find their way inside through the vents. Dad always said he was going to put screen wire over the vents, but he just never had the time."

"A chipmunk?" I said. "I love chipmunks, but not sure I want them inside. And this one's keeping me awake."

"Probably. We need to tell your Dad so he can figure out where they are getting in and close up the hole."

The last thing I wanted to do was tell Dad. Suddenly I remembered this was not the first time we thought we had chipmunk problems. Some time back I remembered that Dad had killed one in the kitchen. It had found it's way in from the back porch into the hall closet and had been slipping into the kitchen looking for crumbs to eat. I happened on it one night when I got up from bed to get a glass of water. It scurried under the couch and sat real still, but I saw it anyway. When I knelt to get a closer look, I could see its little heart beating in the tips of its ears. After that, I made sure and left out raw peanuts for it every night I remembered. I'd set up and wait for it to slip under the crack of the closet door and scamper down the hall to the kitchen. It was so cute.

Then one morning, the chipmunk came to the kitchen late, and Dad was up early—about 4 a.m. I didn't see what happened, but Mom told me about it later. Dad sat eating his Rice Krispies and reading the paper when the chipmunk ran under the table to get the peanuts I had left it. Quick, Dad grabbed up one of his work boots, threw it at the chipmunk and killed it with one blow—right in the kitchen floor. When Mom told me about it, she cried into a wadded-up Kleenex, her eyes red, "It was such a cute little thing…never did anything to anyone. I screamed, 'Don't, Louis!' But he'd already sent that big ole boot of his flying! He didn't mean it! He thought it was a mouse. It was just automatic with your father. You understand."

I did understand. But watching Mom cry, I didn't want to.

"He didn't eat it, did he?" I asked thinking that would only make things worse, but I did want to know. I knew how Dad hated to waste meat.

"No, he didn't eat it. Said it wasn't even a mouthful, and he threw it out with the trash."

She looked at me and shook her head.

What could she say? What could anybody say?

Dad was...Dad.

No, I didn't want to tell Daddy about the chipmunks, so I started wadding up cotton and sticking it in my ears at night. I wasn't afraid of a few chipmunks.

For several months my plan of live-and-let-live worked, until one morning a loud explosion woke me!

"Louis Hinkle! What are you doing?" I heard Mom scream.

I jumped out of bed and ran to the back door to see Dad standing in the back yard with a smoking shotgun in his hand.

"Honey some chipmunks have moved into our house and I just saw one come out of the vent on the roof and scamper down that tree. I thought I'd take a shot or two at him and see if maybe he'd decide he needs to live somewhere else."

"Please don't shoot them. They are just trying to get in out of the rain. Besides, you are going to blow holes in the roof," Mom cautioned. "We don't need any more holes."

"Well, I shot high. It was only intended to scare, not kill," he said walking back into the house and sitting the shotgun in the hall closet. "Guess I'll just have to try again tomorrow."

But I could see that now it would be war between Dad and chipmunks until they were gone.

Over the next few weeks, Dad did what he could to roust the chipmunks out of the attic, but once settled into their warm dry home, they didn't want to abandon it. He did put the screen over the gable. They chewed right through it the first night. Then he made a different gable with smaller holes, but they chewed right through the wood. He replaced that gable with one made of concrete. That took longer, but they finally chewed through a loose board at the corner of the house and made a new entrance. I could hear them nesting over my head in the attic at night, but I didn't say anything because I was firmly on Team Chipmunk.

One morning I got up to find the attic stairs in the hallway unfolded and the light on in the attic above. I climbed up a few steps and found Dad in the attic. He was busy removing wads of leaves and fur from a corner and shoving it into trash bags.

"What are you doing, Dad?"

"Why, I'm evicting our new tenants."

"But why?"

"Cause they haven't paid their rent." He kept shoveling.

"But where will they go?"

"Into the cook pot if they stay here! They are pulling out all the insulation in the walls to make their homes—That's going to bring fleas and mites and all kinds of things inside the house. I won't have it!" He kept stuffing the nest collection of chipmunk work into the bags until it was all gone. Then he swept the floor of the attic with a whisk boom and spread out new loose insulation.

After he finished, he got his hammer, some boards and nails and did a rough patch job on the corner of the roof, but because the foundation had settled the corner didn't meet exactly. I could still see daylight when I looked closely.

"There. Now maybe they'll move on to someone else's attic."

But they didn't. Once a chipmunk thinks of your attic as his home, it's hard to make him believe otherwise. Fortunately, most of the time, Dad had bigger things to think about than chipmunks.

A few days later, I heard, "Eeee!"

I rushed to the living room where Mom stood stomping her foot and glaring out the window. "That chipmunk, he climbed right up to the bird feeder, knocked the seed container off, and while I was standing here, stuffed his cheeks with seeds and ran off into the woods. He's ruined the feeder. It broke when it fell!"

"Well, you wanted to nurture wildlife. Isn't he wildlife?"

"Yes, but there are plenty of seeds for chipmunks. That seed was store bought for songbirds! Now I have no way to feed them."

"Didn't you say you wanted chipmunks?" I remembered when our trees were small how Mom would look out the kitchen windows longingly across the street at my aunt's ancient oaks. My aunt had hundreds of squirrels and chipmunks. Now, they were making homes in our yard as well since our trees had matured. I thought she'd be glad.

"I guess you better be careful what you wish for, you just might get it," Mom whispered. "Guess we'll have to get a different kind of bird feeder."

We did. We got the ones that hung from the limb of a tree. However, it didn't fare any better, and soon it too hit the ground and broke spilling all the seed. So next Mom bought a window feeder. That lasted a couple of weeks, but a squirrel jumped on it with enough force that it broke the window.

"I don't know why I'm replacing this window with my hard-earned money over a squirrel," Dad grumbled a few days later as he brought in the new glass pane and puttied it into the old frame. The money should come out of the household allotment I pay you each week."

"If you hadn't killed the cat, then we wouldn't have any chipmunks or squirrels," Mom pointed out. Mom is talking about a stray cat that we had for a while until Dad picked it up to pet it, and the frightened cat scratched him. Dad struggled with it a little, the cat grew even more frightened and really dug into his arm. Dad snapped its neck in an instant and threw it across the fence in front of our horrified eyes.

"Well serves the cat right, I only wanted to pet him, and he clawed me half to death and even bit me," Dad said, clearly feeling completely justified. "He should not have bitten the hand that was feeding him."

I shivered a little when he said this but kept my lips firmly sealed. Didn't want to have done to me what the cat had experienced.

"Well, I may have planted the trees, but I didn't attach the feeder to the window. It's your own fault the window is broke. You shouldn't have put the bird feeder there. Didn't you know that squirrel would have a go at it? Soon we'll have squirrels and chipmunks both living in the attic."

"I thought he would be afraid to come that close to the house," Mom said as she stood nearby to hand Dad any tools he might need.

"If I wasn't afraid, it would fall out this winter, I'd just put masking tape over the crack," Dad muttered as he added more putty with a rounded knife and smoothed it with deft perfect strokes to seal the glass into the frame.

"I know you would, but it wouldn't look very nice."

"I'm a poor man. And sometimes a poor man's got to make do." Dad turned his shoulders inward a little more in his pitiful stance he adopted when he wanted to look put-upon and downtrodden. It worked with the neighbors. They usually felt sorry for him. "Poor Mr. Hinkle," they'd say. "He sure does work hard." However, I had grown used to his posturing and didn't take it overly seriously. I knew right then if I got Dad to open his wallet, he'd have at least 30 hundred-dollar bills stuffed in it. The window glass cost less than three dollars.

"Well, you've fixed it, so I don't know why we're arguing."

"It's the nature of chipmunks and squirrels to store food and find a warm safe place to live. We can't change that. But we are going to have to encourage them to live somewhere else." Dad hefted the newly framed glass up and slid it into the window slot, then screwed in the braces to hold it. "There. Good as new. Don't mount another feeder to it!"

The next day Dad brought home a crude chipmunk trap made from wire, with a little trap door, which he blocked open with a piece of wood. "Let's see if we can catch ourselves a chipmunk dinner," he said. Little prickles of ice tickled the back of my neck when he said this. I thought about Sammy the squirrel, long gone now. Dad did not eat Sammy; he let him go. But you just never knew about Dad. He might really put the chipmunk in stew. He'd already cooked a possum. Walking to the back yard, Dad looked around as if scouting for chipmunk trails. After a few minutes of poking first under one bush, then another, he settled the trap behind one, propped the door open and stepped back, seeming satisfied.

"Now, I'll just add a little seed at the back. He'll go in, bump the stick, the door will fall, and he'll be trapped. One less chipmunk, I tell you—that would be a good thing."

"What will you do with him?"

"I'm going to eat him, that's what I'm going to do!" Dad growled.

"Daddy! You wouldn't? Can't we re-home him down by the tree house?"

"Well, maybe. We have to catch him first! Now, go wash your hands, your mother's almost got dinner ready."

For several days nothing happened with the trap. The fourth day, Dad checked it before breakfast and found a surprised possum blinking up at him. "Another confused varmint! He doesn't even eat this type of seed. Get out of here!" Dad took the possum outside, shook it out of the cage and nudged it along with his boot, then reset the trap. "If not for my wife, I'd throw you in a baking dish. Count your blessings Mrs. Possum. Velma said she'd leave me if I brought home another possum for her to cook."

The possum scuttled off into the bushes without a backward glance, unaware how close she'd come to being dinner.

Meanwhile, the chipmunks seemed to be staying on the ground and somewhere else these days out of reach, as if word had gotten around that Dad wasn't happy with them.

I'd almost forgotten the chipmunk war when one evening after dinner I was in the backyard washing my pony with the hose, and Dad drove up. He got out of the van and walked over to me with the lid of a box under his arm.

"What have you got?" I asked him, adjusting the spray, and watching the white line of soap edge down Bupp's withers and off his muscular legs onto the ground as I sprayed him. The pony wrinkled his whiskers seeming to smile. The weather was hot, and he loved to be sprayed when it was hot.

Dad said. "Want to see? I've got them dressed out to cook." Somehow he didn't look all that happy, and I just knew.

"No."

"It's not what you think, Jane."

"I don't want to hear it," I said.

"Well, we couldn't let them live in the house," Dad said.

I picked up the end of Bupp's halter and led him to the barn, my back stiff because I knew Dad was watching. Inside the barn I slammed the door and fastened the lock then threw myself into the clean straw of the manger and sobbed. I would miss the scurry of happy, little feet overhead that night.

***

2006
Driving to the nursing home the next day I am in a hurry, and it is early. Normally I walk, but this time it is too cool, so I drive. As I pull out of the driveway something darts from the side of the road. I try to dodge but hear a thump under the car that tells me I have struck something. I circle around and there on the road is a chipmunk, crushed. I pull the car off to the side of the road and cry, for the chipmunk, for Dad, and, yes, for me. Regardless of how careful I am, sometimes things just go wrong.

Eventually, I dry my eyes, make myself presentable and arrive at the nursing home where I find Dad sitting on the side of his bed his toes curling around the edge of his shoes. In a moment he takes his foot-long shoehorn and shovels his swollen feet into black tennis shoes. He then washes his hands and slowly pushes his walker out the door to the dining room where lunch is waiting.

I follow him out the door, holding lightly to his belt loops in case he falls. In the dining room the other residents have already gathered. There are 10, including Dad. Jennifer, one of the older residents, is standing. A balloon floats up from a string tied to her chair. She has gift bags before her on the table and is opening a bottle of cologne to sniff.

"Let me smell," Marge, who sits to her right, says. "Mmmm… I like that."

"It's her birthday," Hilda, the cook, explains as I help Dad into his chair. "We have cake for after."

I flip Dad's walker around and sit on the seat so I can remain next to him. He picks up his fork and begins to eat the tuna melt and cottage cheese with pear.

For a few minutes Jennifer opens gifts, and we admire them. Cologne, sugar-free chocolate, a cane patterned in pink camo. Susan, her daughter, hands each gift to her in turn. The other residents exclaim in delight and pass the gifts around to examine. Dad eats but does not take part in the celebration.

Once all the gifts are opened, Jennifer rubs her arm. "My hand feels numb." She shakes it a little.

Marge grabs Jennifer's hand and rubs it. "Arthritis. Sit down and have some lunch."

Jennifer sits.

"Where's your husband today?" Ruth asks me.

"He's in Colorado. Took him to the airport yesterday," I tell them. "He'll be back Sunday. We plan to go hiking when he gets back. I so look forward to exploring the new trail," I tell them. Over time I've gotten to know most of the people at the nursing home, and they know a lot about me and our life. One of the wonderful things about older people is they still seem to care about the people around them. Younger folks do not always make the time to get to know others; so I enjoy my visits to the nursing home more and more as we become acquainted. They know my husband travels and seem to find what we do interesting and often ask me about it. And I know about their families too and all their children. They are happy to tell me about their adventures as well.

"Would you like a glass of tea? Maybe some cake?" Hilda asks.

"That would be great!"

Tammy, the housekeeper says, "I'm going to lay out all weekend, by our new pool. It's too cold to get in the water, but I can lay there beside it with a good book and read."

"That sounds like the perfect weekend," I tell her. Enjoying a good book beside a pool does sound wonderful.

"I don't feel much like eating," Jennifer says to no one in particular. She looks pale to me, and I wonder which birthday she's celebrating. If maybe the excitement is too much.

"Dad would you like to go to the park this weekend? Watch the kids in the paddle boats?"

"Do they charge for that?" Dad asks.

"No. It's free to watch the boats, and it's free for you to come and go here too."

"Let's see how I feel then. I'm still a little tired," he answers. He continues to eat with relish.

"Hilda, Hilda!" Tammy suddenly screams from directly behind me. I turn in time to see her catch Jennifer as she falls. Slowly, she lowers her to the floor directly behind Dad. Jenny looks blue. I'm not sure she's breathing.
Everything happens at once. Jenny's daughter rushes to her side.

"Dial 911" Hilda calls out!

"Is she breathing?" I ask. I rush for a towel to mop up salad and dressing now scattered on the floor. I don't want anyone to fall.

"I feel sick," Jennifer says. From somewhere a small garbage pail appears.

"Mother throw up if you need to," her daughter urges presenting the pail. All the residents around the table except Dad have stopped eating. They watch in horror as we circle around Jennifer who is stretched out on the floor. I rush to Dad's room, pick up a lap rug and bring it back to tuck around Jenny.

All the action is taking place directly behind Dad's chair, but he does not stop eating. Instead, he breaks off a piece of bread and mops up the cheese from the tuna melt.

"The EMTs are on their way," Tammy announces. Her voice shakes with anxiety. "How you doing, Jennifer?" she asks. Jennifer doesn't answer, only nods.

I feel relieved to see she's conscious. "I'll wait outside for the EMTs, to make sure they know what building to come to," I say. I go to the door, and as soon as I step outside, I see the fire engine and ambulance turning down the street coming toward us. I wave until I'm sure they see me.

When I go back into the dining room, I realize Dad is still sitting only a few feet from Jennifer. He's finished the tuna melt and has started on the fruit and Jell-O desert. All the other residences have either gone to their rooms or they've moved their chairs over to the other side of the table to make room for the EMTs.

"Dad, you've got to get up and give the EMTs room to work," I say. I tug gently on his arm. He scoops his plate close to his chest and keeps eating.

I tug his walker over to him, trying to get him to stand. He keeps chewing. The EMTs are at the door.

"Dad you've got to move. Give them room to work."

He doesn't answer.

"Dad!"

Despite my bad back, I pull him, chair, and all, down the side of the table and around the end out of the way of the EMTs.

The emergency personnel rush in and settle their bags and the gurney around Jennifer. They work on her for 10 minutes. Her blood pressure is extremely low, but she's conscious and can answer questions.

Dad sits and watches like he's at a dinner theatre, and he's got a front row seat.

"You just never know when it's your time," he muses between bits of red Jell-O.

"You just can't kill me." He takes another bite. "And they can't throw me out no matter what I do as long as you pay my rent."

"No, Dad, they can't throw you out," I say marveling at his lack of response to everything happening around him and unsure what it means.

Later I take him back to his room and get him settled. As I am easing him into his sweats for the night (Dad still will not wear pajamas in the nursing home), Dad says, "Jane, I was thinking about how the neighbor took possession of the tree house where the chipmunks lived. Remember that?"

"Yes, Dad, I remember that," I say easing first one arm then the other into his top.

"I guess that all worked out in the end," he says.

"How do you mean?" I ask, adjusting his top down around his hips.

"Well, if you remember, that neighbor's son, the one that stole your tree house, when he grew up, he built his house on property that backed up to our new house. And he put a swimming pool at the back of the house without checking the boundaries and accidentally put it on our property."

"I do seem to recall that," I say, content that now his top is on so now I help him step out of his pants and into his sweatpants. He does this carefully before continuing.

"Yes, he did that and when your sister found out about it, we asked him to pay for the property where he put his swimming pool; but he wouldn't. He said we were friends and that I should just let him leave it. But then I remembered that tree house, and I thought, probably we should not just leave it. So, I got an attorney and we sued him and collected the value of the property."

"You did?" I said. I had not heard this part of the story.

"Yes, I did," Dad says. "Your sister helped me do it." He sat down on the side of the bed, and I helped him lift his legs and swing them in and under the covers.

"So, what did you do with the money?" I ask.

"We paid for your mother's cemetery plot with that money," Dad says.

"Pretty harsh, going after him like that," I say.

"Well, maybe. But it was no worse than him taking your tree house. And your mother wanted to be buried next to your brother, and I wanted her to have the lot if she wanted it. I couldn't afford it, and this was a way to get the money. And I just couldn't forget about him taking possession of that tree house and taking that away from you kids. He was a kid with motorcycles, swimming pool, nice clothes, but he was determined to take your tree house, and he got it. And not only that, he evicted the chipmunks too. I was out one day and saw him about to climb up into the tree house and the chipmunks came out of their home at the base and he stomped and stomped and he scared them away. I saw it. It was terrible. Then they got run over. I skinned and dressed them so they wouldn't go to waste," Dad said, his eyes staring far off.

"So that was what you had in the box that day," I said.

"Yes."

"But you've killed chipmunks too," I say to Dad, thinking about the ones he hit with a boot in the kitchen when I was a kid.

"Yes, but never on purpose," he told me. "I thought that one was a mouse."

"I never kill for fun. Only to feed my family or protect them."

"You mean like the cat?"

His eyebrows shot up, as he recalled snapping the cat's neck.

"Yes, like the cat. We could not have a vicious cat around you kids. For all I knew that cat might have rabies. It was not acting right, so I killed it. Kids are more important than cats."

"So why didn't you act shocked when Jennifer passed out this afternoon and the EMTs had to come?" I ask.

"Wouldn't have done any good. How embarrassing to have everyone standing around staring at you when you've lost control of yourself that way. I wouldn't want people staring at me. So, I kept eating trying to be normal. I couldn't do anything for her, but I could give her her privacy, so that's what I did."

"So how did you stay so calm?"

"God takes us away when he wants us. What's to get excited about? We don't have any say. He doesn't need any help setting the clock on life for any of us. It's up to him when we live and when we die."

I take Dad's hand. "I love you Dad."
He squeezes my fingers.

◇

"For I, the Lord, love justice; I hate robbery and wrong; I will faithfully give them their recompense, and I will make an everlasting covenant with them."
(Isaiah 61:8)

◇

Roasted Peanuts

One of our favorite snacks at night when I was a kid was roasted peanuts. We had a peanut farm close to us, so Dad would often buy a huge bag of peanuts; and he would roast them over a fire in a light-weight skillet with a long handle made for this purpose; or Mom would bake them in the oven. We would eat these at night as we read or watched television.

Wash peanuts quickly by pouring them into a colander and running them under the faucet to remove the dust.
Pat dry with paper towels.
Spread on baking sheet.
Sprinkle with salt.
Put in oven at 325 degrees for 30 minutes or until slightly brown.
Allow to cool before eating. Dad ate his in the shell; we shelled ours.
(Note: You may also cook on top of the stove in a salt-water brine for 30 minutes in a pressure cooker (1/2 cup salt to gallon of water,) then drain and bake for saltier peanuts.

Chapter 19 – We All Scream for Snow Cream

"Let's make some angels first, before the snow starts to melt." — Louis

2006

The weather turns cold the week before the auction. So cold that I'm not confident at all that anyone will attend. Despite the cold we continue the cleanup. There is no way to really finish it. We just have to do our best and then, when time for the sale comes, we will just start. I've hired an auction company, and over the last few weeks the owner, Edward, has worked with me to determine how to display things and sell them. Some items will be sold individually. Others in "lots". We know everything won't sell, but he tells me there are always scavengers at the end of the sale that will take things away that remain unsold. So maybe we can at least avoid additional scrap expense. Everything that we have not reserved for Dad's future life, or that he has not designated for family, must go.

My sister and I have the ability to purchase things we want as well from the estate. She indicates she wants to purchase a portion of the property and plans to bid on it. I hope with all my heart, if she wants it, that she will be able to buy it. Every morning I continue to go to the shop and sort and organize. Soon the cold turns my feet numb inside my boots; and periodically I walk to the heater and hold my feet up to the fire to thaw them out. When I see my boots smoking, I pull them away. It helps, but my feet never really thaw out. Neither do my hands. I work wearing leather gloves. The fingers are split, and I've stuffed them with fabric I've found to protect my hands. They are good gloves and keep my hands dry and prevent cracking, but they really are not that warm. Often I put my hands inside my jacket so I can thaw them enough to restore feeling. Before the day is over I begin to experience the tingling of frostbite.

The huge heater glows red in the corner of the shop doing its best to keep us warm. Without it we could not work at all. It makes our lives only just tolerable. Yet there is no option but to continue.

As I sort I think about all the cold winter days when Dad brought one piece of heavy equipment or another into the shop to overhaul, paint, or otherwise prepare for when the weather was good and he could work again. Many times I've worked under similar circumstances to paint and letter a dozer, loader or truck in this very shop. As I work I think back to the 60s which seemed colder even than today. In the 60s we often had to bust foot-thick ice on the pond for the cattle to drink. As my father would say, "Old Man Winter's not always kind."

***

1968

On cold nights when I was a child I often stood in my parent's bedroom peering out the window into the darkness wishing for Dad to come home. He would be out checking the cattle, putting antifreeze in the vehicles, or some other project that forced him out into the impossible cold. One night the snow fell so thick and fast I couldn't see the pecan tree only 10 feet away from the window. Before Dad left to check on the cattle, he cautioned us not to go outside for fear we'd get lost. The thought of stumbling around lost in high snowdrifts only a few feet from my own doorstep gave me the shivers. It felt good to be inside with a bright fire burning in the den fireplace. Still, I worried about Dad and would anxiously wait for him to come home.

Stiff winds drove the snow horizontally across the fields some nights. It piled in huge drifts against the west side of the house and screened-in porch. Inside the house everything sounded muffled, like when Mother stuffed cotton in my ears when I had an earache. It felt cozy inside. I didn't envy Dad having to go out in such bad weather.

In the kitchen, Mother popped corn on the stove in an old red-topped popcorn pot, and she filled our Disney mugs with hot chocolate. Franky had a Goofy Mug. I had Bugs Bunny. We bought them with cereal box tops we saved. I sat around in my blue and pink-flowered footy pajamas and blue housecoat and ate and enjoyed my chocolate. Silently I prayed, *God, take care of Dad and don't let him get lost in the snow tonight.* But I did it with my eyes open because I didn't want my brother to think I was a sissy worrying about Dad.

Finally, I could hear Dad coming up the back steps. He stomped the snow from his boots, then swept it off the top of them with the broom. He dusted the snow from his hat by flinging it against his leg several times.

"Scat cat!" I heard him say. In a rumble of paws Scoop the dog and Tiny and Red the cats jumped up from where they had been curled together on the doormat for warmth to allow Dad room to open the door. In the summer the cats and dog did not get along well, but in winter the cats sometimes slept on top of the dog desperately trying to keep warm. Scoop didn't mind having a live cat coat in cold weather. In fact he welcomed it. But it all looked strange somehow cats and dogs sleeping together. Reminded me of the Bible verse, *"And the lion shall lay down with the lamb."* (Isaiah 11:6) When Dad opened the door, Scoop, Tiny and Red all tried to rush into the house; but Dad wouldn't have it.

"Aah! Get back out a here!" He shoved them back out the door at the end of his boot and firmly shut the door behind him.

"Is that hot chocolate I smell? Velma, I sure could use some!"

"Coming up!" Mom rushed to pour a cup of chocolate from the pan she had simmering on the stove.

"Did you get the cows put up in the barn?" I asked Dad.

"The cows are all in, but the ponies and horses didn't come when I called. Guess they settled down in the hollow behind the barn. If they are too dumb not to come when I call them, I'm not going to look for them in this weather," Dad muttered. He hung up his coat and dusted the last bits of snow from his pants before he put on his house shoes and settled into his leather recliner.

Franky and I continued our game of Monopoly, and Dad took up the local newspaper to read. As we played, I could hear the dog and cats outside crying for us to let them in. The dog howled periodically and the cats took to climbing the screen and meowing, pathetically.

"Can't we let them in Dad?" I asked. "They are cold!"

"They are outside animals. That means they live outside."

"But it's so cold. Can't we let them in, just for tonight?"

"No! If we let them in tonight, they'll think they need to come inside all the time. They have winter coats made for snow. They don't need to come inside."

"But they sound cold!"

"They aren't cold! You kids have spoiled them. That's what you've done. When I was a boy, the animals had enough sense to go to the barn and sleep in the hay. That's what you get for making pets of them. They don't have a lick of sense." Dad looked sternly at us over the top of his black horn-rimmed glasses before again focusing his attention on the newspaper. Every once in a while he'd curl out his lips and sip his hot chocolate. "Mum....mummm.. Velma, that sure is good chocolate."

The contrast between the plight of my cats and dogs and my father propped up in his fuzzy slippers drinking hot chocolate didn't escape me. It rolled around in my head like a loose acorn. I tried hard to think of a way to persuade Dad to let the cats in, but nothing workable came to mind.

The cats continued to climb the screen, setting my nerves on edge. I wanted to run and open the door and let them in, but I knew if I did, Dad would just throw them out and spank me and send me to my room for my disobedience. At that moment, I hated the back porch and wished we didn't even have one. Mother always said that whoever thought to put the porch on the west side of the house was crazy. I was seven before I realized she meant Dad.

Franky once cooked an egg on the floor of the porch in summer to prove how hot it got. In the winter, the wind whipped through it like a freight train chilling anything alive to the bone. Once we'd had a cat give birth out there during the summer. The kittens contracted distemper. I nursed them carefully, but they still died on that porch. So the back porch already had negative memories tied to it in my mind. It provided little protection for either the firewood or the animals. Yet the animals stayed anyway because they liked being close to their humans. Most of the time they just hunkered down on the 'Welcome' mat and toughed it all out. Probably the sound of our voices brought them comfort somehow and gave them hope that eventually we would come out to feed and care for them.

Sometimes if it got really bad, Dad would let us put a cardboard box with a towel on the porch for the animals to sleep in. With its frigid, concrete slab floor, this made about as much sense as putting a cardboard box in the freezer. I thought this to myself, but I knew enough not to say it. Dad fussed about how the dog and cats had a warm barn only a quarter of a mile away they could shelter in. Franky, Mom, or me tried to find the most protected corner to place the box for the animals to sleep in on the porch when they didn't go to the barn—that was the corner away from the door that led into the house. Most of the time they would not sleep in it. I guess the sound of a voice meant more to them than warmth, and they would return every time to the doormat.

So inside, toasty warm from the fire, we sat eating popcorn and drinking hot chocolate. But my mind lingered outside on the porch with the cats every minute of that evening. After we ate, Dad read us a Bible story about how David tended his sheep with care. I liked to hear how David would climb down rocky cliffs to save just one sheep; they were that important to him. Sometimes he had to battle mountain lions to protect the herd. David loved his sheep like God loved us, the Bible said. He even slept with them on cold nights to help keep them warm and protect them from harm. I couldn't imagine Dad sleeping on the back porch to keep our animals warm.

Dad wasn't much like David, I decided, as I lay awake in bed that night listening to the wind howl around the corner of the house. I'd asked Mother once why Dad felt the way he did about animals staying outside. She told me Dad was a farm boy and they looked at animals differently than city people. Mother considered herself a city girl, having grown up in Fayetteville, Tennessee, years and years before. I tried, but couldn't imagine Mom before she became my Mom. The life she described seemed to involve someone else.

While Dad is a "tough love" kind of guy with the animals, he does a lot for his church and fellow humans. He goes out of his way to help the poor. He finds them jobs, buys them groceries, even loans them cars. The color of their skin does not matter to him, in fact he seems to harbor more concern for those of color than he does for whites. He does a lot even when we can't really afford it.

In addition, Dad's always busy building, remodeling or maintaining the church buildings where we attend services. He serves on the board, leads the singing and often serves as youth leader. He frequently takes a turn at teaching adult Sunday school as well. Pretty much any time the door is open at church we are there doing something. Still, I wish he had a softer heart toward animals. I know God gave us dominion over them, but Dad could be kinder I think. It is one of those contradictions in Dad, and in life, I don't fully understand.

Eventually the snow turned to sleet, and the sound of it pelting my windows woke me up during the night. I no longer heard the cats meowing. Probably they settled down in their box after all, or went to the barn.

"Wake up kids! It's daylight! Let's go have some fun! Let's make snow angels! What do you say?" Dad called the next morning. He walked into my bedroom, uncovered my feet and began to pull my toes. This was his favorite way to wake me. It drove me crazy. My feet were ticklish. Just hearing him tramp toward my bedroom could wake me with a sense of dread. I was a light sleeper; he didn't have to pull my toes to wake me.

"Get up sleepy head," Dad gave my little toe one more pull, then headed for my brother's room. I executed a mock kick after him.

"Franky, wake up!" I heard Dad call from the bedroom next to mine.

"Quit it, Dad! I'm awake!"

"Don't talk smart! I thought we'd go make snow angels, but if you don't want to...."

"I want to."

"Then get up!"

I crawled out of bed and dressed in my warmest sweater, two pairs of jeans and boots. Franky and I met out in the hall and followed Dad outside. It was no longer snowing, and we had about 8 inches of fresh snow in the pasture with drifts over a foot high. Sleet topped it all off with a crispy crust that shone like diamonds in the morning sunlight. Ice encased all the tree limbs making the farm look magical, like a picture out of my nursery rhyme book. The air tickled my nose and felt light and crisp on my face. The sun shone so brightly I had to shade my eyes with my hand just to look around.

In the field, I could see the horses huddled together, heads drooping, their backs turned toward the breeze. Frozen icicles hung off their long winter fur. Steam circled their faces when they exhaled. Scoop, our dog, appeared from around the corner of the house, looking pleased with himself. A collie mix, his tail waved out behind him as he ran across the yard toward us. After saying hello, he headed out across the field to bark at the horses, full of doggie smiles that he found us outside.

"Wonder if the cats are with him?" I asked.

I watched the corner of the house, but the cats did not appear.

"We need to look for the cats," I said.

"In a minute, I'm going to make a snow angel first," Franky declared.

Jumping off the porch steps, he cried, "Yee, Hi!" and ran through the snow. I went a lot slower, afraid of falling until I tested the ice thickness.

Once I made it across the patio to the yard, the prickles in my nerves left, and I felt better. We walked down to the gate together and went out into the pasture directly behind the house.

"Well, kid's let's get with it. The day's a wasting!"

Suddenly, I realized I didn't know how to make a snow angel. I'd never made one. I looked at Dad.

"Want me to go first?"

I nodded.

Daddy's voice suddenly sounded almost playful. "Okay, then I'll show you how it's done."

He plopped down in the snow butt first, legs stiff, then leaned back creating a puff of snow on each side. He waved his arms and legs back and forth with a swish. A huge grin spread across his face as he waved back and forth several times looking up at us and at the blue, blue sky. I don't think I'd ever seen my father grin like that.

Then he carefully stood up avoiding touching outside the angel he had made. "What do you think?" Dad asked. "Have you got the hang of it?"

"Yeah!"

Franky threw himself backward into the snow and started peddling his arms and legs side-to-side furiously. I sat down carefully, lay back and began to sweep my arms and legs back and forth too, enjoying the sensation of the snow stirring under me as I looked up at the perfectly clear sky. The cold crept through my clothes slightly, but I didn't mind. I made my angel. Then I carefully got up so I wouldn't disturb the pattern. Three perfect angels lay in the snow where we lay moments before.

"Well that's pretty good," Dad said, studying our work. "But I think we can do better. Let's do it again." We selected another spot and plopped down almost simultaneously. We made three more angels. We laughed as we made the angels and looked up at the sky. There was something magical about the process that we all liked.

Lying on the ground with my arms spread wide, I looked up at the heavens and tried to catch a stray snowflake on my tongue. None. The sky was all out of snow. But I kept my tongue out anyway, just in case.

I watched Dad carefully sit down in the snow and make yet another angel, apparently not quite satisfied with the last one.

Dad didn't play with us much. Most of the time he only wanted us to work. Sweep the floor. Sort these nails. Carry boxes in the house. Feed the animals. Polish his shoes. The list seemed endless. So I savored the moment like a Christmas morning.

After we all made angels several more times, we carefully got up and stepped out of the imprints so we could admire our work. Tired of barking at the horses, Scoop came to inspect them too. He quickly added little doggy footprints around each angel making them look like snowflakes surrounded them. Scoop sniffed at their centers. He sneezed blowing snow all around. Then he plopped in the snow beside one of the angles, rolled on his back and wiggled back and forth as if to make his own dog snow angel.

We all laughed.

"Guess we know what he thinks of our artwork," Dad said.

"He sneezed at it," I said. "Not only that, he thinks he can do better!"

We laughed together again.

"One little, two little, three little angels, four little five little, six little angels..." I sang to myself.

"Those are mighty fine angels," Dad concluded. "No matter what Scoop thinks."

"Do you think the horses will walk on them?" Franky asked. We were inside the pasture with the horses, but at the moment they looked content to stand at the opposite end of the field near the barn and let the sun hit them to melt the ice in their coats. They were beginning to steam from body warmth and sunshine. Soon the ice would melt and they would be back to normal.

"I don't think so. They seem pretty happy where they are. Jane, run in and get a mixing bowl from your Mother. Let's collect fresh snow to make snow cream!"

"Snow cream. Are we going to make snow cream?"

"Sure. Why not?"

"I'll get it," I told Dad, and I ran to the house.

"The trick," Dad said, after I returned and handed him a bowl, "is to make sure the snow is fresh, at least two inches from the ground, to avoid any grass. And we don't want it if it's packed down and icy. We want fluffy snow." Dad searched the ground. When he found a drift he liked, he scooped up a big bowl of snow.

"What you want is the yellow snow," Franky laughed.

"Don't let him fool you," Dad said. "Yellow snow means a dog got there before you did. You wouldn't want to eat that."

Sometimes Dad gave me more information than I wanted.

Dad headed to the house with the bowl of snow tucked under his arm. One of Dad's favorite foods was snow cream. It was almost free, the only store bought ingredients were eggs, vanilla, and sugar.

"No sign of the cats, I guess." Franky concluded, as he watched Scoop roll on his back next to one of our snow angels. Scoop made happy little grunts and wiggles making his own new snow angel.

"I'm worried about them. It was a really cold night," I said.

"You check the barn," said Franky. "I'll check around the house."

Glad for my galoshes, I took off running for the barn. It was an awkward experience both because of the shoes, and because the snow was nearly to my knees. The snow made a pleasant crunch under my boots, like cereal. The air was so still now, with the sun out, I scarcely felt the cold. I did feel the need to hurry. Through the gate, then up to the barn door. I pulled and tugged on the door shoving snow back so it would open; then I went inside. The cows were huddled in the large section of the barn at the back. Easily 35 head of cattle milled around in different sections of the barn, tugging hay from the mangers eating, lying down chewing their cud. Steam rose off their backs. They looked happy to be inside and reasonably warm.

I prowled around the manger and looked underneath. No cats. I climbed the stairs to the loft. No cats there either. I looked out the large opening that lead from the interior of the loft into the larger hay storage area. There was a drop of

Page 303

about 10 feet to the floor where Franky and I would sometimes pile hay and then jump into the pile from the loft opening. It gave me a good view of the larger, newer section of the barn. No cats in sight. It felt eerily quiet in the barn loft. Below me, I could hear the cows chewing, bawling, moving around, but in the loft where I usually found the cats hiding or hunting, I found nothing but straw and some corn waiting to be shelled. Quickly, I checked all the usual hiding places. The corn crib. The rafters behind the tack room. No cats.

Out of options, I slowly walked back to the house.

Inside Mother had almost finished the snow cream.

"Wash your hands and come help me stir in the last of the sugar," she said. I hurried to take off my cap, boots and coat and rushed to wash my hands.

In the kitchen Mother stirred snow cream up in a large enamel tub with a red rim around it. The snow in the bowl Dad brought to the house looked snow-blind white, but the cream Mother stirred turned it an appetizing sunshine yellow, not at all like the yellow Franky warned me about.

"I've already mixed in the vanilla and raw eggs, you just need to finish adding all the sugar there in the measuring cup—slowly," Mom cautioned me.

My face tingled from the cold outside, I pulled a tall stepping-stool over to the counter and perched on it. Picking up the wooden spoon I began to stir the sugar, ever so slowly, into the snow cream mix. As I stirred, I imagined that I'd turned into a magician stirring up some secret mixture in my hat. I wanted it to become something mysterious, beautiful and tasty. At first the texture of the snow cream felt fluffy and stiff, like egg whites, but as I stirred, it melted slightly until is became the fine texture of home-made ice cream. As it melted and I added sugar, I tasted it now and again, just to make sure it tasted okay.

"All done," I emptied out the last of the sugar and stirred it slowly into the snow cream.

"Stir it a bit more, like you are folding it in," Mother directed. "Then we'll put it into bowls and serve it."

"Is it ready yet?" Dad called from his office where he'd been adding something up on the adding machine.

"It's ready," Mother called. "Come and get it while it's cold."

We sat in the kitchen with the sun streaming in the bank of windows over the sink and for the next 20 minutes we enjoyed the heavenly delights of snow cream. I savored each bite, carefully consuming the delicate mixture, trying to create a memory of the exact taste so I could recall it when I was sweating outside next summer.

Somehow the four of us consumed a good half-gallon bowl in just under 30 minutes. I scooped up the last bit with my spoon and savored it, then sat back on the stool. My stomach felt full enough to pop. My lips tingled with cold.

"Wish I could have snow cream every day," I told Mother.

"Did you find the cats?" she asked.

"I didn't," Franky said. "Did you?" he asked me.

I shook my head.

"I looked all around the house," he continued, "but didn't see any footprints except on the porch. It's like they completely disappeared. The only place we haven't looked is the pool area."

"Quit worrying. They'll turn up," Dad said.

Franky and I looked at each other. Neither of us spoke.

Our pool had a 7-foot fence around it, and Dad kept the gate padlocked at all times. Our parents didn't allow either of us inside the enclosure unless one or both of them came with us.

"Well, somebody's got to work to put food on the table. I'm going to the shop and see what I can get done."

After Dad left, I headed to my bedroom. However, on the way, Franky stopped me in the hall.

"I'm worried about them," he said.

"Me too."

"Think we should check around the pool?"

"I don't think there's any place for them to hide around the pool, most of the bushes are bare."

"It's the only place we haven't checked."

"Yeah. But it's locked. You know we aren't supposed to be inside the pool area without Mom or Dad. Besides, I don't know where Dad keeps the key to the lock."

"I do."

We looked at each other.

"Where is it?"

"In Dad's office in the drawer under his harmonica. I found it one day when I was looking for a pencil."

"Meet me outside in 5 minutes," Franky said.

Outside a few minutes later, Franky unlocked the lock that brought two ends of a logging chain together holding the pool gate closed. The chain rattle always made me think of "Dark Shadows" on television. Spooky.

We opened the gate and entered the pool area. The snow had covered everything along the patio. The pool was frozen solid, and several inches of snow covered the ice. We looked around.

"No cats here," I said. "There's no place for them to hide."

Franky didn't say anything. He just starred at the pool.

I followed his gaze but couldn't tell what he was looking at.

Slowly, Franky walked over to the edge of the pool, bent down and brushed some snow away.

"What is it?" I asked.

He didn't say anything. Instead he leaned out over the pool looking closely at something.

"Be careful. You might fall in."

He ignored me.

"Franky what do you see?" I asked. I could barely make out two slight humps in the pool ice, covered with snow—surely nothing.

Franky picked up a rock from beside the pool and banged it down on the ice several times next to one of the humps until the ice cracked.

He bent down again and picked up one of the lumps of ice by a pointy end. He held it up.

At first I couldn't tell what it was.

Then I looked closer. It was Tiny, frozen stiff.

"Cat Popsicle?" Franky said, holding the cat up by its frozen tail. He wasn't smiling. As he said it, the tail snapped and the frozen cat plunged back into the water beside the other lump in the ice.

* * *

2007

Despite the cold of the last few days, the day of the sale dawns clear, sunny and tolerably warm. Our efforts at advertising pay off, and cars and trucks line up all the way around the subdivision. People are milling around looking at the items for sale hours before the sale is scheduled to start. The auction company does a wonderful job. They sell popcorn, hot dogs, hot chocolate, and coffee. People walk around and visit with neighbors and friends. Many seek me out to say hello, many that I have not seen since I was in high school are there. One old boyfriend comes up to me, hugs me and lifts me off the ground telling me how pretty I am. I don't feel pretty, I feel tired and the weight of the responsibility for the sale falls heavily on my shoulders. I have not yet recovered from back surgery and wear a brace under my heavy coat to help me get through the day.

Soon the auction starts. The heavy equipment and tractors sell quickly; the log cabin takes a little longer. The printing press is slow to move, and in the end we almost have to give that away. Then "lots" of things are sold next. Tools, saws, hammers, wood of various varieties, oak, walnut and pecan that Dad cut many years ago and saved to make furniture sell for more than I anticipated. There are tables that came out of stores Dad demolished that one woman is thrilled to purchase. There are good hobby tables. Once things sell, people file by the cashier to pay, and then they load their items into cars or trucks or onto trailers and depart. It is like watching pieces of Dad taken away. I feel numb.

The day passes in a blur. We have done better than I dared hope. In the final stages the shop is nearly cleared out and the scavengers descend and load up the final items that did not sell. There are a few people still milling around. A woman with several missing teeth comes up to me with a set of ice cream bowls.

"How much for the bowls?" she asks. She is holding the set of bowls that we ate snow cream from so many years ago.

I look at her. I look at the bowls. I could never eat out of one of those bowls again without thinking of the frozen cats. Probably that's why they are at the shop. Mom probably threw them out, and Dad salvaged them and brought them here. Bad memory to be sure. I look at her and say, "No charge. You can have them."

"Really? But they're so pretty! Are you sure?"

"I'm sure," I tell her.

As she walks away I wish her and the bowls well. Maybe they will create happy memories in their new home.

◇

"Who knows whether the spirit of man goes upward and the spirit of the beast goes down into the earth?" (Ecclesiastes 3:21)
"And all flesh shall see the salvation of God." (Luke 3:6)

◇

Snow Crème
1 large bowl of fresh, clean snow.
Mix 1 cup of sugar, half cup of whipping crème, 2 raw eggs (beaten until fluffy) and 2 teaspoons of vanilla into snow.
Stir gently until mixed well.
Serve in bowls.
Eat slowly to avoid freeze headache.
(There is a risk of salmonella. But at the time chickens and eggs were produced locally, and the risk was not even considered. Eat at your own risk. We thought it was wonderful.)

Chapter 20 – Ladies Wear Hose
"Your mother would never have been seen in public bare-legged without hose."
— Louis

2007
Over the next few weeks we work with the attorney's and the bank to get all of Dad's debts paid, all of his finances in order, and set up a fund for his care. During this time he continues to improve, and so do I. We expand our activities to going out to dinner and to the movies that he enjoys. In Dad's entire life he has likely only gone to a dozen movies at an actual theatre. The ones I remember were "Gone with the Wind" "Thoroughly Modern Millie" and the "The Ugly Dachshund". Mom and I took him to see "Nine to Five" as well. That one made him angry. He thought the secretaries were very mean to their boss.

For the first time in many years we talk at length about many things. I pick up food and we take it to the park, or just sit in the car if the weather is cold and visit while we eat. I enjoy these talks a lot. Dad takes regular exercise classes and makes friends at the nursing facility and feels much better than he did at home. He enjoys telling me about these classes and the friends he's making.

Meanwhile, between visits with him, I provide extensive pictures, videos, and reports to the court that document the cleanup and account for every penny earned by the estate sale. I even deposit coins I find between couch cushions and when I vacuum out of the closets and cupboards. All personal items designated to go to extended family are divided up and placed in locked storage containers for those members to pick up. Keys are mailed to them so they could pick up their belongings at their convenience. I go over the inventory with Dad to confirm his wishes are carried out, and then these records too are presented to the court which oversees all my activities.

As Dad heals he becomes restless in the nursing home and it grows increasingly obvious he could likely do well back in assisted living without the extensive level of care the nursing home provides. Suddenly, we find ourselves looking into the future unsure how to proceed. Dad is well enough he might live for a long time, and we need to prepare for that in a way my husband and I can sustain ourselves and be with our children while at the same time taking care of Dad. Currently, we are spread thin across two states and two households. Our house in Texas has just sold, and my husband has a nice apartment overlooking a creek lined up for the two of us in Texas.

By this time I had been away from my home in Texas for nearly a year. Moving forward it would be easier to manage our lives if we can take Dad to

Texas with us. In Texas Dad would be closer to high-quality medical facilities than he will be if we move him back to his hometown and into assisted living there. However, moving to Texas will take him away from life-long friends, my sister, her children and many other familiar things. Texas would allow him to spend more time with our kids who he has not yet really had the chance to get to know. It would also allow him to see and do new things, and perhaps make new friends. So there is much to consider.

Dad had never been a particularly cooperative person. And that combined with my recently ruptured disc makes the option of Dad living with us out of the question. In addition to the ruptured disc, I now have torn cartilage in my knee and must wear a brace to remain mobile. I've opted not to have surgery to repair the knee because I do not want to take the risk of anesthesia while Dad is dependent on me. But this means that there are certain things I simply cannot do for him. And while Dad has improved a lot, it is no longer possible for him to live alone.

Still, the need for us to find a lifestyle that we can maintain over the long term is apparent. My husband needs to be back in Texas because of the centralized airport that made his constant travel bearable. Texas is where our life is, but in order for Dad to move to Texas with us he will need to be willing, we will need to find a suitable place for him and the judge will have to agree to allow us to move him. Another option would be for him to remain in Tennessee and my sister manage his care; but she has her hands full with two teen daughters and she is mid-divorce. She is exhausted from her own career challenges as a nurse; and the more we consider this the less we feel it is a good option for either her or Dad. She has already worked extensively to care for Mom and made huge sacrifices to career and family to accommodate Mom's needs. It just does not seem right to saddle her with another elder parent under these circumstances.

Except for the trip to Pennsylvania, Dad has not traveled much in his lifetime. He has largely grown up and lived his entire life within a mile of where he was born; so to move 800 miles cross-country in his 80s is a lot to ask. However, over the weeks we discuss it, and soon Dad agrees that he would like to take the plunge. He has never spent much time with my children and has rarely seen his great-grand children. This will allow him time with them and with me that we had never before been able to manage.

To our amazement the judge approves. So I pack up our things, and as soon as Dad feels he's ready I book tickets to Texas. I rent a truck to haul our belongings home, and Hock flies in to drive the truck back. We met at the airport briefly, Hock coming back from a trip, Dad and I headed to Texas. We hug and then go different directions. Hock catches a cab to the apartment to pick up the truck, and I turn in my rental that I've been using since the back surgery. Then we wait for our plane.

As we wait, Dad and I sit by the window in the terminal watching planes come and go. Dad eats a ham sandwich and sips a Coke. We share his chips. As I sit beside him and eat I wonder what he is thinking.

"Dad, how do you feel about getting on that plane?" I ask him.

"Excited," he says with a smile.

"Really?"

"Yes, I've only been on a plane when we went to Chicago to check out the Cinderella Pool Company, remember? That was before your sister was born."

I did remember. In fact I think Mom got pregnant on that trip, but I don't remind Dad of this.

"Well I booked first-class tickets for us, so you should be comfortable," I tell Dad.

"You didn't need to do that," Dad says. "I'm not made of money, you know."

"I know, but it wasn't that much more, and everyone should fly first class at least once in their life, don't you think?" The room in first class will help keep him comfortable since he is still recovering from a fractured pelvis, but I don't mention this.

He nods. He finishes his sandwich and folds up the paper carefully before sticking it in his pocket to throw away later. When he does this I remember the last time he visited my husband and I in Texas. We took him through the drive-thru at McDonalds for breakfast and without us knowing it he saved his "potato patty" in the glove compartment for "later". We found it a year later. It looked much the same as when he bought it with one bite missing.

Eventually the plane arrives and I push Dad's wheelchair to the gate where he gets up and walks down the skyway to the plane. Once we are settled, he reaches for my hand and holds it until long after we takeoff. His hand feels moist, but otherwise he looks calm when the plane leaves the ground. We both stare out the window watching Tennessee fall away beneath us. We both know this is likely the last time he will ever see it. He looks out the window until clouds obscure the ground and the sun shines in, much like I imagine heaven. Eventually he turns his face forward. He lets go of my hand and stares absently into space. In a way I feel a little like when I brought my daughter home from the hospital. I wonder how he's feeling.

After the plane levels out the stewardess comes around asking if we'd like something to drink. Dad has a Sprite, and I order a small bottle of Merlot. The wine relaxes me.

Dad says, "You know, if things had gone differently I would have liked to take your mother on a lot of trips. I wanted to see the world; and I wanted her to go with me. There were several times I really tried to be somebody. I tried to make investments that would make money; but God just never smiled on me. I'm not sure why," he says. He watches the clouds pass under us, and I search for words to comfort him.

"You did your best. You had a good life. You have a family that loves you,"

I tell him.

He nods. But he does not look convinced.

About the time I finish the wine the stewardess comes back around with lunch.

"Why, what are we having?" Dad asks. I show him how to fold out his tray table and he looks up at the pretty stewardess.

She bends over with a smile and places a meal on his tray. "Chicken and new potatoes," she says. "And what would you like to drink, sir?"

Dad looks at the chicken she places on his tray table, then at her. "Coffee, if you have it," he smiles. "My, this looks good," he says unwrapping the meal and reaching for his plastic utensils.

However, I can also see that he's glancing at the stewardess' legs.

"That stewardess is bare-legged," Dad says as she leaves.

"Yes, people have given up wearing hose these days," I tell him. "They are hot and uncomfortable."

"Your mother would never have been seen in public with bare legs without hose." Dad shakes his head then takes his first bite of chicken. He chews thoughtfully. He swallows. "Your mother was a lady. And ladies do not appear in public bare-legged."

"Yes she was a lady," I agree.

And as I watch Dad eat, my mind flies back across the years to when I was learning what it meant to be a lady and longed to wear hose.

* * *

1969

When I was 12, I wanted to wear hose to church in the worst possible way. In my mind wearing hose meant I was a woman. They looked smooth and neat, and lady like. It was what Mom wore, and I wanted to be just like her. I pictured myself in hose instead of knee socks as I lie in bed at night. Socks were so coarse, and made my legs look shorter. They made me look like a little girl. And they made my calves look fat. Hose made legs look trim, sleek, smooth and beautiful. They made legs look longer too. But of course to wear hose I would need to shave my legs—something Mom thought I was too young to do. While I only had the finest of blond hair on them, I still wanted to shave them so they would be smooth.

So I pilfered Dad's razor one night, and in the bathtub, with prickles of guilt running up and down my spine, I shaved my legs. The next day I wore socks to cover my legs so Mom wouldn't notice. And for the next few weeks I relished the secret maturity of smooth legs. In bed at night I'd run my hand up and down my legs relishing how sleek and smooth they were. Now if only Mom would let me wear hose!

Then one night Dad was sitting in his office adding up the day's receipts. I was in the bathroom taking a bath, and I again picked up his razor, as usual, to shave my legs. A little nervous about it all still, I lathered my legs and quickly drew the razor upward from my ankle. But this time it felt different. The blade dragged. When I looked at the razor I realized the guard over the blade had come unhooked exposing a large amount of the blade. Drawing it up my leg, had sliced the skin all the way down to the muscle in a 3-inch gash. I gasped with pain and fear. Blood turned the tub red in seconds. I sat naked in the tub wondering what to do. And then I clamped my hand down on the gash and yelled for Dad. But not too loud. Mom was asleep and I didn't want to wake her.

 Dad heard and came running. The door was not locked, and I told him to come in when he knocked. I grabbed a towel to cover myself before he opened the door, and then showed him my leg with blood pouring out of the huge gash.

 Dad's face turned white, and he grabbed a hand towel from the shelf and pressed it against the wound. We sat for several uneasy moments on the edge of the tub with him pressing down on my leg trying to stop the bleeding. Suddenly, I realized I was half-naked in front of my Dad—and caught shaving when I was not supposed to be besides. Dad didn't scold though. Instead, he kept pressure on the wound to stop the bleeding. Once in a while he'd lift the hand towel a little so we could see if the bleeding had slowed. Then he'd quickly bear down on the wound again.

 A 3 inch strip of flesh, 1-half inch wide, dangled from the wound. It was clear this would never reattach and heal in such mangled condition. Dad looked at it several times, and then looked at me. "Jane we are going to have to do something about the piece of skin that's hanging."

 "I know, it already looks purple, doesn't it?" I said. My crying had subsided, but now I just felt faint and scared and in disbelief that I'd actually cut myself so badly.

 Dad nodded. He pulled out his pocketknife.

 "You hold pressure on the wound while I wash my knife," he said. Then he took his knife and ran it under steaming-hot water and washed it well with soap. Then he pulled out a bottle of alcohol from the medicine cabinet along with some gauze. Our medicine cabinet was fairly well stocked. Living on a farm Mom often had to cope with minor accidents. He also located some good-sized gauze pads and surgical tape. As he gathered materials, I sat there on the edge of the tub pressing the wound to slow the bleeding.

 "Okay, let's see what we can do about all this," Dad said. He sat back down on the edge of the tub, lifted the towel away from the wound. It was still bleeding but not as much. Dad soaked a pad of gauze in alcohol and cleaned the gash. Then he carefully sliced off the dangling flesh from my leg. As he did this his face turned even whiter, and I got light headed. But we both managed to get through it. Dad took the separated flesh and threw it in the toilet and then pressed down on the wound again with clean gauze.

 "It really needs stitches in the gapped section that's left," Dad said. "But I don't know how to do them, and we'd have to take you to the emergency room to get it sewn up. The only hospital with an emergency room is 20 miles from here and may not even be open. It's trimmed up pretty good, and it's nearly stopped bleeding; and if we pull it together and keep it bandaged real clean, I think it will heal. What do you think?" he asked me, like he was asking an adult. "Do you feel like a ride to the emergency room? Or you want to just bandage it and see how it does?"

It was late. I was exhausted. It did look like the wound would quit bleeding on its own. And, I was flattered Dad was asking me my opinion. I nodded my consent.

He cleaned the wound again with alcohol. I gasped. But then he pressed it with more clean gauze covered with antibiotic creme and found surgical tape to wind around the gauze and all the way around my ankle to keep the bandage on. Once he was satisfied he picked up the waste and bloody gauze and put them in the trash.

"Okay, can you walk on that leg good enough to get to bed?" he asked.

"I think so," I told him. Suddenly, I felt exhausted; and all I wanted to do was go to sleep. We'd been sitting there a long time, Dad in his pajamas, me wrapped in a towel. When Dad finished, I realized just how, when push came to shove, I trusted him and depended on him. My cousin once said Dad was the kind of guy you wanted around if you got stranded on a desert island. And he was right. Dad could do anything. I hoped someday I would be as smart and capable as he was. Someday.

"Thanks, for taking care of it, Dad," I told him.

He hugged me. He didn't ask me how I cut my leg; but he did see his razor on the side of the tub, the guard off, laying in a puddle of blood. He picked it up, put the guard back in place, washed the razor, dried it, and put it back where it belonged. Not a word about what I'd done. He hugged me, and we went off to bed.

For a week I skipped my Physical Education class because every time I exercised the wound would break open and bleed. Mother bought me a pink safety razor the next week. She also bought me two pair of hose, and I wore a pair to church every Sunday and relished how uncomfortable I felt in order that I might look like a lady. And I was pleased to join the ranks of those who had gone before me wearing their uncomfortable panty girdles or garter belts. However, the scar on my leg was long and red and ugly when it healed. It was years before it faded—the price I paid for becoming a lady without asking for advice or permission.

* * *

2007

By the time I pull my thoughts back from this rather complicated memory it is nearly time to land and the stewardess comes around to collect our empty cups and dishes. Dad gives her a disapproving glance that only I recognize as disapproving; but he doesn't say anything about her bare legs.

"Did you enjoy your meal?" I ask.

"Well, it was okay," he says. I can tell he is being polite. He wipes his mouth and folds his napkin that he kept and puts it in his pocket like he used to do with his handkerchief.

"Fair?" I ask.

"Yes, pretty good, but not as good as your mother's," he says. "I wonder if they still have coffee?"

"I'm sure they do." I press the call button to get the stewardess' attention.

"Two coffee's please?"

Then I lean over and hug Dad tight. As I hug him I can smell the Old Spice that he still wears, and I feel a bit of a bristle against my cheek where he missed a spot shaving; but I don't care. Underneath the bristle, is a good man. My heart feels tight, and I feel tears rise. "Dad I love you!"

He pats me on the back in that way he has that's part pleasure part pain. I know now it's meant to be tender.

Our coffee comes. As I sip I reflect. I don't want to think about a world where Dad is not in it. Yet our days are numbered. I resolve that no matter what the future brings, I will remember this moment. I will remember all the times Dad has taken care of me, and I will now take care of him. I look up using an old trick to clear my eyes of tears so he won't see me cry. I don't want sadness to touch us.

We finish our coffee. The stewardess heads our way to pick up our cups.

"When she gets here I'm going to tell her she really needs to wear some pantyhose when she's working so she'll look like a lady," I joke.

Dad looks at me, horrified. "Don't you dare!"

We both look at each other then laugh.

"Ladies and gentlemen, please raise your chairs, stow your tray tables, and fasten your seatbelts, we are about to land," the Captain says.

◇

"An excellent wife who can find? She is far more precious than jewels."
(Proverbs 31:10)

◇

Chicken and New Potatoes
One whole organic chicken, approximately 3 pounds.
Clean and wash chicken, discard giblets.

Place chicken, breast up, in a glass baking dish, folding wings under its back to provide a more stable reclining position.

Rub chicken with olive oil, salt, fresh ground pepper.

Then crumble parsley over the top.

Oil a sheet of foil where it might come into contact with the chicken and use to cover chicken.

Bake at 350 degrees until it reaches internal temperature of 170 degrees (normally 2.5 hours).

Wash, cut and quarter 2 cups of potatoes. Remove eyes.

After 90 minutes of baking add potatoes around the base of the chicken and allow to simmer in accumulated chicken broth.

1 cup of chopped carrots may also be added.

Remove foil for the last 30 minutes to allow chicken to brown.

Serve with steamed green beans and fresh rolls.

Chapter 21 – Sink Strainers

"This family can throw away more food than I can ever put on this table." —
Louis

2007

The plane ride is finally over, and we land in Texas. Dad holds my hand during landing and visibly relaxes once we pull to a stop at the terminal. We disembark, and pick up a rental car, and drive Dad to the new assisted living community we selected in Texas. It is not nearly as elegant as where he stayed in Nashville, but all the same very nice. Instead of looking out over ancient oak trees in a courtyard from the third story window, this window has a view of a Texas sandstone block wall about 8 feet away. However, the facility is ranked highly, and we have personal recommendations about the care available to him there. The buildings are built like small residences with eight residents per building. Each has a covered patio with rocking chairs and large shade trees and there are paths to walk along and many communal activities.

We find his room and settle him in for the night. Furnishings are basic, but his own furniture will arrive soon. I've already seen the fresh salad and lovely soup that the group cook is preparing. The common rooms are well-furnished and homey. The residents are not nearly as old or as ill as they were at the nursing home in Nashville. This is more like a home than a facility; and I'm happy about this.

My daughter arrives soon after we do, and together we dress out his bed in new sheets, and she places pictures on the wall that I sent ahead; so by evening his room looks almost like home. I can tell Dad is a little shell-shocked by the swift changes in his life, and he looks tired. We stay for dinner and then we settle into white rocking chairs on the wide covered porch at the front of the home to relax. After a few moments I can see him visibly unwind.

"Dinner was good, wasn't it?" I ask him.

"Yes, I especially enjoyed the salad," he says.

"Hock will be here in a day or two with your things, and then we can get you completely set up."

Hock is bringing Dad's couch from home, his Craftmatic adjustable bed and a chest of drawers that belonged to him at home so, once his things are in place, his room will feel more like his own."

"It's fine like it is," Dad tells me. But I want things to be the best they can be. We linger a little longer watching the twilight approach and the shadows on the trees grow long. We can hear birds calling. Across the street is a construction site that includes heavy equipment. I can tell Dad is interested in what they are doing, and I'm secretly pleased that there's activity that he's familiar with that will keep his mind busy. Soon it's time to leave, and I tell him goodnight. It feels a bit like leaving a child at summer camp.

"Be nice to everyone, and I'm sure you will make friends quickly," I tell him, giving him a hug and a kiss on his cheek. He nods.

The next morning when I arrive I see Dad outside talking to a man at the construction site. Dad has a toothpick in his mouth and his construction ball cap is on his head. They are deep in conversation, and once in a while Dad waves his hand out at the site as if explaining the finer points of water runoff and how to "cut a grade" on the land so it will drain well. When I walk up I catch the last part of the conversation.

Dad says, "Yes, I'm retired now, but I owned a heavy equipment operation back in Tennessee for 40 years; so I can tell you if you don't get that slope right water will run over on this property here. Before you know it these folks will be suing you for damages."

The supervisor nods respectfully to Dad and seems genuinely interested. I suspect he knows all this, but I am happy the man is treating Dad with respect.

"Dad, I brought you a shower curtain for you bathroom, want to come in and help me hang it?" I ask him.

"This is my beautiful daughter, Jane," he introduces us. "She kidnapped me recently and brought me to Texas. I guess I better go help her now, but I enjoyed talking to you."

The supervisor nods and smiles at the kidnapping part.

Dad tells him he'll see him later, and I have no doubt he will.

Back in Dad's room we hang the shower curtain in the bathroom, and I set up a few additional things I think he might need. He brought some of his belongings, but it made sense to just buy some of what he needs once we arrived. After I get it situated, I turn around and find he's gone. Quickly I go into the kitchen where I find Dad helping the cook to prepare lunch. He is peeling potatoes for her and she seems to like that.

"You see, if you peel a potato with a knife like you've done you waste half of the potato," he instructs her. "Now if you peel it with a peeler like this, the one I found in the drawer, you save a lot of the potato. Now if you are really skilled you can peel it very thin with a little Old Hickory knife or a pocketknife, but in case you don't have one of those a peeler like this is better than nothing. You see, if you aren't careful you can starve to death simply by peeling the skin too thick. You waste a lot and throw enough to feed a whole other family away if you are a careless peeler," he tells her. "And then if you don't dispose of the peelings right, you could stop up your sink." He points his arthritic finger at the sink and peers at the cook pointedly over his glasses to see if she is absorbing his message.

She smiles seeming to enjoy Dad's attention.

* * *

1970

"This family can throw away more food than I can ever put on this table," Dad yelled at us one evening after dinner. He slammed the empty dinner plate he'd been about to place in the sink onto the red-Formica kitchen counter. The impact made me jump in my dining room chair and I slide a little lower into my seat. Anytime Dad got wound up about something, I just wanted to slide right under the table and slither off to my room like a snake.

As I watched, Dad reached into the sink, and held up the sink strainer to prove his point. In the bottom of the strainer I could see bits and pieces of potatoes, sliced tomatoes and tiny little soggy pieces of pot roast we'd just had for dinner–maybe a tablespoon full in all. The sight truly disgusted me, and I tried not to look.

Not Franky. "Look Dad, I finished all mine," he said. He held up the plate to show he'd licked the last drop of roast off and polished the rim with his tongue.

"Well it's a good thing because if you leave anything your Mom's going to use it to destroy the plumbing!" Dad added just as sincere as if he'd told us Mom had a drinking problem. "Like I have time to crawl under the house and fix the pipes, after I've worked my fingers to the bone to feed the lot of you! And what thanks do I get?" He made a production of scraping every bit of food out of the sink strainer and onto a paper towel. For a minute I thought he might make us eat it! But he just passed it under our noses for a minute on its way to the trash to impress upon us how dangerous the little pile of garbage really was. Franky gagged. "Ew, Dad. Don't!" He jumped up from the table and ran to his room. I watched to see if Dad would go after him, but he was well into his evangelistic phrasing now about the strainer and seemed not to notice.

"I'm just showing you," Dad shook his head and looked innocent. He continued, "This is what your mother makes me do. Because of this, she expects me to crawl under the house and take all this out of the pipes, and fix the sink just so she can stop it up again!" He lifted his arms as if he might start praying, then let them drop to his sides in defeat and tossed the rolled-up-paper-towel full of waste in the trash.

"Louis, I don't think what's in that sink strainer is enough to wreck the plumbing. And it's not me that wrecks everything. Take a look out in the front yard. That new riding mower you got has been sitting out in the rain for months! Four hundred dollars for that, and you've left it out in the rain to rust. So, don't start on me about sink strainers and how I'm the author of destruction. You do your part in destruction and neglect too!"

I already knew that our pipes were put together weird from previous episodes of sink strainer drama. Most people had a loop in the kitchen pipes under the sink called a "trap" where, if something went down that wasn't supposed to, you could empty the trap into a bucket under the sink and not have to crawl under the floor. However, Dad put our trap under the floor so a sink stoppage became a serious matter for our family—especially in winter.

Dad moved again to show Mother the sink strainer remains, now in the trash. She pushed him away, "Louis, put that sink strainer down and leave me alone," she said. She busily continued to put leftovers into clean, plastic margarine tubs to store in the refrigerator and tried to ignore Dad. But he wouldn't have it. "Well, see here Velma…I'm just trying to show you why I have to work so hard!" he began.

Mother's face turned red, "There's not enough in that sink strainer to keep a bird alive, let alone another person. Now leave it alone and go watch television." Dad hung his head, as if only he knew and understood what lay at the bottom of the sink strainer. It was as if the weight of the world settled on his lonely shoulders. I almost felt sorry for him, but not quite.

"Woman, you have no appreciation for how hard I work so you can eat," Dad growled.

Clearly, his day had not gone well and he needed to "vent," Mother would say. But the question of why he selected the sink strainer to make a big deal of left me completely baffled. This was only one of at least a dozen sink strainer dramas over the last few months. Mother said he'd become fixated about it. While I didn't know what fixated meant, I pictured the sink strainer somehow glued to Dad's brain when she said it. Lately, Dad had been fixating on lots of things. I tried to avoid doing anything that would set him off. Yet, most of the time he still caught me off guard, and the outcome at such times was never pretty. I hunched down in my chair a little further still wanting to disappear.

Mother's day had not gone well either. Recently Dad had bought us a horse. The horse, named Misty, was a large, strawberry roam about 16 hands high and gentle as a lamb. She came with a yearling colt we named Lady who was, as yet, unbroken. Misty had taken a serious dislike to my brother and had, as a result, become mine. I totally loved her and spent every free minute with her. However, Misty, had run under a fully loaded clothesline that day, hooking it with the saddle horn and she dragged several loads of towels and bed sheets far down the driveway before I'd managed to catch her. The frame of the saddle broke before the clothesline poles. Both appeared to be a total loss. You might say my day had gone no better than that of either of my parents. Without the saddle I couldn't ride my horse, and I knew without asking we had no money for a new saddle. I'd been hoping to show it to Dad to see if he knew of a way to fix it, but now was certainly NOT the time for that conversation. And I wondered why Dad had picked this night to fuss at us about what lay at the bottom of the sink strainer.

However, it did not take long for me to learn the why of it.

The next morning I got up to find Mom in the kitchen with a plunger trying to unstop the kitchen drain and having no luck. Soon Dad came in and tried plunging the sink with a stronger arm. Still no luck. So he went outside got his tools came back in and began to take the kitchen sink apart. He went under the floor and cleaned out the trap but the water still would not drain. He ran a plumber's snake down the pipes but that didn't help either.

"Let's try boiling water, maybe grease has stopped up the pipe below," Dad said. He was sweating, and Mom looked unhappy as she pulled out a pot and began to boil water.

While the water heated, Dad put the trap back together and once the water boiled, Dad poured it down the sink. This helped some but did not completely clear the blockage.

"I guess I'm going to have to go under the house again and see if I can unclog it from down there," Dad said.

"Louis be careful, there's a snake living under there," Mom said.
Dad kissed her behind the ear and said, "Well, my Great Big Beautiful Doll, I wish you'd thought about that before you let the grease and potato peelings go down the drain."

Mother turned red but didn't say anything. She really did feel guilty about the sink, and what should have been a quick fix appeared to be turning into an all day project.

"Jane come with me. I will need you to hand me tools while I work under the house. And if I get into trouble I need you there so you can run and get your Mom," Dad told me.

Helping Dad was not my favorite thing to do, but I followed along with him and obediently sat on the edge of the concrete next to the crawl space that led under the house as Dad crawled under dragging his toolbox behind him. Once underneath, I could hear him unfolding the toolbox and getting his tools out. I could even see the reflected glow of the flashlight as he positioned himself in preparation to take the pipes apart yet again. Eventually, I heard the pipe wrench turning the pipe. Suddenly, I heard a gush of water and Dad swearing in the way that he had, "Lord Almighty, come upon the scene. What I have to put up with! Jane, bring me a large bowl, I think a bucket is too tall. I don't want all this to pour out under the house."

Why he didn't think about this before he crawled under the house I'm unsure, but I was glad for something to do. I ran into the kitchen and asked Mom for a large Tupperware bowl, which she provided. I ran back and crouched down next to the access and looked into the dark underbelly of the house. I could just make out where Dad was under the low floor. There he lay, stretched on his side in the dust, dirt and gravel.

"Toss me the bowl," he instructed reaching out his hand toward me.

I tossed. He managed to get a foot on it and drag it to his hands, and then I could see him begin to pull things out of the pipe under the floor. He pulled, scraped potato peelings, hair, and gunk out of the pipe for about 10 minutes and put it into the bowl. Then he ran the plumber's snake up the pipe and when he was satisfied that he'd cleaned it all out, he put the pipes back together. Once he had this all done, he put all the tools back into the box and began to crawl back out from under the floor. Just as he approached the exit door King the snake, a brown snake that lived under the floor, made an appearance. He slithered across the ground between Dad and the crawl space door.

"Dad! Watch out, King's down there with you," I warned him.

"Yes, I see that." He paused considering his position.

King paused too, raised his head and looked at Dad as if unsure if he should go deeper under the house or out the trap door toward me.

"Jane, back away from the trap door, and let's see if I can scare him outside," Dad said.

"Okay," I told Dad backing away.

I could hear Dad scraping around under the house. Then I heard what sounded like a rock hit the dirt. Then more scraping and another clunk.

"King, I don't want to hurt you, but I need out! Get out of here!" Dad said, and I could hear him throw a third rock.

About that time I saw King lift his head higher to see out the trap door. He paused, looked at me for a moment. I could see the confusion in his brown, glistening eyes. I backed away a little further. "Come on King. I won't hurt you. You really need to get out of Dad's way so he can get out from under the house." King actually seemed to understand. I backed away even more, and he came out a few more inches, then paused again. I backed up more. He inched out more. Then a rock bounced on the ground next to him, no doubt thrown by Dad. As soon as it hit, King cut to the right and slithered off disappearing into the flowerbed at the corner of the house.

"He's gone," I yelled. I heard more scraping and tools clanking. Soon Dad crawled out through the trap door with dust and mud all down his side. He was grasping the bowl that contained all types of slushy things, and I did recognize potato peelings.

"Blasted snake, I really need to fix the trap door so he can't get back under there," he said while dusting himself off.

"You can't do that, that's King's home," I told Dad.

"Well if it's his home he needs to participate in the upkeep," Dad said.

"How about that!"

"Well, he keeps mice away! Isn't that good enough?"

Dad considered this. "It would be better if he could fix pipes."

"But he doesn't have hands!"

"Well then I guess keeping mice away is good enough," Dad said. "So he's not a plumber's snake then, is he?"

"Not much of one."

We laughed as we went in the house to show Mom what Dad got out of the sink drain.

* * *

2007
Hock's trip from Tennessee to Texas to bring Dad's things to him has not gone well. The truck has something wrong with the window and door. Whenever the truck is placed into gear, a hammering sounds in the driver door blasts away like a jackhammer. The faster Hock drives, the more it hammers. The sound is deafening and relentless. He drives the entire first day with the hammering sound. He tries to drop the truck off at another truck rental place and change vehicles en route, but no other locations has a truck the same size. So he must continue on his way with this horrible hammering. Finally, somewhere in Arkansas the glass in the driver's door shatters and the sound stops. A blessed relief for Hock. At this point he can barely hear, and we are wondering if damage to his hearing may be permanent. While he's glad for the hammering to stop, now there is no glass in the door. Instead, it's on the seat and all over the truck floor. He also must deal with the noise the wind makes blowing through the truck cabin when large trucks pass.

Like a good ex-soldier Hock continues on his mission to bring our things back from Tennessee. Hock is an amazing man. Many husbands would be angry with their wives for putting them in such a position, but he never complains. When he arrives at assisted living and gets out of the truck, the first thing he does is fold me into his arms and kiss me. Then he shakes Dad's hand.

Sherry again comes to help us unload, and before long we replace the issued furniture with Dad's own. Sherry sets up his television while I put his clothing away. When it's all done, she kisses him goodbye and leaves.

I sit on his couch and program his remote control as Dad showers. He takes a long time. Finally I call to him, "Dad, are you okay in there?"

"Yes, I'm okay but the shower won't drain. Wonder if they have a plumber's snake around here somewhere?"

I think about King and I cannot stop laughing at this.

Dad looks at me when he walks in the room and sees me still laughing. Tears run down my cheeks. Soon he starts laughing too.

Finally he asks, "What are we laughing about?"

"Life, Dad. We are laughing at life."

◇

"... the LORD said to Moses, 'Make a fiery serpent and mount it on a pole. When anyone who is bitten looks at it, he will live.' So Moses made a bronze snake and mounted it on a pole. If anyone who was bitten looked at the bronze snake, he would live." (Numbers 21:19)

◇

"Just as Moses lifted up the snake in the wilderness, so the Son of Man must be lifted up." (John 3:14)

◇

Texas Hash

Saute 1 cup of loosely cut onions in 1 tablespoon of bacon grease or Crisco until clear.
Brown 1 pound ground beef.
(You may also use leftover roast cut into small pieces.)
Add
one bag of frozen mixed veggies,
2 peeled and diced white potatoes,
1 cup of water.
Add 1 16 oz. can of peeled, stewed tomatoes.
Simmer for an hour with lid on.
Serve hot with salt, pepper, and crackers.
Freeze leftovers.
(Note: Some people keep a quart container in their freezer and add leftover veggies to it after each meal. When the container is full use these veggies in the stew rather than buying frozen mixed veggies. A cost saving measure, but very tasty.)

Chapter 22 – Gopher Stew

"I'm going to see if I can find some of that old dynamite that I got to blow up the tree stumps on your uncle's place." — Louis

2007

It doesn't take long for Dad to settle in. In the mornings he helps cook meals and washes dishes afterward "making myself useful" he tells me. I wonder how much the cook enjoys this. She smiles when I ask and doesn't comment.

Dad says she's a "fleshy woman", and I wonder if she reminds him somehow of his mother, and if being in assisted living reminds him a little of living at home with his parents.

I work in the mornings, and in early afternoon I drive to his place every day to see how Dad's doing. When I am at home, I sort through paperwork, old letters and medical records that belong to Dad that I did not have time to organize while in Tennessee. Among some of his letters I find a piece of leather that Mom sewed "Velma Loves Louis" on, presumably during a break when she worked at the shoe factory before they married. I give it to him on my next visit. He holds it rubbing his thumb over the stitches several times. I ask him if he's glad to see it?

"Not particularly," he says and places it on his nightstand.

I never see it again. For weeks I look for it thinking maybe he stuffed it between the mattresses, or it fell under his chair; or maybe it fell behind the bed. I wonder, did he throw it away, or did someone from the housing staff take it? Maybe he gave it to someone? Regardless, I am sad that it is gone. It is a genuine relic of my parents' love.

Frequently I take him to run errands with me. I take him to Sam's Club where he enjoys riding around in the electric cart. I enjoy watching him operate the cart with the skill once reserved for operating a bulldozer or loader. Dad still understands the dynamics of speed, forward, and backward motion. He enjoys the large selection, the organization, and all the diversity of goods Sam's offers.

"Jane, who has all the money to buy all this?" he asks me on one visit.

"Dad, I just don't know, but I guess some people do. We are here, aren't we?" But I see as he looks around that the sheer volume overwhelms a man who is accustomed to subsistence living either outdoors on a farm, or later on a bulldozer.

It's not long before Dad's feeling well and settled enough to go to Sherry's house and visit his granddaughter and great-granddaughters. They greet him at the car door and show him inside. Together they give him a tour of their house.

He inspects all the recently remodeled features, and comments on the fine workmanship Sherry and her husband have poured into the house, doing much of the work themselves. Dad recognizes good work when he sees it, and both Sherry and her husband appreciate his compliments. After a complete tour, we head out to the back patio overlooking a large expanse of green lawn bordered by a high plank board-on-board fence. Sherry brings ice tea to all of us.

Dad settles into a chair at the edge of the patio, and in only a moment one of the two chocolate labs brings Dad a ball and drops it at his feet. He looks down at the ball in surprise, then looks questioningly at me. I am not sure Dad has ever had a dog that would play fetch. He looks delighted at the prospect.

"I think he wants me to play."

"Well throw the ball for him."

He picks up the ball and throws it for Mocha, who immediately zips off at full speed, retrieves the ball and brings it back to Dad. Meanwhile Snickers, the other chocolate lab, a little younger, is sniffing around as if wondering where his ball is. Did he miss it being thrown?

Dad and Mocha become fast friends, and he throws the ball for her until I worry that Dad's arm may suffer permanent strain. Meanwhile Snickers helps Mocha retrieve a ball or two then goes back to sniff the yard and even dig a little here and there.

"There are gophers in that yard," Dad says as he watches Snickers.

It's a beautiful yard and I'm taken aback at Dad's quick assumption. "How can you tell?"

"Well, I can see they have gophers. Can't you?" Dad asks. He looks at me incredulously for a moment, then says, "Just look there, and there, and there at that humped up ground. They have gophers."

* * *

1967

"What are you standing on?" Dad paused in his hoeing to stare at my bare feet. It was 6 a.m. and we were hard at work hoeing the garden before it got too hot. The soil felt moist with dew making the job only slightly less irksome.

"I don't know. It's just a row of soft dirt." I paused glad for a reason to lean on my hoe and rest my arms. The handle was broken making it just the right length for my height, but the top was sharp and jagged making it a less than ideal place to rest my chin.

Dad walked the few steps across the garden to where I stood, his heavy work boots making dusty puffing sounds. He jammed his hoe into the row closely in front of my toes making me jump!

"That's not a normal row, that's a gopher cave! That varmint is right under the dirt, digging his way along the radishes and eating them from underneath. Look!" He reached down and plucked a fluffy radish top out of the ground and dangled the end in front of my nose. No radish, only teeth marks on the stalk.

"See? They ate the entire vegetable! The varmint's eating out all the bottoms and leaving us the tops! They are smart, I tell you. They try to hide the fact they are here; but I'm too smart for them. I know gopher teeth marks when I see them."

He threw the green top down beside the row of radishes and pulled another. It looked the same. He pulled up more—the same. I picked up one of the discarded leaves and saw tiny little teeth marks in what was left of the white radish top.

"What's a gopher?"

"It's a nuisance, that's what it is! No doubt they are coming over from the neighbor's field. He turned the dirt in his entire pasture last week. Ran them over on me—that scoundrel! I got a strong inclination to give him a piece of my mind."

Dad respects our new neighbor who had built a house just down from ours but sometimes he got on Dad's nerves. He hadn't wasted any time fencing in a pasture for horses he planned to keep there. He'd taken possession of the tree house Dad built Franky and me at the edge of the garden saying it was really on his property. His son told us we couldn't use the tree house anymore. I am friends with the neighbor's daughter. We often go for walks and talks but sometimes I think she there in part to see my cute brother. Running gophers over on us creates a strain on the relationship between families, even though it's not intentional

"What do we do?"

"We're going to kill the varmints!"

"Wouldn't it be easier to just run them back across the property line?"

"Gophers don't understand property lines, and now that they know the garden's here, there's really only one way to get rid of them."

"How's that?"

"Just wait. I'll show you." Dad smiled.

That evening Dad came home with some of the cruelest looking traps I'd ever seen. Out on the back porch he demonstrated in front of Franky and me how we would place the traps in the ground over an underground gopher path and how, when the gopher went through the path and tripped the switch, long spikes like pitchforks would slam down and poke the gopher right through the neck, trapping him underground. I shivered as Dad showed us how it worked. Poor gopher. I didn't know exactly what a gopher looked like, but I didn't think any animal deserved to have a pitchfork thrust through its neck! But I knew better than to tell Dad that.

The next day Dad set out several traps around the garden. After he left for work, I went down and tripped them all.

That night Dad checked the traps. "Blasted traps," he said as he walked up the steps of the back porch stomping the garden dirt off his boots. "Every one of those traps was thrown, but no gopher."

"You don't say," I said, twirling a curl of my hair around my finger doing my best to look innocent.

"You didn't do anything to them, did you?"

"Me?" I looked innocent, not exactly telling a lie, but close enough. *God please don't cast me into hell for lying, I'm only trying to save one of your defenseless creatures,* I prayed silently. *Did the end justify the means?* I wondered.

The routine went on for about a week. Dad set the traps in the mornings before going to work. I tripped them after he left. He came home and checked them at night. No gopher. Then he went to bed fuming mad. In the meantime, the gophers worked their way through all the radishes, the onion sets, the baby carrots and then made a soft dirt trail up from the garden through the yard and started working on mother's chrysanthemum roots. Guilt settled heavy on my shoulders. God would surely open the earth under my feet, and I would slide down an express route to the fiery pit of hell. I didn't dare walk into church on Sunday with this deception on my soul. Beads of sweat popped up on my upper lip when I thought about my deception as I hoed the potatoes. I was thinking that making it to the end of the potato row probably wasn't going to get me into heaven. I needed to confess my sins to Dad, but that meant the gophers would die. I'd looked up a gopher picture in the *Encyclopedia Britannica*. It was so cute with a stubby little nose, soft brown fur, and shiny eyes. They only ate roots and vegetables. I just couldn't turn them in. We had enough food to spare, didn't we?

Hanging up my hoe on the back porch, I met Dad coming out of the house that evening.

"Want to go over to the shop with me?"

"Sure," I said, dusting off my hands on the back of my shorts. "What for?"

"I'm going to see if I can find some of that old dynamite that I got to blow up the tree stumps on your uncle's place."

"What are you going to do with dynamite?"

"You'll see. Come on!"

I crawled into Dad's big dump truck and he started the engine and it roared. In 5 minutes we pulled up in front of the shop. He got out and slammed the door, and I did the same and followed him inside. Inside, Dad turned on the lights. He moved things around on his workbench and swept the floor and a few things he always liked to do. Straightening, he called it. I tried to pull a Coke out of the old Coke machine that sat behind the door, but it took dimes, and I didn't have a dime. Dad had installed the machine to make money off his workers, and it really did work. They would actually pay for their drinks, and Dad would earn back some of the money he paid them. But it was frustrating as his child to have to pay for drinks at the shop Dad owned. My uncle, my mother's brother, owned a small roadside grocery store, and he let all his kids have all the Sun Drops and junk food they wanted for free.

Sometimes Franky or I could jimmy the coke machine so I could get a drink out without paying for it. It wasn't really stealing if the drinks belonged to your Dad, Franky told me. And he'd shown me how. But this time it didn't work. My mouth watered for that Coke, but I didn't want to ask Dad for a dime. Hellbound people didn't deserve Cokes, I decided. Thirsty? Get used to it. This was nothing like the thirst in hell. I needed to toughen up. I sat down on a wooden crate and waited, mouth sawdust-dry. A few minutes later, Dad walked over and pulled a box out from behind the Coke machine. Inside were things that looked like large firecrackers, wrapped in dirty red paper. Franky and I would sometimes amuse ourselves by rolling them around on the floor or tying the little strings together and forming daisy chains out of them. Sometimes we'd bury them in the sawdust underneath Dad's table saw.

"What's that?" I asked.

"That's dynamite?"

When he said that, my heart stopped for a second. I couldn't tell you how many times Franky had held one and looked in the workbench for matches saying, "I'm going to light this, and throw it to see what happens. I bet it's a big old firecracker. Maybe it will pop real loud."

"Yes, it looks like it would pop real loud if it worked, but it looks old and like it's been wet once or twice. I bet it's a dud," I replied.

"What are you going to do with dynamite?" I asked Dad when I was fairly sure my voice wouldn't shake. No point in letting him know about our former firecracker play. That was water under the bridge.

"We're going to dynamite some gopher holes," Dad said with a smug tilt of his mouth. He picked up the box of dynamite and walked to the door shutting off the lights before I'd quite gotten half way there. I hurried through the dimness in the building toward the door lit from the outside by the evening sun and wondered on the way what it was like to die and see the light of heaven.

Outside, we followed the path between various hunks of junk, which included the old broken-down school bus that had been there for what seemed like forever. Dad threw the dynamite behind the seat of the truck, slammed the seat back on it like it was nothing, and got in with a squeak and clatter of springs. I was more careful climbing in, and I sat down softly conscious that what lay behind us in the seat could blow us completely out of the truck given the right circumstances. A little bead of sweat trickled down the side of my face, even though it wasn't hot at all. Things weren't looking good for the gophers. Their fate was in God's hands now.

"Dad, what are we doing?" Franky asked when we got home. He stood on the porch with his hands in his pockets until Dad asked him to unload the case of dynamite. Franky picked up the box and placed it on the lawn. He cut his eyes toward me, "So that's dynamite?"

I nodded.

"We're going to get rid of some gophers." Dad unwound some fuse from a spool he'd brought from the shop and began to cut it into 18 inch sections.

"How?" Franky asked. He dusted his hands on his jeans and dropped down on the grass beside the dynamite.

"Why, we're going to jam it down all the holes we can find and blow them up. Maybe the blast will launch a few of them right into the frying pan. At the very least, maybe they'll be a bit scarce around here after this."

"Shouldn't we tell Mother you're going to set off some dynamite?" I asked. Surely if Mother knew, she'd bring a quick stop to this madness.

"She'll find out soon enough!" Dad kept measuring and cutting fuse.

"Yeah, this is man's work," Franky grinned.

They were insane. Both of them. But I couldn't help myself—I had to see how it worked out.

Poor gophers. I'd tried to save them, but they just hadn't had the sense to take the hint when I'd gone around collapsing all their gopher traps and crushing all the gopher underground trails with my feet. As I watched Franky and Dad, I took a few steps back toward the house, but couldn't tear my eyes away from the box of dynamite. Some of it looked old and dusty. I wondered how long dynamite lasted. Did it work after it'd been rained on?

I'd seen Dad blast stumps out of the ground. Sometimes they blew 10 feet high. Somehow stealing a few radishes and the random carrot didn't seem enough to justify such a dramatic cure. I carefully used my bare foot to crush down one of the gopher trails in the yard. Working quickly, I collapsed a full 10 feet while Dad wasn't looking. If the gopher was at the other end, maybe he'd make a run for it and get away in time.

Together Dad and Franky worked for the next 30 minutes in the side yard and down into the garden, then through the radish beds, carrots, onion sets and into the peas. Franky set the charges, and Dad attached the fuses.

"How are we going to set all these off?" Franky asked.

"We're going to tie all the fuses together and attach them to one long cord. Then I'll light it from up there," Dad pointed to the front yard a full 30 feet from ground zero. I watched with one eye squeezed shut and kept crushing the gopher trails with both feet. Neither seemed to notice my latest efforts to save the wildlife.

Finally, all the charges were set. Sweating, we all retreated to a safe distance pulling the main wire with us. When Dad felt we were far enough away to be safe, he stopped. He reached into a box of matches he always carried in his overall pocket. He scratched it across a stone in mother's flowerbed to light it. The wind blew it out. I exhaled, not realizing until then that I'd been holding my breath.

"Jane, get back," he yelled.

"I'm behind you!"

"Get back on the porch out of the way."

"I want to see."

"You heard me!"

"Franky, you go with her?"

"I'm not scared!"

"One more word, and I'll send you both to your rooms!"

He lit a second match. It hissed into life, flared briefly, but not long enough to light the fuse.

Not even a bird chirped when Dad lit the third match. He cupped it in his hand and lit the fuse. I covered my ears and squatted down behind the porch steps and waited. The fuse smoked and sizzled across the yard. My legs ached from crouching. My nose itched. I scratched. Here and there a stray bit of grass caught fire then flared out along the path of the fuse. It seemed to take a year for the fuse to make it to where Dad had tied all the separate lines together. We watched. Minutes ticked by.

I had just sucked in a large breath when the first charge went off. The blast nearly deafened me. It looked like fireworks, only with dirt instead of sparklers. Radish plants, complete with red radish bases, flew into the air as if in slow motion. Apparently the gophers had not eaten ALL the radishes. The second charge fired scant seconds later. I stood awed by the spectacle as dirt clods flew into the air, shattered then fluttered down on the afternoon breeze. Soon all the other charges did their work, and the entire garden, and most of the side yard, flew into the air.

"Do you see any gophers?" Dad yelled over the sound of raining dirt, roots and vegetable particles.

"Nope," Franky responded. He jumped to his feet and did the first steps of an Indian dance he'd learned in Boy Scouts. "Not sure if I'd recognize one if I saw it. Wouldn't they be in pieces or vaporized?"

"Likely so!"

Silence fell after the last explosion. Dust filled the air and then drifted out over the pond like evening mist. The garden was a complete loss. So was most of the side yard.

I looked up to see Mom standing on the back porch, an expression of utter shock on her face. "Louis, what on earth are you up to? I thought war had been declared."

"Just exterminating."

"Louis Hinkle, you are crazy. Kids, get in the house. You're father's crazy. You don't need to be around him."

"But what about the gophers?" I asked.

"I expect we've seen the last of them." Dad smiled.

Mom shooed Franky and me into the house by shaking a white cup towel at us. Just before I went inside, I glanced back over my shoulder. Dad was sitting in the yard, legs outstretched in front of him, leaning back on his hands surveying the damage. He was smiling with a piece of grass clenched between his teeth. "I guess I taught those gophers a thing or two."

We bought our radishes in the grocery store that year. Onions too. Dad plowed the side yard, ran over it a time or two with the harrow and reseeded it in grass. The grass grew lush and green before the end of the summer. I don't know if we killed any gophers or just scared them off, but we never saw another gopher. It was also the last year we tried to raise a garden.

* * *

2007

Dad doesn't tell my son-in-law about the gophers or the dynamite. I am relieved because I don't want my son-in-law to think we are crazy people. And, truthfully so many of my childhood memories are so bizarre sometimes I wonder if I made them up. Much of it seems so preposterous, even to me. But then I realize no one could make up the stories I recall. They are simply too strange. Truth is… stranger than fiction.

We sit on the patio and watch the sun set. The dogs eventually lie down and chew their tennis balls and look at us, happy. Eventually, my daughter brings us dinner that we relish. She is an excellent hostess and cook.

When the street lights start to come on we say goodbye. On the drive to take Dad home I can't help myself, I have to ask. "Dad, why didn't you tell him about dynamiting the gophers in the garden when we were kids?"

Dad looks out the window, then says, "Jane, it's a different time. He's too sophisticated to stoop to the likes of dynamiting his fancy yard and garden to get rid of gophers."

"Well it did a lot of damage to our yard too, wiped out the entire garden. So why did you dynamite our yard?" I asked.

"It was a long time ago," Dad says. "Life gets tough and sometimes a man just needs to blow off a little steam." He smiles.

◇

"If there is famine in the land, if there is pestilence or blight or mildew or locust or caterpillar, if their enemies besiege them in the land at their gates, whatever plague, whatever sickness there is, whatever prayer, whatever plea is made by any man or by all your people Israel, each knowing his own affliction and his own sorrow and stretching out his hands toward this house, then hear from heaven your dwelling place and forgive and render to each whose heart you know, according to all his ways, for you, you only, know the hearts of the children of mankind, that they may fear you and walk in your ways all the days that they live in the land that you gave to our fathers." (2 Chronicles 6:28)

Cucumber Radish Salad

Wash and peel 1 large cucumber.
Wash and top/and/tail 10 red radishes.
Place in half-and-half mixture of water and white vinegar sufficient to cover veggies in small white bowl and allow to marinate.
Add 1 teaspoon of salt, dash of pepper, and dash of dill.
Let rest in refrigerator all day.
Serve as a side dish for fish or roast.

Chapter 23 – Thanksgiving Gobbler
"Yes, everything is lovely. It all looks so perfect." — Louis

2007

"Would you like to attend Thanksgiving dinner with our friends?" I ask Dad. We are sitting in his room having just finished dinner. It seems like the right time for us to make plans for the holidays.

Since moving back to Texas and since the sale of our house, Hock and I have moved into an apartment, and don't have room to host Thanksgiving for family. Our apartment is on the second floor with the only access via a steep set of stairs that Dad would never be able to navigate. Fortunately, some very kind friends have offered to host all of us this holiday.

"Sure, if that's what you want. Might give me a chance to see how the other half lives," he tells me with an ironic smile. While he does not say it, his personal world has shrunk considerably in the last two years—from acres of land, multiple cars trucks and storage facilities, to one room, a few treasured items and a single closet of possessions—and a bank account. However, the world outside this room likely feels much bigger to him than the old one, coming from a small Middle Tennessee town to the suburbs of Dallas. While the move has increased his standard of living and encompasses more choices in the way of restaurants, medical care, and entertainment, his friend base is now much smaller. But, the opportunity to make new friends seems to appeal to him. I hug Dad's neck, tell him what time we will pick him up for Thanksgiving dinner tomorrow, and we say goodbye.

The next day Dad dresses carefully with my help and tops off his outfit with a tweed Kangol hat like the one his father from Germany wore. It makes him look classic. He also wears a warm sweater over a clean plaid shirt. He looks nice I tell him as we drive to the friend's house. Hock is not with us this year having left for a seminar in Europe; so it is the two of us and Sherry and other family members who will meet us there.

Everyone is nice to Dad when he arrives, but he is quiet as he sits in front of the window and watches several dogs play with the children outside. I bring him tea, and he sips as he watches. Friends stop by and make light conversation. Soon we are called to dinner. We circle, hold hands, and pray together before we eat. *"Lord, thank you for the opportunity for us all to safely gather together today. We thank you for your many blessings this year, for this food, and for each other. Bless the hands that prepared our meal in order that it might nourish our bodies and sustain us. Amen."*

I prepare a plate of food for Dad, and he sits down at the formal dining room table where he has a view of the pool and the kids. Many join him. Others gather at a long table in the kitchen around the corner, also by a window, and some take plates of food outside to eat in the outdoor-seating area by a warm fire.

Our friends are kind to Dad. I mingle, but come back often to check on him. I think of many Thanksgivings we've shared over the years. Some of those Thanksgivings were pretty sparse. Yet, in our eyes, the tables were full and prepared with hard work and with love. I know, likely, neither of us can think of Thanksgiving without recalling that Franky, brother and son, died two short days after Thanksgiving in 1976. While we are ever-thankful each holiday for those of us still living, we also feel the loss of those who are gone. Now with Dad's health declining, I wonder if this will be his last Thanksgiving.

"Are you enjoying yourself, Dad?" I ask him.

"Yes, it all looks so perfect," Dad says.

It does look perfect, at least on the surface; and I think how glad I am for Dad to have a perfect, peaceful Thanksgiving.

* * *

1967

Thanksgiving in Tennessee when I was a child came wrapped in a rustling swell of red, brown and orange maple leaves swirling around us whenever we went outside. The leaves often seemed to scamper as the wind carried them across lawns and piled them up against abandoned tractors, toys, barns and fence posts. Eventually their sheer numbers buried the garden and lawns under a crackly coat that insulated plant roots from the cold snow certain to come.

On such days wood smoke filled my nostrils and smudged the air with a swirling haze that I didn't mind at all because it smelled warm and inviting, like hearth and home.

Rising at 3:00 a.m. Thanksgiving morning, Mom removed "Tom Turkey" from the Frigidaire where she had him thawing. After setting aside the less-desirable bits to boil to make broth, she scalded the turkey in the sink underneath a hot faucet spray of near-boiling water. Then she washed Tom, much like a mother washes a child, in the sink. After she felt certain Tom was clean, she'd sit him upright on a linen towel and rub him dry all over talking to him all the time saying, "What a lovely fellow you are! You are going to look wonderful on the table, aren't you?" Not waiting for a response from Tom, who was headless anyway and unable to comment even if he had been alive, she'd remove any lingering pinfeathers and give him a rubdown with olive oil equal to any professional massage. It was enough to put Tom to sleep—if he were alive. After she had him settled, Mom applied salt, pepper, garlic, parsley and sage until he virtually shimmered in spices. Finally, looking completely satisfied with herself, Mom placed Tom, new spice coat and all, gently into his roasting pan. Then onto the oven rack he went where he cooked slowly until Thanksgiving lunch.

While Tom cooked, Mom went back to bed for two more precious hours of sleep. At 5 a.m. she began her Thanksgiving Day of assembling, cooking, serving and, finally, cleaning.

No one made Thanksgiving dinner like Mom. It wasn't so much that we had fancy things like—say—oyster stuffing. Thumbing through her cookbook, I mentally drooled over the recipes while Mom worked feverishly combining magical ingredients in an ancient crockery bowl. She executed her moves like a magician about to pull a fluffy white rabbit out of a hat. I didn't even know what an oyster was, but it sure sounded good. I'd heard my brother refer to "mountain oysters" with a crude laugh that made me automatically know I'd better never ask him what they were. So I was left to thumb through the non-illustrated recipes of the *Better Homes and Garden's Cookbook* and imagine what they were and how they tasted instead. If they came from the coast, I was certain they were wonderful. I had never seen the ocean but I intended to go as soon as I could. I already knew I would love it.

Mother made cornbread stuffing instead of oyster stuffing. And I found it fragrant, and magical, and so light it virtually dissolved in a cloud of complex flavor on my tongue. In part, what made it magical had something to do with the way she worked with her wrists as she prepared it. Sitting on the corner counter in the kitchen watching her work (Mom would protest my sitting there but eventually she'd forget and I'd sneak back so I could see better), I would imitate the quick turns and twists she made crumbling the warm cornbread up and then mixing in all the wet ingredients by hand with a large spoon. However, I never got it quite right. Mixing cornbread took a lighter stroke than mixing biscuits.

Mom's method looked more like fluffing as opposed to my unsure squeezing. Mother handled food like a professional dressmaker swirls fine fabric between her fingers—with sighs and satisfied smiles imagining all the possibilities.

Men weren't allowed into the kitchen on Thanksgiving until Mom called, "Come and get it!" That rule had been "The Rule" as long as I could remember. It also didn't mean that the men folk didn't try to amble through and "sample" things anyway. Sampling usually resulted in furrowed brows and a stiff wrap on the knuckles with a wooden spoon. Mom meant business with tasters. "Leave that alone! Did you wash your hands?" The line of questioning was sometimes enough to run them off—but not always. Dad or Franky would run their hands under the faucet with lots of soap and a nailbrush as if that would make them acceptable for "sampling". Of course it did not. If they appeared again, Mom would use whatever was available to swat the offending hand. A tea towel or a fly swatter often appeared out of nowhere as she chased the men out of the kitchen where they would linger just out of reach milling around like a pack of stray dogs, mouths watering.

Mom was not without sympathy and did, however, always keep a beautiful crystal bowl in the refrigerator with loosely chopped veggies for us to snack on in a way that would not ruin our appetite.

Waiting for Thanksgiving lunch had its rewards. Sometimes there was a cake bowl or a mixer beater that needed to be licked clean. This, we could have. Mom scrapped them, but she'd leave enough to make the wait worth it. My brother and I, and sometimes Dad, would dive in trying to select the one containing the most batter, and then we'd polish it clean with our tongues before dropping it into the sink-full of soapy water.

At least once during the Thanksgiving preparations, Dad would try to insert himself into the preparations. "Honey, can I do anything?" he'd ask in a syrupy voice, at least a half-octave higher than his normal everyday voice. Anyone could see that his offer had ulterior motives. All he wanted was a better angle to sample when she was not looking.

"Everything's under control," Mom would say. But she'd start getting nervous from the perceived pressure. Her hands would begin to tremble, and she'd move a little faster knowing her well-timed preparations were at risk. The pressure to get the food done before Dad inserted himself underfoot would start to heat up the already warm kitchen. Sometimes she'd finish in time before Dad got in the way and caused a calamity. Sometimes he'd startle Mom and she'd drop the freshly whipped mashed potatoes or perhaps the rolls. Other times, it would be Dad who turned over the pitcher of tea as he tried to take the turkey out of the oven. Usually the incident ended up with him stepping on the cats tail with his boots or some other misstep. The cat would jump into the air and knock the chair into the cake cooling on the counter and sending it flying across the kitchen; and all would be ruined.

The drama could, in fact, trickle down even if I stayed well out of the way. "Janie, what's the cat doing in the house?" Mom would scold. I was always the one letting the cat inside. We weren't allowed to have animals in the house because of my allergies, but sometimes I missed them so much, I'd sneak one in hoping she wouldn't notice. As if they knew, the cat usually took up a position in an inconspicuous areas like under the couch, or under the kitchen table. Things went pretty well unless Dad stepped on a protruding paw or tail. Or sometimes it would be one of us kids he'd trip over. The kitchen was small and crowded; and, with several operations under way at once, it was easy to forget the pie browning and burn it, or beat the potatoes too long until they got overly glossy—like glue. The calamity, whatever it turned out to be, would make Mom cry. Sometimes she'd grab up a cup towel, press it to her face and run crying to the bedroom, slamming the door behind her. We'd look at each other and wonder who would finish Thanksgiving dinner? —*not Dad,* we prayed!

"Mom! What can we do to help?" We'd run to the bedroom door and pound on it with our fists. Sometimes the weeping would continue, only louder—which wasn't a good sign.

"I wanted Thanksgiving to be *perfect*," would float out from under the door! Eventually we would coax her out. Mother wouldn't let us kids starve for the price of a ruined pie or cake. But by then the food would be a mixture of hot things gone cold and tea with melted ice leaving circles on the good linen tablecloth. Thanksgiving could be really tricky to carry off *perfectly*.

Sometimes Franky or I would try to distract Dad. "Can you help us with this game of Scrabble? What is a good four-letter word that begins with 'w'?" That would keep him engaged for about five minutes; then he'd be back trying to "help" Mom again. All the time his eye was on the coconut crème pie cooling on the kitchen window ledge with the window cracked to let out the steam. If only he could nip a tiny spoonful of the topping he would be a happy man.

Until I was 10, Thanksgiving went about the same every year. Things would go well for a while. Then it would all go to "Hell in a Hand Basket" Franky would say, if we weren't careful.

I was 10 the year Dad bought the electric knife. Mother had just taken the turkey out of the oven and placed it carefully on the serving platter in the center of the table. Dad got up and went to his office briefly and came back with a box that he handled with loving care. He placed it on the table, opened it, and drew out and assembled a GE electric carving knife which he immediately plugged in. Whurrrrrr…..a high pitched hum came from the blades as they whipped back and forth at lightening speed.

"What's that?" Mom asked turning from where she was preparing the cranberry salad.

"I bought an electric knife, dear," he said. The blades whirred again as they both watched him test it out in mid air. "I thought it would make slicing the turkey easier." He smiled. Whirr…Whirr… for good measure, then he sat the knife down on the table.

" Louis, that thing looks dangerous."

"It is dangerous, so you need a husband in the kitchen to use it and protect you my Great Big Beautiful Doll," Dad said. He hovered over the turkey tugging gently on the leg trying to find a place to begin slicing as Mom watched nervously. Carefully, he inserted the knife and it cut through the warm turkey like butter. He cut enough slices for our meal in only a few moments, gently folding them down beside the body of the turkey on the serving platter. Then he cleaned the blades and sliced some cheese to serve alongside the turkey. After that was done, he turned to Mom and asked, "Honey, would you like for me to slice anything else?" He waited, knife in hand, expectant. A lover of all new shiny tools, his excitement at an opportunity to use the knife ignited a small fire in his eyes. That mixed with a good reason for him to be in the kitchen and "help" caused him to smile happily.

"No, I think that's enough." Mom looked at the perfectly sliced turkey and appeared to be considering how she could inch him back out of the kitchen.

Dad reluctantly set the knife down on the counter, adjusted the platter on the table and headed back toward his chair to wait until Mom finished the salad. She turned back to her work just as he passed the coconut crème pie. He reached out and took a tiny bit of the topping with his finger and stuck it triumphantly into his mouth on his way out of the kitchen without Mom noticing.

Clearly Mom was now queen of her domain again, but the knife made her uneasy. Perhaps she sensed she was losing her grip on her domain.

For once, it looked like Mother's dream of a perfect Thanksgiving dinner would come true—even with Dad's help—just *perfect*. Mom seemed to sense it and straightened her back. I noticed the pearls around her neck seemed to glisten more than usual. Her dress seemed more crisply ironed. The tablecloth seemed whiter. All the tea glasses sparkled in the light.

As if on cue to do our part to complete the perfect family holiday picture, Franky and I sat down on the rug in front of the fire and exchanged Scrabble for Checkers. Dad sat in his chair reading Bible stories to us and nibbling on expertly sliced cheese and crackers as we waited for Mom to call us. Some time passed with Mom humming to herself in between finishing the salad and dishing up the veggies. All was nearly ready. The cat slunk to a spot under the asparagus fern stand nearer the kitchen, looking optimistic, hoping for a random slice of turkey to fall to the floor.

I could feel that at any moment, Mom would say, "Dinner's ready!" She was just tidying up a bit before she made the announcement. A few stray dishes were cast into hot soapy water. She took off her apron. My mouth watered at the thought of that juicy turkey just waiting. I could see little wafts of steam rising from its crisp, brown, fragrant breast.

Staring at the lovely scene in anticipation, I saw it all happen like a movie in slow motion. Mother reached for a plate of leftover breakfast biscuits sitting on the counter that she'd turned a pie tin over to keep them fresh. No doubt she did this to clear the clutter before we all sat down. As she picked them up a mouse jumped from under the pie tin where it had obviously been hiding most of the morning, no doubt gnawing away at the leftover biscuits in a mixture of hunger and nervousness. No matter how pristinely clean, all farms have mice from time to time, and we were no exception.

"Ahhh…" Mom screamed! "A mouse! Louis!"

She flung the plate, biscuits, pie tin and mouse up in the air in the kitchen. The plate and biscuits rose in the air, flew across the kitchen and landed about midway to the stove with a crash. The mouse, went up with the plate and biscuits, but somehow managed to make an acrobatic leap and caught hold of the kitchen chandelier overhead where it clung only briefly as the fixture swayed heavily. Then it slid slowly, awkwardly down the side of one brass sconce before our horror-stricken eyes. From there it jumped and landed on the counter next to where Dad left the electric knife. There it sat for a startled moment, blinking in surprise. Mom's scream spurred it to action. The mouse jumped again sending the electric knife flying into the air at the same time Mom jumped back. As she jumped back she reached out and caught the knife by the handle in mid-air with one hand, and with the other arm raised high to balance herself she accidently struck the chandelier a glancing blow. For a moment it wobbled, then broke free of its mounting and fell directly into the middle of the dining room table.

When the chandelier fell, the cat shot out from under the fern and across the house toward the door hitting the door screen at a full run causing it to open. The cat ran out of the house followed closely by the mouse who just made it out before the door slammed shut.

"Louis, help me!" Mother grabbed the chandelier which wobbled around on top of the table and threatened to fall to the floor likely taking tablecloth, turkey, and everything else with it. Now she stood balancing the chandelier in one hand and holding the knife by the handle in the other.

I turned to Dad, expectantly. He looked paralyzed.

"Help me, Louis!" Mom screamed which seemed to unfreeze Dad who shot quickly into action.

He flew into the kitchen, took the knife from Mom, unplugged it, and placed it back on the counter. Then he took the chandelier out of her hands, lifted it gently off the table without upsetting anything, and carried it outside. When he came back in, he helped Mom settle things back in their proper place. By some miracle nothing had been seriously damaged. By changing the tablecloth, placing most of the food into fresh bowls, and pouring new tea, order was soon restored.

My brother and I sat in amazement watching our parents work in tandem to salvage Thanksgiving. After all the food was back on the table, Mom ran to the bedroom, changed clothes, came back to the kitchen and lit candles to add light now that the chandelier was gone.

"Dinner's ready," Mom finally called. We all washed our hands and sat down at the table to eat by candlelight. Mom's hair looked a bit frazzled, and her cheeks appeared pinker than normal. Dad had some mashed potatoes on his white shirt, but otherwise he looked tan and handsome, and in charge. Somehow together they had saved Thanksgiving.

"Would you like to say the blessing, Louis?" Mother asked.

We bowed our heads, joined hands, and Dad offered a prayer: *"Lord, thank you for this food, and for all your blessings this day and every day. Thank you Lord for Velma and all her hard work. Amen."* When he finished, we ate the best Thanksgiving dinner we ever shared in the little green house on the hill that overlooked Aunt Gretta's orchard and backed up to lush pastures, banked by a deep pond, fenced with cedar posts that sometimes contained escape-artist cattle. It was a place called home by a diverse group of people and a menagerie of animals on any given day.

* * *

2007

"Time for dessert," our hostess calls. She is busy in the kitchen with her husband who is trying to help. She slices pumpkin pie, adds whipped topping to each slice, and hands the pie resting on beautiful plates to her husband who distributes each to a waiting guest.

"Would you like some pie, Dad?" I ask.

"Yes, and some coffee too, if they have it."

"I'll check."

Dad looks contentedly out the back window from his position at the dining table. His location is around the corner from the kitchen yet within sight of the kitchen table where many other guests are also waiting on pie. As I round the corner, a popping noise sounds overhead. We all look up, curious. At that moment, the chandelier over the table wobbles and falls into the middle of the kitchen table. There are a few screams. Chairs are pushed back? There are still more screams of surprise and shock. Dogs and cats run away from the table nearly tripping people trying to get out of the way themselves. The hostess jumps to the rescue and grabs the top of the chandelier to keep it from falling to the floor and taking everything on the table with it. I stand shocked for a moment. Then I look back at Dad who is watching with an amused look on his face. "A *perfect* Thanksgiving after all," he says. "Is anyone hurt? No? Well good!" He picks up his fork and cuts a huge piece of pie, then pops it into his mouth. "Just like home."

◇

"Love never ends. As for prophecies, they will pass away; as for tongues, they will cease; as for knowledge, it will pass away. For we know in part and we prophesy in part, but when the perfect comes, the partial will pass away. When I was a child, I spoke like a child, I thought like a child, I reasoned like a child. When I became a man, I gave up childish ways. For now we see in a mirror dimly, but then face to face. Now I know in part; then I shall know fully, even as I have been fully known." (1 Corinthians 13:8-12)

◇

Turkey Dressing
Cornbread
*In a cast iron skillet on top of stove melt 1 tablespoon Crisco.
In mixing bowl combine,
1 cup plain flour,
1 cup plain cornmeal,*

1 large egg beaten (2 if small),
1 tablespoon of sugar,
2 teaspoons baking powder,
1/3 cup melted butter,
1 cup of milk,
Mix all ingredients, pour into greased skillet while it's still warm.
Back at 375 degrees until bread is brown and you can press on the middle and it springs back.
Remove from oven.
Flip onto large plate and allow to cool.

Broth

Take giblets from turkey and simmer in quart of water for one hour.
Strain, and retain broth. Discard giblets.
Saute 1 cup chopped celery and 1 cup of chopped onions in stainless steel skillet on stove top in 1 tablespoon of Crisco until translucent.
Set aside.

Dressing

Crumble cool cornbread into a bowl.
add
celery, onions,
1 tablespoon of parsley,
1 tablespoon sage,
1 teaspoon salt,
1 teaspoon of pepper,
enough broth to easily stir and mix the mixture.
Mixture should be wet but not runny.
Once it's mixed,
press into large, greased, glass baking dish.
Press gently into the dish with fingers.
Cover with foil.
Bake at 375 for 45 minutes.
Remove foil last 10 minutes to brown.
Serve in same dish as a side for the turkey.

Chapter 24 – Turnip Greens and Wire Sculpture
"Will this make my heart bionic?" — Louis

2007
It is only a few days after Thanksgiving dinner. Hock is back from his teaching trip, and we have just settled down to our lunch at McAlister's in McKinney, Texas, when we get the call. I've taken the first bite of turnip greens and cornbread. I pull out my cell phone and answer the ring.

"Jane, it's about your Dad. His oxygen level dropped right after lunch and he collapsed," Hilda from assisted living says. She is from South Africa and speaks with a thick accent. I hear serious concern in her voice. "His blood pressure is high. We think he's had a stroke. He's en route to the Allen hospital by ambulance. Can you meet the ambulance there?"

"Of course, I'm on my way."

I look down at the turnip greens and cornbread. A meal I'd had so many times as a child. Comfort food. It is a simple meal that brings back good memories of home.

"We have to go," I tell Hock as I push my chair back.

"What's wrong?"

"It's Dad. He collapsed after lunch, and they took him to the hospital." I throw my jacket on and grab my handbag.

"Do you want to take the food to go?"

"No time. And, besides, I've lost my appetite."

On the way to the hospital I think about comfort food, but also about what comforts the heart. There is comfort in family and in belonging to someone. But what is it exactly that binds a family together? Family isn't any one thing, it's more a collection of small things that happen as we work, play, eat and wind down for sleep at night repeatedly together. It's what happens when we face life challenges as a collective. Soldiers bond as brothers under foxhole stress. Co-workers become like family as we solve challenges as a collective. Nuclear families bond over shared happiness, but also over tragedy. A family is not so much knit together by large decisions or events but by small everyday shared occurrences. We generally think of family as blood relations, but many families have no genetic connection yet the bond is just as strong. Family is part fate, part circumstances, and sometimes part blood, but mostly it's a decision and a commitment. What bonds us together may seem arbitrary, even incidental, but over time it's what makes us who we are.

Yet, what comes together must inevitably come apart. All families unwind eventually over time. Some families break apart early in life unable to withstand tragedy, misunderstandings, differing opinions or social pressures. Others do not break apart until death or beyond. What continues to hold us together after death are our shared memories and the love we feel for one another. Real love is the only thing that lasts. It is a gift few ever possess. Despite everything that's happened, I love Dad.

Suddenly, every minute seems precious. I have much yet to learn about life, death and love before Dad and I part. I want to write down what I remember and what I've learned. There is comfort food for the stomach but, more important, comfort food for the heart through shared life experiences and memories.

* * *

1970

Mom and I stepped outside the house and into the early morning sunshine. I wore an old tee shirt and blue jean shorts that were fringed along the thigh for several inches. Mom wore a red and navy plaid shirtwaist dress, belted around her slim waist. We both wore Keds tennis shoes. We walked under the pecan tree that shaded the driveway and prepared to go pick greens in the turnip patch. It's the same tree where I received my first kiss, recently. But I don't tell Mom that. Rain had washed the dust off the trees and fields the night before leaving the air sweet with the smell of the alfalfa hay that grew across the road. I inhaled and held my breath for as long as I could enjoying the scent. I loved living in the country.

Mom and I both had several brown paper sacks tucked neatly under one arm. We were off on our first morning to pick turnip greens on Dad's old-home place about a mile away. We picked in the mornings before the sun got too hot. Everyone in our family liked turnip greens. We all looked forward to eating a pot full that night with pork chops, warm cornbread, and cold buttermilk. But as much as we loved them, we also know we'd soon be sick of them, all of us except Dad.

Dad loved turnip green season for a number of reasons. He saw it as a time when we could do something, "as a family". Whenever he said this, it made me cringe. It always meant extra work. Mother and Franky would make excuses and sometimes outright rebel, or he'd just find them scarce. But not me. I hadn't quite figured out how to get out of doing things Dad wanted me to do without hurting his feelings.

Besides, I liked turnip-green picking better than other family projects he thought up, such as frog killing and dodging in the road in the middle of the night to pick up busted cases of nails he had dropped on the road. By comparison, this was a cake walk.

So we waited. Dad who had gone to the shop to get his favorite pair of boots he liked to wear turnip green picking. They were the ones with deep tread that Mom banned from the house because they carried dirt clods in and scattered them across her clean floors. They gave him extra traction so he could walk faster than the rest of us.

Mom and I didn't wear boots. I'd outgrown mine, and Mom thought they were unbecoming to a lady; so our plan was to take our tennis shoes off and pick greens barefoot, then wash our feet in a bucket of water when we were done. Some people might think this country, or silly, but feet were easier to wash than boots; and I kind of enjoyed the feeling of wet earth working its way between my toes as I picked. And, at the moment, it felt good to stand with nothing to do but think about that and enjoy the feel of the early morning sun on my face and smell the fresh air.

"What's that?" Mother's question stirred me from my thoughts.

She pointed at something small and red in the driveway a few feet from where we stood.

"What's what?" I asked, more to pass the time than any real concern over what I'd find in our driveway at 7:30 a.m. I walked over and picked up the object she indicated. Rolling it over in my hand, it looked like an intricate, red sculpture made out of red rubber coated wire. It had many small twists and turns, each of these rolled up into a larger ball. I considered it for a moment, about the size of a car key. To me it looked like a miniature brain made of colored wire.

"I don't know what it is!" I said. "But it's really neat. Look."

I handed the object to her. She rolled it around in her hand a time or two.

"It's interesting and pretty, don't you think? But I wonder what it is and what it's for?" I peered over her arm to get a closer look.

"I've never seen anything like it. It is pretty." Mom looked around the driveway. She stooped and picked up several more.

"Look here's a green one."

"I found a blue one!" I held it up for her to examine.

"Maybe it's something Louis found and brought home, and it rolled out of his truck." Mom said. Dad was forever bringing things home and tossing them out in the yard without explanation. One time Franky and I found a sawbones kit that contained all the tools an old-time doctor would need to remove arms and legs. When we asked him about it, he shrugged and said, "Yes, I found that inside the wall of a house I tore down last week. Thought you kids would like to play with it." I couldn't imagine what he meant. What were we supposed to do with it? Maybe we could practice sawing each other's limbs off?

"I don't know what they are, but I think they would look interesting as an ornament for the table. Don't you?" Mom rolled the collection of rolled wire balls around and around in her hand, to clean the dirt off them. Soon they began to shine attractively.

"Why not? We could put them in the white cut-glass bowl that belonged to Mama Hickson," I said. Mama Hickson was my grandmother who now lived with my cousins in Texas.

"They would look nice on the dining table," I added.

"Brummmm." Dad drove up to the end of the drive in the van. Mother stuck the balls into her pocket as we slid into the van, me in back, Mom up front with Dad.

Fifteen minutes later we stood knee-deep in fresh greens. I bent and picked alongside Mom and Dad. The sound of the turnip greens tearing in our fingers made me hungry. Honeybees buzzed around a nearby row of beehives that belonged to Uncle Dave who owned one side of the field. A wide stretch of purple clover surrounded the turnip green patch. Uncle Dave always made sure the fields had plenty of clover to flavor the honey his bees made in the white hives placed along the edge of the field. There were 12 hives. I thought of them as bee condominiums. I'd never looked inside, not having a bee hat my size. But in my mind I already knew what they looked like from reading about them in *Popular Science Magazine*. The buzzing made me nervous; however the bees looked relaxed enough today. They'd buzzed around me but none settled on me. They only seemed curious about our intrusion into their world.

Dad pulled a shovel out of the bed of the truck and began to dig the turnips from a row that had gone to seed and the greens were no longer good to eat. We quickly filled our bags with greens, and Dad filled a large burlap bag with purple and white turnips.

Having filled all the bags I brought, I walked over to the green pepper beds that belonged to Uncle Dave. After he put out the tobacco sets in the field he'd replant green peppers in their place in the raised beds. I picked a pepper knowing Uncle Dave wouldn't mind. I'd asked once and he told me anytime I wanted a pepper I could pick one. I bit into the crisp green flesh and savored it. Sweet! Peppers were my favorite.

Uncle Dave was a WWI vet who still grew tobacco sets in a bed covered in muslin, and plowed his farm with a mule named Maude. Everyone else had a tractor, but Dave had plowed so long with Maude, his black plow horse, he said it would hurt her feelings if he bought a tractor. "She'd pine, and feel useless," he told me one Sunday when I went over to get the funny papers to read. He always saved these for Franky and me because our parents didn't subscribe to the Sunday paper. I learned to ride horses when I was two years old when Uncle Dave placed me up on Maude's back as he walked her to the barn. I still remember the slow long-legged sway of riding Maude. She was a gentle horse with thick, long mane and tail and soft, intelligent eyes. It was instant love between us.

"Jane, you ready to go?" Dad called, bringing me back to the present.

I swallowed the last of the pepper and picked up my bags of turnip greens.

"You bet."

"Mom?"

"Coming!"

We washed our feet off in the bucket of water Dad had in the back of the van, put our tennis shoes back on and headed for the house in the van.

At home we set up turnip green freezing production. Dad washed the turnips and greens outside on the patio and lay the leaves on towels on the well house roof to drain. The roof of the well house was about waist high to me now. Soon it looked like the well had a leafy hat. Then he took the greens inside the house towel-full by towel-full to Mom in the kitchen. While he went outside for a second load, she would rinse them again in the sink.

"I can't stand biting into turnip greens and finding grit!" She shook her head. Mother never trusted anyone to wash anything as well as she washed it. After the greens got their second bath, she folded them into a huge pot of water boiling on the stove. Soon the whole house smelled like turnip greens, and a cloud of moisture swirled around the kitchen fogging up the windows. Mother's face grew pink and moist from the heat. Once she blanched the leaves, mother scooped them out of the pot and drained them in huge colanders in the sink. Then they became my responsibility.

"Here Jane. Take the greens with the tongs and put equal amounts into these freezer bags. Then, squeeze all the air out and seal the bags shut with these yellow twist wires." Mother did one while I watched to show me how it was done.

"Got it?"

"I think so."

"Good."

While I worked out of one side of the sink, Mother worked out of the other. Before noon, we'd prepared 50 quart bags of turnip greens.

"Congratulations! A good day's work." Dad beamed.

"Now Velma, what's for lunch?"

Mother stared at him a moment, her face glowing with steam and perspiration. Dad had long ago finished washing greens and, while we'd worked in the kitchen all morning, he'd sat in his office working on the adding machine doing bookwork. Mom had tiny flecks of greens on her pink cheeks, and her crisp plaid dress from the morning now looked damp and wrinkled.

"Tuna sandwiches!" Mom said with an over-bright smile. "We'll have sandwiches."

That night we had a lovely dinner of pork chops, turnip greens, mashed potatoes, and buttermilk just like I'd hoped. In the middle of the table sat my grandmother's white cut glass bowl full of the little wire sculptures we'd found lying in the driveway. I loved the different shapes and sizes and different colors of the twisted wire. I wondered where Dad had gotten them, but with all the turnip green picking on our minds, no one had asked him.

The turnip greens tasted sweet and almost melted in my mouth. I skipped the buttermilk because I had not yet acquired a taste for it, but mother loved buttermilk and drank two glasses.

"My favorite dinner." Dad scraped up the last bite of greens and cornbread from his plate and popped it into his mouth with satisfaction.

The next day, we did the same thing all over.
And the next day.

By day three, my hands were stained dark from picking greens. The smell of turnips wafted from my hair when I turned my head. My pillow even smelled like turnip greens. All the towels were stained green. Mother started letting the towels set in the washer in bleach trying to get the turnip green stains out. Our patio looked green and the well-house roof was green for sure. When we opened the front door in the morning, rabbits sat expectantly in the yard waiting for Mom to toss out another washtub full of turnip ends and roots.

"I think we've frozen enough turnip greens to last us a lifetime," Mom said sitting on the back-porch steps waiting for Dad to bring the van to pick us up. "The freezer's completely full. We can't put up anything we picked today. It'll have to go to the neighbors."

"I don't care if I ever see another turnip green as long as I live!" I plopped down beside her to examine my green, mosquito-bitten ankles. I couldn't go swimming in public until some of the green faded. Who wanted to swim with a girl with green ankles?

Dad drove up in the truck. "Good news girls! I bought us another freezer! The hardware store will deliver it this afternoon!"

"You've got to be kidding," Mom and I said simultaneously.

"I'm done!" I tossed down my bags.

"Louis," Mom said, "we can't possibly prepare another bag of turnip greens! I'm sick of turnip greens! Why can't you do anything in moderation?"

"Well if you won't put them up, I'll do it myself." Dad glared at Mom for a minute. When she didn't get up from the porch step where she sat, he got back into his truck and drove away.

The freezer arrived that afternoon. The deliveryman hauled the heavy appliance up the back steps and sat it alongside our other freezer on the back porch. Dad arrived soon after with a dozen bags of wilted turnip greens. He washed them outside, and stuffed them into freezer bags without blanching them and closed the bags. Then he put them in the freezer.

"Louis, they'll spoil. They are full of bacteria." Mom told him over dinner.

"They'll be fine." Dad continued to eat his dinner without stopping.

"I won't have something like that in the freezer. You'll get ptomaine poison. Are you willing to risk your life or the life of your children on some lousy turnip greens? Don't we have enough turnip greens?"

Dad stopped chewing. He reached out and picked up one of the little wire figures in the pristine white bowl that belonged to my grandmother.

"What's this?" he asked.

Exasperated, mother leaned back in her chair. "I don't know what it is. We thought you'd know what it was."

"Where did you get them?" Dad asked.

"We found them in the driveway, Dad. Don't you think they look like beautiful little wire sculpture?" I picked one up and rolled it around in my hand.

"In the driveway?" Dad repeated.

"Yes, in the driveway," Mother repeated.

"You're kidding, right?" Dad looked at Mom and started to laugh. Dad laughed until tears rolled out the corners of his eyes. He laughed so loud and so hard he made me start to laugh. He laughed and wiped the corners of his eyes with his napkin and then laughed even harder.

"Why are you laughing? What's so funny?" Mom asked.

"You're so worried about germs!" Dad said. "Do you know what these are?"

"No!" Mother said. "I don't! We only thought they were pretty and unusual."

"Well, I agree. They are unusual!" Dad wiped tears from the corner of his eyes with is handkerchief.

"Louis, I demand an explanation for this!"

"It's just so funny! Here you are worried about the bacteria on a few turnip greens in the freezer when you have put telephone wire that the dog ate and pooped out in the driveway sitting on the table as a centerpiece for our dinner."

* * *

2007

When Hock and I arrive at the hospital, Dad is just returning from testing. They roll him into the room, settle him into his bed, and I kiss his forehead. "How do you feel, Dad?"

"I've had better days!" he says. He fusses in a loud voice, "These doctor's, they don't know nothing. The just want more money—that's all!"

I pat his hand. I can tell that his mouth has drawn down to one side which indicates another stroke. Soon the doctor comes in and confirms this.

"Your father has multiple blood clots in his legs and lungs, we need to admit him. And we believe he's had a minor stroke. With blood thinners, these should dissolve, but we feel this could happen again due to his prostate cancer. People with cancer tend to develop blood clots," the doctor tells us. "We need to admit him, put him on blood thinners and antibiotics and keep him for a few days."

"Will blood thinners prevent future clots long-term, or is this just something we must deal with moving forward?" I ask the doctor.

"Well, there is another option that we feel might be helpful to prevent the clots," the doctor says. "We recommend your father have a Greenfield filter implanted in the artery leading to his heart. The filter works like a mixer and busts up the clots so they are less likely to migrate to the brain."

He pulls a wire filter out of his pocket and hands it to me. I take it in my hand and look at it. It looks like a little bit of twisted wire with curls on the end, kind of like a Japanese lantern or a piece of wire sculpture. As I roll it in my hand I see how fluid flowing through it would develop sufficient force and perhaps it would break up the clots just like a mixer. But as I roll it around in my fingers I also cannot stop thinking about the little bits of colored wire Mom discovered in our driveway so many years ago. Under different circumstances the memory would have made me laugh. But right now Dad's life is literally in my hands. This filter could save him. Or at least keep him alive for a while longer. But I wonder if the benefits are worth the risk.

"Is it dangerous to implant the filter?" I ask.

"It comes with some risk, but your father is at risk anyway. We feel the filter would reduce the risk of future clots causing substantial damage," he tells me.

"Okay, if Dad is okay with putting the filter in, then so am I," I tell the doctor.

"Dad, how do you feel about that?" I hand him the filter.

"Looks like a good idea to me," he says rolling the filter around in his hand.

"Maybe it's time your old man became part man, part machine. Will this make my heart bionic?" Dad asks with a twisted smile.

We all laugh.

"A little," the doctor says and smiles as he pats Dad's shoulder.

The next day they implant the filter in the inferior vena cava leading to Dad's heart. After the surgery, the nurses soon have him sitting up on the side of the bed back in his room. I walk into the room and find Dad facing away from the door so he can look out the large hospital window. From the back his gown hangs open from his neck to the bed, and his buttocks are visible reminding me of a small child. The gown has faded almost white with the faintest of prints that reminds me of clouds. Dad wears white compression hose pulled all the way up to mid-thigh, and his feet dangle from the opposite side of the bed not touching the floor, toes pointed which makes him look even more childlike, almost angelic.

In this position he sits intently focused on what he sees outside the window using a very large pair of binoculars that I brought him at his request earlier. He wanted them because there is construction and site preparation going on across the parking lot from the hospital. Dad intently watches the bulldozers moving earth and does not at first hear me. Looking at him I cannot help but think he looks like some sort of very strange cherub with his gown spread out all around him, long white hose over thin legs and bare feet hanging down not touching the floor. The image is ethereal, and a bit comical, yet his focus is so intent it all culminates into a bizarre visual contradiction. My very masculine, manly father dressed up in a white dress and white hose totally preoccupied with a manly job of dozer operation. That visual pretty much sums up Dad on any given day. Full of contradiction.

I smile. I marvel about our future together as we travel this uncertain path God's put before us. Despite our differences, somehow fate has conspired to join us as father and daughter—until death do us part. Standing there, I do not know what the future holds; but I know. despite all the wrongs, all the craziness, all the misunderstandings, anger, misgivings we've experienced over the years, there is something right here too. Each of us finds in the other something to love and maybe even something we need. We are still learning about life and death; and we are learning together, even now in our own crazy mixed-up way.

"Dad?" I call to him. He jumps, and draws the binoculars away from his eyes and turns so he can see me. He feels the draft in back where the gown is open, and he reaches to pinch it closed with one hand.

"Jane, when did you get here?" he asks me. "Good to see you." Still holding the gown closed with one hand, he sets the binoculars on the bedside table, then reaches toward me to collect his hug. His face still droops, but not as bad. I find this encouraging.

"What were you doing?" I ask him.

"I was just looking out the window at that job site across the street. They are not cutting the grade right on that earth work. They will have problems with rain water collecting on the north side and it will create foundation problems later," he tells me with confidence, swinging his white-stockinged legs back and forth like a child.

Amazed that he feels so well so soon after surgery I just look at him, then out the window, then back at him. "So how do you feel?"

"Pretty good for an old man," he says. "That little piece of scrap wire they put in my artery is supposed to make all the difference," he says.

He picks up the sample Greenfield filter and rolls it around between his fingers, then tosses it at me. I catch it in my hand and roll it between my fingers too remembering that long ago day when Mom picked up the colored wire in the driveway, and said, "Wonder what this is? It's interesting, and pretty, don't you think? Wonder what it's for?"

This time we know what the pretty, interesting piece of wire sculpture is for. We are hoping it will prolong Dad's life.

◇

"O Lord, you hear the desire of the afflicted; you will strengthen their heart; you will incline your ear." (Psalm 10:17)

◇

Turnip Greens and Cornbread

Pick greens fresh from the garden, or buy fresh at store.
Wash individual leaves thoroughly.
Pull off tough stems and discard.
Place into 5 quart pot of boiling water along with a 2 strips of bacon or ¼ cup of cooked ham, ¼ cup finely-chopped onions, 1 teaspoon salt.
Cook until soft (about 30 to 40 minutes).
Place in serving dish retaining enough 'pot liquor' from turnip greens to cover the greens.

Cook Cornbread (Recipe elsewhere in this book.)

Take one piece of cornbread, slice horizontal, open and place on plate.
Dish turnip greens along with 'pot liquor' over cornbread.
Top with splash of white vinegar, salt and lots of pepper to taste.
Serve with side of small, new red potatoes.

Chapter 25 – Fresh Roasted Corn and Plum Pits
"What's the best thing you ever did?" — Jane
"Married your Mom." — Louis

2007

"My bed is leaking," Dad tells me. He sits on the edge of his bed after lunch, studying the subject of our conversation with dark accusing eyes. When I pull back the covers the bed is wet along the edge, as if someone poured a glass of water on it.

"I don't think it's the bed leaking Dad. Perhaps you are missing the urinal at night?"

"No. It's the bed leaking. They need to fix it."

Dad's eyesight is failing and his hands are twisted from arthritis until he can no longer button his shirt or pants. The Greenfield filter installed in his chest has helped with the blood clots. There have been no additional strokes, but now he seems to be retaining fluid and his face appears puffy. His skin looks blotchy and he seems to be growing weaker. I'm at a loss to know the reason. Lately he's been running a fever and does not want to get out of bed in the morning.

I've seen him in action with the urinal and know he's missing it more often than not. I've looked for creative designs for urinals on the Internet hoping to find a new model that's accident proof. But inspiration has yet to enlighten the urinal industry about what works best for a patient like Dad. Until it does, we'll have to make do. I help Dad changes his clothes, then settle him in a nearby chair with a blanket and his favorite fuzzy slippers. Then I pull sheets from the laundry cart in the hall, at the nursing home, disinfect and change his bed while he watches looking at me as if he still does not believe me but will humor me by allowing me to change the sheets. The task is complicated by the fact that I am still wearing a brace on my knee to keep it from turning sideways.

While the Greenfield filter seems to keep Dad free of clots, he is experiencing cognitive decline post-surgery, perhaps due to micro strokes from clots too small to show up in scans. It has not taken us long to understand that he needs more care than assisted living can provide. So once again we have changed Dad's living circumstances to fit his needs, and I've moved him to a nursing home not far from where I live. It is a lovely place and he has a private room. His view is of the entrance lined with Bradford pear trees and he can see people coming and going from the facility.

My sister and her daughters come for a visit and make a book for him with pictures that he can point to and indicate how he feels. Many contain funny phrases and sayings to make him smile. He is sad when they leave.

I've decorated his room with cards, many left over from the holidays. He has two televisions. The weather is cool outside, so on one TV I keep a virtual fireplace playing most days. Other days I play DVDs of beautiful music with pictures of lovely scenery. He likes the fireplace the best. The craft table that we've had in his room at all the places he's lived is still an active spot, and when he has visitors they often sit down to paint, color, or build on a birdhouse. Dad works on them too when his hands are steady enough.

On Thursdays the local church choir comes and sings and someone plays the piano to accompany them. Dad and the other residents come together and sing along with their musical guests. Dad likes this. It reminds him of his days leading singing at church. Sometimes people bring therapy dogs to visit with residents. Once even a therapy pony visits. I make sure he has dog biscuits in his room so when they come he has a treat for them. Still, with all this, Dad sleeps more than he did, and he looks pale and tired. His eyes lack the luster and interest they had only a few weeks ago.

"Want to go outside?" I ask.

"No."

"Why not? It's beautiful out there and unseasonably warm; you'll enjoy the fresh air."

He looks skeptically at the bed from the chair where he's sitting. I know he only wants to crawl back in it, but he seems to not quite have forgiven it for it's earlier betrayal.

"If you insist." He throws a pit from a plum he's just finished toward the trash and misses. He can't reach to pick it up, so instead he wipes his hands on his pants, ignoring the washcloth I hold out to him. Carefully I ease him into the wheelchair.

Outside I wheel him from one end of the sidewalk to the other. The nursing home does not have the extensive grounds of the facility where he lived in Nashville. There we had squirrels, chipmunks and robins to entertain us. Here we are privately counting the days until he will no longer be held a prisoner by Medicare's rules regarding skill care and we can drive to the park for fresh air. Until then we will make this sidewalk and the park bench at the entrance next to the pots of pansies our getaway retreat. There is a courtyard behind this facility and patients who have rooms on the back can see into it, but they are not allowed to go there. I do not know why. It is one of the many dark ironies of assisted living that patients are so often walled away from nature under the "guise" that it's not safe for them to venture out. It is one of the most senseless and infuriating things that aging people must face. Often I think most die from lack of fresh air and Vitamin D more often than any other medical condition.

I resolve to not allow this to happen to Dad and take him out almost every day to sit in the sun regardless of the weather. Despite the many setbacks, Dad's better than he's been for the past few weeks, so we don't bother with leg rests on the wheel chair. Instead, he holds his legs out as we roll along. When he gets tired of holding his feet up, I pull the wheelchair to a stop.

"Right here," he indicates a place underneath a Bradford pear tree that's just beginning to flower; and we settle there. I put the lock on the wheelchair and plop down on the sidewalk beside him so we can talk. There are no benches at this spot. Again I wonder why. Dad looks at me in surprise when I sit down on the sidewalk, making me feel a bit surprised myself. I am now 51. Perhaps most 51-year-olds would not sit down on sidewalks. But it is the way I've always been, and I cannot change now. This is how I'm most comfortable—sitting cross-legged on the ground. From here I can see what's in the grass next to me. Often I find something interesting to watch as we talk. A ladybug, a worm or even an ant.

"Are you glad to get rid of your white hose and gown you wore at the hospital?" I ask, tugging at his tan kaki pants so they cover his leg above his socks.

"They don't know nothin' in these hospitals. Like blind dogs in a meat market. They know everything except how to cover up your backside." He shakes his head in disgust recalling the gowns with no fasteners in back.

"Do you like it better here?"

"Well at least they don't let a fellow embarrass himself."

We sit in silence for a moment watching traffic. People hurry home to cook meals. A teen track team jogs by. Running the neighborhood is part of their distance training, and we see them often. I can hear their regular whoosh of breathing as they pass.

Wearing his oxygen mask, Dad watches. "Those legs have gone many a mile."

"Yes they have." I study the last runner until he's out of sight. Then I look up at Dad. He is not looking at the runners. Instead he is looking at his own legs, now so thin. The sun has dropped in the sky and shines through the tree branches and down on my father giving him the effect of a leafy yellow halo from where I sit. Rays of light sparkle out from behind his head making his white hair glow. He looks angelic. I hold his hand pretending to study his nails so he'll let me hold it.

"So what do we do now?" Dad asks.

Mother asked me the same question the day the ambulance brought her home from the hospital for the last time 5 years before.

* * *

2000

Thirteen years of bone cancer left Mom vulnerable to infection. My sister and I found a drug we could import from Canada that put Mom's cancer into remission, but we could not find an antibiotic that would cure the methicillin-resistant staph infection.

During the last days Mom slept a lot. I set up my desk in her room and worked to pass the time. My husband took care of all he could from home and continued to go out and conduct seminars to keep the money flowing in. We needed lots of money to keep things running at home and to help take care of Mom. He never, ever, complained about the money or my long absences. Neither of us talked about how long we could go on like we were. There was no clear timetable for dying.

When Mom felt like it, she and I talked.

"There's a woman who sits beside me," Mom told me once. "She doesn't talk. She only sits. Works."

Shocked, I realized she was talking about me. The realization that she didn't recognize me sometimes or didn't know I was really there made me sad.

"Maybe she thinks you're sleeping and doesn't want to wake you," I suggested.

She seemed to consider this for a moment.

"What's happening to me?" she asked, as if hoping this time my answer would be different than all the other times she asked.

I told her the same thing I always told her. But every day she asked me again. I considered lying to her. I could tell her a pretty story. I wondered if it would be easier on us both if I lied. But I had never told a boldface lie to Mom. And I couldn't make myself start lying now.

"You have bone cancer, Mom. It's in remission, but when you were in the hospital you contracted an antibiotic-resistant infection. We can't cure it. So we've brought you home to die. You wanted to die at home, remember?" She looked out the window where she could sometimes see me jogging down the road in the morning and considered what I'd said.

"I'm not sure I'm up to it," she said.

"How about if I fix you some lunch? Maybe that will make you feel better."
"What do you have?"

"Fresh corn from the corn field down the road."

"With lots of butter?"

"Lots!"

I do many things well. Cooking is not one of them. Mother forgave me, but she wanted the corn the way she wanted it. She waited patiently for me to cook it. I fixed the corn three times before I made it right. And when it was done, I sat at my desk in her room and Mom sat on the edge of her bed with her tray and ate yellow corn with butter running down her chin and between her fingers. "I supposed this is the last corn for this summer," she said between bites.

"Yes," I said. "The very last."

* * *

2007

"What's the best thing you ever did?" I ask Dad out of the blue as the sun finally touches the horizon.

"Married your Mom," he says.

This shocks me as my memories of their marriage are not always particularly good ones. I've come to relate their marriage to Jackson's purge of the Creek Indians from Middle Tennessee. A scorched earth kind of thing at times. Take no prisoners. To say my parents didn't get on sometimes would be a gross understatement. But as I've grown older, having faced my own marital challenges with previous spouses, I have come to understand a little more about married life. Marriage isn't always smooth sailing. Sometimes things get rocky. Sometimes people don't agree. Sometimes they talk about their differences loudly. But that doesn't necessarily mean they don't love each other. Often people fight, not because they don't care, but because they care too much. I feel blessed that by the time I married a third time I had also come to realize that allowing others to be themselves and allowing yourself to do the same is key to a happy marriage. After this realization there was no more fighting.

When he tells me marrying Mom is the best thing he ever did it makes me tear up.

"Really? Not something else?"

"That and going into the dozer business."

"You loved it, didn't you!"

"Yes. I loved it. But I loved your mother more."

"A man got out of that door yesterday," Dad indicates the front door to the nursing home. The one that's combination-coded to keep residents from wandering out and getting lost.

"He got all the way down the street and out of sight before anyone noticed."

"You're kidding!" I say.

"He could have gotten run over." Dad says, a note of optimism in his voice as if that would be preferable to being locked up.

"He could have gotten lost!" I say.

"A person could leave here, go away and never be found—they'd never notice," Dad says.

"Is that what you'd like? To run away and get lost?"

"Sometimes."

"The food's good here," I say. The sun is sinking fast behind the horizon, and now when I look up at Dad the bright yellow is turning to a deep gold behind his head.

"So what do we do now?" Dad asks me again. He shakes his head.

"You must get better," I tell him. "We need to have a few more adventures, don't you think? Maybe see some fun things?"

"Everything's bigger in Texas," Dad says. "That reminds me of a joke."

There was a workman from Oklahoma who came to Texas to build houses. He fell into a swimming pool by accident. When he came to the surface he started screaming, "Don't flush it, don't flush it!" He laughs at his own joke. I smile and hand him a fresh plum from my pocket. He takes a bite and juice spurts like golden drops glistening in the rays of the setting sun.

"My goodness," he says. "I can't remember the last time I had a plum." I smile. I get up from my place on the sidewalk and roll him back toward the nursing home door. As I roll I think I probably need to collect the plum pit from where it skittered under his bed when he missed the trash can before someone moves the bed and slips and falls on it.

◇

"She is far more precious than jewels. The heart of her husband trusts in her, and he will have no lack of gain. She does him good, and not harm, all the days of her life. She seeks wool and flax, and works with willing hands. She is like the ships of the merchant; she brings her food from afar..." (Proverbs 31:11-31)

◇

Fresh Roasted Corn

Pull corn (Silver Queen if you can find it) from stalks when it's ripe enough that when you press a kernel with your fingernail it spurts fluid that looks like milk.
No liquid? It's too far gone to eat.
Kernels should be large and fully developed. If they are pale and small, corn is not mature.
Take ripe corn home and shuck and silk with silking brush.
Rinse shucked corn in sink, cutting off any damaged kernels or any worm damage.
Bring water to boil in 5 quart pot on stove top.
When water is at a rolling boil, add 2 teaspoons of salt.
Gently lay corn into pot.
Cook covered for 10 minutes.
Remove corn with tongs and place on dish.
Rub corn with Land of Lakes butter.
Salt and serve.
(For children sometimes it's best to take a knife and slit the kernels of the corn the length of the cob after cooking to make it easier to eat. Some people prefer to cut the corn off the cob and serve without the cob. If you eat the corn on the cob, use corn cob holders to make the process neater and easier. Corn is good with pork chops and greens, at picnics, or with nearly any country meal.)

Chapter 26 – Diapers and Knives
"Why are there knives all over the floor?" — Jane

2008
Much as we hope for things to be different, Dad continues to decline. The nursing home sends him to the hospital again to treat the Methicillin-resistant staphylococcus aureus. It is the same type of infection that killed Mom. We are unsure how he contracted it, but likely at the nursing home.

Mother contracted MRSA in the hospital during her surgery to fix a broken thighbone. She had a metal plate inserted in her thigh to hold the fractured bones together, and that prevented the antibiotics from completely clearing the infection. We could give her antibiotics, but the bacteria would hide out around the artificial metal in her body during treatment. As soon as we stopped the antibiotic, the infection came back. She was not well enough to survive the removal of the pin in her leg. It would require her to lie in bed with a broken leg for 6 weeks on heavy antibiotics. So, eventually, we just had to let God take her home.

Now Dad's facing something similar. He has artificial knees and a plate in his fused ankle. The infection is extremely dangerous for Dad, as it was for Mom. Some people can fight the infection back. But it never completely goes away. However, if the quality of life is good, the inevitable can be postponed—for a while. But Dad is weak from his prostate cancer, and his heart appears to be rapidly growing weaker perhaps due to the infection. It may also be that he has grown tired of living and simply wants to go home.

When I arrive at Dad's hospital room, I find him asleep. He lies half-curled up on his side, his outstretched hand dangles limply in the air off the edge of the bed. He snores softly. His lips quiver as if he's remembering something wonderful like the taste of fresh strawberries or the heart-shaped peaches I bring him.

Wearing the gown and mask the hospital demands that I wear since Dad was diagnosed with MRSA, I sit in his wheelchair close to the bed and watch him sleep. We are unable to keep the bed from "leaking", and the problem seems to have spread to all the beds he sleeps in; so now he wears diapers to protect him from his beds. He runs a continual fever. Several rounds of IV antibiotics have failed to bring the infection under control. He has grown septic. Gone is the fluid his tissues seemed to hold onto a few weeks ago that made him look chubby. Now he is gaunt. His temples look sunken, and his skin feels clammy.

I've been visiting Dad as often as possible, but the truth is, there are many demands on my time. I have two young granddaughters that need my time as well. I try to make the soccer games and the cheer camps and keep things as normal as possible despite Dad's illness. I have a company that needs constant attention to keep money flowing. And I try to meet with my daughter at least once a week to catch up with her life. Often we do this by walking at a local park. I visit Dad nearly every day, but most of the time I only stay an hour or two. No matter how much time I spend at any of these things, it never seems like enough. Hock gets the smallest part of me of all, but he never complains. Instead, he is always eager to help.

Recently a barn cat has appeared at Sherry's barn. She already has two cats and cannot keep a third; so she and the girls beg me to take the cat home. Hock doesn't think it's a good idea with our busy schedules, but soon, as he says, "he has all the girls crying," so Shadow comes home with us and becomes a part of our family as an inside cat. She takes to us immediately and sleeps curled around Hock's head at night eternally grateful for her home. She also warms my lap when we watch TV at night; or when we sit on the patio outside she sits beside me curious about everything. Together we look out into the woods and down at the creek and relax. She is a great joy to me, and I cannot imagine life without her.

Looking at Dad as I wait for him to wake up, I am reminded of how Mom looked just before she passed. The dream of having him move out of the nursing home and back into assisted living has faded. As I watch him, it seems unkind to wake him even though I know he would be pleased to see me. So, instead, I slip my hand into his and wait. He smiles in his sleep at my touch. We have time to just sit before the doctor arrives to talk to us during evening rounds. Gazing around the room, I notice a butter knife under the edge of a chair, another against the wall. A third knife sticks out of his house shoe on the floor. A fourth sparkles under the dresser. Why are there butter knives everywhere?

Eventually he stirs, wakes and releases my hand. With great difficulty he sits up, pivots, and hangs his legs off the edge of his bed, then he pats the side of his bed indicating for me to sit next to him. I do even though with MRSA we should limit contact. How many more opportunities will I have to sit by Dad and look out the window? We gaze out at the parking lot, at the air conditioning units lined up against the building across the lot.

"Why are there knives all over the floor?" I ask, pointing at the butter knives in various places around the room.

He smiles. "Well, my beautiful daughter, they are there because they keep bringing me knives, and I don't need a butter knife. I need a steak knife to eat my steak. They waste time, energy and money bringing them to me, so I must put them to some good use. So, I throw them."

"You throw them?"

"I throw them!" He smiles again. "I need to throw something. I like throwing them. Throwing them does me more good than you can imagine!" He laughs a soundless, shoulder-compressing laugh.

It's then I notice pockmarks in the walls where he's hit them when he throws the knives. "But what if someone walks in and you hit them? What if someone steps on a knife and falls when they come into your room? What if your doctor falls? Are those dents in the walls from you hitting the wall with knives?"

"Maybe." He considers the dents, and then shrugs. "That's their tough luck!" He picks up a smashed, used straw from his bedside table and begins to pick his teeth. We watch a grackle outside on the window ledge devour a grasshopper. In the background the oxygen machine inhales, and exhales, inhales, and exhales.

I look around the room and recall one of the new lamps needs a bulb. I wonder what will happen if a knife inadvertently strikes the lamp socket in an oxygen-filled room. I recall tuning in to the news some years back to discover the building where my mother-in-law lived in New Jersey had caught fire when a woman thoughtlessly lit a cigarette while visiting a friend who used oxygen. The blast took out three floors of the high rise. Both women were burned beyond recognition. My mother-in-law never even felt the blast that happened in her own building.

Dad might be fading, but it appears he still likes to take chances to blow off steam occasionally when he can—even now. I'm grateful they didn't give him a steak knife when he needed a butter knife, or someone might have really gotten hurt. I hope that the oxygen machine won't explode in his face if he hits it, and maybe take out the third floor, its occupants, maybe even me. Yet secretly I'm a little happy about his knife throwing. It means there's still some fight in him, even yet. I never thought I'd miss the grumpy, gruff side of Dad; but now I realize I miss it more than I ever thought possible.

Just then a nurse walks through the door and says, "Mr. Hinkle, would you like some milk and crackers to tide you over until dinner?"

"Yes, I think I would," Dad says.

The nurse turns to leave and then stops, "Why are all these knives laying on the floor?"

"I wanted a steak knife," Dad says. "And while you are at it, bring a steak to go with it."

Dad and I look at each other and laugh.

* * *

1964
I never liked milk. But I liked going to the barn with Dad when he milked the cow. When I was seven we would go to the barn to milk every morning. Dad would often pick me up and carry me through the muddy barn yard so I would not get my feet muddy. Once inside, he'd set me down beside the long manger that extended the length of the barn. The cow would insert her head into the stile, and Dad would begin the process of rubbing down her utter with a clean burlap sack in preparation to milk her. Franky usually helped Dad milk, or he

cleaned out stalls next to the milking parlor.

"Jane, jump up in the manger and spread some feed for the cows," Dad instructed. Now that I was older and could climb into the manger by myself, he no longer helped me. "Franky, shell me a couple of pails of corn."

"Do I have to?"

"Snap to it, son," Dad shouted, "Don't have all day!"

Franky scowled, and started up the stairs to the loft. "I don't know why I always have to shell the corn. I'm getting blisters!"

"Because your sister's hands are too small and soft, that's why!" Dad yelled after him.

I hurried, not wanting Dad to yell at me. The wooden stiles separated the manger from the rest of the barn. These were set up so when the cow stuck her head through the gap between the bars and into the manger, you could slide one of the braces over and insert a wooden block at the top to hold it closed. This held the cow's head inside the manger until you decided to turn her loose. All the cows were trained to stick their heads through the stile and stand, and they ate from the wooden manger while Dad milked them.

My job was to dip feed out of the concrete bin next to the manger with a scoop, and place a pile in front of each cow so she would stand and eat contently while Dad milked her. In cold weather we would sometimes add a block of hay to the oat mix. The end of the manger contained a salt block, and cows would wander in when milking was not going on and lick the salt block. Dad said this kept them healthy. In addition to salt it contained other minerals they needed. I had been known to chip a piece off a new salt block and sample it to see if it was fit for the cows. A time or two I'd sampled their sweet feed as well. It really wasn't bad! It tasted a lot like Grape Nuts cereal. And I would not feed any of my pets anything that I was not willing to eat myself.

Once the cows were eating, I'd tiptoe over and lock their heads in the stile. After all the cows were locked in I'd watch them lap up their food with long, pink, muscular tongues. Sometimes I'd pull up an upturned bucket and sit at one end of the manger and just watch them. In the winter it felt nice to sit next to the cows because they were warm, and the rest of the barn felt cold. Sometimes I'd sit in the manger and pat their heads, or even braid the hair on the top of their heads. Sometimes Dad would loan me his comb, and I would even comb their hair.

Once in a while a cow would eat up all her grub in a hurry and decide she wanted to leave early. She'd try to back out, freak out and then shake the manger around with her head making loud banging and crashing sounds. This would jerk the entire manger up and down and make me feel like I was on a wild sled ride. Most of the time they gave up real fast because it hurt. And it would make my heart skip a beat. We'd all freeze expecting something terrible to happen. But more often than not the cows would roll their wet, brown gaze toward me and let me do whatever I wanted. As a reward I'd flip away pesky flies for them.

My favorite cow was White Socks. She was a Jersey mix with four white stockings and delicate features of her mother who was a purebred Jersey, but she had the lovely brown coat of her father, who was Hereford. I always brought a special something for White Socks in my pocket and would sneak it into her feed. Sometimes I brought a bit of bread crust saved from my breakfast. Sometimes-old cornbread from the night before. Often Mother saved leftover cabbage or wilted lettuce or radish tops from the garden. Dad taught me how to milk a cow on White Socks. She patiently waited, and didn't turn over my bucket or put her foot in it or anything, even though I was slow and cold, and my hands got tired easy.

Lately, I'd noticed that White Socks had not been looking as good as she once did. She'd grown thin and sometimes I thought she looked tired. She ate even more than she usually did; and when I could I would slip her extra treats. But it seemed like the other cows had lost respect for her and would push her aside from the hay outside whenever they could. For these reasons I tried to spend as much time with her as possible to make sure she felt loved. Mom said love was necessary for all living things.

In the winter, we fed the cows silage. Silage was really just corn cut up in the field by a large machine designed for that job. Some people would load it into silos for winter feed where it would ferment for several months until cold weather. The fermenting made it possible to store it for the entire winter. We had a ground silo, which was really just a big trench dug into the side of a hill. Dad would store the silage there and cover it with black paper and thick plastic. He'd weigh this down with old tires to keep the wind from blowing off the plastic. When we were ready to use it for feed, we'd peel back the plastic, throw away the top layer of chopped corn and stalks that had turned black and looked decayed—about 2 inches deep. Underneath the fermented silage looked green and golden and smelled fragrant, like a mixture of wild flowers, corn, and fresh vinegar.

The cows loved it. So did the field rats. With such an abundant food supply, the rats could grow a foot long, and sometimes longer. We had a lanky, wild, calico cat with only three legs that stayed at the barn. I named her Peg. She had the spirit of a warrior, and she wouldn't let anyone touch her. Many times I'd seen her kill a rat larger than herself and carry it off to eat later in a place where she felt safe.

On this particular day I had just finished locking the last cow's head in the stile when I heard a tiny "meow".

"Kittens," I breathed. My heart fluttered. I wanted a kitten to keep in the house more than anything else in the world! I did not know it yet but eventually I would have a cat of my own named Tigger, but for now I was still in the wishful stage of kitten adoption. For now all we had were barn cats that were really just strays that lived at the barn.

I loved White Socks, but I couldn't take her in the house with me. I couldn't cuddle her, so she didn't really qualify as a pet. Often when I said my prayers at night, they included, "And Lord, please bring me a kitten of my own. I promise I'll take good care of it."

I must have been saying it to myself because Dad suddenly said, "What?" He was sitting on a short stool milking White Socks.

"I hear kittens!" I said, scarcely able to breathe, my heart pounded with excitement. I tossed the scoop that I'd used to feed the cows into the feed bin with a crash, and headed off into the back of the barn. This area of the barn was newer, having only been added a few years before. It was about the size of our grade-school gymnasium. It was here that we stacked bales of hay from front to back for winter feed. The front of the stack was lower where we'd pulled bales to feed the cows, but the further back you went, the taller the stack grew until it reached the ceiling of the barn about 2 stories high. Franky and I often played in the hay constructing tunnels and caves to play hide and seek in.

"Meow." I heard it again. I headed toward the noise. Climbing over bale after bale of hay, I stopped often to listen for the sound. It wasn't easy to find the kittens. The backside of the barn was huge, and the kitten's call sounded weak. "I know I'm not hearing things," I muttered to myself. I picked around through the straw. I continued to look. I reached into a few cracks between bales. No kittens. I might reach into a hole and find a snake instead of a kitten if I wasn't careful. We had chicken snakes, one at least eight feet long who loved to eat eggs. The thought of grabbing a snake creeped me out! I picked up the broken end of a rake and used it to prod into some of the darker holes where I didn't want to stick my hand.

I was about to give up when the kitten meowed one more time. Suddenly, I knew where to look. I scrambled over several bales, and looked down into a little cavern about the size of a single bale of hay.

"Oh!" I clutched my hands to my chest—delighted! "I found them!" I shouted to Dad. There were four kittens two yellow, one gray and one spotted calico like its Mother, Peg. Their eyes were just opening, and were a cloudy blue. The kittens stared at me and struggled to keep their little heads from wobbling. They looked like furry starfish, fat bellies laid flat against the hay, legs all stuck out. Love for each clutched at my heart. I picked up the gray one first. He hissed!

"Don't hiss at me! I'm your friend." I tucked him close into my chest and stroked his little warm head with my finger. He settled down and sniffed at me with a wiggly nose. I could see him trying to focus his eyes on me. I smiled.

I sat and held him stroking his forehead with my finger. His brow wrinkled as he struggled to focus on me. He knew I was not his mother, but he no longer tried to scare me away. Instead, he settled down into my warm hand and soon I felt him purr. My heart instantly expanded 10 times its normal size. How could Dad think cats were pests? All a cat wanted was food and a warm place, like the barn, to sleep. And maybe a cat wanted a mouse now and then to chase. I wondered why the chicken snake hadn't eaten the kittens.

Maybe their mother knew just how high to put them so the snake wouldn't find them. Or maybe they'd just been lucky. I hated to put the kitten back for fear the next time I visited he wouldn't be there. The snake might get him, or something else. This end of the barn was open to the outside on one end.

I could tell by the milk buckets clanging and the sound of Dad turning the cattle loose from the manger that it was almost time for us to head home. With a sigh, I placed the kitten back in the nest with his brothers and sisters. I gave each a pat and resolved if I could to come back later and maybe move them to a safer place.

At dinner that night, I asked Dad again, "Can I please have one of the kittens for a pet and keep it in the house?"

"No. Don't ask me anymore! They are barn cats. They need to stay at the barn. They help keep the rats down."

My heart sank, and I struggled to keep my lip from puckering up.

That night after everyone went to sleep, I crawled out of bed in the dark, pulled on a shirt and shorts and my saddle shoes, then got a flashlight from my bottom drawer and tested it to see if it worked.

Quietly, I opened my bedroom door and crept down the hall to the white French doors that lead out onto our back porch. Mom had left one door standing open to allow the night breeze into the house. Only the screen door separated me from the darkness outside. But it was a squeaky screen door.

I knew Mom and Dad might hear me. The key to getting past the screen door without making a lot of noise was to open it real fast and lift on it a tad at the same time. I had practiced the technique many times—now came the test. Carefully, I lifted and pushed. Not a sound. I smiled and slid through the open doorway on silent feet, then closed the door in the same way. Outside the crickets sang. Frogs croaked their thoughts. It was a bloody chorus, I could scarcely think! As I walked to the barn, I saw a bat dart over the pond hunting insects. I'd heard girls at school talking about vampires, but I didn't believe in them. Still, I walked a little faster down the path I couldn't see but my feet knew by heart.

Once I reached the barn, I felt that any moment the big chicken snake might bite me. But he didn't. The barn creaked now and then. All the cattle slept outside in the field, but I heard mice scurry as I opened the side barn door.

The kittens were right where I left them only now they snuggled up against their mother, Peg. She seemed pleased I'd arrived rather than fearful as I'd expected. To my amazement, she let me pick up each of the kittens and pet them without protest. Maybe she knew I wanted to help. Once I was sure they were okay, I thought about where a safe place might be for them to live until they got strong enough to take care of themselves. Probably the loft would be safer. It could be closed on both ends but Peg could come and go under the door that led down the stairs. I picked up two kittens and put them in one baggy pant pocket.

Then I picked up two more and put them in the other. Quick, before I chickened out, I grabbed Peg before she realized what was up.

"Got ya!" She struggled only a little, then settled in under my arm, resigned. I carried them all upstairs to the loft. Moonlight streamed in through the loft window and lit the entire upstairs, bright as day.

I sat Peg on the loft floor, and switched off my flashlight. By moonlight, I could see into the corners. Near a huge pile of shelled corn there were several bales of last year's hay. Behind it a low protected corner nestled under the rounded barn roof. I pulled a pocket-knife from one of the shelves and sawed through the strings on a bale of hay. Carefully I scattered it around under the eve of the barn, then mashed some into the shape of what I thought would make a good nest for a barn cat. Peg sat on top of a bale of hay and watched me. No doubt, she could hear her kittens mewing in my pocket. She wasn't about to leave. When I felt satisfied the nest looked inviting, I picked Peg up and sat her there. She sniffed around, then looked at me as if to say, "This is acceptable, but where are my kittens?"

I dug them each out of my pocket. Their little legs swirled in circles trying to find the ground. Gently I set each one in the nest. They grunted and mewed, and each got quick, reassuring licks from its mother. She examined them all as I set them out as if to make certain they were really hers and I had not substituted someone else's kittens. I knew she might just pick one up and take off down stairs with it again preferring her own nest to the one I made her. Cats liked to pick their own homes, Mom always said. But amazingly enough she didn't. Soon she settled down into the straw, stretched out, and the kittens began to nurse. Peg purred. Her eyes squinted down. I watched for a while until I realized how sleepy I felt. For a while, at least, the kittens should be safe. I resolved to check on them every day until they were old enough to fend for themselves. I wanted them to become familiar with me with the hope that they would grow up tame.

It was Saturday, a full three weeks since I'd found the kittens. Nothing had happened to them in all that time. I'd spent a lot of time playing with them rather than combing White Sock's hair and had really kind of forgotten about her as I'd been so focused on the kittens. She's gotten skinnier, but I didn't know what to do about it; so I tried to just think positive. And the kittens kept me busy and made me happy. One gray one in particular was growing into a fine cat. I still thought maybe Dad would let me keep him at the house. I looked forward to playing with him whenever I went to the barn; and sometimes I took him to the house and played with him on the back porch.

That afternoon, I sat on the back porch petting the kitten and watching from a distance across the pasture as Dad and Franky loaded several cows into the back of the truck. Dad said they planned to make a run to market. I really didn't know what market was, but Dad made trips there a couple of times a year and took cows and calves.

Today he'd asked me to go along, and I wanted to go and see what it was all about. Soon he pulled up in the truck next to the house, and Franky jumped out to let me slide into the seat beside Dad. I asked Dad if I could take the kitten, and surprisingly he said yes. So, I got in and settled the cat on my lap. Franky jumped back into the truck beside me and slammed the door, and we headed off to market.

The trip took about an hour, and we went up and down hills and along winding tree shaded roads. It was a peaceful. As we drove I heard Franky and Dad talking about market prices, but I didn't really listen or understand. Instead I played with the kitten, teasing it with a string I'd unraveled from the sleeve of my sweater. Once I turned around and, to my surprise, found White Socks pressing her face up against the rear window of the truck looking at me.

"What's White Socks doing in the truck?" I asked Dad.

"We are taking her to market."

"But why?"

"She's not producing much milk, Jane." And that was all he said. Busy with the kitten, I didn't think much about it. I guess I thought market meant "treatment" and White Socks would be coming home with us again after she was better.

We'd finally reached the town where the market was, and Dad wrestled with the steering wheel of the truck to make the sharp turn into the market parking lot. Expertly, he backed the truck up to a ramp that led to a series of chutes and gates that led around to the back of the building. Dad and Franky jumped out of the truck, and Dad removed the tailgate. Franky picked up a stick and began to poke at the cows and whistle until they took off down the ramp and through a series of gates around the side of the market. White Socks was the last to go. She stopped briefly and raised and turned her head to look at me before Franky poked her with a stick one last time, and then she went around the corner out of sight.

A few weeks later Dad said, "Velma, the butcher is delivering the meat today. Make sure you are home to load it into the freezer."

"I will! I'm always here." She rolled her eyes. "I don't have a car, remember?"

"Yeah, right!" Dad said. "Well, keep an eye out for him."

The butcher came about 3 p.m. He pulled up to the house in a white delivery truck, still dressed in a white apron speckled with blood. He was a large, heavy man with giant hands and red cheeks. He laughed a lot at nothing, and I tried to stay as far away from him as possible. He smelled of manure and blood. Mother and I loaded all the white packages from his truck into the freezer. T-bone steaks, hamburger, roast. The packages were all labeled neatly with a black grease pencil.

"Ummm. This is going to be good," I told Mom.

"Our own beef. It's always better than store bought. In the store, you never know what they put in there. What would you like tonight?" Mother asked, as the butcher truck pulled out of the driveway and rumbled down the road.

I considered all the packages. "A steak," I told her. I hadn't had steak but maybe one time that I could remember.

That night Mother grilled the steak in the stove under the broiler. She added onions, salt and pepper. It smelled wonderful and made my mouth water.

We gathered around the table and Mother served up my steak first. It steamed fragrantly, next to the green beans and mashed potatoes. I looked at it, and for the first time in my life I felt rich. She also served my brother, Dad and herself steaks as well. Then she sat down.

"Well. Taste it!" Mom told all of us.

I didn't need to be told a second time. I cut into the steak and took a bite. Then another.

"How is it?" Mother asked.

"Yeah, how is Old White Socks?" Franky said, stuffing a huge piece of steak into his mouth.

I stopped chewing, and looked at Mom. She glared at Franky, her mouth drawn in that 'how could you?' line.

Suddenly my stomach clawed its way into my throat. I spit the second bite of steak into my napkin.

"White Socks? What do you mean, White Socks?"

"You dim wit! What do you think I meant! That's White Socks you're eating!" Franky told me. "She's great, isn't she?" He took another bite. "Delicious!"

"But I thought she was coming home, or maybe we sold her to another farm?"

"You ding-bat! You're thinking about another kind of market!" Franky laughed, took a big bite of meat, pouched it out in his jaw and said, "Mum, good! Nothing better than a good steak!"

"Eat your dinner now, before it gets cold," Dad said, chewing his steak vigorously between words.

With tears pooling in my eyes I asked no one in particular what I already knew, "So White Socks isn't ever coming home?" Suddenly I realized I'd been so occupied with the kitten that I'd missed what was happening to White Socks. Maybe if I'd been paying attention I could have prevented what happened. But now it was too late. Guilt descended on my soul like a dark weight.

"Well, in a way she is home," Mom said, rubbing my back a little. "She gave us milk during her life, now she will give you strength and strong muscles even though she's gone. So in a way, she's still here. It's the circle of life."

"I don't like the circle of life," I cried.

"I know," Mom said. "I don't like it much either sometimes."

"Why did God make it so everything dies?" I asked. "I don't want things to die."

"I know, honey, but it's just the way it is," Mom said. She rubbed my back some more. It was quiet for a minute.

Then Dad looked at me and said, "Eat your steak. It will make you grow up to be big and strong."

Looking at them in that moment I resolved that if someone or something had to die so I could grow up to be big and strong, I never, ever wanted to grow up and be big or strong! And I wasn't too happy with God for setting up life that way. Why did he do that? I resolved to add that question to the top of my list of things I wanted to ask God when I saw him.

* * *

2008

The doctor comes to see us on his rounds, and he examines Dad. Then he motions for me to meet him in the hall. We move down the hallway a little way where Dad cannot overhear us.

"We've given your father three rounds of IV antibiotics. We've given him the strongest antibiotics we have, and we still have been unable to clear him of infection," the doctor tells me. He is looking intently at my face to see my reaction.

I listen to his words, but it takes a while for them to sink in. "Why do you think they aren't working?" I ask.

"It's hard to tell. Possibly he's just tired. Possibly his own immune system is too weak to pick up and help the drugs clear his system. Perhaps the strain he has is just not going to respond to this drug or to the combination of drugs we've given him. Whatever it is, I'm afraid we are out of options. I suspect as soon as we stop the antibiotics the infection will come back, and quickly. He's already demonstrating symptoms of sepsis."

"We had a similar situation with Mom," I tell him and explain what happened with her.

He nods.

"What exactly is sepsis?" I ask. "Is there any way to treat it in someone with artificial joints?" I ask.

"Well, we are doing what we can. But the bacteria is attacking his organs, and they are shutting down. His kidney function is greatly reduced, his heartbeat is irregular. His lungs are full of fluid. I'm afraid, it's only a matter of time," the doctor says. He reaches out and puts his hand on my shoulder to comfort me.

"So, what do we do now?" I ask. They are words I've asked myself several times. Words that both Dad and Mom have asked me at critical points in their lives.

"I'd take him home. Make him comfortable and say whatever you want to say to him."

"Do we tell him? Or is it better not to tell him? Will he live longer if he doesn't know? Will he be happier?"

"Some people want to know, some don't. What type of person is your father?"

"He's the type of person who will want to know."

When I walk back into Dad's room, I see they've brought him another tray of food. In his hand, Dad is holding the butter knife as if weighing it in his hand.

"Dad!"

◇

"For his anger is but for a moment, and his favor is for a lifetime. Weeping may tarry for the night, but joy comes with the morning." (Psalm 30:5)

◇

Minute Steak
4 Minute Steaks
Break an egg in a bowl and mix with ½ cup of milk.
In a large, plastic Ziploc bag mix ½ cup self-rising cornmeal, ½ cup of self-rising flour, salt and pepper to taste (I like heavy pepper).
Dip the steak in the milk/egg mixture, then drop into the Ziploc bag.
Zip the bag and shake the steak until it's coated in flour/cornmeal.
Heat 1 tablespoon Crisco in a large iron skillet.
When heated but not yet smoking, place coated Minute Steak in grease and cook until done on medium heat browning well on each side.
Remove steak, add more grease and 2 tablespoons of flour.
Stir until brown.
Add 2 cups of milk and stir quickly until gravy forms, adding salt and pepper to taste.
Serve steak promptly coated with milk gravy.
Serve with sides of asparagus, or green beans, and mashed potatoes.

Chapter 27 – Amazing Grace Cookies

2008
Things have not been going well for Dad since he returned to the nursing home. They have not been able to cure the infection. His fever rises, and he continually sweats despite powerful antibiotics the doctor sends him home with. We change his pajamas frequently to keep him dry. I still hope God may work a miracle and allow Dad to live a while longer. Part of me really wants to believe the doctors are wrong and that he will pull through. That this is just another setback among many, and that Dad will beat off the infection and recover. There is still so much we have to do. I want to take him on trips. I want him to spend more time with his great grandchildren. I still have so many unanswered questions about him and his life.

We fall into a routine again where I come and sit with him every day. We talk some but mostly he's quiet. I bring books and magazines to read when he's asleep and straighten his clothes in his drawers. I go out and buy things I think will tempt him to eat.

The 7th of March starts off as a clear, sunny, cool day. I drive to the nursing home to be with Dad. On my way I picked up a health shake that has wheat grass, protein, and vitamins in it thinking it might tempt him to eat something. When I walk into his room he is sleeping. In sleep his features are relaxed and once in a while his eyebrows raise as if he is receiving a compliment or waiting for a laugh after he has offered up a particularly witty tidbit of conversation. There is nothing about him that indicates he is suffering. Yet the slight dew on his brow persists. The shake is warming up in my hand and will spoil if he does not drink it soon, yet I hate to wake him. He looks happy in his sleep. I set the shake down on his nightstand and start to take off my jacket, carefully and quietly, yet he senses I am in the room and stirs. He opens his eyes.

"Good morning, sleepy head!" I say to him, like he used to say to me when I was small.

"Good morning," he says, his voice rough with sleep. He struggles to pull himself up in the bed a little, then lays back with resignation, too weak to sit up. I finish removing my jacket than help him up and brace his back with pillows.

"I've brought you a health shake for breakfast, would you like that?" I ask him.

"I'm not really hungry," he says, not commenting about how unusual it is for him to have a health shake for breakfast. But when I extend the shake within reach he takes the straw between his lips and sips. He smiles encouragingly to let me know he appreciates my efforts. This is the first food he has taken in days, and I am relieved to see him even sip the shake. But after only an additional swallows or two he motions me away.

We spend the day watching the electric fireplace and looking out the window as the weather changes from sunshine to overcast. Then he dozes, and I read. I sit in a chair next to his bed across from the window with him in between so I can still observe him without appearing to. He sleeps on his side facing me grasping the rail of his bed in both hands as if he is trying to avoid being thrown off of a carnival ride. Beads of perspiration form on his brow and, several times, I wipe them away for him with a tissue. I recall doing this as a child when he had been working on a hot day or on some project that required a lot of energy, or when his hands were too dirty for him to wipe his own brow.

He looks up at me for a moment drifting up from a nap. His eyes questioning as if he's not sure why I am there.

"How you feeling, Dad?" I ask, as I always do.

"Pretty good, for a dead man."

"You don't look dead to me." I smile, mock poke his arm, as if testing a pie to see if it's done.

"Look closer." His mouth twists in a self-satisfied smile.

"How'd you sleep?"

"Sleep? I don't sleep. I just lay here with my eyes closed so they think I'm sleeping. That way they don't bother me."

"Why don't you sleep?"

He shakes his head from side to side. "Bad dreams. Hallucinations," he confides. "The oxygen machine in the corner—is deafening and that little white light keeps flashing." He strikes out at the surroundings as if to cover up the impact of his uncharacteristic disclosure.

He glances at me again to see how I'm taking his words.

"Tell me about the bad dreams," I say.

He thinks a moment.

"Different things. Sometimes about your mother."

"What's she doing?"

"Oh. Things she always did. Cooking. Cleaning. She fusses at me sometimes. I know it's her, but I can't see her face. But I can feel her presence."

He still doesn't look at me.

I think about this for a moment. Mom used to say Dad rarely met her gaze. It was something she said indicated his guilty conscience. Now I wonder if that habit has extracted an unexpected price from him. Because he rarely looked directly at her face, now, when he recalls things about her, he can no longer remember what she looked like maybe?

"I dreamed about Mom once after she died," I tell him. "She was wearing an apricot dress with a fluffy chiffon skirt. She had on strappy, silver high heels, and she was laughing an infectious laugh, saying 'Look, I can dance!'"

My heart aches at the memory. Mother lost her ability to walk those last few weeks of her life. The dream somehow made me believe somewhere in heaven Mom now dances, laughs and smiles.

"I dream about bad things," Dad says. He reaches over and pats my leg.

"What kind of bad things?"

He doesn't speak for a moment. "I remember things that weren't good. When I lie down, the memories flow through my brain. Can't seem to stop them. They are just as real as you are—sitting here. And then I wake up, and I'm in this room. I know I'm here, and they are about to call me to dinner. But that other world—it's as real as this is one. I don't even have to close my eyes to see it. Is that crazy?"

I see fear in his eyes.

"Not crazy. Maybe just vivid memories. You've been so busy all your life, maybe you never had time to process all that happened to you. Maybe it's good to remember. Puts things in perspective."

"Maybe. But maybe God won't let me die and go to heaven because I remember bad things. Maybe I wasn't always as good as I should have been."

I hug his shoulders again and wonder if he's talking about his bad memories about what others have done, or about what he's done.

"None of us are always as good as we should or could be. We are only human. God knows that. He forgives us for our humanity. We are saved by grace, not works."

There's another pause. He rubs his arthritic hands down his leg as if to press the wrinkles out. He does this over and over until I begin to wonder if his legs hurt.

"Sometimes I wasn't very good to the dog," he whispers.

Memories of him stepping on the dog, kicking the dog, picking her up by the collar and throwing her out of his way flash through my mind. Memories of how he wouldn't take her to the vet after she got hit by a car and broke her back. How she lay in the garage for weeks, how my mother would dip graham crackers in milk, scratch them against her teeth to get her to eat.

"Sometimes I wasn't good to your mother."

I think about what happened when Mom told him she had cancer. He told her she'd have to take a taxi to her chemo treatments because he had to work. He'd refused to buy her medicine because he said he couldn't afford it. How my sister and I had to find ways to get her meds for free. I recalled how he'd cooked chicken livers some mornings for breakfast and how the smell made her throw up. The memories flooded back of a thousand different things he'd done that troubled her; yet now I wonder, was it intentional? Or did he really not know? Was it that he didn't care? Or was it that he cared too much! Did he feel saving and making money to pay for her care was more important than actually being there?

Was work possible for him, and staying with her impossible? How many of us can stand by and watch the person we love most die? We all have our limits. We all have our failings. There were of course things he'd done to trouble me too. But I do not mention them now. I realize I've caused him quite a bit of trouble and worry myself too over the years. A lot. Too much. The last thing I want to talk about are all the things I've done to trouble him and for which now I am *so very sorry.* We are all broken, I realize. All of us have fallen short of what we'd like to be.

"Everyone just does the best they can at the time, Dad. Have you asked for forgiveness?" I ask him.

"Yes," he says, rubbing his leg.

"Then have faith that God's forgiven you. You did the best you could, Dad. Sometimes you lost your temper. Sometimes you gave up hope. It's something we all do. God's going to understand that when you get to heaven. And it's not good for you to lie here all day and dwell on all this. You need to find a hobby," I tell him, pulling a loose string from the cuff of his red checked shirt. He continues to sleep in his clothes as he has ever since he came to the nursing home. He refuses to wear pajamas because he doesn't want people to see him in something so casual.

He holds his hand out. I drop the string in his hand. He tosses it into the trash like a hot potato.

"Next week let's go to Hobby Lobby. Maybe you can find something you'd like to do there in the way of a craft."

"I don't need a hobby. My hobby is laying right here in this bed."

"Dad, if you try I really believe you can beat this. You may never shake the infection entirely but you can get better. You must try. The best way is to find something that interests you. Find a new purpose. Something that makes you happy."

"Dying interests me. Nothing else. I'm done working."

He looks me in the eye, takes my hand. "You need to get on with your life and let me die," he says, his eyes drift toward the window, the abandoned bird feeder hanging on the outside of the window.

"Letting you die isn't a decision I can make." I put my arms around him, hug him tight. "Life and death decisions are above my pay grade. It's my job to take care of you and try to keep you with me as long as I can."

He nods. Then shakes his head from side to side. "All I want to do is stay right here and keep this bed warm." He pats the bed with his twisted arthritic fingers.

We pass the day in this way. A quiet day. A peaceful day. Toward evening he stirs again when the hospice service comes in to see how he is doing. A tall, dark-haired, pleasant woman comes through his door and introduces herself. She is cheerful. She is kind. When she asks him if he is in pain he tells her he is. This surprises me, first because I have not detected that he is hurting, and second because he admits it to her but has not admitted it to me.

"Mr. Hinkle, we'll get you something for that," she says; and off she goes to speak to someone about that "something".

Shortly, a nurse comes in and gives him a shot. Within 10 minutes of receiving the shot, Dad visibly relaxes. We sit for a while longer in companionable silence and watch the fire flicker on the television and listened to it crackle. It has become almost life-like. Almost like a third person in the room. I guess it reminds us both of so many other fires, so many other years where we'd sat in our den in the family room together in front of a fire. Sometimes roasting popcorn over it. Sometimes peanuts. Sometimes Dad would read us Bible stories by the fire, and we would pray before bed. I remember great fire "back sticks" that Dad rolled into the den and placed at the back of the fire to keep it burning through cold nights.

The fire was the center of our house as a child. Dad had always been very good to make sure it never went out in winter, even rising at night to feed it. Like the great backstick, Dad has also been the center of the family. He has been what held us together, and also what held our attention throughout life. Around his room where we are now I have placed pictures and cards on the wall from family members. Out the window we can see the sky growing darker as evening falls. The sun will set soon. I have not eaten since breakfast.

"Dad, I'm going to run down the street and get a bite to eat. Do you want something?"

"No, I'm fine, but you go ahead," he says. He does not open his eyes.

"I'll be back in just a few minutes," I tell him.

"Take your time," he says. He turns his head toward the window, opens his eyes and looks out again. "Looks like it may snow," he says softly.

"Not tonight. Maybe tomorrow?" I say, looking out the window. There is no snow in the forecast, and I see no snow; but I half-agree with him just to be agreeable. It is, after all, March and the Bradford pear trees are already blooming. Rarely do we get snow in Texas in March.

I drive to Long John Silver's and eat dinner all the while thinking of all the Captain D dinners Dad bought us over the years. He was fond of taking people to Sunday lunch after church and often we would go when we were home visiting. We looked forward to those dinners; but, in hindsight, I realize Dad did this just to get us to spend time with him. As I eat I think about wrapping up one of my pieces of fish to take back to him. Maybe he would take just a bite, I reason. So I set some aside. Perhaps just the memory of all the fish we'd shared together might entice him.

"I will make you fisher's of men." (Matthew 4:19) The words of Jesus come to mind at that particular moment. Dad is not a perfect man, but he did what he could for others, and he tried to bring the people he encountered to Christ. Over the years he's gone out of his way for family members supplying them with

food, care, cars, dental work, rent, even houses. Most of the time he's done this with no word of thanks in return. Often the only thanks he's gotten has been for them to abuse him or take advantage of him. Yet he continued to reach out to others to help when he could. He taught us all a lot by example. He taught me to try to live a good life not so much by verbally telling people I was a Christian, but more by living as an example. I, of course, am far from perfect too. But I try. I believe that's all God asks of any of us. To do our best.

Now I'm trying by doing my best for Dad. As I eat I realize there is really precious little I can do for him now except be with him and wait on the Lord, and maybe try to tempt him to eat!

After I eat what I can, which is not much, I collect the piece of fish I've saved for Dad and head back toward the nursing home. On the way I stop at the store, and pick up fresh-baked coconut oatmeal cookies from the deli. Maybe these will appeal to him.

When I arrive back at the nursing home Dad is no longer grasping the rail of the bed. Instead he lies on his back with his head turned away from me. I sense he is waiting. I sense he is longing. It is dark now. I wonder if he is counting minutes, days, weeks? What is he waiting on? Is each sunset a celebration of another day lived? Or is it regret at another day gone?

"Did you have a good dinner?" he asks without turning.

"Yes, I had fish, I brought you back some," I tell him holding out the box. "Do you want it?" I ask. "I also brought you some coconut oatmeal cookies!" I say and hold up the bag.

"No, I'm fine," he says, not turning to look at either me or the food containers.

"Are you hurting?" I ask him.

"No. Not hurting."

I sit back down in the chair. The nurse comes in to check on us. I tell her we are fine. Dad drifts off into sleep. My back is aching from sitting in the chair all day, and my knee hurts.

Finally, it gets to be too much. "Dad, I need to go home. There's a nurse coming to sit with you tonight. She's very nice. I met her earlier. You'll like her."

"That's nice."

I've hired a private nurse to be with him at night when I cannot be there. This will be her first night.

"Okay, you go ahead," he says. "Try to get some rest."

I linger for a moment trying to think of something else to say to prolong the moment. I feel reluctant to leave. He turns to me, and I can see he is perspiring again. I reach for a tissue and gently mop his brow. Then I place the tissue on the nightstand.

"Okay, I'm going. I'll leave the fish and cookies here for you in case you get hungry. Have them put the fish in the refrigerator if you don't feel like eating it now. Maybe later?"

"Maybe later," he says. He looks at me for a moment, then says, "You've done all you can for this old man."

My eyes mist up. "I'll see you in the morning," I say again.

He doesn't answer.

I lean down and kiss his damp brow. Despite the perspiration, his brow feels cool. I run my fingers through his hair and sweep it back from his forehead the way Mom did for us as children.

Then I limp to the car. The knee brace on my knee hurts. On the way to the car a song comes to mind. "Amazing Grace". On the way home I hum it. Mom and Dad used to sing the song together. Mother would play it on the piano, Dad would sing tenor, Mom soprano. I hummed the song all the way home, over and over.

* * *

1966

"I want to make some oatmeal cookies," I told Mom one Saturday afternoon. "Are you sure you don't want me to make them?" Mom looked up from the copy of the local newspaper she'd been reading.

We were sitting on the white wrought-iron bench under the maple tree in our front yard. The afternoon breeze lifted my hair and tickled the back of my neck. For more than an hour I'd hauled our cocker spaniel, Rusty, around in the wagon pretending she was a fine lady from New York coming to see her country cousins. The wagon wheels were stiff, and it took a lot of effort to roll the wagon and keep Rusty in it at the same time. Now, sitting under a cool breeze my stomach grumbled with hunger.

"No, I'd like to make them myself. Maybe I could surprise Dad when he comes home?" I'd never cooked before, but I'd been reading the cookbook I got from the Scholastic Book Club. I'd watched Mom make coconut oatmeal cookies lots of times. It looked simple enough.

Mom gazed at me, as if suddenly noticing I'd grown. "Okay, let's go do it!"

I took the rose-printed dress and straw hat off Rusty. I'd once worn the outfit on Easter, but I'd outgrown it long ago, and Mom had put it in the rag bag. I'd dug it out for play that morning thinking it made a perfect outfit for Rusty. As soon as I removed the dress, the cocker spaniel shot off the wagon like she'd been let out of prison. Sniffing out the first dust hole in the drive, she rolled in it grunting with satisfaction. She up and sneezed with satisfaction.

I ran to my room, put up the dress and hat, and got down my cookbook.

"Do you have a special recipe you'd like to make?"

"Yes, this one." I pointed.

"Coconut Oatmeal Cookies." Mother read the directions. "I think we have all the ingredients. Here, let me tie an apron on you so you won't get flour all over your clothes. Do you know what to do first?" Mom asked.

"It says I should gather all the tools and ingredients."

"Do you know where everything is?"

"Yes, Mama."

"Well, go ahead and get started, only let me know when it's time to pre-heat the oven. I don't want you messing with the oven heat, understand?"

"Yes." I nodded, anxious to begin and feeling very grown up.

Mother settled down in the den to finish reading the newspaper. I began to open up cabinets and took out a bowl, a pan and the mixer. I also found measuring cups, mixing spoons, flour, baking soda and baking powder. I looked in the canister for sugar, but there was not a lot in the canister. I searched the cabinets, but could not find a bag. Then I saw a large quart jar on the counter that contained what appeared to be sugar. I put it, along with the rest of the ingredients, on the kitchen table together.

"Do we have any coconut?" I asked Mom.

"It's in the back of the cabinet in a can."

I searched and found the coconut along with the oatmeal, vanilla, and salt and lined them all up. Taking a deep breath, I read the directions carefully one more time.

About that time, Dad came in from work.

"What's my little girl doing?"

"I'm baking cookies, but you aren't supposed to see them!" I tried to stand between him and the table where I'd begun to prepare so he couldn't see what I was doing.

"What kind of cookies?"

"It's a surprise!"

"Oh, I see. Well, then I'll go to my office until you finish your surprise."

"Thanks, Dad."

I mixed the soft ingredients with the mixer. Then combined and mixed the dry ingredients. Then put the two together and stirred them by hand. The dough was stiff, and my arms ached from stirring, but I didn't want to ask Mom for help. Finally, after I'd mixed everything thoroughly, I washed my hands, then greased and floured the pan.

"Do you need help pouring them into the pan?" Mom asked.

We planned to make them in the form of bars. "I can do it. But can you pre-heat the oven?"

"Sure." Mother got up and turned on the oven. "What temperature?"

"It says 375 degrees."

I told her I could transfer the dough to the pan, but I had my doubts. The bowl was heavy. Eventually, grunting like Rusty in his dust hole, I managed to complete the task.

"Want me to put it in the oven for you?" Mom asked.

"Please."

Dad came into the kitchen, just as she closed the oven door.

"Why don't you play me a piece on the piano while your mother makes us some sandwiches?"

My heart sank to my tennis shoes. I had not been practicing like I should. During the school year, I'd come home from school, have a snack and play the piano for 30 minutes before homework. Usually Mother would set the timer on the stove, and listen to me play from the kitchen as she prepared dinner.

"That's good!" she'd call. Or, "That one needs a little more work."

Dad was a different story. He paid money for lessons; he wanted results. I hated to play for Dad. The only songs he wanted me to learn were hymns. None of my friends wanted me to play hymns. I wanted to play something cool that my friends would like to hear.

Besides, now that it was summer, I hardly ever practiced. Who wanted to sit inside in the heat and practice piano when they could be outside running in the fields, climbing trees or playing with the dog?

I tried to think of a logical excuse not to play. "I don't know if I can play with people listening." It sounded weak, even to me.

"Well then pretend we aren't here." Dad led the way into the living room where the piano was and pulled up a chair.

My fingers dragged as I took off my apron and folded it over a chair. Looking down at my scuffed sneakers, I followed him into the living room and slid onto the piano bench.

"Want to hear 'Jingle Bells?'" I asked hopefully. It was one of the first songs I'd learned to play, and I knew how to play it real well.

"How about 'Amazing Grace'," Dad said. "Didn't I hear you practicing that the other day?"

"But, Dad, I don't do that one very well," I begged. My heart sank even lower than my shoes. "Amazing Grace" had sharps, and my fingers got hopelessly confused. I'd never do it right!

"I'm paying a lot of money for music lessons, and all I've asked is that you play me one hymn. It's the least you can do, young lady."

I was sunk. What little time I had spent at the piano lately I'd spent practicing Beatles tunes, not hymns. *That's where deception gets you*, I thought darkly as I thumbed through the hymnal. It got you in big trouble.

"I can't find it. Are you sure it's in this hymnal?" I made one last effort.

"Page 32."

I settled the book on the book rest and found the keys with trembling fingers.

Tentatively, I hit the first few notes.

It went pretty well for a while. Well enough that Dad started to sing along, " *"Amazing grace, how sweet the sound. That saved a wretch like me..."*

Then it all began to break apart. I tried to pick the tune back up in the middle, but failed. Then I started over, *"Amazing, Grace, how sweet..."* I went off again.

My third try was so terrible I gave up in disgust and collapsed my head down on the keyboard and started to cry.

Hearing me from the kitchen, mother came into the living room and said, "Jane, go to your room."

"Not until she plays the song!"

"She's had enough. She's had a long day. We can try it again tomorrow."

I turned around, and glared at Dad through my tears.

"You don't love me! All you want is for me to play for your friends to impress them!" I said.

"That's not true," Dad said. "I want you to learn the song for you."

I looked up at him. Dad's face was filled with disappointment. I threw myself off the bench at a run and raced to my room where I collapsed across my bed sobbing. I never wanted to play the piano again as long as I lived. Why had I ever begged for lessons? I pounded my pillow. Stupid! Stupid! If I had never wanted to play, I wouldn't feel so humiliated now.

Thank goodness Mother remembered the cookies, or I might have burned down the house.

After about 30 minutes, Mom came into my room.

"Dry your eyes, and wash your face and come eat your sandwich."

"Where's Dad?"

"He went out to put the cows in the barn. It looks like a storm is coming."

"He doesn't love me," I sobbed.

"Yes he does. He just doesn't always know how to show it. He just wanted to show you he was interested in your music. He feels music is a lifelong skill that will bring you joy."

"He has a funny way of showing he loves me."

Mother didn't say anything. She only pulled my hair back from my face and combed it with her fingers.

My heart hurt because I'd been so ugly to Dad. I needed to apologize, and I knew it. As I was thinking I walked into the kitchen. Dad joined came in from outside and joined me.

"Are the cows okay?" I asked filling the awkward silence.

"Yes, they're all in the barn, got them in just before it started to rain." He met me halfway.

"Dad, I'm sorry for what I said—what I did."

"That's okay. However, you must practice more. I work really hard to pay for your lessons, you know. Music is a gift that will last a lifetime."

"I know."

There was silence for a few minutes.

"Did you try my cookies?" I asked, hoping to change the subject.

He reached down and hugged me. "Those were the best cookies I ever had."

I hugged him around his thick shoulders.

"Now I've got some work to do at the shop."

After he'd gone, I ate my sandwich and washed it down with luke-warm milk.

"Want a cookie?" Mom asked.

"Yeah!" I was excited to take a bite of the first cookie I'd ever baked.

She put it on a cake plate and handed it to me. I picked up my fork and cut a big chunk and took a bite.

"Ugh!" It was terrible. I spit it out in my napkin!

"What's wrong?" Mom asked.

I wiped my mouth on the corner of the napkin and drank down the last of my milk. "They're awful!"

Mother pinched a corner from a cookie and tasted it. Making a face, she spit it back out in a napkin.

"Jane, where did you get the sugar for these?"

"From the canister, and from the quart jar sitting on the counter!"

"Salt! You used salt, Jane. I had salt in the quart jar measured to put in the pickles I planned to make tomorrow!"

"Oh no! I thought it was sugar! I made the cookies with salt instead of sugar!"

We both looked at each other.

"How many cookies did Dad eat?"

"Three."

We exchanged glances again.

In that moment I realized if I'd only finished the song, Dad would have complimented me. But because I quit in the middle I never got to hear him praise my work. He ate those terrible cookies and complimented me on them instead. How could he have done that? The lesson in all of it was not how well I did something but that I stuck it out and finished the job. Dad would have been happy with any result as long as it was the best I could do and as long as I finished what I promised to do.

"I guess he really does love me!" I said to Mom.

* * *

2008

The phone wakes me from my dream. It is a nurse at the front desk at the nursing home.

"Mrs. Eden, if you want to see your father before he passes, you need to come right away."

"But he was fine last night," I say in disbelief.

"He took a turn a few hours ago," she responds.

"I'll be there as soon as I can," I say and click off the phone.

For a few moments I sit on the side of the bed. I recall the feeling I had the moment Mom died as I knelt on the floor by her bed holding her hand. It was like her spirit lifted out of her body and, for a moment, entered my body. It was a feeling of total love, but it was also a frightening moment too. Eventually the feeling passed and her spirit seemed to lift away, leaving behind it a loving feeling. But it also scared me. As much as I lov Dad…I am afraid to share a similar experience with him.

I jump in the shower and head to the nursing home. On the way I call my daughter and ask her to meet me there.

Thirty minutes after the call I walk into Dad's room. The nurse is standing on the far side of the room. The sun has just come up. She looks calm. Dad is in bed facing up. He is still. I raise an eyebrow to the nurse.

"You just missed him," she says. "He is gone. I was about to clean him up."

"Can you leave us for a moment?" I ask.

"Sure," she says.

As she passes me she touches me on the shoulder. "I only got to work with him a short time, but I enjoyed the time I had with him," she says.

She is tall, graceful with a cloud of dark hair much like my sister. I suspect Dad noticed this too.

The nurse leaves the room, and I sit down on the edge of the bed. I place my hand on Dad's leg. It is still warm, soft. I begin to rub it like you would rub the leg of a child with a leg ache to give comfort. The container of coconut oatmeal cookies sits on his nightstand. One cookie is out, one bite taken.

This is how my daughter finds us. She come in and hugs me. Then she sits in the chair I have sat in so many times before. I continue to rub Dad's leg as it grows cold, and my daughter and I talk. We share many memories.

Finally the dark-haired, cheerful hospice woman comes in and she has the minister with her that I've met before. We join hands and he prays for Dad's spirit and for us. Then the nursing home staff come and clean Dad up and place him on a gurney as if he is making a trip to the hospital. Once he is ready, they go down the hallway and close all the doors to the other rooms so no one can see what is happening. Then they roll Dad down the hall and out the door at the end into the sunshine. It is a cool March morning. My daughter and I follow Dad out. As they roll him into the bright sunlight snowflakes begin to fall.

"It's snowing! And the sun is shining! It wasn't supposed to snow today!" the dark-headed hospice woman says.

I look at Dad, his face still uncovered. He looks peaceful. Snow is landing on his face, his eyelashes, his pale skin. We wait for the ambulance to back in. It will take him to the funeral home where he will be prepared for his last flight back to Tennessee. There he will rest in a plot near his parents. The snow sparkles on his skin, on his lashes. It does not melt, instead it remains on his face; his blanket glitters in the sun with it until they slide him quietly into the ambulance. As I watch, they close the door and pull away without a siren. Finally, Dad's earthly adventures are over. Finally, he is headed home.

◇

"For we know that if the tent that is our earthly home is destroyed, we have a building from God, a house not made with hands, eternal in the heavens."
(2 Corinthians 5:1)

* * *

Conclusion

I still to this day do not know the true details of the death of my paternal grandfather's first wife. To me it mattered more to have companionable time with my Dad than to learn the details of her death.

In 2010 I had my skin cancer checkup and routine chest X-ray to see if the melanoma had spread. It had not. I remain cancer free at this time. Leaving the doctor's office I wanted to sing with gratitude. A song came to mind, but I couldn't remember the second and third verses. So, once home, I leafed through some hymnals that once belonged to Dad trying to find the song, and the page for "Amazing Grace" fell open. Paper-clipped to the page were several 20-dollar bills. I guess Dad was saving the money for a few more piano lessons for me.

◇

"When you pass through the waters, I will be with you; And through the rivers, they will not overwhelm you. When you walk through fire, you will not be scorched, nor will the flame burn you." (Isaiah 43:2)

◇

Amazing Grace Cookies

Combine the following dry ingredients
1 cup white sugar,
1 cup brown sugar,
1 teaspoon salt,
1 teaspoon baking powder,
1 teaspoon baking soda,
2 cups plain flour,
2 cups steel-cut oatmeal,
1 cup coconut.

Briefly soften 1 cup of butter in microwave for 10 seconds.
Beat together
2 eggs,
1 teaspoon vanilla extract.
Add butter and stir to blend.
Add the rest of the ingredients and stir.
Grease glass baking dish and pour mixture in dish.
Bake at 375 degrees for 35 minutes or until firm to touch in middle.

www.ingramcontent.com/pod-product-compliance
Lightning Source LLC
Chambersburg PA
CBHW050310120526
44592CB00014B/1850